Signs of Life:
Jews from
Wuerttemberg

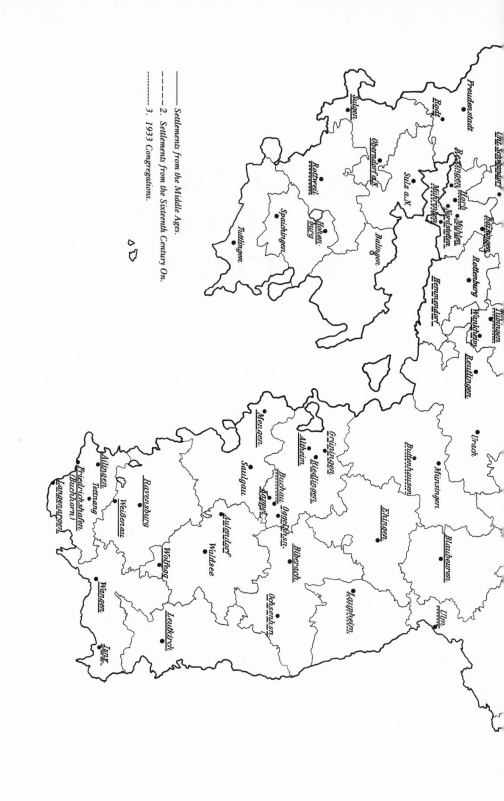

Settlements from the Middle Ages.

2. Settlements from the Sixteenth Century On.

3. 1933 Congregations.

Freudenstadt

Sulgen

Rott

Rottweil

Oberndorf a.N.

Sulz a.N.

Hohen-
burg

Spaichingen

Tuttlingen

Balingen

Horb

Mühringen

Nordstetten

Unt. Schwandorf

Rexingen

Müh...

Hechingen

Rottenburg

Wankheim

Tübingen

Reutlingen

Urach

Münsingen

Blaubeuren

Ulm

Mengen

Altheim

Grüningen

Riedlingen

Buttenhausen

Saulgau

Buchau

Oggelshausen

Kappel

Biberach

Ehingen

Laupheim

Allmendingen

Ravensburg

Weißenau

Aulendorf

Waldsee

Ochsenhausen

Friedrichshafen
(Buchhorn)

Langenargen

Tettnang

Wolfegg

Wangen

Leutkirch

Isny

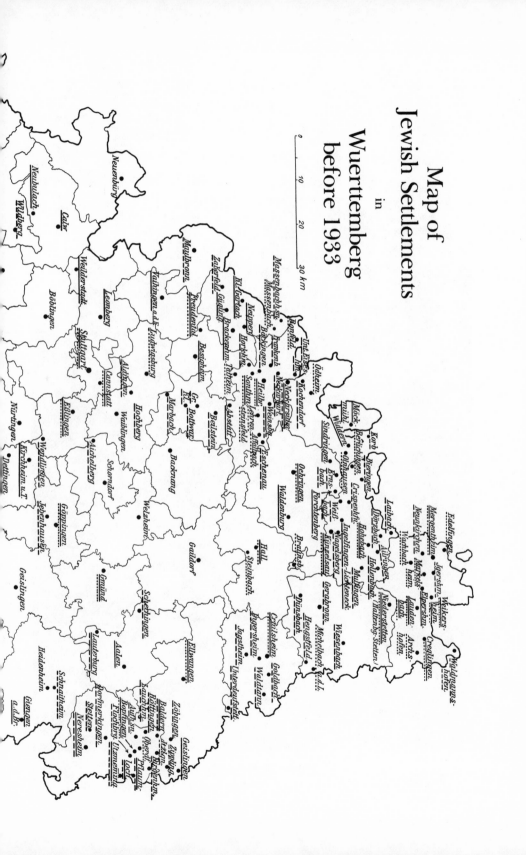

Map of
Jewish Settlements
in
Wuerttemberg
before 1933

0   10   20   30 km

Stuttgart Synagogue Exterior

From Festschrift zum 50 jährigen Jubiläum der Synagoge zu Stuttgart, *Israelitischen Kirchenvorsteheramt Stuttgart, 1911*

Signs of Life: Jews from Wuerttemberg

Reports for the Period after 1933
in Letters and Descriptions

Edited by
Walter Strauss

KTAV PUBLISHING HOUSE, INC.
New York
1982

Library of Congress Cataloging in Publication Data
Main entry under title:

Signs of life, Jews from Wuerttemberg.

  Includes index.
  1. Jews—Germany—Württemberg—Biography. 2. Jews—
Germany—Württemberg—Persecutions. 3. Holocaust,
Jewish (1939-1945)—Germany—Württemberg. 4. Holocaust
survivors—Biography. 5. Württemberg (Germany)—
Ethnic relations. I. Strauss, Walter, 1905-
DS135.G37S56   943'.47'004924022 [B]   82-6631
ISBN 0-87068-201-6   AACR2

Manufactured in the United States of America

Contents

List of Illustrations   viii
Foreword   ix
Introduction   xi
Acknowledgments   xv
Editor's Note   xvii

Main Text   1

Appendices:
   I Fate of Students from the Karlsgymnasium   375
  II 1965 Karlsgymnasium Reception for Walter Strauss   378
 III Persecution and German Popular Opinion   380
Index of Cities, Towns and Villages   381

List of Illustrations

Map of Jewish Settlements in Wuerttemberg before 1933
Stuttgart Synagogue Exterior   *frontispiece*

(following page xvii)
Otto Hirsch Memorial Shave Zion
Shave Zion
Memorial at the Pragfriedhof, Stuttgart, for the 2,498
  Killed Jews from Wuerttemberg, 1933–1945
Memorial in Buttenhausen
Memorial in Laupheim at the Location
  of the Former Synagogue
Former Synagogue of Rexingen
  Today Used as a Church
Memorial Plate for Berthold Auerbach in Nordstetten
Remains of the Stuttgart Synagogue
  after Kristallnacht, November 9, 1938
The Pragfriedhof Cemetery, Stuttgart

Foreword

Aufbau, July 1980, "Gruss an Walter Strauss" ("Greetings to Walter Strauss") by Will Schaber

Some time ago hundreds of questionnaires flew to the four winds. The New York-based Organization of the Jews from Wuerttemberg was inquiring about the life histories of the Jewish emigrants from this part of Germany. It was looking for information about the European years of the refugees, about the persecution by National Socialism, their beginnings in their new countries, personal and occupational developments, and the problems of the new life. The responses were unexpectedly numerous; not less than 250 [ed. note: eventually 500] substantial answers, partly in German and partly in English. The organization decided to publish them as its "Roots" contribution in the form of a book.

The chairman of the group, the Stuttgarter Walter Strauss, said in an interview, "The time has come to compile a chronicle of our experience. We owe that to our children and grandchildren. They will want to know their roots." Strauss, who will be seventy-five on July 25, founded the organization shortly after his arrival in the United States. It immediately outgrew the limits of a purely social group; for years one thought first of all of the ones who still remained in Hitler's Germany, affidavits of supports were collected, human lives were saved.

After the war money was collected for the people who returned hungry to Stuttgart from the concentration camps. The conductor Fritz Busch, who was in New York at the time, conducting the Metropolitan Opera, helped the action by giving a special benefit concert. Busch meant a lot to Strauss. Strauss had met and admired him when he was a student of twelve and Busch was general music director in Stuttgart. After the early death of his friend in 1951, Strauss single-handedly organized regular Busch memorial concerts. These were memorable events: outstanding music, singers like Alexander Kipnis, Birgit Nilsson, and Jon Vickers, and instrumentalists like Rudolf Serkin and Bruno Eisner donated their time. Donations went to the Busch Foundation at the Marlboro School of Music. The last of these concerts took place in 1979.

His hobby, music, takes a large space in the life of Walter Strauss, the former German lawyer and today a New York insurance broker. His studies were divided between personal interests and business, as his two doctorates (philosophy and literature under Karl Jaspers and Gundolf in

Heidelberg; law at the University of Tuebingen) indicate. By the way, Strauss set an academic record. At the age of twenty he was the youngest doctoral recipient in Heidelberg.

The jubilee is connected with the *Aufbau* in a special way. Walter Strauss has been president of the "Blue Card" organization for twelve years, and our readers esteem his knowledgeable reports on Social Security and medical insurance.

To our friend greetings, thanks and best wishes!

Introduction

In September 1979 we wrote to all of the Jews from Wuerttemberg whose addresses we could locate:

> We feel that the time has come to create a record of our experiences. We owe this to our children and grandchildren, who are entitled to know their roots. They should remember how a group of immigrants and persecutees . . . started from scratch and began new lives in their new homeland.

We asked them to write down what had happened to them and their parents. We were interested in their background in the old country and the kinds of persecution they had encountered, but also in their life experiences in the new country.

An additional value was finding out what had become of friends we had not heard from for a long time. For instance, I received a letter from a man I had had no contact with for a very long time, who mentioned his surprise at finding me still alive.

Honestly, we were surprised at how many responses we received and were soon convinced that these accounts could be published as a book. In May 1980 we sent another letter to the same people and many others we had just located. Since many had asked us for more details of what we were actually interested in, we said that we were mainly concerned with the names of parents if they were still alive in 1933, their places and years of birth, occupations, and possibly dates of death. In reference to the people to whom we wrote our letters, we also wanted to know how they had established their lives in the new country, where they presently lived, and the names of the members of their families. If of any importance, we asked for their involvement in social organizations of any kind. Up to our final deadline of June 30, 1981, we received, to our own surprise, close to five hundred replies, which we herewith present to the public.

Our organization was founded in 1939. When at that time we held our initial meeting in New York City, the hall had to be closed by the Fire Department because eight hundred people wanted to get in and it held only six hundred! Among others we got a greeting from Professor Albert Einstein, who as everybody knows was born in Wuerttemberg:

Mein Wunsch—moege es euch scnell gelingen
den Leuten hier das Schwaebeln beizubringen.

My wish—O may you succeed in speeding
to teach Americans Schwaebisch reading.

Actually we came together strictly for social reasons, but almost everybody who came to the States at the time had requests from friends and
acquaintances to help with immigration. In most cases that meant visiting
relatives and friends and asking them to sign the necessary sponsorship
papers. Many of the ones still in Wuerttemberg had written and never
received an answer from them. During those weeks many of us did little
but visit American relatives. We tried to explain to them the deep serious-
ness of the situation in Hitler's Germany, since many of them did not see
clearly what we knew very well most probably meant a question of life and
death.

Of course, what some of the Jews in Wuerttemberg did not know was
that the American relatives had to prove some not insubstantial means of
their own in order to make their sponsorship acceptable to the Immigration Service. It was also possible to get professional people—such as
teachers and rabbis—into the United States by proving an employment
contract. In some exceptional cases even this was possible for us. We must
mention in this connection the name of our good old friend Sigmund
Kahn, who certainly gets the credit for saving the most people. I remember one case where a wealthy American relative said that he had finally
signed the sponsorship papers only to end the daily visits of Mr. Kahn.

With the entry of America into the war in 1941 this immigration help
became more or less impossible. When the "Thousand Year Reich" collapsed after twelve years, we heard that at least some Jews had survived
the Holocaust and returned to Stuttgart but had nothing to eat. We
decided immediately to send food packages to Stuttgart and started
forthwith the collection for that purpose. By chance I mentioned this fact
to Fritz Busch, who immediately offered to hold a benefit concert to help.
[See FRITZ BUSCH biography for details.]

The Organization of the Jews from Wuerttemberg is really the only
Landsmannschaft of the Jews from Germany which has remained together.
From time to time we actually received phone calls from Wuerttemberg
Jews who asked us to arrange another Wuerttemberg meeting, since they,
especially the older ones, would like to see their old friends again. When-
ever we had a visit from friends from abroad—for instance, Leopold
Marx and Landgerichtspraesident Alfred Marx—we took the opportu-
nity to call a meeting.

Our intention in collecting the emigration and immigration stories of our circle was approved by an overwhelming majority of the Wuerttemberg Jews. We originally sent out six hundred letters and received close to five hundred answers.

However, there were quite a few who told us that they found it superfluous to build up such personal history. Some also explained that for reasons of principle they did not want to have anything to do with Germany, which had killed their closest relatives. Of course, we fully understand such an attitude, especially when the closest relatives like spouses or parents were killed.

On the other side, there seems to be a great majority of people who feel that the crimes of the parents should not be transferred automatically to the children, and that there were a great number of Germans who helped Jews. For instance, without Bosch and Company many would not have had the money to pay the expenses of their emigration, which not only included the train but also the boat. Hans Walz, as the head of Bosch, would have immediately lost his own life had it ever been found out that, without the knowledge of the Gestapo, he gave very substantial amounts of cash to Karl Adler. The same is true of my former classmate Egon Braun, who was a confidant of Hans Walz. Such events should never be entirely forgotten, even by the ones who hold all Germans equally responsible without exception.

In Israel there is a Jewish memorial park on one of the hills surrounding Jerusalem, Yad Vashem. It is a reminder of the Holocaust and of the six million Jews killed by Hitler. In this hall are also the names of a few Germans which the Jews put there in deep gratitude for saving Jewish lives. The first name is that of the first President of the new Germany, Theodor Heuss. One of the following is Hans Walz, the head of Bosch and Company (by the way both men came from Wuerttemberg). In the hall we find a very true and moving line which might perhaps lead to a future understanding between Germany and Israel. "Forgetfulness leads to exile, while remembrance is the secret of redemption."

Actually, what this means is that forgetfulness leads to estrangement, while remembrance is the secret of reconciliation. An important German educator was once asked by young Germans what he thought about the guilt of Hitler's Germany for the deaths of the millions of Jews. He answered, "No, you do not have to feel guilty for the sins of your country. But it is your privilege to blush for it."

Walter Strauss

New York—Stuttgart
Spring 1982

xiii

From Paul Sauer, *Demokratischer Neubeginn in Not und Elend* (Ulm: Vaas, 1978)

Ministerpresident Maier tried to make contact with the Jewish emigrants from Southwest Germany. He wrote a letter to the Organization of the Jews from Wuerttemberg in New York. Walter Strauss, the chairman of the organization, answered on September 13, 1946, at the "First demonstration of an official German representative towards the Jews from Germany." In the letter one feels the sorrow and the disappointment of the Jews violently expelled from their homeland even to speak to their former countrymen. Strauss wrote that he was happy about the personal attitude of Reinhold Maier, but since he and his fellow victims so far had no proof of a change in the German attitude towards the Jews, they would be very cautious in their possible new relations with Germans; "it is not easy to forget when it was not a question of personal suffering but of deliberate murder of beloved friends." Strauss then mentioned the Jews who came from the concentration camps to Wuerttemberg. He wished that the restitution laws would be enforced as quickly as possible, so that real help would be possible for these people. "We are convinced that an energetic effort from the German officials could not only accelerate this legislation but beyond this would show to the world that Germany really tries as quickly and fully as possible to make good the harm they have done." Strauss finished his letter with the wish, "May the German people, under a leadership of men like you, experience in a time not too far ahead not only industrial reconstruction but also a human regeneration which will make the occurrences of the last twelve years impossible for all time to come."

Acknowledgments

I want to thank especially Dr. Herbert A. Strauss, Director of the Research Foundation for Jewish Immigration, Inc., who not only gave me the courage to compile this book but was of tremendous help during its first months when its publication was still doubtful. Furthermore, I want to thank Fritz Lebrecht and Johanna Wernicke, who were extremely helpful in translating and correcting some of the partly unreadable letters, and Doris Kabat, who besides innumerable others, did the main typing of the book. Thomas Naegele was of enormous general assistance and particularly helpful with the preparation of the German edition. At the end I want to thank my last and maybe best assistant, Steve Mead, who not only helped in typing and compiling the book but also gave me some excellent ideas and contributed to its warmth, humanity, and English style. The book would never have been possible without the cooperation of the close to five hundred people who actually wrote it.

We received financial assistance from the Government of Baden-Wuerttemberg, the City of Stuttgart, and many German banks and industrialists and their foundations, mainly the Bosch Foundation, which saved the lives of so many Wuerttemberg Jews during the Hitler period, as this book clearly shows.

Editor's Note

This book is a special kind of history in which people tell about their own lives in their own words. Thus in most cases, in order to preserve the original style and flavor, we have not corrected grammar except where necessary to clarify the meaning. Unfortunately, extensive deletions have been necessary for space reasons.

Items marked by an asterisk (*) are mainly taken from the booklet *The Fate of the Jewish Lawyers in Wuerttemberg 1933–1945*, which the then Wuerttemberg Secretary of Justice, Dr. Wolfgang Haussmann, asked Landgerichtspraesident Alfred Marx to compile. We want to take this opportunity to again thank Mr. Marx for the great help he has given us with his work.

Otto Hirsch Memorial
Shave Zion

Shave Zion

Memorial at the Pragfriedhof, Stuttgart, for the 2,498 Killed Jews from Wuerttemberg, 1933–1945

Courtesy Landesbildstelle Wuerttemberg

Memorial in Buttenhausen

Memorial in Laupheim at the Location of the Former Synagogue

Former Synagogue of Rexingen Today Used as a Church

Courtesy Willy Leygraf, Reutlingen

Memorial Plate for Berthold Auerbach in Nordstetten

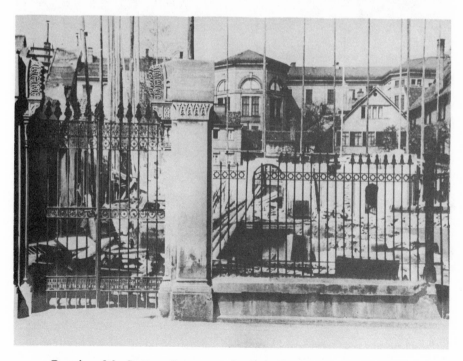

Remains of the Stuttgart Synagogue after Kristallnacht, November 9, 1938

The Pragfriedhof Cemetery, Stuttgart

From Festschrift zum 50 jährigen Jubiläum der Synagoge zu Stuttgart, *Israelitischen Kirchenvorsteheramt Stuttgart, 1911*

HANNA ABENDSTERN (née Feldmann)
16 Dovehouse Close
Whitefield, M25 7PE
England

We used to live in Neumünster/Schleswig-Holstein, where Martin worked for a leather firm. We left Germany for Luxembourg. During the September crisis in 1938 we left for England. During the war he spent three months in an internment camp. Our two sons went to school in Rochdale and the older one became an engineer. The younger one is a doctor. In 1941 we bought a house in Rochdale which a few years ago got too big for us and we moved to a modern flat in Whitefield, an outspoken Jewish district, where we felt very happy.

We joined the newly founded Reform synagogue and made many friends there, especially with the many former German-Jews.

My Parents: Lilly Feldmann, born 1877 and died in Jerusalem, 1967. Dr. Gustav Feldmann, born 1872, died in Jerusalem, 1947.

My Own Place of Birth: 1904 in Stuttgart.

Martin Abendstern: 1903, Stuttgart, died 1978 in Whitefield-Bury.

I hope these facts are kept short enough and I thank you for sending the questionnaire to me.

Thank you for your letter. You want to know a bit more about Martin's parents. His father died already in 1923 and his mother and his brother went through hell.

My mother-in-law used to live in a big flat in her own house. She refused for a long time to join us in Luxembourg or England as she wanted to keep her house for her children. She was sure Hitler did not do any harm to people of her age. She had to share her flat with more and more people and after her sixtieth birthday she had to leave Stuttgart for Oberdorf-Bopfingen. On the 1st of December 1941 she was transported to Riga, and on March 26, 1942, she was shot by the Nazis together with twelve hundred women and children. We had a letter of a deaf-and-dumb eyewitness of the massacre who survived. This letter is now at the Yad Vashem in Jerusalem. Martin's brother, Otto, was on business in Brussels when the Germans overran Belgium. All foreigners had to go to the police. Some went straightaway underground; my brother-in-law went to the police, was interned, landed in Gurs, and was from there taken to Auschwitz. We were later told by the Red Cross that nobody of that

1

transport came back. His wife and son went underground in the South of France. Both are alive and I am expecting my sister-in-law the day after tomorrow. The son is a psychiatrist in New York.

I am sure you got similar stories from many people. The time did not heal our wounds and it is most important that the coming generations will get some information. For many grandchildren our experience belongs already to history.

It was nice to hear from you after such a long time.

AMELY ADLER (née Zippert)
253 Garth Road, Apt. 6A
Scarsdale, N.Y. 10583

I was very pleased to receive your letter, outlining the plans of the Organization of the Jews from Wuerttemberg to create a permanent record of the history and experiences of the Wuerttemberg Jews during and as a result of the Nazi regime.

Let me say at the outset that I wholeheartedly welcome your plans to document these experiences of the Wuerttemberg Jews during their years of emigration and resettlement. This will contribute, I am sure, to focus attention on a memorable period in the history of our people. In addition, it will provide some answers in the minds of our second, and now third generation of descendants of the German-Jewish immigrant community to learn about their background and find a response to the often-recurring question: How did you manage to survive the years of Nazi persecution and rebuild your lives in a new home?

As to my own background, I was born during the pre-Hitler years in Stuttgart and grew up there with my family, parents and my older brother, Paul. My father, Max Zippert, originated from North Germany, but during World War I he was wounded and was stationed in Stuttgart to recuperate. It was there that he met and later married my mother, Helene née Kaufmann, who belonged to an old established Stuttgart family. My maternal grandfather, Richard Kaufmann, owned a Buchhandlung and Antiquariat in Schlosstrasse, Stuttgart. My maternal grandmother, Amalie, was the youngest daughter of Kirchenrat Dr. Moses V. Wasserman, who was Chief Rabbi of Wuerttemberg during the second half of the nineteenth century. My father traveled throughout Wuerttemberg on business. My mother was a music teacher and pianist by profession and was well known in the Stuttgart Jewish community and beyond. I attended the Stuttgarter Juedische Schule. As a family, we were involved in many of the functions and activities of the local congregation and other Jewish groups. The traumatic experience of the Kristallnacht, November

9, 1938, brought a drastic change into our lives and left a lasting impression on my memory. There is no need to go into detail; everyone who has lived through it remembers the burning of the synagogue, the breaking of the shop windows in the Jewish stores, and the arrests and transport to concentration camps of the Jewish men. My father was arrested and, fortunately, sent to one of the "milder" places of incarceration, the Police Prison in Welzheim/Wuerttemberg. He was released after seventeen days on the condition that he would expedite our emigration and, moreover, register weekly in person at the local police bureau. We were very fortunate to obtain an affidavit to emigrate to the United States, from distant relatives, but our waiting number was high and we were compelled to seek an interim stay in England. Thus, we managed to leave Stuttgart at the last moment and arrived in London a few hours prior to the official Declaration of War in September 1939. At the end of the war we were able to follow our original plan to immigrate to the United States. We settled in Baltimore and struggled to find a footing in our new country. A few years after our arrival, I relocated to New York City, where I met, and later married, my husband, Erich Adler. We raised two children, a son and a daughter, both now grown up, leading successful lives of their own. My son, Mark, is married and lives in Farmingdale, Long Island. He is assistant district attorney in Nassau County. My daughter, Vivian, is a licensed registered nurse and works in a large hospital in the Bronx. My husband and I left New York City for Westchester County a few years ago. He is working as a tailor, not far from where we live. As for myself, I still commute daily into the city and am working at Columbia University for a psychiatric research training program. [*Ed. comment:* Helene Zippert passed away meanwhile.]

We are happy and grateful to have been given a chance to reestablish our lives in this great country, to be able to live here in peace and safety, and to be able to contribute our share of the progress and upkeep of its democratic principles.

CARL ADLER

Carl was the youngest of the five children of Julius Adler and Bertha née Schafer. The Adlers had been vintners in Bad Mergentheim, but Julius came to Stuttgart in about 1890 to start a winery with his brothers and cousins. The business flourished, and Carl and his cousins started their working life in the winery. Carl married Lise Flegenheimer in 1921. Later he was the manager of a chemical-manufacturing concern. Carl and Lise emigrated to England in 1939 where Lise died in 1943. Carl moved to New York with his children and met his second wife, Edith. They operated a cleaning store in New Jersey. Carl died in 1963. Carl and Lise had three daughters. Ellen married Harry Carsch from Stuttgart and had a daughter and two sons. Marion married Edgar Grossman. They operated a cleaning business in Jew Jersey. They have two daughters, both married and living in New Jersey. Sybil married Fredi Jakob and has four sons. They live in Sacramento, California, where they teach at the university.

GRETE ADLER (née Marx)
24 Linden Terrace
Leonia, N.J. 07605

As the first girl after three brothers, I was pampered by everybody. I attended the Kunstgewerbeschule Stuttgart (bookbinding). I also did voluntary work at a home for babies of unwed mothers.

Singing in Karl Adler's chorus as a young girl, I was not the only female who fell in love with the tall, dynamic, witty, yet strict conductor. But what a shock when one evening after chorus, without any overture, he told me I would become his wife. Even my protests that I was medically unfit for marriage due to a heart problem could not change his mind. So it happened that the beloved "dictator" opened the way to a new life, never easy but always full of rich experiences, for a rather shy and sheltered girl.

My roles were: creating a relaxed home atmosphere; becoming mother to our son, Fritz; also Karl Adler's private secretary (keeping class records, copying music, designing programs, proofreading, mediating in ticklish situations and backstage worker). All these responsibilities helped me to develop unexpected strength intensified during the Nazi years.

When we emigrated in November 1940, Karl Adler was able to take his parents along, but I had to leave behind my mother, my uncle, and two brothers; the youngest, Alfred Marx, became Karl's successor at the Auswandererstelle.

Karl's sisters, Irene Adler and Fanny Neumann (with husband Simon and sons Walter and Harold), had preceded us and took the parents into their apartment in Astoria, New York, while we stayed in a nearby furnished room (without even a table) at the home of Jewish policeman.

I helped mother Adler as family cook for eight or nine people until we moved to a furnished apartment (as caretakers) in Riverdale, New York. When the owner moved out his furniture, I replaced it with a wall unit of fifty orange crates, topped with house plants and ceramics. We spent our first vacation working on farms. My greeting card depicting Karl Adler with a pitchfork so impressed a designer that she hired me as a silk-screen printer. Thus, I got my first paying job. Another odd job took me to Macy's huge department store to demonstrate handprinting on textiles.

4

Most rewarding, however, was my secretarial work at City College, which brought me in close contact with all of Karl Adler's students. All along I helped him with his vast correspondence, both official and private. When I was once in the hospital, instead of flowers, he brought my little type-writer to my room.

When Karl Adler, upon the recommendation of Walter Strauss, be-came the American representative of the Kuenstlerhilfe (relief fund for refugee artists, sponsored by the Suddeutsche Rundfunk, Stuttgart) we tried to handle these "cases" as unbusinesslike as possible.

After Karl became ill and we moved to Leonia, New Jersey, our own garden became the healing balance of our lives. The closeness to nature helped me, especially after his death, to overcome loneliness. Having been his "right hand" for almost half a century, I now began to use it to express myself more fully, and at seventy-five, taking up painting became far more than a mere pastime. Some of my work was even warmly received in local exhibitions. Another "first": after a Bach concert, an American doctor's family asked me to teach their little boy German in word and song.

Life in Leonia, the small community of artists and scientists, is full of surprises for me. What next . . . ?

IRENE ADLER

Born 1898 in Buttenhausen, graduated from high school and had to leave home at age sixteen to further her education at a business school in Stuttgart. After completion she found employment as a bookkeeper in that city. Was the first member of the family to emigrate to the United States—in 1936. For many years she worked on the assembly line in a bakery, mostly on the night shift. Aside from taking English courses she did some part-time work in a catering establishment, washing dishes and waiting on tables. A grant from the Blue Card enabled her to take a course in handling electric bookkeeping machines, after which she found a job as a bookkeeper. Notwithstanding the daily ordeal to spend hours on the crowded subways and the feeling that her work was not properly appreci-ated, she stayed there for thirty years, until her retirement in 1975.

As a real pioneer—denying herself many necessities—she left no stone unturned to prepare the soil for the imigration of the rest of the family (her parents, Louis and Mathilde Adler; her brother, Professor Karl Adler, and wife; her sister, Fanny Neumann, with husband, Simon, and sons Walter and Harold). After this goal was achieved, she still put her own well-being in the background. In order to contribute as much as possible to the mutual household she took part-time jobs in a coffee shop and did babysitting. For many years she was a board member of the Organization of Jews from Wuerttemberg. Being unmarried, she made all the problems of relatives and friends her own, to such a degree that she hardly ever found the time to enjoy herself and reap the harvest of her labors. She remained so attached to her *Landsleute* that she never failed to visit them on all happy as well as sad occasions, even when she became so weak that she hardly could walk any more. After a hip fracture, some heart ailment, and pneumonia, she lingered in and out of the hospital for a full year until death came as a blessing to her in 1980.

A model of loyalty, conscientiousness, reliability, concern for others—that was Irene Adler.

[*Ed. remark:* In her last will she left $1,000 to the Organization of Jews from Wuerttemberg.]

*JAKOB ADLER

Born 1885 in Mergentheim; went to Stuttgart in 1922 as an attorney. In June 1943 he emigrated to Brazil, where his wife, Dr. Hilde Adler, had already gone in May 1933. In 1950 the family moved to the United States. Only after he had learned the Portuguese language was attorney Adler able to make a modest living as a commercial employee. He died in 1964 in the United States.

Lawyer Jakob Adler was sometimes confused with lawyer Jakob (Julius) Adler II, born 1895 in Stuttgart and admitted to the bar there in 1923. Jakob Adler II resigned in 1925, when he got married and joined an industrial firm. He too had to emigrate. In August 1939 he went to the United States and died there in 1949.

KARL ADLER

The following biographical sketch by his wife, Grete, gives just a bare outline of his life. The limited framework only hints at the full stature of the man. Fate confronted him with great tasks and several times destroyed what he had built up, but it also endowed him with strength to overcome the most difficult, often dangerous situations.

From his father, Louis Adler, who served as honorary cantor in his hometown, Buttenhausen, Karl Adler inherited a beautiful voice and learned the traditional synagogue melodies (*negunim*). After completing his studies at the Lehrerseminar Esslingen, he taught in Ulm, at the same time studying at the Musikakademie in Stuttgart. After graduation (1911) he became baritone soloist at the Hoftheater Stuttgart until the outbreak of World War I. [*Ed. note:* I remember as a very small boy having heard him as "Heerrufer" in my first *Lohengrin*.] In 1915 he joined the Army as a volunteer, was awarded the Iron Cross. Severe head wounds later prevented his singing career. A fellow officer, Theodore Baeuerle (later boss, friend, and Wuerttemberg Kultminister), gave Karl Adler a new direction in life. Baeuerle initiated the Wuerttemberg Adult Education Movement, asking Karl Adler to establish its music department (1919–21).

In the Ides of March 1933, an attack on Karl Adler with an iron pipe caused a head wound next to the scar from his war injury, making hospitalization necessary. Police offered "protective custody" (*Schutzhaft*) in prison, which he declined.

His dismissal as director of the Conservatory (April 1933) caused the trustees and many students to resign in protest and the whole chorus to serenade him in front of our house. Robbed of his life's work, he never showed self-pity. In the framework of the Juedische Lehrhaus, whose director he had been since 1926, he founded the Stuttgarter Juedische Kunstgemeinschaft (1933–38), which gradually involved the whole Jewish community. Of the two thousand members, two hundred became active in the chorus and orchestra. Our concerts, plays, and art exhibits became the only bright aspects in our lives, especially after Jews were barred from all public performances. In the face of doom, this not only saved us from despair but awakened pride in achievement and self-confidence.

But there were great difficulties connected with these productions, all attended by a Gestapo official. Each program had to be approved. Just one day before a certain concert, the major work (for chorus and orchestra) with its Psalm-text "Oh, let not my foes destroy me!" had to be deleted from the already printed program, and Karl Adler was warned that if he made any inflammatory remark to the audience in announcing the omission, he would be arrested right at the podium.

As director of the Zentralstelle fur das Juedische Vereins- und Veranstaltungswesen he had to report *all* Jewish gatherings in Wuerttemberg.

In 1935 Martin Buber, head of the Mittelstelle fur Juedische Erwachsenenbildung, put Karl Adler in charge of music pedagogical courses for youth leaders in all greater Jewish communities in Germany (mostly on weekends).

During Crystal Night, November 1938, he was arrested but released from the Stuttgart prison after a week, on the demonic condition that he stop all cultural activities and instead speed up Jewish emigration—except his own! While in prison, his office was completely demolished and occupied by a Nazi organization. So his new task, to organize the Mittel- und Auswandererstelle, began with not even a desk. Under the watchful

7

eye of the Gestapo, he developed a network of services: housing, employment, rationing, emigration, which was run by twenty co-workers. The most urgent and risky task was to free the prisoners and to get them—at whatever cost—out of Germany. For this purpose, secret financial help came from the non-Jewish industrialist Hans Walz, director of the firm of Robert Bosch, Stuttgart. This action, if detected, would have meant the death sentence for the donor.

When the original local Nazi officials, who knew and respected Karl Adler from way back, were replaced by outsiders, accomplishing anything by reasoning became almost impossible. To protect our son Fritz from the atmosphere of constant tension, we sent him in the summer of 1939 to an English boarding school (with a children's transport), hoping to be reunited with him in the near future. Meanwhile, our friend Walter Strauss in New York, aware of our plight, succeeded in obtaining a teaching contract from the New York College of Music for Karl Adler, which entitled him to a non-quota visa and saved him from the tragic fate of Otto Hirsch, whose task paralleled his.

The Jewish community gave us a farewell party, the saddest gathering of our lives in view of all those left behind, among them my own mother.

The loyalty of some of our non-Jewish friends helped us keep our faith in humanity. At his last "visit" to the Gestapo, Karl Adler was warned not to spread any horror stories about Germany, whereupon he promised that he would strictly stick to the truth.

In late October 1940, we left Stuttgart with Karl's parents—with some books and music but no furniture.

In Stuttgart, former chorus member bid us tearfully goodbye by singing some of the canons which had opened and closed our rehearsals. When we walked down the gangplank in New York on Thanksgiving Day we were greeted with the same canons, *Viva la Musica* and *Shalom,* sung by some choral members who had preceded us to the United States, among them Walter Strauss, who definitely had saved our lives. Keeping his promise to explore emigration possibilities for about three hundred Wuerttemberg Jews whose pleas he had brought with him, kept Karl Adler—and me, with the help of the Organization of the Jews from Wuerttemberg—busy for months. He had to supplement his income by teaching children in ghetto neighborhood schools. His lot improved when he was appointed director of music and ski instructor at Briarcliff Junior College in upstate New York (1942–48).

Finally we managed to get passage for our Fritz, but his New York–bound boat was caught in a hurricane and disappeared without a trace. Shortly thereafter we got word that my mother and my favorite uncle had died in the Theresienstadt Concentration Camp. To help us

8

cope with our grief, the president of Briarcliff Junior College invited me to join my husband in organizing a music library. Karl received an honorary doctorate from New York College of Music "For outstanding achievement in music education." Took charge of the vocal program of New York City College, Extension Division, 1946–62. Many public performances with the chorus, composed of members from different ethnic backgrounds. Thanks to our social hours after each rehearsal and our outing group, it became a kind of mini–United Nations.

The combination of Karl Adler's Jewish, pedagogic, and musical background led him to the last stage of his professional life: Yeshiva University, New York (1945–68). He founded and built up the Music Department and the Cantorial Training Institute. Innovation: making general music studies and participation in chorus mandatory for all cantorial students, thus widening their horizons and upgrading their cultural standards. He held this post until he became ill (long beyond retirement age).

We moved to Leonia, New Jersey, where we had bought a little house and garden, and where he was still granted a few good years until excruciating pain, due to poor blood circulation, made amputation of one leg necessary. The following day, his heart gave out. And now, among thousands of gray stones in the huge Beth-El Cemetery, there is one inscribed: "Viva la Musica!"

LEO ADLER (by Lotte Adler)

Born in 1884 in Braunsbach, Wuerttemberg. 1908–1938: Religionsoberlehrer und Oberkantor in Stuttgart; also conductor of Synagogen Choir, head of Oberrat Library, president of Berthold Auerbach Verein.

Publications: "Heinrich Sontheim" (with whom he had a lifelong friendship), *Ein Kuenstlerleben* (1916); "Die Bibliothek des Isr. Oberrats," in *Juedisches Gemeindeblatt* (1938); "Isr. Religionsgemeinschaft of Wuerttemberg: Its Development and Changes," in *Year Book of the Leo Baeck Institute,* London (1960); "Wandlungen bei dem Oberrat der Isr. Religionsgemeinschaft," in *Feiertagsschrift der Isr. Kultusvereinigung Wuerttemberg und Hohenzollern,* Stuttgart, September 1962 and April 1963. Many essays, mostly in Jewish papers.

1933: He married Lotte Levy in Stuttgart. 1938: Arrested by SS man. Prison in Stuttgart. 1938: Concentration camp—Dachau. 1939: Prison in Asperg as a hostage.

We already had affidavits to enter the United States. Only through Professor Karl Adler's connections and helpfulness could he be freed. The same night we left for Rotterdam. We arrived in New York in 1939.

He looked and felt like a prisoner, hair shaved! He was not able to follow his profession in America and made a living as a watchmaker. He got very sick due to the treatment by the Nazis and passed away in 1966 in New York.

Leo Adler was always deeply connected with the Jews from Stuttgart in Stuttgart when he was there and in New York. He received many letters from former pupils, wherever they had emigrated to. He was always very grateful to be in the United States as a citizen.

LOTTE ADLER (née Levy)
73–37 Austin Street
Forest Hills, N.Y. 11375

My parents, Paul and Dora Levy, arrived in the United States in 1939. My father was imprisoned in Stuttgart for a short time. Here they lived with us.

My father was a board member of the Blue Card and of the New World Club, Brooklyn section. My mother took care of the house while I was working as a licensed masseuse. My parents passed away 1944–1945.

OTTO S. ADLER
11 Berkeley Road
Springfield, N.J. 07081

When I was born in 1921 in the village of Duensbach, Kreis Gerabronn, there lived thirteen Jews in this village, of which six were my family. I am the only survivor from my family and this village Jewish heritage. Everybody else perished in the Holocaust: my father and brother in Auschwitz, my mother and sister near Riga, and my grandmother in Theresienstadt, where she was deported to at the age of seventy.

I myself received my American visa in 1940 in Stuttgart. On the following day, I left Stuttgart to start my journey to the United States. I was to meet my brother on May 10 in Rotterdam. He was in a Jewish Youth Home in Holland. But on that day in the morning, German troops marched into Holland and Belgium. I got as far as Cleve. Luckily I could return to Stuttgart. I tried to get out via Italy. Too late. Italy entered the war. I tried to get out via Russia, China, and Japan. Almost at the last moment my passage was cancelled. They had made a mistake. The berth alloted to me on a Japanese boat was an "Arier berth."

Then the American Export Line started a service from Lisbon to New York. But time was running out fast. On September 8, my American visa expired and an extension was not given. Just before expiration, a cousin of mine in the United States paid the passage in dollars and somehow I managed to get a Spanish and Portuguese transit visa. By the time I got air passage to Lisbon and got there in 1940, my American visa was actually expired. I had hoped to get an extension from the American consul in Lisbon. However, promptly upon arrival in Lisbon Airport I was arrested by our allies, the Portuguese police, and the following morning on the next plane deported back to Germany, with stopover and change of plane in Madrid, Spain. If this would have happened, I would not write this today.

In Madrid, which at that time was practically a German colony, however, things were different. Contrary to all official rules, employees of the German Lufthansa Airline helped me in every way. I did not get on the next plane to Germany. I went to the American Embassy with my American visa, asking for an extension. A cigarette they offered me, but flatly refused any help. In desperation I went to the German Embassy. There I received the help which I never expected. Despite the big "J" on my passport, they helped me to get a temporary residence permit in Spain and advanced funds, which I later repaid. These German people, in spite of Hitler and in sharp contrast to the Portuguese authorities, were human beings, and I will always be thankful to them. There in Spain I waited for six months. Then again I received my American visa, and finally, on March 21, 1941, I arrived in the United States.

Immediately I started to work for the same people I had worked for in Stuttgart. Two years later I was inducted into the U.S. Army. I served until November 1945 in Military Intelligence, interrogation of prisoners-of-war, and after the Armistice, Civil Administration and Counter-Intelligence in Europe.

I had married in November 1941 a girl I knew from Germany. When I returned from the war, we had a baby girl of sixteen months. I continued to work for the same people I had worked for before. In 1954 my former boss died. His partner then took me in as a junior partner. This is my situation today. We are happily married. My daughter is married and now we enjoy the pleasure of our little granddaughter of two years. I only hope that the future for them, our children and grandchildren, will be bright and they shall never experience what we had to go through.

TRUDY ADLER (née Oppenheim)
Elkins Park Home, Apt. 406A
7900 Old York Road
Elkins Park, Pa. 19117

I was born in Tuebingen in 1911. My father, Jacob Oppenheim, was born in 1874. My mother, Karoline, was born in 1883. My parents owned the "Fashion House" Ed. Degginger, in Tuebingen, where they moved to in 1906.

My brother, Heinz, born in 1907, became a physician; married Dorothy Hayum, daughter of Dr. Simon and Hermine Hayum, from Tuebingen; and emigrated to the United States in 1936. He practiced in Louisville, Kentucky, and was teaching also. A daughter lives in Louisville as well, and married a physician too.

I myself, in 1935, married Dr. jur. Otto Friedrich Adler from Frankfurt a.M. We moved to Burgsteinfurt in Westphalia, where my husband worked as a counselor for a big firm. We emigrated in 1938 to the United States and lived in Philadelphia. My husband became a certified public accountant. My parents came to us in Philadelphia in 1940 and lived with us until they passed away; my mother in 1942 and father in 1947. When my sister-in-law passed away in 1950 I brought up my niece until my brother remarried. He died in September 1969 and my husband passed away in 1971—sixty-one years old. He was president of the Heinrich Goetz Lodge of B'nai B'rith, and we were and I still am a member of the Congregation Shelon in Philadelphia. I always was a housewife.

We have a daughter, Evelyn Rose, born March 5, 1941. She married Robert Sunray. He was born in Harrison, New York, graduated from Columbia University, and is an exporter. They lived in New Rochelle, New York, until 1970, when they moved to Ramat Gan, Israel. They have two boys now thirteen and one-half and sixteen and one-half years old.

GERTRUD (TRUDE) AMBERG-MEYER
26 Yavniel Street
Givatayim, Israel

Born 1903 in Heilbronn as the only child of Alex Amberg and his wife, Anna (née Hirsch).

I had a wonderful, warm childhood. My father, highly intelligent and of deep human understanding, guided me in his gentle way. Together with his brother Albert, he owned a leather shop, which often served as a place for informal meetings and discussions, especially about politics. My father was an active Democrat of the Friedrich Naumann school. At the

12

same time he was a practicing Jew, serving, along with Dr. S. Gumbel, as deputy in the Council of Württemberg Congregations at Stuttgart. He also took great pride in presiding over a local organization which supported the poor, in particular of the itinerant category. "Rather waste money on five undeserving people than refuse it to one really needy!" he used to say. His death at an early age (he became only sixty-one years old) was a heavy shock to me and to my mother, who had loyally helped him in her practical ways.

I graduated first from the Heilbronn Lyceum for Girls, then from the Oberrealschule (Abitur). In 1926, I got married and moved to Nürnberg, where my husband operated a large tin toy factory. We had two children, Ellen and Hans-Josef. In 1933, right after the seizure of power by Hitler, I for the first time visited Palestine. The following year, the Nazis forced my husband into heavy digging labor. It was only for a day, but the experience was enough. Gleefully the Nazis shouted to him: "Tell it in Palestine that we taught you to work!"

We acted quickly. For three years we lived in Tel Aviv with my mother, then ran a nearby chicken farm—hard work under very primitive circumstances, with kerosene ovens and no electricity, and a mule carriage to take the children to school. To earn more money, I took care of a children's camp for twelve years. After twenty-three years we sold the farm; my mother had died, my husband became seriously ill. My son, a lieutenant in the Independence War of 1948, went to study in the United States, where he graduated and worked his way up to his present position as biometrics director of the Squibb Laboratories of Princeton, New Jersey. His wife is a native of Jerusalem. My daughter married a controller of the Port Authority in Israel.

After my husband's death I did linguistic work for a private company taking care of international meetings in Israel.

Today I am a great-grandmother and live alone in Givatayim.

SIEGFRIED ARAM (ABRAHAM)
[As told by his friends]

Siegfried Aram was born in 1891 in Heilbronn and died in New York in 1978. His father's name was Siegmund Abraham, and his mother was born Gruenwald from the brewery Loewenbrau. His grandfather was the consul to the United States. He must have inherited much from his grandmother Gruenwald. He studied law and was a lawyer of some repute. He was a Doctor of Law, a Ph.D., and a Dr. per. pol.

The story goes that during World War I there was a dangerous order

13

given to eliminate a mine to an officer who had five children and that Aram, who was not married, offered to take over that order. When doing so, the mine exploded and killed the horse under him and Aram became deaf. He received a special reward from the King of Wuerttemberg.

Being deaf, he changed his profession after the war to be an art dealer with galleries mainly in Berlin and Baden-Baden. His friends called him an excellent buyer and a very poor seller. The man, who was one of the richest art dealers in Germany, came to the United States quite poor and could never make a living, especially because he was deaf. He, who was in Germany friend and advisor to famous personalities like the Thomas Mann family and Erich Maria Remarque, had to be helped by his friends, who even let him sleep at their apartments. He wrote, around 1933, a book, *Hitler Treibt Zum Krieg.*

[*Ed. comment:* I had met Aram in Germany and saw him several times in New York fundamentally changed and in miserable condition mentally and physically.]

RICHARD ARNSTEIN
801 West 181st Street
New York, N.Y. 10033

My father, Gustav Arnstein, was born in 1865. In 1896 he married Netty Luber, born in 1874. In 1907 he bought the Nachtwach und Schliess-dienst Gesellschaft in Stuttgart. At that time I was three years old. I joined the concern in 1927 and at the same time I married Charlotte Heymann. Her father, Berthold Heymann, was a member of the Wuerttemberg Landtag for over twenty-five years and Minister of Culture and Education for a number of years after the revolution in 1918. Faced with the boycott on April 1, 1933, we sold the firm to a Christian friend and I continued to work there for four more years. In September 1938 I emigrated to New York alone, as my affidavit was found insufficient for the entire family. My wife and children followed in May 1939.

My parents had tickets for the S.S. *Manhattan,* which sailed from Genoa on June 6, 1940. However on June 1, Mussolini closed the border, as Italy was about to enter the war. My father did not survive that blow. He died on June 1, 1940. Later on, my mother was able to go to Spain. For one year she lived in Barcelona, and after overcoming many obstacles, she came to New York in 1943. She died in 1958.

Our son, Walter, has been professor of history at the University of Illinois in Champaign/Urbana for the last twelve years. His textbook *Britain, Yesterday and Today* appeared in its third edition and has been introduced in more than two hundred universities and colleges. He is married to the former Charlotte Sutphen, who has a master's degree in music and is teaching piano. Their daughter, Sylvia, is studying for her master's degree in art at the Pratt Institute in Brooklyn. Their son, Peter, is a teaching assistant and studying for his Ph.D. in music at the University of Wisconsin in Madison. His wife, Pamela, is also teaching at the university and working on her master's degree in music.

Our daughter, Laura, was a fashion buyer for Ohrbach's for twelve years and made yearly trips to Paris and Florence. She married William Altschuler, who is a fund manager with Oppenheimer and Company. She is now retired from business life and active in school and civic affairs (League of Women Voters Educational Priority Panel). Their son, Ted, will begin his studies at Brandeis University in the fall. He wants to become a biologist. Their daughter, Susan, is attending the High School of Music and Art in Manhattan.

In January 1933 my father-in-law, Berthold Heymann, was warned by a member of the Nazi party that his arrest was imminent. He fled to Switzerland, where asylum was granted to him and his wife as political refugees. He died in Zurich in 1939. His wife, Anna, returned to Stuttgart, where she died in 1965.

LORE AUBURN (née Kauffmann)
3 Coronation Road
Epson, Auckland 3
New Zealand

My father was Professor Hugo Joseph Kauffmann, who for years worked at the Technische Hochschule in Stuttgart and at the Textilforschungs Institute in Reutlingen. At the time of the Hitler takeover my parents moved to Stuttgart and later emigrated to the United States. My father worked up to his death in 1956 as research chemist for Becco Buffalo; he was then eighty-five years old and mentally completely alert. My mother, Martha, née Schloss, was born in 1881 in Stuttgart and married my father in 1902. She helped my father in his chemical work. I saw her last in 1970, when she was mentally alert but already depressed, and as the distances in New York prevented her cousins and friends from visiting her, she became depressed and withdrawn. She died in 1976 at the age of ninety-four. My brother, Hans Kauffmann, lives on.

I was born in Stuttgart in 1907 and went to the Olgastift after two years in the Waldorfschule. I went to the Realschule after attending Girls School. Already at that time anti-Semitism was rife. I was the only Jewish girl at the school. Once I ran home, and only after my mother had spoken to the very nice headmaster did I go back.

15

After Maturum, I studied medicine in different universities: Tuebingen, Berlin, Zurich, Heidelberg, where in 1928 I met my future husband, who was a few years ahead with his medical studies. In 1933 we were both employed by the Neukoeliner Hospital in Berlin at the time of the Reichstag fire. As my husband was given notice because he was *fremdstämmig*, we left for Holland on the last train on March 31 from Berlin overflowing with refugees. We had relatives in Holland, and my husband, after some difficulties, went to England and with the help of a Russian doctor found out that he could qualify for a Scottish degree in a year in Edinburgh. I had only done two months of my practical year as a doctor and, therefore, was not admitted. My husband worked for an Indian doctor as underpaid, overworked assistant in Manchester, and then we settled and after some difficulties got permission by the Home Office to start practice in Whitefield, Lancashire. My husband volunteered for the British Army and was actually in the Normandy landings. Also, apart from working as field officer for the evacuation of the wounded, he enjoyed being able to work as interpreter of German prisoners-of-war. I contracted TB while he was overseas, so after the war we decided to emigrate to New Zealand, where my husband established a good medical practice. I had volunteered during the war for service in a hospital and was put on the Permanent English Medical Register. After ten years, my husband took a position as director of student health at the Auckland University and, when he retired, worked medically part-time. I was able to help him with his medical work and also with his interest in old prints, book translating, etc. I have three children. One son is associate professor of law. After spending ten years in Israel, mostly working on a kibbutz, he qualified in New Zealand. The second son, after qualifying as a diesel engineer, also spent time overseas and in Israel. He is now running an antique shop. Both sons were in Israel on active service during the 1967 war. We adopted our daughter, who is now married and has three children and also lives here.

I have never been back in Germany after short visits in 1934 and 1935. I have a few relatives in New York, also in Berkeley. My mother's cousin and her daughter, Hede and Ev Schloss, live in New York, 514 West 211th Street, New York, N.Y. 10034 [*Ed. comment:* Hede Schloss died recently.]

ALBERT BACH

Kibbutz Ruchama
79180 Doar Na Chof Ashkelon
Israel

My mother, Mathilde Bach, née Frankfurter, was born in 1873 in Stuttgart and died in 1932 in Tuebingen (in the home of my sister, Mrs. Hanna Bernheim). I emigrated with my family to Paris, France, and from there to Israel in 1951. Since then, we are living with our son and his family in the kibbutz Ruchama. I am still working part-time. During World War II, I was interned for a short time as a German and was, from 1940 until 1942, with the Légion Étrangère in Morocco. I myself was born in 1899.

While living in Germany, I belonged to the Jewish Youth Organization (Juedischer Jugendbund). After the war, in Paris, I was active in the KKL and we were members of the Consistoire Israel de France. My wife, Elisabeth, born 1905, was a member of the WIZO in Paris. For many years after the war, she was assistant director of the children's home of the Éclaireurs Israélites in Moissac (France). In the kibbutz in Israel my wife worked as a kindergarten teacher for ten years.

*ALFRED BACH

Lawyer Alfred Bach was born in 1874 in Ulm and admitted to the court of Stuttgart in 1901. He took the increasing restrictions against the Jews so much to heart that he put an end to his life. He died of gunshot wounds in 1935, shortly before the proclamation of the notorious Nuernberg Laws.

While his son managed to emigrate to South Africa, his widow, Anna, née Steiner, was deported in 1941 to Riga, from where she never returned.

HANS I. BACH

Born 1902 in Stuttgart. First son of Albert and Bertha Bach. Died 1977.

Family: Father partner of D. Bach & Soehne, men's shirt factory. Business founded in 1858 by grandfather David. Mother born in Neustadt a.d.W. Her father, Moses Samson, wine merchant, later in Stuttgart. Mother founded sisterhood of B'nai B'rith lodge.

Education and Career in Germany: Eberhard-Ludwigs-Gymnasium to

Abitur 1920; University of Freiburg; employment in bookstore in Stuttgart, then university of Leipzig; Frankfurt; Dr. phil., Berlin, 1928. Co-editor of Jean Paul edition, Lector Reichsinnenministerium Schundpruefstelle, co-editor *Der Morgen* 1933–1939.

Marriage: 1938, Berlin, to Suse R. Fleischhacker, born 1902; no offspring.

Emigration and Career: 1939 to England; interned on Isle of Man, then factory worker; employment with Foreign Office Board of Trade; teacher at boarding school; lecturer, Institute of Jewish Learning; editor, *Synagogue Review of Great Britain*, 1958–1960; science editor with publishing house; after retirement free-lance writer on psychological, cultural, and Jewish subjects.

Publications: Critical edition of Jean Paul's *Hesperus* (1929); book on Jacob Bernays, 1974 (Gold Medal from Bonn University, 1977); numerous articles in scientific and popular magazines and periodicals.

Jewish Interests and Activities: Kameraden Youth Movement; Juedisches Lehrhaus Frankfurt a.M. (Martin Buber, Franz Rosenzweig); Reichsvertretung (Otto Hirsch); personal friendship with Leo Baeck.

Hobbies: Jewish genealogy, piano-playing.

RUDI (RUDOLPH DAVID) BACH
5 Tanners Road
New Hyde Park, N.Y. 11022

Born 1904 in Stuttgart, second son of Albert and Bertha Bach.

Family: Father partner of D. Bach & Soehne, men's shirts factory, business founded 1858 by grandfather David. Mother born in Neustadt a.d.W. Her father, Moses Samson, wine merchant, later in Stuttgart. Mother founded sisterhood of B'nai B'rith.

Education and career: Eberhard-Ludwigs-Gymnasium to Abitur; apprentice at Brueder Landauer; studies at TH, Stuttgart; with Gebr. Simon, Berlin, then with ladies dress manufacturer; studies at Berlin University. 1926–27, cutting assistant in New York; joined family business; became partner in 1929.

Marriage: 1929 to Ruth, daughter of Hermann and Rose Mayer née Hirsch; father partner in Hirsch & Mayer Mercedes Weinbrennereien. This business had been founded in Cannstatt by his father together with the father of his partner and brother-in-law, Alfred Hirsch. The business moved later on to Stuttgart-Feuerbach, where the partner also founded the SWF Spezialwerkzeugfabrik Stuttgart-Feuerbach.

Emigration: Although we suffered no personal harm and the business but minor economic damage, we decided to leave. This necessitated the

sale of our company, in which I was the first member of the third generation. The sale was effected in 1936 under comparatively reasonable
terms. My wife and I emigrated with two and one half children to Palestine; we could let my parents follow in 1938. Established import-agency;
when World War II ended imports, job with auditor, then assistant manager in cosmetic factory; 1947 emigration to United States; worked first
with father-in-law; established business importing machine-knives in
which I am still active.

Children: Son Michael, immunologist with pharmaceutical company;
his wife, Shirley, university professor; two sons, one married. Daughter
Dori married to John W. Beckhard, both with me in Bach & Co.; three
daughters. Daughter Rachel married Steven Kaplan, both university
professors in psychology; one son.

Jewish interests; in Germany: Kameraden Youth Movement—for some
time as member of Bundesleitung; Committee of CV, Juedische Kunstgemeinschaft; (upon wish of Otto Hirsch) secretary of Juedisches Lehrhaus,
which I helped to reorganize into an adult education institution with
accent on preparation for emigration. In Palestine, Haganah and German-Jewish organizations. In United States wife very active in Hadassah.

Hobbies: writing, Jewish studies, plants, gardening, traveling, photography.

In Memory of Rabbi Dr. SIMON BAMBERGER by Ilse Roberg

As much as I would like to oblige your request by writing you about our
dear, dear friend, Rabbi Simon Bamberger and his wonderful wife,
Trude, I find myself in the awkward position of not being a historian at all.
To write an article abut this truly religious and very human individual, I
would need a complete and exact background which I do not have and
which most likely cannot be obtained in a hurry.

Dr. and Mrs. Bamberger were not blessed with children of their own
and, therefore, many young people, especially the young teachers of the
Jewish School and the students of the School of Sports, became their
boarders or their steady Shabbos guests. If, on occasion, food seemed a
little scarce because of too many guests, one could hear a sweet little
warning, "F H Z," which meant *"Family Haelt Zurueck,"* and we were the
family. Unforgettable are the delicious, hard-crusted chalot, baked by
Trude Bamberger, who was severely plagued by diabetes. The cake was a
very plain one, and Dr. Bamberger delighted in putting a little bit of jam
on it, inevitably remarking, "I am the only one allowed to do this because I
have a French grandmother."

19

When the friendship between me and Alex Roberg, one of the boarders in the Bamberger household, and my esteemed colleague at the school where both of us taught, started to bloom into courtship, Dr. and Mrs. Bamberger were delighted and sent the most cordial letters of recommendation and encouragement to my parents.

However, dear Walter Strauss, all these little incidents cannot convey a picture of the man whose learning achievements bore fruit in publications, whose human relationships created a warm and congenial bond between his congregants in the Israelitische Religionsgesellschaft, whose deep concern for the well-being of fellow Jews in these most trying times, brought about a sincere respect between the "Polish Shul" and its congregation. He supervised the teaching of religious subjects in our school and took delight in seeing our achievements, especially those of the children of our Polish brethren. These children were brought up in the finest sense of tradition, studying the Talmud at a very early age. Instructions from *Seidis* (grandfathers) like the *Talmud Chochom* Lehrmann, Engelberg, Schluesselberg, Tanne, Engelmeyer, etc. (May they forgive me if I did not mention them in the order due to them for their prestige in knowledge.)

What an imposing personality remains our revered Shoichet Engelmeyer and his wise wife, who, unfortunately, was rendered helpless by cripling arthritis.

Let me mention also our beloved Cantor Zanger and his large family, an integral part of the Religionsgesellschaft, who beautified every service with his touching renditions of our holy prayers. May they all rest in peace, and may surviving children and grandchildren take pride in these noble and brave forefathers, *sichronom liv' rochoh.*

We met the Bambergers later in Israel, where he was the principal of the Mizrachi School in Bne-Brak. Rabbi Simon Bamberger died in 1957, shortly after our first reunion. Mrs. Trude Bamberger passed away around 1970 after a heroically fought life of afflictions. This would have deprived anybody else of every ounce of love and confidence in God, had he been in a similar condition. All these people around her remained lovingly in attendance; may they be rewarded for such extraordinary human kindness.

RENATE BARTH (née Kahn)
4499 Henry Hudson Parkway
Bronx, N.Y. 10471

I, Renate Barth, was born in 1905 in Baisingen, Wuerttemberg. Both my parents, Albert Kahn and Bertha Kahn, née Weinberger, were also born in Baisingen. My father was very active in community affairs and was president of the Jewish congregation. My father passed away in 1922 at the age of forty-seven. My mother experienced Kristallnacht in Baisingen, hiding in the forest with some other Jewish neighbors. She passed away in her home in Baisingen in December 1940 because she was unable to get a doctor while she had a high temperature. We were advised about her passing because the affidavit that we sent for her came back, "Party Deceased."

I was married in 1929 to Jakob Barth. My sister, Sara Kahn, and my brother, Herman Kahn, and I all attended the Juedishe Schule in Baisingen, where teacher Strassburger taught for a whole generation. A son, Walter, was born in 1931 to us, and in 1938 my husband, son, and I migrated to the United States and we settled in Richmond Hill, New York. My husband worked in a metal-manufacturing company, but unfortunately passed away in 1944, a short while after we had received our United States citizenship papers. My son attended City College and received a degree in electrical engineering and after a two-year tour in the U.S. Army, attended New York University and received a master's degree in business administration. He is now president of his own firm in financial consulting here in New York. He married a Jewish girl who was raised during the war in Holland by non-Jewish people while her parents were deported to the camps in 1941. They have four children.

I took various dietician courses and worked in summer camps and schools in charge of food and kitchen management. I am now retired but still active as a volunteer to nursing homes, temples, and various other Jewish causes.

My sister, Sara, was married to Ludwig Adler, living in Markelsheim, Wuerttemberg. They migrated to this country in 1938. Her husband passed away in 1959, and she and her two children with their families settled in Israel in 1969. My brother, Herman, left Germany in 1935 and settled in Israel, where he raised a family of three children.

My uncle, my father's brother, was Rabbi Dr. Moritz Kahn, whose congregation was in Bad Mergentheim and the surrounding area. He was very respected and loved by both the Jewish and Gentile communities for over thirty years. I was informed that during Kristallnacht, he was severely mugged and mishandled and soon after left Germany to settle in Israel.

A particularly tragic story relates to the brother of my mother, Max Weinberger, who was called to serve in the German army in the First World War. At that time he had been recently married and had two children, two and four years old. He lost his life in the war in 1915. But the major tragedy was that his wife and both children, who were later married, were killed in the concentration camps in World War II. My uncle was buried in Baisingen, and when I visited there a few years ago to see the graves, his grave was in such bad condition that I could no longer recognize it. My grandfather had a brother, Rabbi Ludwig Kahn, who was the rabbi in Heilbronn for many, many years.

FRITZ BAUER

"If I were in a position to change the terminology of the legal profession I would call the state attorneys the law attorneys. . . . The state attorney does not represent the state. He is not the lawyer for any state position or interest but of human beings and their social existence against aggressors from private or state interests. He is bound by the laws of which the most important are the rights of man." For that reason Bauer fought for the institution of the ombudsman, which already in many progressive countries protected the citizen against abuses of power. He dedicated a book to the right of resistance. He defended the duty of resistance to illegal orders. He did not for the reasons of the Old Testament defend the right of "an eye for an eye" but he defends the Nazi trials of the German government in the spirit of obedience to God over obedience to man. In publications like *The Crime and the Society* (1957) and *Searching for the Right* (1966) he has given his opinions on reform of the penal law. He desires a law which is in harmony with modern natural and social sciences and social order of the restitution.

Born 1903 as the son of a family which lived in Stuttgart for a long time, he studied law and began in 1927 as a judge. In 1933, of course, he lost his positions because he was a Jew and a liberal, came with Kurt Schumacher to a concentration camp, and emigrated to Denmark and Sweden in 1936. In 1949 he returned and since 1956 was the general state attorney of Hesse. In 1968 a few days before his sixty-fifth birthday he died in Frankfurt, Germany.

For more details write to his sister: Margot Tiefenthal, Dahlheimersgatan 4 a, S-413 20 Goteborg, Sweden.

It is well known how Fritz Bauer helped the Israelis in the trial of Eichmann. Fritz Bauer wrote books not only about law but also economics and politics. The Germans also made a film about him which his sister saw on TV but cannot remember the name of.

GRETE BAUER
formerly Hoelderlin Strasse 57
Stuttgart

Grete Bauer, born 1883 and died 1974, came in 1917 to Stuttgart, where she married Moritz Bauer. Son Ernest to Italy before Hitler. Daughter Trude and her husband, Alfred Kahn, with their daughter, Anne Marie, emigrated to Holland, from where they were deported later and perished.

Mrs. Bauer earned her living as an alteration seamstress for many years and later became an occupant of the Jewish Home for the Aged.

MARGO BAUER (née Eisinger)
316 Second Street West
Tierra Verde, Fla.

Born 1920 in Stuttgart. Mother: Julia Eisinger (Gidion) Horb, born 1895, died 1964 in Chicago. Father: Philipp Eisinger, born 1884, died 1945 in Chicago. Sales representative and importer of pipes. Husband: Henry Bauer, born 1907 in Stuttgart. Mother: Elizabeth Levy (maiden name), born 1885; died 1968 in Chicago, Illinois. Father: Julius Bauer, born 1874 in Ellwangen, and died 1965. Children of Henry and Margo Bauer: Joan Bauer: Born 1945, attorney-at-law, Morehead, Kentucky; Nancy Bauer Much: Born 1947, three children: Jeremy Philipp, born 1969; Mellicent Fae, born 1972; Joel Ashley, born 1975.

HELGA BAUM (née Dreifus)
83 Weaving Lane
Wantagh, N.Y. 11793

My father, Max Dreifus, was born in Stuttgart in 1891. He and his father, David, owned and operated a men's clothing factory, first as Dreifus und Lehmann and later under the name of Gebrueder Kramer. The firm was liquidated in 1938. He emigrated to the United States in March 1939 and lived in Chicago for two years. In 1941 he moved to Columbus, Ohio, and opened a Dr. Scholl's shoe store. He retired in 1956 and has lived in Columbus since that time. His second wife is Doris Jacobson, who was born in Scotland and is Jewish. My mother, Else Loewenstein Dreifus, died in Stuttgart in 1930.

I was born in Stuttgart in 1925. I attended the Rhoderthsche Maedchenschule and the Heidehofschule until November 1938. I graduated from high school in Columbus in 1943 and from Ohio State University in

1945. In 1946 I married Newman Baum, who was born in Missouri and is of German-Jewish descent on both paternal and maternal sides. I worked as a chemist until our children were born—Philip James in 1951 and Eric Daniel in 1954.

In 1965 I received a master's degree in secondary education. For six years I taught German part-time and for the last ten years I have been a full-time teacher of science on the junior-high level.

As far as religious affiliation is concerned, we belonged to a Reform congregation while our sons were in school, and both were confirmed, but not Bar Mitzvah (neither was their father). In the community I have been active in groups such as University Women, Home Bureau, teachers' union, etc.

KURT J. BAUM
7 Fallbrook Park
Canandaigua, N.Y. 14424

Father: Emil Feigenbaum, born 1893 in Binswangen. Educated in Noerdlingen. Partner at Lippmann Wolff & Sohn GMBH in Stuttgart-Zuffenhausen (Lumpensortieranstalt) with about 120 employees. Family emigrated in September 1938 to Belgium. Partner at Benselin & Henrotay in Vilvorde-Brussels, same type of business. Arrested 1940. Died 1940 in German air attack.

Mother: Claire Feigenbaum, née Reis. Born 1892 in Niederstetten. Educated in Schwaebisch-Hall. Taught secretarial work in adult education classes in Frankfurt/Main during World War I. Married in 1920. Spent about six months in Belgian camp Malines. Liberated during Allied invasion. Emigrated to United States in 1952 to join us and her future grandchildren in Rochester, New York. Changed name to Baum. Died 1972 in Rochester.

Myself: Born 1921 in Stuttgart. Educated at Hohensteinschule (later Horst-Wessel-Realschule!), Zuffenhausen. Emigrated September 1938 to Belgium. Attended business college in Brussels until 1940. Arrested with father, 1940. French internment camps and Foreign Labor Battalions (Compagnies de Travailleurs Étrangers): St. Cyprien, Argeles-sur-Mer, Chateau de Tombebouc, Camp Plaisance-Losse, Sauveterre-de-Guyenne, Casteljaloux, Prison Drancy in Paris. 1942 shipped to the following concentration camps: Kochanowitz, Borsigwerk, Auschwitz-Blechhammer (Tattoo No. 177132), Gross-Rosen, Buchenwald. Liberated 1945 by U.S. Third Army.

Work History: U.S. Military Government Wuerttemberg-Baden in Stuttgart, 1945–47. Comptoir Textile de Liege, Brussels, 1947–50. European-

American Bank Corporation, New York, N.Y., September 1950–51. 1951–present: Labelon Corporation, a manufacturer of office supplies. Current position, vice-president, international sales.

Member of Congregation B'rith Kodesh, Rochester. Co-founder and trustee, Sonnenberg Gardens, Canandaigua. Past president, Rochester Purchasing Management Association. Past president, Rochester Small Business Association. Founder and past president, Canandaigua Industrial Management Council. Co-founder and past president, Canandaigua Lively Arts Council. Past director, Canandaigua Chamber of Commerce. Member, Canandaigua Country Club.

Married Margot Baum, née Alt, in 1948. Born in Koeln 1925. M.A. degree, University of Rochester. Chairperson, Foreign Language Department, Canandaigua High School and Junior High School. Teaches German at Canandaigua Academy. Member, Hadassah.

Children: Peter David, b. 1952 Rochester, New York. B.A., University of Pennsylvania, M.B.A., University of Florida. Account executive at Dean Witter Reynolds, Ocala, Florida.

Michael Daniel, b. 1955 Rochester. B.A., Sarah Lawrence College. Currently secretary in the practice of two doctors of psychology, San Francisco.

Susan Esther, b. 1958 Rochester. B.F.A., Syracuse University, with textile design major. Currently employed at Thomas Strahan Division of National Gypsum Company, Boston, Massachusetts.

I hope this gives you most of the information you are seeking. My wife and I are happy to have had the opportunity to build a new life for ourselves and our children in our new homeland. Canandaigua (Seneca Indian word for "the Chosen Spot") is an especially pretty little resort town in the Finger Lakes region and we love it here. We are within only thirty-five minutes drive from Rochester, three-and-one-half hours from Toronto, and six-and-one-half hours from New York City. We are most thankful for the opportunities this country has given us.

ERWIN BECKHARD

Born 1893 in Stuttgart. He died in 1973. He lived in New York up to his death, on Elmhurst Avenue in Elmhurst, Queens. His wife, Eleanor, died in 1972. His son, Ted, was born in 1933. His wife is Madeleine. He is an engineering designer and they have a child, Alan, born in 1967. They live at 2 Hillcrest Avenue in Dover, New Jersey.

JULIUS BECKHARD (widow Vera Beckhard)
80 Park Avenue
New York, N.Y. 10016

Born 1896 in Stuttgart. Son of Gustave and Mathilde Beckhard. Married to Erna Sinn in 1922. Left for the United States in 1923. Business executive and head and founder of the Beckhard Line since 1924. Erna Beckhard passed away in 1946. He remarried in 1948 Vera Krueger. Children: Mrs. Hanna M. Aron, Herbert Beckhard, and Mrs. Eva Hommel. Eight grandchildren: six girls and two boys.

Julius Beckhard was very active in philanthropic work. He was on the executive board of the Federation of Jewish Philanthropies. 1949–50, special gifts chairman for UJA; member of board of founders of the Long Island Jewish Hospital; on the board of trustees at the National Jewish Hospital in Denver. Board of governors of the Joint Defense Appeal, ADL. Member of the New York Advisory Board, B'nai B'rith. President, Long Island Lodge, B'nai B'rith, 1954–55. Vice-president, Metropolitan Council B'nai B'rith, 1947–49. District representative, National Service for Armed Forces and Veterans, since 1947. Creator of the Henry Monsky Memorial Athletic Field at the Veterans Hospital in Northport, Long Island. National commissioner of the Vocational Guidance Service of B'nai B'rith. President, Inwood Police Boys Club. Trustee of the Metropolitan Synagogue. Board member of Leo Baeck Lodge, B'nai B'rith.

Passed away in 1976.

ERNEST L. BERGMAN
1421 Harris Street
State College, Pa. 16801

After my father, Willi Bergmann, passed away in 1925, when I was three years old, and my brother Willy, an infant, my mother, Julia (née Steiner), moved back with us to her home in Laupheim, where we lived in the house of my grandfather, Simon L. Steiner. I attended the Jewish Grade School there and in 1933 entered the Laupheim Latin School. With increasing cruelty on the part of the Third Reich, it became impossible to continue, and in 1936 my uncle, Helmut Steiner, took me into his home in St. Gallen, Switzerland, so I could finish high school there. From there I went to the Bern State Agriculture School, to study agriculture for two years. During the following four years I worked on Swiss farms doing every farm chore, including milking eighteen cows by hand. My training and work in agriculture kept me out of a Swiss Refugee Labor Camp, but nevertheless, I was subjected to severe travel restrictions imposed by the

Swiss Federal Police. Then, with the help of my employers and friends, I got a chance to study and work for nearly a year at the Swiss Central Station for Fruit Growing in exchange for taking care of the heating system.

In 1946 my mother and brother, who had both followed me to St. Gallen prior to the war, and I immigrated together to the United States, followed a few months later by my grandmother. My grandfather had been killed by the Nazis. My first job in the States was pruning apple trees near Poughkeepsie, New York. After that I worked for three years for S. S. Steiner Hops, Inc., on their farm near Independence, Oregon, and for two years as horticulturist on a large Oregon vegetable farm. After receiving my citizenship in 1952, I was able to get a state job as an experimental aide at Oregon State College, and it was there, with the urging by my employer and my wife Alice (née Adler of St. Gallen, Switzerland), that I decided to go back to college and get an American degree. By continuing my job, my wife working full-time, and with some credit for my studies and experiences in Switzerland, I could complete the requirements for the B.S. degree in pomology in two years. Afterwards, with the help of a research assistantship and my wife working, I earned an M.S. and Ph.D. degree in horticulture–plant nutrition from Michigan State University in an additional three years.

In 1958 I joined the Department of Horticulture, Pennsylvania State University, as an assistant professor of plant nutrition and am now a full professor in that field. Currently, I am teaching a course in plant nutrition to upper-class students with an average course enrollment of 140. My research is concerned with nutrition of horticultural crops, especially vegetables, virus-plant nutrition relationships, plant and soil analyses, etc. I am a graduate and undergraduate student advisor and have many published scientific and semi-popular papers. During the late sixties, I have been three times, each time for three months, in Argentina on assignment to help improve the country's apple production, a project co-sponsored by the government of Argentina and Penn State University.

I am a member of many honorary and professional societies, including a fellow of the American Society for Horticultural Science and of the American Association for the Advancement of Science. The University Faculty Senate, to which I was elected for the first time in 1968, elected me its chairman for 1974–75. During the last eighteen years I have also been very active in civic affairs as elected member and/or chairman of various local and regional councils, authorities and commissions.

We consider ourselves extremely fortunate that most members of the family got out of Germany alive and were able to create a new satisfying existence in this country.

LEA BERLINER (née Fischmann)
14 Gordon Street
32764 Haifa,
Israel

As for my personal experiences, well . . . How can one put forty-five years of Israeli life into words? The first adventure of a *haluza,* vintage 1934, who felt responsible for—and carried the "fate of Palestine" on her shoulders? In complete identification with the Socio-Zionist ideas of the time, the fervor of communal living, the dancing of exciting new dances like hora, and krakoviak into the early hours of the night on an empty stomach—barefoot, shoes gone.

We lived a myth, in intensity comparable only to hot religion, and it was deliriously delicious. Who remembers the backbreaking work of road-building with one's own hands? Who knows today of the fight for working places with Jewish farms to supplant cheap Arab work? How to describe the hot-house atmosphere of the harassed Jewish community? The ups and downs, everybody involved.

The horror and the heroics as Arab disturbances began with constant sniping. The bloodletting. The clandestine Jewish weapons. The physical toil. Or worse, no work at all. With the nightmare of going hungry.

It was all there, it was all me—and my family—my husband, my little boy. Lea Berliner, née Lea Fischmann of Stuttgart, daughter of Karoline and Michael Fischmann.

Tent—shack—kerosene lamp. Primus-cooker. Awareness of slowly ac-quiring the mentality of the very poor.

With agriculture bogged down, struggle for a job, opening and closing of a shop. Though at the end, fifteen years of successful and satisfying office work on an advanced level.

Today, at sixty-eight, I occupy myself by drawing, painting, and taking university courses.

Personal achievements? Whether an intense, full, and active life counts for that—or being the mother of a senior lecturer at the University of Jerusalem with a Ph.D. from Berkeley? Or of a kindergarten-teacher daughter? Or perhaps six clever, beautiful granddaughters will do? The decision is yours. Dear Mr. Strauss, mine is the life of a foot soldier. But then there is no army without its foot soldiers. Even today.

HANNA BERNHEIM (née Bach)
4518 Barbara Place
Cincinnati, Ohio 45229

I was a member of the board of our Cincinnati Gate Club, formed by immigrants from Germany, Austria, Hungary, and Czechoslovakia, where we got very informative lectures by American leaders to acquaint us with American history, literature, religious developments, and election procedures. I was also co-founder of Our Neighborhood Help, which assisted members of our group in sickness. After the war ended in 1945 we collected clothing and sent it to survivors in Europe for several years. I was instrumental with some members of the Cincinnati Section of the National Council of Jewish Women who "adopted" European families, sending packages and encouraging letters which I translated. This organization also sent me as a friendly visitor to a lady in a hospital who suffered from muscular dystrophy until she passed away after several years.

My husband's father, Rudolph Bernheim, born 1847 in Hechingen, lived in Stuttgart from 1899 to 1934. At the age of ninety-five he was threatened to be transferred to a concentration camp but a friend could prevent it by giving money. However, he was transferred to an old-age home, and when his money was confiscated at the bank, all this got him so upset that he suffered a heart attack and died.

MARGIT BERNSTEIN (née Oppenheimer)
Hagdowd Naivri 31
Kiryath-Chaim
Israel

My husband, Philipp Bernstein, was born in Bad Cannstatt and grew up in Kirchheim/Teck. We met in the orphanage Esslingen, where my brother and I were put after the arrest of our beloved father, Moses Oppenheimer. My brother is living at present in Miami Beach, Florida.

We were three children of a mixed marriage which ended in divorce already in 1929, before Hitler. Our mother, who married again, is still living in a senior citizen home in Stuttgart/Berg. We grew up in the home of our Jewish father and naturally belong to the Jewish faith. My sister, Anne Berger, was lucky to get out of Germany in 1940 and lives here in Haifa. She has been widowed for fourteen years and has two married daughters.

My brother, Joseph Oppenheimer, and I had been sent to Theresienstadt, later were separated and sent to different camps. After my release, the 8th of May, 1945, I went back to Stuttgart, where after a few weeks I was reunited with my brother. In September 1945 I emigrated to Palestine with the help of the Jewish Brigade and the man who later became my husband. He had been with the Brigade throughout the war. These were soldiers who served under the English military.

The first part of my journey led me to Antwerp, where I stayed about four months. Then came the illegal trip on a boat on which seven hundred passengers, former concentration-camp inhabitants, were herded together. It was a miracle that we survived, and in 1946, the boat *Tel Chai* landed in Haifa. We did not come to a "land of milk and honey," which it is not even today. Israel demands a great deal of her inhabitants. But, having been twice on a visit to the United States, I still believe that Israel is the best country for us Jews.

During the first week in Haifa, I lived with my sister and brother-in-law until my husband was relieved of his military duties and we went to live in his kibbutz. We were married in 1946. Our son, Dani, was born in 1947. I was a very happy mother and hoped that my baby would make me forget all the misery I had endured, but this was not the case. I was a nervous wreck and still am to this day. My condition does not make life easier for my husband or my children.

I receive a pension as compensation for the damage to my health. This does not give me back my health, but makes it possible for us to raise our standard of living a little. We spent twelve years in the kibbutz, but I could never get used to this kind of living, so finally, on my doctor's advice, we left the kibbutz. It had been a very difficult decision to make, especially as my husband had lived in this group for twenty years and our daughter, Jael, would not easily get used to a different life. But we made it. Our son, Dani, is living in a newly founded kibbutz in Galilee with his wife and two sons. Our daughter is also married, has two boys, and lives near us. We derive great joy from our grandchildren and only hope they will never in their life experience the tragedy we had to suffer.

In 1966 our son was dangerously injured in the military, driving a command car over a mine. Miraculously he escaped with third-degree burns over 60 percent of his body. For weeks it was a matter of life or death, and he is now 50 percent disabled. He has studied Oriental sciences and is a "kibbutznik." My husband works daily in a firm which buys and sells agricultural products. I am a housewife and cannot undertake any other work.

HILDE BLANK (née Schlessinger)
99 Hillside Avenue
New York, N.Y. 10040

I was born in 1908 in Stuttgart, as the youngest child of Max O. Schlessinger and Hermine Schlessinger, née Hoffer. Both my parents were born in Vienna in the 1860's. Our father died in 1921 in Stuttgart. My mother kept house for us until she passed away in 1935. Thank God that she did not see anymore the forced separation and decimation of her family, the usual emigration to England, America, and death camps. It would have broken her heart.

I studied at the Conservatory in Stuttgart and became a pianist and music teacher, and I am still busy teaching, though performing was stopped by arthritis some years ago.

In 1974 I married a New Yorker, Sidney Blank. Our son, Harvey, made me a very happy "Grandma" of Jeffrey exactly two years ago. Too bad my husband didn't live to experience this; he died of cancer in 1960.

My family and I joined the Reformed Temple Beth Am, and I am still active in our Sisterhood, as much as my failing health allows; hopefully for some more years to come.

ALICE BLOCH (née Rothschild)
Zurich, Switzerland

Born in Canstatt-Stuttgart, 1894. Married in 1919, Swiss Nationality, since 1939 in Zurich.

My parents: Isak Moritz Rothschild, born 1864; died 1938. Thekla Rothschild née Reis, from Niederstetten. Born 1866, lived from 1940 with daughter, Alice, in Zurich, and died 1961.

Brother: Otto Leopold Rothschild, born 1891, lived in Stuttgart, and murdered in Auschwitz in 1942.

Husband: Oscar Bloch, born 1882, died 1937; Swiss citizen.

Our children: Ruth Pappa Bloch, born 1920. Gardening technician since 1936 in Switzerland, graduated from Gardening School, later directress of leisure-time activities in Adliswil. Lost her husband, Karl Pappas, from Thusis, in 1978, due to an accident.

Heinz Bloch, diplom technician. Since 1937 in Switzerland, in machine factory. Studied evenings at Technicum, Zurich. Worked in Baden until death in 1980. Lived with wife, Ruth, in a one-family home in Baden with a big garden, which he loved to work in during his free time.

Hanna Bloch, born February 1929. Seamstress. Arrived after November pogroms in 1938 in Zurich and lived with relatives while still attending school. Later learned *haute couture* and worked in that profession, even after marriage to Josef Baumann, a book printer. Died in traffic accident.

I, Alice Bloch, when first in Zurich in 1939, took a six-room apartment and took three student boarders, which helped financially. I also did translations from English and took in sewing. After the children were married and the house in Stuttgart was sold, moved into a three-room apartment in 1950, at Haneldweg 25.

*ROBERT BLOCH

Dr. Robert Bloch was born in 1888 in Stuttgart and served in the judiciary of Wuerttemberg since 1916. In accordance with the Law for the Preservation of the Civil Service he was dismissed, without pension, in 1933. In 1942 he was deported to Auschwitz.

After the war it became known that this was an extermination transport from which no one returned. Robert Bloch was severely ill when he had to start out on this journey, and it seems certain that his life was ended shortly afterward in the gas chamber.

ARNOLD BLUM
1322 Hillsdale Drive
Monroeville, Pa. 15146

Born: 1922.

Father: David Blum, born in Noerdlingen, died in Nuernberg.

Mother: Melanie Blum, born in Horb a/N, died in Pittsburgh, Pennsylvania.

Life in Germany: Lived in Stuttgart, 1925–1939. Attended Dillmann Realgymnasium. Prisoner in Dachau at age sixteen. Witnessed burning of Stuttgart Synagogue, November 9, 1938. Member of Werkleute.

United States: Arrived in 1939, worked as a janitor, shipping clerk, etc., until 1943; entered U.S. Army, and trained as combat engineer. Wounded twice while serving in European theatre. Entered Columbia University in 1946, graduated with B.S. in metallurgy in 1950. Married Rita Strauss in 1949, also from Stuttgart, graduate of Hunter College. Received M.S. from Stevens Institute of Technology in 1954 after evening studies. Resided in New York City, Scotch Plains, New Jersey, and for the past twenty years in Monroeville, Pennsylvania.

Children: Two sons, David, now M.D. in endocrinology, and Ralph, a chef. Both are married and have two children each.

Israel: From 1974–1977 in Nahariyah, while technical director of local tool plant.

Jewish Life: Long-time member of Temple David, Monroeville, Pennsylvania; past congregational president and teacher in religious school.

Professional Life: Engineer and industrial manager. Patents and publications in metallurgy and nucleonics.

MARIANNE BLUMENTHAL (née Leiter)
422 Silverlake Scotchtown Road
Middletown, N.Y. 10940

My name is Marianne Blumenthal. I was born in Ulm a/D, Germany, in 1926. I am the daughter of Charles (form. Sally) Leiter and Auguste Leiter. I am married to Fritz F. Blumenthal, a physician, and reside in Middletown, New York. Two children, John Blumenthal and Stephanie Blumenthal. I have one brother, Max Leiter, also born in Ulm, in 1922. He is married to Susie Kasper, is a business executive living in Forest Hills. Two children, Richard and Steven Leiter.

My father, Charles S. Leiter, born in 1893 in Stuttgart, Germany, to Ernestine and Edward Leiter. He had a brother, Max. My father apprenticed in the textile trade at Wolfsöhne, until he entered the Army in 1914. His younger brother, Max, was killed in the war. After my father returned from the war he married Auguste Braun; they settled down in Ulm a/Donau.

My mother, Auguste Leiter, née Braun, was born in Niederstetten, to Sophie and Samuel Braun in 1903. She grew up in Niederstetten and later went to a music conservatory in Stuttgart to study voice, where she met my father.

Upon settling in Ulm, my father, together with his two cousins Albert and Julius Sanger, bought a textile-manufacturing business by the name of Heinrich Glaeser Nachfolger, GMBH. After having lived in Söflingen for several years, after their son was born, they moved to Lichtensteinstrasse 12 in Ulm. Four years later their daughter was born. My parents had many friends, enjoyed their musical interests. My father played the violin, had regular chamber music evenings, and my mother continued her singing and performed at various functions. My parents were active members of the congregation as well as the Kulturbund. My brother and I went to local schools until the Nazis appeared on the scene. In 1937 we were expelled from German public schools, whereupon the Jewish community started their own school, where I went until emigration in 1939. My brother was sent to Switzerland to a private school.

On the famous Kristallnacht, my father was picked up at daybreak by the Gestapo, brought to jail, ending up in Dachau for four weeks. Only because of having a quota number for emigration was he released.

We left Germany in October 1939 via England to the United States. We had no money—all our belongings, including furnishings and clothing, were confiscated by the Nazis. At first we roomed with friends until we found an apartment in Washington Heights. My father started a small textile business with a former colleague; everyone in the family worked. We became United States citizens in 1945. My brother was drafted and served overseas as a sergeant.

After the war was over, my father was able to reclaim his business and property in Germany. He rebuilt his business once more until it was sold in 1979. Between the years of 1950 and 1978, my parents made yearly trips to Germany. My father passed away in 1979, and my mother is living in New York at 35–35 85th Street, Jackson Heights, New York.

HANS BONHEIM
32–11 Nicholson Drive
Fair Lawn, N.J.

Born 1911 in Pforzheim; son of Max Bonheim and Elly Bonheim. Father was officer in the German army and was killed in Flanders in 1916. Sister Lotte married Dussling, left in 1928.

My mother tried to find employment for me and applied at the Hahn & Kolb Machinery. She looked totally Aryan and only at the last moment did she inquire if there would be an objection to my being Jewish. The application was denied. I obtained employment with J. Bauer & Co., Stuttgart, as correspondent, salesman, etc., until my emigration to the United States in October 1937.

In the United States, I found a job with my brother-in-law, who had a small factory in Canton, Ohio. I had a chance to learn English properly and attended night classes. Family friction caused me to leave Canton and return to New York City. My fiancée, Inge Meyer, had a job on Staten Island, and we were married in February 1939. I worked as a Fuller Brush man, assorted other sales jobs, and finally found employment through the Jewish Federation as a machinist in a small machine shop. The company grew. I advanced as toolmaker, and because of my technical training in Germany, I advanced to draftsman and designer. I have some patents to my credit and was instrumental in designing a line of engraving machines for the now-prominent New Hermes, Inc., of New York. In 1939, I left the smaller company and worked for New Hermes, Inc., until my retirement in 1977. After that I did some consulting work for this company.

In 1950 our family moved to Fair Lawn, New Jersey. We are members of the Fair Lawn Jewish Center, charter members of B'nai B'rith, and I am a commissioner of the Boy Scouts of America.

A daughter, Carol Bryk, lives in New City, New York, and has a boy and girl. Another daughter, Frances Lipowitz, lives in Evergreen, Colorado, has two boys; and a son Ralph, twenty-six, lives in New Brunswick and works in New York. With Karl Adler's training, I sang in our synagogue choir for twenty-six years.

My mother, Elly Bonheim, came to the United States in 1939, lived in various places, worked as a practical nurse, and lived in the Isabella House until her death five years ago at the age of ninety-three.

LUISE HELEN BRONNER
30 Kilsyt Road
Brookline, Mass. 02146

Luise Helen Bronner was born in Germany in 1912 and emigrated to the United States in 1938. She is unmarried. She attended the Oberrealschule in Heilbronn—graduating in 1932—and a private chemistry school in Stuttgart. From 1939 to 1959 she was employed in the chemical industry in Rhode Island. The work consisted of assisting the research director in the lab as well as translating technical articles from German into English. At her last position she was in charge of the control and analytical lab. She studied chemistry at the University of Rhode Island from 1959 to 1961 when she got her B.S. Since then she has held various instructional positions in the German departments of several universities. Since 1975 she has been an associate professor in the German Department of the University of Massachusetts in Boston.

She is an educator, published poet, Bertolt Brecht and Eduard Mörike (another German poet) scholar, philologist, and student of German literature. She has published a number of articles, book reviews, poems, and translations in these fields. In 1978 a book of her poetry, *Mosaik,* was published by Bläschke in Darmstadt. Her poems have appeared in *Aufbau, Lyrica Germanica,* and *Skylark,* among other publications.

About herself she says:

Education is—in my opinion—the only shield against anarchism or totalitarianism. I would like to see it happen that every student has a background in the humanities and regardless of his major knows enough of the basic principles of the natural sciences to enable him to take a responsible stand in a society baffled by technological advances. Furthermore, if the home can no longer instill ethical conduct, the schools will have to fulfill this task.

Thanks to coming to these shores, I escaped the holocaust in Germany. I was penniless, but after working for twenty years in industry, plus restitution money from Germany, I could afford to go back to college. I entered the teaching profession, believing in this field I could make a contribution to the country which saved my life. I have served on various committees, and also in the senate, and I have written several proposals concerning education which sprang out of my varied experience and my unusual background. I would like to continue serving the University of Massachusetts at Boston, preferably in the field of continuing education.

In Germany, I had attained the Abitur and the training as laboratory technician at a private chemistry school. I also had gained experience by working in the laboratory of the soap factory which my father, Berthold Heilbronner, had founded together with his brothers, Siegmund and Karl, at Heilbronn. They came originally from Laupheim; probably they settled in Heilbronn because their uncle (Max Rosengart) was practicing law there. My mother, Franziska Rosenstein, was born and raised in Heilbronn, the daughter of a well-to-do merchant. She loved literature and music, and one of her brothers, Ernst (who went to his brother Max in Argentina), composed songs and wrote the lyrics himself. My younger sister, Lotte, emigrated to Israel (she has five grandchildren). My older brother, Emil, felt too "fenced in" and left for the United States as early as 1928. He has become a very successful businessman. (He has six grandchildren.) He helped me to come to the United States in 1938.

I would like to close these remarks with some lines taken from my booklet of poems, *Mosaik* (St. Michael, Austria: Bläschke, 1978), p. 9:

> Du spielst Dir selber auf zum Tanz
> Bist Du gesund und frei—
> Im freien Land!
> Glück oder Unglück ist dann
> Nichts als Resonanz.

[*Ed. note:* See the entry for MAX ROSENGART for another sample of Luise Bronner's poetry.]

ARNOLD BRUNSWICK (Braunschweiger)
80–09 35th Avenue
Jackson Heights, N.Y. 11372

Father: Julius Braunschweiger, born 1871, died 1935 in Stuttgart; business activity: manufacturer of men's clothing.

Mother: Leonie Braunschweiger, née Rosenthal, born 1879 in Rottweil a/Neckar; deported to Riga and killed there around 1943.

I was born in 1900 in Rottweil a/Neckar. In 1936 I married Anna Braunschweiger, née Katz, in Yugoslavia. In 1939 we left Yugoslavia for England, and we lived there until 1947, when we emigrated to the United States. Upon arrival I changed my name to Brunswick.

LEO BURCKHARDT
2601 Henry Hudson Parkway
Bronx, N.Y. 10463

My parents, Theodore and Fanny, were alive in 1933. Mother was picked up in 1942 and sent to Auschwitz. Never heard a word from her. Father committed suicide.

I was born in 1902. I was department-store manager, Isidor Augsburger, Rottweil/N., until 1934, then from 1936 to 1939 was department-store manager of Brueder Landauer, Heilbronn/N.; business manager, S. Rothschild Soehne, Stuttgart.

I was present on the night of November 9, 1938, when vandals destroyed the apartments of the Landauer families in Heilbronn. Vandals hit me on this terrible night with an iron pipe over the head for which I received hospital treatment in Stuttgart.

On September 15, 1939, I arrived in New York via Rotterdam with my wife, Lina, and son, Werner (four years old). I started working in New York immediately as a luncheonette counterman. My wife did housecleaning in order to help support the family. Starting in 1948 I was food manager at Mount Sinai Hospital for ten years, after which I was restaurant manager until my retirement in 1970.

From 1934 until 1939 I was president of the Sports Division Schild (Reichsbund Juedischer Frontsoldaten), Heilbronn and Stuttgart. From 1945 until 1950, Sport-Redakteur of the Aufbau, also manager of the Sports Division of the New World Club.

For forty years soccer (football) referee in Germany and the United States. In Germany officiated at the First Division (Oberliga). After 1940 continued as referee for twenty-five years in the Professional and Amateur Leagues. In 1945 I was voted as best referee in the United States.

One of my brothers who lived in France fought with the underground against the French who supported the Nazis and was killed in action. My son, Werner, born in Heilbronn in 1935, was in the U.S. Army for two years (Field Artillery) stationed in Germany.

My wife, Lina, died in 1974 of cancer after forty-two years of marriage. I married again. Her name is Margaret (an immigrant from Yugoslavia). She is a painting teacher at the Riverdale Senior Center.

We are members of the Tabernacle Congregation.

My son, Werner, lives in Peabody, Massachusetts, and is district manager for Honeywell, Inc.

ILSE BURGHEIMER (née Sommer)
16 Shelomoh Hamelekh
Tel Aviv, Israel 64378

I was born in Stuttgart in 1908, the oldest daughter of Bernhard Sommer, businessman, and his wife Elise, née Nathan. My father's birthplace is Freudenberg/Main near Wertheim, and my mother's, Kuenzelsau near Heilbronn. They also lived in Cannstatt.

In 1934 I married Julius Burgheimer, whose parents had moved from Strassburg to Stuttgart in 1918.

Our son, Frank, was born in 1937. In 1938 we emigrated to Palestine after my husband's business at the Stuttgarter Slaughterhouse had been taken over by Aryans. In July my husband left alone with the Lift, and I followed a few months later with our fifteen-month-old child. My husband had rented a two-room apartment in which I am still living. As I understood from my husband's letters that he could not find any kind of work, I was determined to earn our living by taking in washing as soon as possible after my arrival. On September 28, I arrived and two days later began to work. Fortunately, I was allowed to have my child with me. I had to work on an open roof and to cook on a "Primus" cooker under the washkettle.

When our child was eighteen months old, he was accepted (as an exception) in a kindergarten in the morning, and I was able to get a job as a maid, four hours daily, and stayed for four years. Evenings I worked in a catering place where I learned the trade, and after four more years, I established my own catering business, which was very successful for twenty-one years. The best-known politicians and business people were among my customers.

My husband had worked all this time as a taxi driver, but in 1953 he contracted tuberculosis and spent seven months in the hospital, during which time I was the sole breadwinner. In 1964 he passed away.

At this time my son was already in the United States. After three years of military service he went to Cornell University, received his Ph.D. in food technology, and worked for the Nestle Company in Ohio. In 1972, after fourteen years in the United States, he returned to Israel, where he works at the Standard Institute of Israel. He is married and the father of two small children.

I am almost seventy-two years old and stopped working in 1973 (Yom Kippur War) and am enjoying my family very much.

I have a sister ten years younger than I who emigrated from Stuttgart to the United States and married an Orthodox Jew.

FRITZ BUSCH (by Walter Strauss)

Innumerable memories tie me to Fritz Busch, the musical mentor and master of my young years in Stuttgart.

Here, I wish to report of one, which is especially characteristic of the deep human feelings of this great artist. With a sad heart I saw Fritz Busch leave Stuttgart, long ago, as general music director of Stuttgart, and nearly twenty-five years had passed when I met him again in New York. He just had opened very successfully the Metropolitan season with *Lohengrin* and was very busy preparing performances of other operas. The war had just ended, and I told him that I, in my capacity as chairman of the Organization of the Jews from Wuerttemberg, was engaged in sending food packages to the refugees who survived the concentration camps. Spontaneously Fritz Busch offered to give a charity concert in the framework of our organization in favor of these refugees. Soon hereafter, this concert took place. The three brothers Fritz, Adolf, and Hermann Busch played piano trios by Mendelssohn and Schubert; Fritz Busch accompanied his son-in-law Martial Singher, who sang Schubert *lieder*, and his wife Grete read the chapter about "Stuttgart" from his then-still-unpublished memoirs. The conductor of the most famous orchestras of the world was at that time somewhat out of practice as a pianist, and I know that he studied hard for many hours. With his customary twinkle of the eyes, full of humor, he assured me several times how happy he was to save the expenses of an orchestra in this manner. This concert lived on in the memory of all who attended, not only as one of the most beautiful musical events, but as a deep-felt human deed. It was the last time that the three brothers Busch made music together in public, called by the *New York Times,* "A Musical Event," and as so many times before, they devoted their time and their art for others. The three Busch brothers, who had left Hitler's Germany due to their convictions, played for the Jews driven from Germany.

One can imagine how great our gratitude was and will be for all time.

*HERMANN CARLEBACH

Lawyer Dr. Hermann Carlebach was born in 1900 in Stuttgart, since 1925 at the Landgericht and Oberlandesgericht Stuttgart, emigrated to Palestine in 1935. As a good lawyer he succeeded in opening a law office in Haifa in 1939 despite the rather complicated legal situation during the time of the British Mandate. In 1942 he joined the Civil Service.

ROBERT CARSCH

Robert was born in Stuttgart in 1887. He entered his father's sewing machine business as a young man and married Grete Kann Weil in 1918. A son, Hans Helmuth (later known as Harry), was born in 1919.

Robert and his family emigrated to England in 1936. Sewing machines remained the chief source of income, and Harry, too, apprenticed in this field. Harry married Ellen Adler, also from Stuttgart, whom he met in London during World War II. They and their daughter came to live in the New York area in 1948. Two sons were born in 1962 and 1965.

Robert and Grete died in England in 1968. Harry was active in the sewing machine business until his death in 1978.

*ERICH DESSAUER

Lawyer Erich Dessauer, born 1887 in Tuebingen, was admitted to the Landgericht and Oberlandesgericht of Stuttgart in 1917. The license was revoked in 1938. However, he was able to continue to act as a consultant and representative of Jews. When, in connection with the pogrom of November 9, 1938, the majority of the male Jewish population was for several weeks taken into so-called protective custody, he was one of them. Later he was again arrested by the Gestapo for "consorting with enemies of the state." The "enemy of the state" was a Catholic cleric who at that time, 1941–1942, still befriended him. In 1943, Dessauer was deported to Theresienstadt, together with his wife, Emma, née Levi, a well-known violinist. From Theresienstadt, a few preprinted postcard forms still arrived, from which it could be seen that he suffered hunger.

In 1944 he was deported to the extermination camp Auschwitz. Despite an attack of typhoid, his wife survived Theresienstadt.

RABBI HERMAN DICKER
57–12 Parsons Boulevard
Flushing, N.Y. 11365

Born in 1914, Hungary. Son of Osias and Sara (Spindel).

Education: 1920–32 Gymnasium Stuttgart; 1932–36 Hildesheimer Rabbinical Seminary, Berlin; University of Zurich, Switzerland, 1937, Ph.D.; Library School, Pratt Institute, Brooklyn, New York, 1968, Master of Library Science.

Married Eileen Last in 1945; children: Anna Rachel and Eli Jay. Chaplain, U.S. Army, 1943. Retired Lieutenant Colonel 1967. Recipient: Bronze Star, five Campaign Stars, Commendation Ribbon with Oak Leaf Cluster.

Member: New York Board of Rabbis, Association of Jewish Chaplains; Association of Jewish Librarians, Beta Phi Mu, International Library Science Honor Society.

Publications: History of Jews of Ulm, Germany, in the Middle Ages, 1938; *Wanderers and Settlers in the Far East: A Century of Jewish Life in China and Japan,* 1962; *A Jewish Family Trail: The Dickers and Their Mates,* 1977; *Piety and Perseverance,* 1981. 1967–1968: director of research, American Joint Distribution Committee, presently head of reader services, Library, Jewish Theological Seminary of America.

SOFIE DREYFUS (née Ries)
1031 Chesworth Road
Philadelphia, Pa. 19115

Born 1894 in Stuttgart. My parents were: Hermann Ries, who died in 1902, and Meta Amalie Ries, née Kahn, born 1870 in Bamberg. She was deported from Amsterdam, Holland, to Camp Westerbork in 1943, from where she was deported to Auschwitz. According to a report from the Netherlands National Tracing Bureau of the Dutch Red Cross, she is considered to have been killed in Auschwitz in 1943.

I went through eleven years of school and worked as a secretary until I got married in 1925 to Friedrich Dreyfus, born in 1889 in Ulm a. D. In 1938 my husband, who was working as an accountant, was deported to Dachau; he was released one month later as a war veteran with the order that we had to leave Germany within three weeks. Since we did not have our visa to the United States yet, we spent ten months in Rotterdam in a camp for refugees. In 1939, we left Europe on the *Veendam* and arrived in Hoboken in 1939, together with our daughter, Erika Anna Dreyfus, born 1927.

First I worked at all kinds of jobs, whatever I could get. Finally, my husband got a job as an accountant until, after a long illness, he died in 1950 in Philadelphia. Since then, I am living with my daughter, Erika, who is married to Charles Sonnenberg. They have a daughter and a son, both married, and I am enjoying my five great-grandchildren.

For many years we are affiliated with Temple Zion in Philadelphia, and I am working as secretary for our rabbi, Dr. Daniel P. Parker, and the synagogue. This activity is my whole life, and I hope the Almighty gives me the strength to do it for a long time to come.

ALFRED DREYFUSS
c/o Dreyfuss Metal Co.
1220 East 75th Street
Chicago, Ill. 60619

Born 1908, son of Arthur and Regina Dreyfuss, née Wiesenbacher, in Ulm Donau. My father, Arthur, died in 1935. My mother, Regina, died in 1921.

After leaving the Realgymnasium, I joined Wolf Strauss Iron and Metals Company in Ulm and Nuernberg. In the year 1937 I left for the United States and settled in Chicago, where I found a position in an aluminum-smelting concern, which I left in the year 1951 to form a company under the name of Dreyfuss Metal Company.

Concerning my personal life, I am married to Elsbeth, née Wertheimer, from Goeppingen. We have two children, a boy and a girl. My oldest, Charles, is married and the father of five daughters. He is associated with me in business. My daughter, Ruth, is a dental hygienist, married to a dentist, and the mother of two sons.

HECLA DREYFUSS (née Gideon)
408 Cortelyou Road
Brooklyn, N.Y. 11218

Born in 1908 in Rexingen, the first child of Moritz and Sophie Gideon, née Zuerndorfer. Father born in Rexingen 1878, mother born 1886. Has one brother, Richard, and two sisters, Hilde and Gretel.

I was married in 1929 to Sally Dreyfuss, a master butcher in Bretten. We had our own store until 1938. Our daughter, Margot, was born in 1932.

We came to the United States in 1938. We lived first in Brooklyn, then moved to New York. In the beginning I worked as a cleaning woman, and my brother and brother-in-law lived with us.

My husband bought a butcher store, where we made our own delicatessen, just like in Bretten. I learned to help with whatever work there was. Later I worked as a machine operator, then for over fifteen years in the lunchroom of the Franklin D. Roosevelt High School.

My daughter, Margot, married Henry Lowenstein in 1956. She studied to work in medical fields and still works for a specialist for blood diseases. I have two granddaughters, Fays and Lyn.

MARGARETA (GRETEL) DREYFUSS (née Gideon)
617 East 5th Street
Brooklyn, N.Y. 11218

Born in Rexingen in 1916. Worked as an apprentice for four years in the Loewengart Leather Company in Stuttgart. From February 1938 to November 1938 in charge of the Jewish Kindergarten in Rexingen.

Emigrated to the United States in 1939, working as a housekeeper until marriage to Kurt Dreyfuss, 1943. Two children. My daughter Susan, a teacher, married Frank Halfer. We belong to the same German-founded congregation as my brother, Richard Gideon.

MARGARET DRIEVES (née Maier)
61–48 78th Street
Rego Park, N.Y. 11379

Father, Julius Maier, born in Buttenhausen. Mother, Bertha Maier, born in Walldorf near Heidelberg. They lived in Stuttgart, Moserstrasse 7, until their emigration to the United States in 1941.

Julius Maier died in 1962. Bertha Maier died in 1958. My husband, Fred Drieves, lost his parents and went to the Waisenhaus (orphanage) in Esslingen a M Neckar. At some later date was with the United States Army in Europe. We married in Stuttgart and came to the United States in 1939.

Gretel Drieves, née Maier, and son James are living in Queens, New York.

OLGA DRUCKER (née Lenk)
65 Nancy Boulevard
Merrick, N.Y. 11566

My father, Dr. Richard Lenk, was born in 1880 in Stuttgart and died in 1972 in New York. My mother Martha, née Hirsch, was born 1891 in Wiesbaden and died in 1967 in New York.

The family business, founded by my grandfather, Maximilian Levy, was the Herold Books, formerly Levy & Mueller, publishers of juvenile books. It was stolen by the Nazis in the late thirties. During the Crystal Night, November 1938, my father was sent to Dachau concentration camp. He and my mother tried after his release, approximately six weeks later, to emigrate to whatever country might accept them. They fled Stuttgart for the United States in 1941, one day before the U.S. Consulate was closed down.

I was born in 1927 and was sent to England in March 1939 with a children's transport. My older brother, Hans Herbert, already lived in England for some time as a student. I lived with several gentile families, which puzzled me, since we did have relatives in London and Oxford. Why did they not take me in? I was soon converted to the Protestant religion of my benefactors and for six years was a regular church attendant. I returned later to my faith, but this experience taught me tolerance. I am still in contact with one of the families, and we have visited mutually several times.

My parents came to New York via Lisbon in August 1941, and worked in various positions to make a living. However, the adjustment was difficult for my father, who retired soon, leaving to my mother the task of supporting them. I could join my parents in March 1945 and we moved to

Kew Gardens in Queens. Life became gradually easier, with the beginning of German restitution payments. Before mother passed away, they made a few cruises to the Caribbean and to Europe and saw her brothers and sisters again. They lived to see five grandchildren grow up.

I married a Berliner *Landsmann*. Rolf is director of engineering and operations at WNET-TV, after being with ABC for twenty-nine years. I went to college at the age of thirty-nine, obtaining B.A. and M.A. degrees. I do community relations work for the Foster Grandparent Program on Long Island and play the cello in a community orchestra. Some time ago I wrote a so-far unpublished book about my family, beginning with my great-great-grandfather Herz Levy of Herxheim, at the beginning of the eighteenth century. My three children, Jane, Robert, and Alice, enjoyed reading it. I also became the editor-owner of *Elder Leaves,* a senior digest publication. I belong to several writers organizations, including the Children's Book Writers Association and the Long Island Poetry Collective.

My brother, Herbert Lenk, lives in Cincinnati, Ohio, is married, and has two children.

JEAN H. DUBIN (née Oberdorfer)
Philadelphia, Pa.

Born 1923 in Stuttgart, where I also attended school. I emigrated with my parents to the United States (Philadelphia, Pa.) in 1940 via England. I married Paul S. Stern, chemical engineer, and have two daughters, Carol-Lynn and Joyce Renee—both married—one grandchild. After Paul Stern's death in 1962 I married Irving Dubin, chemical engineer, in 1965. My affiliations are: Temple Beth Am, Springfield, New Jersey, Hadassah, and B'nai B'rith.

Father: Hugo Oberdorfer, born 1889.

Mother: Berta Oberdorfer (née Harburger), born 1902.

My mother was a housewife. My father was associated with Saenger & Harburger, 105 Rotebuehl Street, Stuttgart, (machinery dealers). They emigrated in 1940 to Philadelphia.

Business Activities: Gifts and religious goods (wholesale).

Social Organizations: Congregation Tikvoh Chadoshoh, Heinrich Graetz Lodge B'nai B'rith, German Jewish Club of Philadelphia, Sisterhood of Congregation Tikvoh Chadoshoh, Hadassah.

ELSE DWORZAN (née Henle)
Hospital Street 36
c/o Israel Religiongesellschaft
7000 Stuttgart 1
West Germany

Born 1903 to Moritz and Emma (née Lowenstein) Henle. Parents born in Buttenhausen and lived in Stuttgart.

Emigrated to United States with mother in 1941. She worked as an infant's nurse. Mother worked in household and died in 1965. Returned to Stuttgart, where she lives now. Her grandmother and uncle Lowenstein with the rest of the family perished in Theresienstadt.

BERNARD H. ECKSTEIN
8930 Albion Road
North Royalton, Ohio 44133

Born in Ulm in 1923, the son of Hugo and Hedwig Eckstein (née Pressburger). Emigrated to England in 1937 to be able to continue schooling. Arrived in New York in 1939.

After graduation from Newtown High School, Queens, New York, I went to work as a laboratory assistant in the research laboratory of Sun Chemical Corporation in 1941 and then started the formal study of chemistry at New York University evening session. In 1943, I joined the U. S. Army and served until 1946, chiefly in the Field Artillery. As a soldier I returned to Germany and even spent one day in Ulm in 1945. Between March 1946 and 1948 I earned an A.B. degree in chemistry from Princeton University, and over the next four years a Ph.D. in physical chemistry from Cornell University. Then, I thoroughly enjoyed two years as a post-doctoral fellow with the great Professor Peter Debye, Nobel laureate in chemistry, still at Cornell.

In 1954 I joined the Du Pont Company as a research chemist at the Experiment Station in Wilmington, Delaware. In 1957 I took a similar position with Union Carbide Corporation at its Parma Technical Center, near Cleveland, Ohio, where I now hold the position of research scientist. Over the years I have enjoyed varied research-and-development activities ranging from polymer chemistry and physics, through electrochemistry and inorganic chemistry, to the study of reactions at high temperatures. In recent years I have been particularly concerned with carbon fibers and advanced composite materials, and would correctly be classified as a materials scientist. These investigations have led to more than a dozen publications.

In 1958 I married Sheila J. Rubin, an accomplished artist from Brookline, Massachusetts. We have no children. Together we enjoy music, theater, travel, and particularly the great outdoors; we have spent many vacations hiking in the mountains, and nature inspires most of Sheila's work.

HEDWIG ECKSTEIN (née Pressburger)
35–51 85th Street
Jackson Heights, N.Y. 11372

My life has nothing unusual in it. I was born in 1900, Hedwig Pressburger, in Rexingen; married Hugo Eckstein in Ulm. We left Germany in 1939, spent eight months in London with my husband's family, and then came here. Having no connections, little means, and a limited knowledge of the language, we did not have an easy life. But we had steady jobs and the determination to give our sons the best education possible. With the help of the G.I. Bill, we could send them to Princeton University, for graduate studies to Cornell and Harvard. One is a chemist and one an economist. They made good careers.

OTTO ECKSTEIN
24 Barberry Road
Lexington, Mass. 02173

In late September 1938, during the Munich crisis, my parents sent me to their relatives in England. They, Hugo and Hedwig Eckstein, followed in April 1939. I attended school in New York, particularly started in high school, served twenty-one months in the United States Army, and then entered Princeton University. After completing my bachelor's degree there I went on to Harvard to obtain a Ph. D. in economics. Since 1955 I have been on the faculty of Harvard University and am presently the Paul M. Warburg Professor of Economics.

I have also had some exceptional opportunities outside of academic life, including the direction of a study for the Congressional Joint Economic Committee in 1959–60 and service as a member of the President's Council of Economic Advisors in 1964–66. In 1969, I founded Data Resources, Inc., the first major economic-information company, and have been its president since then.

I cannot claim to have suffered any great hardships, because of the extremely protective nature of my family. They sent me out of Germany as conditions deteriorated badly in the fall of 1938 and war was seriously threatening, so I missed the Kristallnacht. My father's sister took good care of me in England and sent me and my brother, Bernard, to an excellent school. While my parents were wiped out economically by the migration and had to work very hard to make a living in New York City, they never asked my brother and me to divert our energies away from our educational efforts and encouraged us both to study hard and obtain the Ph.D. With this kind of encouragement, my brother and I were able to benefit fully from the enormous opportunities, and hope that we have given this country something in return and are able to be as supportive of the next generation.

MARGOT EHRENFELD (née Meyer)
Flintenmarken 83
2950 Vedback, Denmark

I was born in 1906 in Stuttgart. My father, Dr. Adolf Meyer, died in 1912, but his pharmacy continued until the Nazis took it from us. In 1926 I married Harry Ehrenfeld from Frankfurt. We lived in Berlin until 1937.

I am a member of WIZO and served by making visits to old and lonely people. Unfortunately, the three I had passed away, and I have no one at present, except an old (Christian) lady who is lonely despite her three children and some grandchildren.

My mother, Estella Meyer, née Haas, escaped to England after terrible difficulties in 1939 and lived with her brother. My husband and I tried everything to get her to Denmark. The Danes at that time were not very favorably disposed towards Jewish immigrants. One of our Danish friends knew the Minister of Justice at that time, and because of that we obtained a residence permit, but no working permit, and had to wait seventeen years—that was the law—until we could get Danish passports. Now, thousands can come here; they can obtain citizenship, work permits, and even apartments at once. (We are not wanted anywhere.)

Mother came with an English residence permit to us in 1940 and died while being with me. Shortly before, we had to flee to Sweden in a rowboat.

ALBERT EINSTEIN (privately by **Bruno Eisner**)
(From the book *Aufbau*, edited by Will Schaber.)

The pianist Bruno Eisner and his wife were close friends of Albert Einstein. Einstein was, according to the Eisners, an enthusiastic but bad violinist. When Eisner came in 1936 as a visitor to New York, Einstein had rented a room for him and paid the rent.

Einstein neglected his appearance badly. Mrs. Einstein told him once, "What is relative with your theory I don't understand, but your sweater is positively dirty." Einstein answered, "But I cannot part with it. I've had it already for twenty years."

He was never vain, with one exception: his violin playing. Music was just as important for him as science. He was basically very musical. If Einstein was playing chamber music and lost his place, it was never necessary to stop. He always came in again at the right moment. They once played a benefit concert for Israel with two very difficult Bach arias. Einstein was supposed to play the violin, but at the first rehearsal it became clear that the part was much too difficult for him. Einstein was asked to resign. Next morning early the telephone rang. Mrs. Einstein said in her usual Schwaebisch dialect, "Albert practices since six o'clock. Please come over at ten for a rehearsal." In ice and snow we went there. Einstein said, "I know I played very badly yesterday. Let's try it today." And really this time everything went perfectly.

By the way Einstein was also a poet. He wrote to us for our very first overcrowded meeting in 1939:

> Mein Wunsch—o moege es euch scnell gelingen
> den Leuten hier das Schwaebeln beizubringen.

> My wish—O may you succeed in speeding
> to teach Americans Schwabisch reading.

[The piece below was in the *New York Times Book Review* on May 24, 1981.]

Albert Einstein: The Human Side, Dukas and Hoffmann (Princeton). From the archives of the great physicist Albert Einstein . . . Helen Dukas, his longtime secretary and trustee of his literary estate, offers a small selection of letters and other personal writings that illustrate his development as a human being. The connecting passages are by Banesh Hoffman, a mathematician who collaborated with him on research. The entries from the period around the turn of the century, in particular, are novel and fascinating.

*ALFRED EINSTEIN

Lawyer Alfred Einstein, born 1887 in Stuttgart, practiced law there since 1915. After he lost his admission to the bar in 1938 he continued as a consultant until 1943. After the pogrom of November 9, 1938, he was in Dachau until January 1939. Later he was able to work as a helper for a wine merchant.

He died in 1945 of the aftereffects of pneumonia.

He was a brother of Dr. Gustav Einstein, who had married Irene (née Strauss), daughter to the banker Stephan Strauss.

*ERNST EINSTEIN

Dr. Ernst Einstein, born 1892 in Stuttgart, was since 1920, acting district court judge in Stuttgart, Bad Cannstatt, Stuttgart and Besigheim, as well as assistant district attorney at the Office of the District Attorney in Stuttgart.

Since 1927 he was district judge at District Court Stuttgart. In 1929 he became an assistant judge at the Landgericht, Stuttgart.

On August 1, 1933, he had to resign in accordance with the Law for the Preservation of the Civil Service. In August 1938 he emigrated to the United States. There he worked in a foundry and as a paper salesman.

HANSI EINSTEIN
50 West 97th Street, Apt. 14L
New York, N.Y. 10025

My name is Hansi Einstein. I am the widow of Alfred Einstein. We had two children: Hans-Peter and Lorelinde. My husband was a lawyer. I was a pianist and a piano teacher. We lived in Stuttgart. It was a beautiful city and we were very happy there until—but everybody knows that. I played with our Jewish orchestra, directed by Karl Adler. How lucky we were to have him. He was a wonderful person and a first-class musician.

In 1939 my husband was for three months in the concentration camp Dachau. He came back sick and very weak. To save the children we decided to send them to England. It was the hardest decision I had to make in my life. They left with the last children's transport before the beginning of the war.

If I remember right it was Julius Baumann who conducted the Bunte Stunde concerts. We had at least one every month. There too I played the piano parts with the orchestra, then directed by Mr. Colm. I also played solo and accompanied singers and instrumentalists. It was a busy time for me, but it gave me great satisfaction to be able to give some pleasure to the people of our community.

In January 1945 my husband died. He never got his health back after Dachau. It was too horrible to be alone. Almost all my friends and relatives were already gone, so I went to my mother in Fürth/Bayern. There I worked in the Jewish community as registration officer especially for displaced persons. I also taught some of their children how to read and to write. They had been living in camps and had never attended school.

Finally in July 1948 mother and I got our visa for America. We arrived in New York in August. My mother stayed with my sister and her family in New Jersey. They came over in 1937 already. I went to New York and lived the first year with the family of my husband's brother, Dr. Gustav Einstein. The next year in March my daughter came over from England to join me.

I tried hard to get work. I gave piano lessons again, but that did not suffice to make a living, so I became a baby nurse. That means I took newborn babies home from the hospital and took care of them for several

51

weeks. Lorelinde soon found a job. She worked during the day and went to college at night. Soon we could afford our own little apartment, but the worst blow was still to come. In January 1952 my son, Hans-Peter, was killed in England in a motorcycle accident. It was the most painful experience of my life. I never saw him again since the day he left Stuttgart. He was fourteen years old then.

KURT EINSTEIN
22 Oxford Road
Elmsford, N.Y.

Born in 1924 in Stuttgart. Owner of Einstein Associates, Personnel Agency, 122 East 42nd Street, New York City. Went directly to Riga in 1941 and was liberated in 1945 in Danzig. Parents: Leopold and Lisbeth (née Gerstman), brother: Fritz, sister: Inge.

*WALTER EINSTEIN

Attorney Dr. Walter Einstein, born in Buchau in 1902, was admitted to the Landgericht and Oberlandesgericht in Stuttgart in 1929. In 1933 his admission was annulled. In 1936 he emigrated to France, where he has been active in the textile industry since. However, his work was interrupted in 1940 when, as an alien, he was imprisoned in a camp that came under German control with their invasion. A successful escape saved him from deportation to an extermination camp in 1942. Thereafter he went into hiding with French farmers and lost a finger as result of blood-poisoning. With the retreat of the Germans his dangerous existence as an illegal came to an end after exactly two years. In 1944 his father was shot as a hostage in France.

*FRITZ ELSAS

Dr. Jur. Fritz Elsas was born in 1890 in Cannstatt. Elected to the Wuerttemberg Assembly in 1924, he was a member of the German Democratic Party during World War I; counsellor of law for the City of Stuttgart, and active in organizing the food supplies of the city, 1926; managing director of the Organization of German Cities, 1931; deputy mayor of Berlin. The former President of West Germany, Professor Theodor Heuss, who was a very close friend of his, called him in a speech in Stuttgart in 1954 "one of the outstanding experts and most instrumental in the German social and economic communal politics." Deprived of his offices in 1933, he refused to accept offers from abroad because, again according to the words of

Theodor Heuss, "he knew that Germany was his country and the country of his children."

After the failure of the attempt on Hitler's life on July 20, 1944, he took Dr. Carl Goerdeler into his home, one of the leading men of the German resistance. Dr. Elsas was later arrested and sent to Mauthausen Concentration Camp, where he was murdered in 1945. The Fritz Elsas Strasse (formerly Gartenstrasse) in Stuttgart was named in honor of his memory.

THE FAMILY OF LENA AND THEODORE ELSAS
(Ludwigsburg and Cannstatt)

Arrived in United States, 1937. Place of residence, New York City. Theodore worked as a bookkeeper until his retirement (over seventy years of age). Lena worked in a factory for some years. Theodore died in 1973. Lena died in 1977. Their two daughters:

KAY ELSAS BROUGHTON
Brecksville, Ohio

First woman graduate in chemical engineering, day session, City College of the City University of New York. M.S. in industrial engineering, Columbia University. Works as engineer for the American Gas Standards Association. Active in local politics. One of six elected selectmen of Brecksville. Married to Steve Broughton, engineer. Four children.

HANNAH ELSAS MILLER
25 Manitou Road
Westport, Conn. 06880

Born 1926. B.A. Hunter College, City of New York. M.A. Columbia Teacher's College. M.S. library science, Southern Connecticut State College, New Haven, Connecticut. Resident Westport, Connecticut, twenty-two years. Teacher, New York City schools, ten years. Author, *Films in the Classroom: A Practical Guide*. Writer and artist. Active in community affairs. Presently member Executive Board, Southwest Regional Health Systems Agency. Married to William Miller, professor of physics, City College of the City University. Physicist, inventor. Three sons.

*HANS G. ELSAS

Attorney Hans G. Elsas, born in Stuttgart in 1894, was admitted to the bar in December 1923. He pursued a lively and successful literary career: in 1927 *Lamentation,* a tragedy published by S. Fischer, appeared in a stage version and was performed, among others, at the Landestheater; in 1934, *The Decent Chap (Biedermann)* was published in Berlin by Propylaean Publishers under the pseudonym Gaupp-Turgis; was republished in a revised edition by Schuler, Stuttgart, in 1961. Part of his literary production appeared in leading newspapers and journals such as *Frankfurter Zeitung, Berner Bund,* and *Jugend.* He also contributed to theater on the air in its early stages.

In 1935 the authorities (Reichsschrifttumskammer) prohibited any further literary activity. He left Germany in 1936 and arrived penniless in Brazil. At first he subsisted as a language instructor at a mission school. Later on he lectured about literature and art history. Thereafter he became a tutor of Greek until finally, in 1959, he was appointed director of the Goethe Society and president of the Goethe Academy in São Paulo. Since 1958 he has been professor of Greek language and literature in the Department of Philosophy and Literature in Assis (São Paulo), Brazil.

SUSANNE ELSASSER (née Rosenfeld)
500 West University Parkway
Baltimore, Md. 21210

I am a daughter of Dr. Fritz Rosenfeld, born in 1876 in Stuttgart and died in New York City in 1942. His wife was Toni Rosenfeld, née Lublinski, born in Berlin in 1884 and died in New York City in 1959.

My older sister is Annemarie Rohan, M.D., born in Stuttgart in 1911, now living in Illinois; she has one son, James Rohan, born in 1947.

My younger brother is Howard Rosen, born in 1921 in Stuttgart, now living in Denver, Colorado; he has three children: Debbie Kaufman, born in 1952; Greg Rosen, born in 1954; and Mark Rosen, born in 1960.

I was born in 1912 and have two children: Thomas Brill, born in 1942, and Ellen Brill Levine, born in 1945.

MARTHA EPPSTEIN (née Levi)
University, Boulevard
Building W, Apartment 618
Silver Spring, Md. 20902

I am one of the twin daughters of Leopold and Minna Levi of Stuttgart. My father was the president of the Wuerttemberger Oberrat after Otto Hirsch.

We were educated in Stuttgart, finished ten years of Hoehere Toech-terschule, which was Realschule the three last years. Until I married, I worked in my father's office. He owned a men's clothing factory.

I married Julius Paul Eppstein, who was a learned banker and was vice-president of a Barmer bank. Later he studied accounting and tax law. I helped my husband in his office which he opened in Stuttgart.

In those frightening years between 1933 and 1938 the only highlight was the Stuttgarter Juedische Kunstgemeinschaft, created and skillfully led by our good friend, Director Karl Adler. Julius Paul and I were very enthusiastic singers in the choir. My sister, Gertrud Fuld, played the violin in the orchestra.

In 1938 Julius Paul was interned in Dachau. After his release, we prepared to emigrate to America, and in 1939 we arrived in New York. Our daughter, Lotte, and Julius Paul's mother, Mrs. Caroline Eppstein, were with us.

The beginning in New York was difficult, and after more studying in English and accounting, Julius Paul found a position in Philadelphia as an accountant with the well-known Sun Clothing firm until he retired at seventy-two years of age. I worked in Philadelphia the first few years. Later I took care of the household and my family.

We joined a German congregation and were quite involved in all the religious and social activities. My husband and all other former B'nai B'rith Lodge brothers founded a B'nai B'rith chapter, which still exists. We bought a house and had this big, fine house for twenty-six years. Besides all these goings-on, my husband was always very interested in politics and wrote frequently to Senators and Congressmen. We certainly were really interested in our new homeland. In 1971 my husband died suddenly of a heart attack.

In 1975 I sold the house and my daughter Lotte and I moved to a newer, quite Jewish section of the city into a modern apartment. My parents, who lived in New York more than twenty-five years with my sister, came twice a year to us for several weeks and loved it here. We found many good friends here whom we knew from Germany and, of course, found new ones here.

My daughter Lotte and I live together and never will forget our Stutt-garter and Wuerttemberger friends. I am in close touch with my sister, Luise Blumenthal (passed away meanwhile), and her children, who live in Silver Spring and Rockville, Maryland. My sister Gertrud Fuld and her family unfortunately were not able to emigrate and lost their lives. So did my only brother, Emil Levi, who fell in the First World War. We now consider Philadelphia, which is a very nice *gemuetliche* city, our home even though we think fondly of Stuttgart.

*CARL ERLANGER

Attorney Dr. Carl Erlanger, born in Ulm in 1906, was admitted to the local Landgericht in 1932. In 1933 his admittance was voided. In the same year he emigrated to Spain, but forced by the Civil War he returned to Ulm in 1936. Soon thereafter the Gestapo ordered him to leave the country within forty-eight hours.

After a short sojourn in Basel he proceeded to Argentina, where he scraped through as a laborer on odd jobs, as a bookkeeper for a savings and loan company, as a sales representative, and as the secretary for a refugee organization until, in 1957, he was able to return to Germany, where he died some time later.

*FRITZ ERLANGER

Lawyer Fritz Erlanger, born 1904 in Stuttgart, was the son of lawyer Hugo Erlanger of Stuttgart. He was admitted to the Regional Court and the Higher Regional Court of Stuttgart in 1930. In 1933 his license was rescinded. That same year he emigrated to France. There he again managed to become a *licencié en droits.*

At the beginning of the war he was interned in the South of France as a German citizen. Because of severe diabetes he was at a hospital in Perpignan when Hitler's hangmen swarmed into the South of France. In 1943 they took him to the notorious transit camp Drancy, a stopping point on the way to Auschwitz, where his life was ended on a date that cannot be determined.

*HUGO ERLANGER

Attorney Dr. Hugo Erlanger, born in Stuttgart in 1868, admitted to the Landgericht Stuttgart in 1893, and later on also a public notary (Oeffentlicher Notar), lost his admittance in 1938. Within a month he left for France. There he died of the flu in 1941 and was spared seeing his wife Frida and his son, attorney Dr. Fritz Erlanger, transported to a death camp in 1943.

*WALTER ERLANGER

Walter Erlanger was born in Buchau in 1911. He emigrated to Switzerland in 1933 and was trained as a teacher for problem children in Arlesheim. In 1935 he left for Holland. He survived the second wave of persecution in the underground, although his health was seriously undermined.

FRED ERLEBACHER
Huntington Woods
Michigan

My father, Abraham, born in 1869, moved with his family of three brothers (two teachers) and three sisters to Baisingen, in 1898. He married my mother, Jenny Phillipp, in 1900; she came from Nordstetten, born 1879. They had thirteen children, nine girls, four boys. He owned two large houses on Main Street and was a very successful cattle dealer. He died suddenly in 1935 from pneumonia; mother lived her last twelve years, from 1940 to 1952, in New York, financially independent and very happy.

I was born 1912 in Baisingen. At age twelve I entered the school in Hoechberg, and finished seven years later as teacher at the Teacher Seminary in Wuerzburg. I received scholarships from B'nai B'rith and the rabbinical council in Stuttgart for the purpose to become a teacher of religion in Wuerttemberg; however, the great Otto Hirsch permitted me to teach in Bavaria, to become a public school teacher. When the Nuernberger Laws in October of 1935 forbade public offices to Jews, the Catholic school commission in Moenchen-Gladbach certified me to teach for the Jewish Public Elementary School in Cologne.

End of March 1938, I was fired as a Jew, and started the next day in Mr. Salomon's Jewish bakery. I taught his wife English, to emigrate to Australia, and I learned baking bread and rolls within three months. I was admitted to the famous confectionary school of Mr. Heckmann (secretly) for a three-month course for master-confectioners. During that time, the Nazi leader of the confectioners hired me to work for him, from 4 A.M. to noon, and then I finished the school until 4 P.M. I was cantor from Friday afternoon until Saturday night in Neuss, on the Rhine, and Sunday, I was the only confectionary baker in Cologne, to bake for opera singers and other artists. My chef was very satisfied with my work. When he asked me, after four weeks, why I did not work Saturdays, I told him that I was Jewish; he was shocked at first, but then started to pay my weekly wages in advance, so as not to owe me, in case I should have to flee across the border.

In 1938 my mother surprised me around midnight and ran me across the border into Holland, to a super-Orthodox cousin of my father, who lived there since 1933, originally from Nuernberg. He did not want to keep me, but finally, after I refused naively an offer of a chance Dutch partisan acquaintance to come to his house and family free of charge, I made a deal with the cousin, that he will keep me in return for my mother sending 1,000 marks to his brother in Frankfurt for a month room and board.

When the HIAS Committee refused me railroad fare to Le Havre and bus fare to Scheveningen, I received, following the advice of a Swiss refugee, $40 from a philanthropy in the Hague, which enabled me to come to New York via Le Havre.

Disembarking in New York in 1938, I found a job immediately as a porter in Brooklyn: the pay was $10 per week, sixteen hours work per day. After three years I rose to be a pastry chef at $55 per week, then served in the infantry as a line sergeant, later as baker, for three years in the Pacific from New Guinea to the Philippines. In New Guinea a Catholic base chaplain ordered me to decorate a cake with two crosses and two Mogen-Davids, for the dedication of a church, whose steeple showed both emblems! In Manila I opened a partly destroyed synagogue in battle dress with sixteen more Jews; the cantor was a colleague from Wuerzburg! On Pesach we held Seder for 4,500 Jewish soldiers and officers in a large stadium, with matzoth from Australia.

My first wife died in 1959; my two daughters were twelve and eight years old. I returned to Wayne University, made my bachelor, became an elementary teacher, and after the master degree a high school teacher, made a doctorate in comparative literature at the University of Michigan in my spare time. For twelve years I was a board member of the German Jewish Congregation, then the president for a year. So far I made eight six-week trips to Israel helping Russian Jews to learn English.

Since 1977 I am retired but still active in the city and with correspondence to our Senators and Congressmen. They like to hear our opinions and advice and speaking out for Israel and our interests.

*GUSTAV ESSLINGER

Lawyer Gustav Esslinger was born in 1875 in Stuttgart, where he was admitted to the Landgericht and Oberlandesgericht. As early as 1933, he was attacked in Streicher's dirty rag *Der Stürmer*.

In 1933, Gustav Esslinger was for a time interned at the protective-custody camp Heuberg. In 1936 he was sentenced to one year and two months in jail because of alleged infringements of NS laws. However, when he had finished his sentence he was not released; instead he was sent to the concentration camp Dachau in 1938. In 1938 he was killed by shooting at the SS artillery range in Prittlbach near Dachau.

*KARL ESSLINGER

His brother, lawyer Karl Esslinger, born 1871 in Stuttgart, was admitted to the Regional Court Stuttgart in 1898. He resigned in 1934. At the end he was in a hospital in Munich. Critically ill, he was deported to Theresienstadt and never returned. After 1945 he was declared dead.

ERNESTINE FARBER-STRASSER

From 1927 to 1933 she was first alto at the opera house in Stuttgart with many guest engagements. Immediately discharged in 1933 for political reasons, she went to the United States and later on to Switzerland. Her voice is preserved on Vox and Polydor recordings.

*HERBERT FAY (formerly Feigenbaum)

Herbert Feigenbaum, born in 1910, was no longer admissible to Referendardienst when he passed his first examination in 1933. He left for France in August 1933, but returned to Germany once again in 1934. In Ulm his only chance for work was to be employed as a shipping clerk. He left for good for the United States in 1936, where he had to struggle to make a living as janitor, shipping clerk, and business employee.

HILDE MARX-FEIGENHEIMER
9 Kew Gardens Road
Kew Gardens, N. Y.

The Feigenheimers from Backnang

Erwin already wore the proud cap of the upper classes of the Real schule; I was eight years old. On the day we met I told my mother: "I have fallen in love today, and I will marry him." The family was highly amused about my cute decision. I made it come true twenty-three years later in America, after two emigrations.

Erwin was the youngest of twelve children of the well-to-do owner of the leather factory of Backnang, Julius Feigenheimer, and his wife Emma (actually, there had been thirteen, but one had been born dead). Julius' brother also had twelve children, most of whom were brought up in Julius' house. It was a big family, and Backnang, at the time, was a small place. The children were sent away for their education. Erwin grew up in a boarding school until he went to various universities to study medicine. Times had been getting worse and worse. He had to earn most of the money for tuition himself. When he received his diploma he was one of the youngest physicians ever in Germany. Eventually he became first assistant at the Innere Abteilung of Cannstadter Krankenhaus, and he was in line to become chief; only, Hitler happened unto the world. Erwin

59

was one of those who realistically judged the dark shadows moving in. In 1934 he emigrated—he was supposed to go to Chile, but sheer accident kept him in the United States. His dream to specialize he could not make come true; he succeeded in having some of his sisters and brothers—his parents had died by then—join him in his new country. For many years he was the provider of the family—for those, that is, who had not become victims of the Nazi terror. For those others he had borrowed the money one needed for visas to Cuba; it took him a long time to repay his debts.

At this writing, there is one Feigenheimer left in Backnang: Berta, widow of one of Erwin's older brothers, Emanuel. It was a mixed marriage, and Emanuel was deported to a concentration camp at a fairly late date. His wonderful wife, Berta, succeeded in getting him out of there, and they lived in Backnang until he died in 1969. Berta will never leave the place. There is not a single Jew left in Backnang.

I have never known the parents Feigenheimer personally. I only know the many tales about the strict father who allowed his children unlimited funds for books but otherwise kept them on a very short leash. And about the mother who is said to have owned nothing but maternity clothes. And about the two cousins Bonna and Bella, who owned the most elegant dress establishment in Stuttgart.

Erwin practiced medicine in a modest neighborhood in Brooklyn. Two of his sisters lived in his house, one of them with her husband. Erwin did not have a room of his own. A sofa in the living room, a chair with the telephone on it next to that—that was his. He had been told to borrow money in order to drive a black Cadillac, but he walked on all his house calls. The practice was excellent. He was not only a blessedly gifted diagnostician—he was a father confessor, tax consultant, psychiatrist, friend to his patients. "If he comes in the room one feels much better already," they used to say. His knowledge, his calm, and his goodness made him the ideal doctor.

The moment the Second World War broke out he volunteered, twice. Both times he was rejected because he was a naturalized citizen entitled to a high rank. We decided to marry, and nine months and a few days later our first daughter, June Barbara, was born. The night after the day when I had come home with the baby from the hospital, we received a telegram by phone from Uncle Sam, for "Lieutenant Feigenheimer." We both felt this fight to be our business, and Erwin accepted the commission, which was far too low. He served in the Medical Corps of the U. S. Army, first in the American South, then in England. On VE-Day he was on the troop ship bound for Japan. The ship turned around when the Japanese surrendered.

Erwin came home, only to start from the very beginning, all our savings having been exhausted. The family had gotten older, the financial support more demanding. A year later our second daughter, Irene Joy, was born. Two years after that, our third daughter, Aviva Jo. We were a very happy family of three generations together with my parents who lived with us, who had helped us to get over the worst years of the war, and who gave our children a beautiful additional share of love.

One of Erwin's student dreams had been a "Sanatorium" in the European sense. We owned and managed one in Saratoga Springs, from 1953–71. Then we moved from the decaying Brooklyn neighborhood to Kew Gardens, for the sake of the children. They grew up beautifully. Two of them finished college with Phi Beta Kappa, one left before graduation to become a dancer. They all are successful and, by now, happily married. I have three grandsons, fifteen, twelve, and one (at this time, 1981).

Erwin took care of his old Brooklyn office and the one in Kew Gardens, until very shortly before his death in 1971; this despite a horrible terminal illness that lasted six years; we both knew.

At the funeral one of his friends said: "If ever in life I should be in need of a lot of courage I will think of my friend Erwin." The cemetery where he rests is located almost exactly between our two houses in Brooklyn and Queens. There is a very plain footstone. Next to Erwin's name, there is a caduceus on one side, a star of David on the other. Engraved above that is the Hebrew word *Ahavah*—that means LOVE.

Hilde Marx-Feigenheimer

ALBERT FLEGENHEIMER
(Information by Mrs. Henry H. Herzog, daughter
9 Gainsborough Road
Scarsdale, N. Y.)

Albert Flegenheimer, born Schwaebisch Hall, 1890. Died New York, 1972. Industrialist, active in the sugar industry in Germany, Italy, Canada, and then in the United States.

[*Editor's remark:* In spite of the fact that we wrote to Mrs. Herzog that we were not just printing names and dates but the stories of real people who had to emigrate due to the Nazis, we did not hear from her any more. ("Even if your father was one of the happy ones whose emigration was relatively easy due to international connections, his life was still changed by Hitler. This change should appear in your report.")]

*EUGEN FLEGENHEIMER

Attorney Dr. Eugen Flegenheimer, born in Schwaebisch Hall in 1888, was admitted to the Landgericht Stuttgart in 1915. In 1934 he surrendered his admission, left for Holland that very month, and proceeded to the United States in 1938. Disregarding his advanced age (he was fifty at the time), he took up the study of law once again and achieved such success that he finally became a judicial assistant at the Supreme Court of the State of Washington, a position he had to relinquish for reasons of health in 1949.

MOSES FLEGENHEIMER

Moses was born in 1862 in Schwaebisch Hall, the youngest of eleven children of Joseph and Caroline Flegenheimer. As a young man, he moved to Stuttgart and founded a grain-trading business. He married Emma Lowenthal. Moses was an astute businessman and well known in the community. He served as president of the Stuttgart Commodities Exchange and was active in the Jewish community. Both Emma and Moses died in Stuttgart, in 1932 and 1939, respectively. They had four daughters.

Anna married Louis Schwabacher and had two sons. Kurt moved to Holland and married a Dutch girl in the early 1930's. He died there several years ago. Manfred, now known as Fred Stevens, is a chemist and lives in Rochester, New York. Anna joined Kurt in Holland in 1939, was deported in 1941, and is thought to have died in a concentration camp.

Martha married Julius Schlessinger. They had a son and a daughter. Martha died in 1979 in New York.

Helene married Robert Bernheim, a banker. They moved to Berlin and had a son and a daughter. Later they divorced and Helene spent some of the war years alone in France. She came to New York in about 1943 and soon after married Max Rothschild, who had a smelting business. Helene died in New York in 1979.

Lise married Carl Adler and had three daughters. Lise died in England in 1943.

*BERNHARD FLEISCHER

Lawyer Bernhard Fleischer was born in 1879 in Goeppingen. In 1937 he was excluded from the bar. In the following years he became almost blind due to severe eye trouble. A non-Jewish woman, on whose care he depended, was arrested in 1942 and sent to the women's concentration camp Ravensbruck because she had guided the Jew Fleischer across the street. Fleischer himself, who had already been imprisoned once during the pogrom of November 1938, was arrested again in 1942. He died in the concentration camp Buchenwald in 1942.

ILSE FRANK (née Rosenfelder)
31–16 90th Street
East Elmhurst, N.Y. 11369

Father: Sali Rosenfelder, born in Noerdlingen in 1893, died in Argentina in 1947. Mother: Bella Rosenfelder, née Strassburger, born in Rexingen in 1897 and died in Argentina in 1970.

I was born in 1924 and left in 1938 for Argentina. I came to this country in 1959 and married in 1960. We have two sons, fifteen and sixteen years old.

Our youngest son, Jeffrey Frank, was chosen last year quite accidentally (the casting director went to his school—Hunter) to ask for boys, among two thousand, to play Michael Caine's son in the movie *The Island*.

We belong to Tifereth Israel in Jackson Heights, where our boys had their Bar Mitzvahs.

My husband is Leopold Frank; the boys are David and Jeffrey.

ILSE FRANK (née Prager)
1163 Weber Street
Union, N.J. 07083

My parents, Sol (Sally) Prager and my mother Johanna, née Sichel, are still alive, and are living in New York. My father moved to Bad Mergentheim in 1923 when he married my mother.

I was born in 1924, and my brother, Ernest, in 1926. He also lives in New York City.

We operated a housewares store which was liquidated on Kristallnacht. In 1940 we emigrated to the United States. We moved to the Bronx, and later on my parents moved to Washington Heights. They belong to Kehillas Yaakov on Fort Washington Avenue, where my father is active and is a part-time chazzan, which he had been in Germany.

In 1945 I married Henry (Heinz) Frank. We have a son, Sheldon, who is twenty-three years old and is presently studying computer science in Oswego, New York. My husband's and my interests are our synagogue life. We are very active. I served as sisterhood president; my husband was financial secretary and vice-president at Congregation Beth Shalom in Union, New Jersey. My other love is Hadassah, the largest Zionist women's organization in America. I also served as president of the Union chapter.

We also belong to the Chevrah Kadisha Derech Yeshoroh of Irvington, New Jersey, the Jewish Family Service of Union County. I belong to the B'nai B'rith Women and Jewish War Veterans Auxiliary. My pastime is sewing, and my husband is office manager with a distributing firm in Union.

HERMANN FREUDENBERG
151 Taber Avenue
Providence, R.I.

Born 1894; school from 1899 to 1910, then apprentice at Landauer Brothers in Ulm a.D. Entered my father's manufacturing business as a salesman in 1913. When the war broke out in 1914, I was attached to the headquarters of General von Below's section as a motorcyclist (which I owned since serving in New Ulm). In October 1914 I was commanded to drive to the front to deliver an important letter. The letter instructed the troops to retreat at once, as French troops are moving from Lunéville Baccarat, with the intention to cut off the entire 26th Division. On the way, a grenade hit the cylinder of the motorcycle; I was badly wounded but managed to reach the next village, to get a car to drive to the front. I delivered my orders, and fainted. The general ordered the first medal for me! This ended my motorcycle duty and I was sent to my regiment; on patrol during the battle on the Somme in 1916, I was badly wounded, losing my right eye. I was discharged from the army in 1917. I married in 1920.

In 1936 I emigrated to the United States and had a position as a designer. The next job was with the Fashion Institute of Technology, School of Designing. In 1967, as the economic situation was difficult, I moved to Providence, where my two daughters live. My wife died in 1975.

ELSE FUERST
299 Altamont Place
Somerville, N.J. 08876

My mother was alive in 1933—Helene Gideon Loewengart. Came to U.S.A. in 1938. Birthdate: Rexingen, 1881. Death: 1970.

My first husband, Martin Wolf. Born Koenigsbach-Baden, 1897; death: 1935 in an automobile accident.

I was born in Rexingen, 1909. We came to this country in September 1938.

64

I married Ernest Fuerst in 1940 and live in Somerville since 1943. Mr Fuerst was a partner of Sunrise Milling in Somerville, New Jersey. Died 1970.

My children: Bert Wolf, born 1930 in Pforzheim; Steven Fuerst, born 1945 in Somerville, New Jersey.

I belong to Temple Shalom, Hadassah, Sisterhood, Rexinginer Benevolent Association, and am a member of the Auxiliary of the Home for the Hebrew Aged of Central New Jersey.

My brothers: Manfred Loewengart. Born Rexingen 1902; died 1940. He was a cattle dealer in Germany and had a farm in Boundbrook, New Jersey. Theo Loewengart. Born 1905; died 1951. In Germany he was an executive for Jacobi Cigars in Mannheim. In New York he was a partner of Loewengart & Co.

GABRIELE GATZERT (née Moos)
2 Atrium Way
Elmhurst, Ill. 60126

I was born in Ulm in 1926, the second child of Karl Julius Moos and Grete Moos, née Lebrecht. Both my mother and my brother, Gerhard Moos, have sent reports, so I shall write mostly about myself.

I lived on the Koenig Wilhelmstrasse and attended the Au-School. I was the only one of sixty children in the class with a telephone at home; therefore I had to answer the principal's phone. Slowly things changed and anything that went wrong I was blamed for, as I was the only Jewish student in the entire school. When chocolate rabbits were stolen from someone's satchel, I was immediately accused of it. Later they were found elsewhere. No matter how hard I tried, the Nazi teacher criticized only my work in front of the class and called me names. Everyone in the class greeted "Heil Hitler"; I did not. I was upset not to be allowed to wear the uniform of the BDM (Bund of German Girls) like the rest of the girls, although I felt that I looked very "German" with my pigtails! Children like to belong to a group but my girlfriends were not permitted to play with me anymore. Then came the night of November 9, the terrible Kristallnacht! My father, awaiting a telegram, went downstairs at 4 A.M. when the bell rang, thinking the telegram came. Instead some S.S. men picked him up in his pajamas. He was not even allowed to get dressed or say goodbye to us. From the window I saw him marched off. My mother saw him before he was sent to Dachau and told me he was beaten severely (he was a World War I veteran!), and we did not know if we ever would see him again. My father met my sixteen-year-old brother who had been arrested in Munich in Dachau.

Meanwhile I entered a private Jewish boarding school in Herrlingen near Ulm, later a Jewish school in Ulm with one teacher for all ages and only about twenty-five children, as many had already left Germany. I remember well how they shouted in our classrooms about us being Jewish and how afraid I was to attend school. I also will never forget the signs in restaurants and stores: "Juden unerwuenscht" (Jews Not Wanted). We loved to go swimming in the city indoor pool and in the Danube; everything was forbidden! All valuables, including a silver jar which my father received for his wounds during World War I, had to be handed in.

While my father was in Dachau, my mother arranged for me to go to

England with a children's transport and attend the "New Herrlingen School" which emigrated meanwhile to England. While waiting for the permit, I broke my leg and was terribly worried that the notice would come while the leg was still in the cast. Finally in June I left at night to meet the rest of the transport; our first stop was in Stuttgart; my parents came along. While awaiting for the train to Frankfurt at 2 A.M. we ate in a restaurant with the sign "Jews Not Wanted," but we had no choice. Luckily no one realized we were Jewish, but what a horrible feeling to eat where one is not wanted! I left my parents in Stuttgart, not knowing when, if ever, I would see them again. I was not yet thirteen years old. An acquaintance brought me to Frankfurt, where I was one of several hundred children to leave Germany. Only later did I realize how lucky I was, as several of my school friends did not survive, as they could not leave Germany in time.

HERMANN GIDEON
Shave Zion, Israel

I was born in Rexingen and emigrated with the first group. Leopold Levi and Karl Adler, personally known to me, did a lot to enable our emigration.

MAX GIDEON
Dover B 222, Century Village
West Palm Beach, Fla. 33401

Born 1906 in Rexingen, I emigrated to the United States in 1924. In 1934 I helped a girl from Munich to come here after I saw a newspaper photo in which a lawyer was paraded in the streets of Munich with a sign on his neck "I am a Jew." I married that girl, and we managed to help forty people from Rexingen to come to this country. We formed the Rexingen Benevolent Association, and we collected contributions to the Otto Hirsch Memorial Park in Shave Zion, Israel.

After years as a salesman, I started the Fort Tryon Bakeshop in 1940 and retired to Florida in 1970 for health reasons. I am still active as director of the Village Mutual Association, the Non-Partisan Political Action Committee, and I am treasurer of the Men's Golf Club.

My son, Stephen, is chief engineer with Loral Electronics. My daughter, Susan, is a teacher and now lives in Scarsdale, New York. During the time I lived in New York, for five years I was treasurer of Jordan Lodge 15, B'nai B'rith, and on the board of our temple.

MAX GIDEON
79 Murry Hill Terrace
Bergenfield, N.J. 07621

My father, Josef Gideon, was born in Rexingen and passed away in Shave Zion. My mother, Sofie Gideon, née Schweizer, was born in Baisingen and passed away in 1958 in Shave Zion. My brother, Victor, was born in 1910 in Baisingen and passed away in 1936. My sister, Resi Schwarz, née Pressburger, was born in 1910 in Baisingen and now lives in Shave Zion.

I, Max Gideon, was born 1916 in Baisingen, went to grammar school and business school, was an apprentice for three years in leather and skins (Feigenheimer, Horb.), worked in my father's meat place until leaving for the United States in 1937, worked in a box factory until called to service 1942–1946. I went to work with Sally Pressburger (Rexingen) and married Sally Wolf in 1946 (Baisingen), daughter of Wilhelm and Betty Wolf (Baisingen), went into my own wholesale meat business until 1968. I am now working in a supermarket as a butcher.

I have two daughters and one granddaughter. Diane, the oldest, is married and lives in Fair Lawn, New Jersey, with her husband, David, and daughter Rachel.

Joan lives and works in West Orange, New Jersey, for the Jewish Center and manages the Senior Citizen Program and newly arrived Russian immigrants.

RICHARD GIDEON
621 East 5th Street
Brooklyn, N.Y. 11218

I was born in Rexingen in 1910. My parents were Moritz and Sophie (née Zuerndorfer), both also born and died in Rexingen. I attended the Hebrew Day School, later the "Real" school in Horb, and at the age of fifteen, I joined father's cattle business in which he was associated with a Mr. Waelder. Three years later I traveled to the markets in Germany, mainly Bavaria, and when father died in 1931, I had to take over his business. I emigrated to the United States in 1938.

My first job was on a chicken farm in Toms River, New Jersey, paying $20 a month. I quit soon and worked nights at a butcher wholesale firm. I married Irma, née Frank, in 1944.

I quit the butcher firm and with six other Rexingens became a Fuller Brush man. We all became successful. I started my own business about eighteen months later and am now retired. I have two children, both teachers. Sonja married Gary Nadritch, has two sons, and lives on Staten Island. Jeffrey and his wife, Dawn, live in Fishkill, New York.

I have been the vice-president of a German-founded congregation for twenty-five years, the Chevra Gemiluth Chesed. My wife is also active in the sisterhood for many years.

RUTH M. GIDEON (née Meyer)
5816 Sheridan Road
Chicago, Ill. 60660

I remember that my late father made you a Bar Mitzvah. He was Ober-rechnungsrat, Lehrer Max Meyer. He attended the Teacher's Seminar in the city of Meiningen and was well known in the Stuttgarter Jewish Congregation. My mother was born in 1867 in Bad Bentheim.

I was born in Stuttgart in 1906. My sister Tesi, ten years older than I, lives in Enschede, in the Netherlands. She lost her only son through the Nazis, and she and her husband lived a gruesome life underground during Hitler's invasion. My sister is living in a Jewish Old Age Home in Enschede.

In 1927 I married Adolf Sichel, and in 1937 we emigrated to the States and lived in Chicago, where my father joined us in 1939. My husband has been in baker's machinery business in Stuttgart and also in Chicago. In 1944 we moved to Albany, New York. My husband died of a heart attack in 1957. Four years later I married Willy Gideon from Horb am Neckar, and moved back to Chicago. In 1967 I lost my second husband.

I have one son aged fifty-two. He is Professor Dr. Martin Sichel at the University of Michigan in Ann Arbor. He had a Guggenheim Fellowship and received his Dr. degree in aeronautical engineering in Princeton, New Jersey, in 1961. He and his wife, Ann, have three sons; aged twenty-five, twenty-two, and nineteen.

I am an active member of our Self-Help in Chicago and of Temple Ezra-Habonim. Our congregation was founded by German Jews.

I was thrilled about your high esteem for my father. He was a personality, loved to teach, and the "Stuttgarter Congregation" was his congregation. You want me to write a few things about his life. I hope I give you the right stories!

I will tell you some episodes from his life, which are funny and I am sure you would like to hear.

After my father graduated from the Teacher-Seminary in Meiningen, his first job was to be a teacher in Bad Bentheim. There he also met my mother. It was Friday evening and my father went for the first time to the Bentheim Synagogue. He wanted to make an impression in the small city by wearing his striped pants and the formal *Gehrock* that goes with it. To have such an outfit was obligatory in the seminary. The village children

69

were running after him and cried: "Look here, there goes the circus director!"

In good old Stuttgart my father counted among his friends also many people not of the Jewish faith, and this mixed group was called "The Wednesday Society." It was a joyful group, who liked to drink a *Viertele* wine together after the day's work and troubles.

My father was a heavy smoker—everything, cigars, cigarettes, pipe. When we celebrated his eightieth birthday in our home in Albany, New York, we had a lot of visitors. One of them, who knew that he was a heavy smoker, said to him: "Meyer, if you would not have smoked so much, you could be much older!" My father enjoyed this immensely.

My father had always a positive attitude towards life, and he surely was a "learned man." But you know this.

My sister, who lives in the Netherlands, is eighty-four, and I am seventy-four. Time waits for no one.

My father passed away in Enschede, Holland, and is buried there.

FRITZ GLÜCK
Nahariya 22 406
Herzl Street 47
Israel

Background in Germany: Born in Stuttgart, 1910.

Parents: Moritz Gluck, merchant, deceased 1932. Helene Gluck, (née Roselfelder) deported and killed by the Nazis.

Education: Graduated from Dillmann Realgymnasium in 1928. Studied law in Heidelberg, Munich, Berlin and Tübingen. Passed first state law examination in 1932.

1932–1933	Referendar Amtsgericht Stuttgart.
1933–1934	"Hachshara" (Lotze, Winkelhof)
Oct. 1934	Emigrated to Palestine ("Capitalist's Certificate"), continued "Hachshara" in Kvutzat Hefzibah and met there Dr. Max Cramer and his family.
1935	Moved with the Cramer family to newly founded Nahariya. Lived with Cramer family and worked as agricultural laborer.
1936	Trouble broke out in Palestine. I enlisted with Jewish Settlement Police and served with them until 1940.
1937	Married Deborah (née Safier) from Krakow.

1938   A son was born and named Moshe. Our son is now professor for theoretical physics at the University of Dortmund (West Germany).

1939   We built our own house in Nahariya.

1940   Volunteered for service with the British Army. Served first with the Infantry and from 1941 until 1946 with Operational Intelligence (HQ 8th Army). Took part in North African campaign, Sicilian and Italian campaigns, and ended up with British Forces in Austria.

1946   Released from army service. Worked as postal clerk in Nahariya and prepared myself at the same time for Foreign Lawyers Examination. Was very active in Haganah underground movement.

1947   Served with Israel Defense Forces and its forerunner.

1952   While serving with the army I passed the Foreign Lawyers Examination.

1952   Quit the army and opened a lawyer's office in Nahariya.

1957   Appointed judge.

1977   Retired.

At present I am an old man, not too healthy and taking it easy. The Germans pay me a pension as a *Landgerichtsrat*, and this, together with my Israeli pension, enables us to live without worries. What really worries me is the future of this country, both economically and politically, and the fact that there is no vacancy in this country for my son.

ELIZABETH GOLD (née Heibronner)
4754 198th Street
Flushing, N.Y. 11358

My father, Karl Heilbronner, was born in Laupheim in 1879; my mother, Grete, née Bruehl, was born in Nürnberg 1891. My parents lived in Heilbronn, where my father together with his brothers Sigmund and Berthold owned a soap factory. I was born in 1918; my sister Lore in 1921. My father came to the United States in 1935, and the rest of the family followed in 1936. My father's last job was as manager of a Castille soap factory in Waltham, Massachusetts; the parents and my sister moved to Cambridge, Massachusetts in 1938, but I stayed in New York. Mother

71

worked in the Window Shop in Cambridge, a nonprofit restaurant and gift shop, employing refugees. My sister trained to be a nurse in Beth Israel Hospital in Brookline, Massachusetts. I myself, learning to be a dressmaker in Germany, continued in this profession in the United States and was working up in a theatrical firm to assistant designer, fitter, and cutter.

My father died in 1939; he was one of the founders of IMAS in Boston. My mother worked until a month before her death in 1967.

My sister Lore married in 1941; she lives now in Overland Park, Kansas, she still works as anesthesist in Memorial Hospital, Kansas, Missouri. Her husband, Sam Turner, was a salesman for a drug company and later in electronics, is now invalid. They have three children: one daughter, married, having two boys, and two sons.

I got marrried to Phil Gold in 1944; my husband is now a teacher. We have two daughters; the older one, Suzanne, is a portrait photographer, and Karen is a pediatric occupational therapist. I am still working at home as a dressmaker.

*EDUARD GOLDSCHMIDT

Attorney Eduard Goldschmidt, father-in-law of former Minister-president Dr. Reinhold Maier, was born in 1869. He was admitted to Landgericht and Oberlandesgericht Stuttgart in 1897 and lost his admission in 1938. In 1939 he left for England and proceeded to the United States in 1943. In 1950 he returned to Stuttgart. There he died in 1955.

His daughter is still living in Germany. Son Rudolf committed suicide in England.

EMIL P. GOLDSCHMIDT
2239 Gables Avenue
Merrick, N.Y. 11566

I was born in 1913, the son of Paul M. Goldschmidt and Paula Goldschmidt, née Eltbacher, and am the brother of Olga Goldschmidt, now residing in Forest Hills, and of the late Julius Goldschmidt. I attended the Heidehof Schule, the Wilhelms and Friederich Eugens Realschule, terminating my education at the Hoehere Handelsschule. After finishing my apprenticeship with the Export-musterlager, I was employed by the Sueddeutsche Durchschreibebuecher Fabrik in Renningen which employment was terminated under most unpleasant circumstances created by the prevailing restrictions in 1936, forcing me to emigrate.

Early in 1936 I arrived in the United States. I was fortunate to find employment as a page with the Bank of the Manhattan Company, and in due time, based on my previous experience with letters of credit, was promoted into their International Letters of Credit Department until 1941.

After leaving the bank until 1971 my knowledge in international trade gave me the opportunity to primarily work for importers and exporters in various fields, such as coffee importers and exporters of textiles and electrical components.

The first time I saw Stuttgart again was in 1948 since I was asked by my employer to visit the various important manufacturers in the electronic and related field, such as Robert Bosch A.G. and Mercedes Benz. I entered my former country with a great amount of misgivings, but was astounded by the courtesies extended to me, the help which I received, amidst the devastated production facilities, the completely destroyed homes—including the former home of my parents—the lack of food—and a town formerly beautiful in complete ruins—sights I shall never forget. I had to remind myself constantly of the tragedy of my father's death and the reason which this nation has brought upon itself.

In 1949 I got married. We have two daughters: Susan, born 1956, and Karen, born 1960.

MARTHA GOLDSCHMIDT (née Lustig)
44–30 MacNish Street
Elmhurst, N.Y. 11373

Born in 1893 in Fechenbach, Unterfranken, as Martha Lustig; emigrated to England in 1939 with late husband, Leopold (formerly partner in Simon Berg in Stuttgart), and in 1941 emigrated to the United States with husband. Upon death of my husband, worked as operator on sewing machines for Pickwick Knitting Mills in Brooklyn, New York, until my retirement in 1977.

OLGA GOLDSCHMIDT
107–40 Queens Boulevard
Forest Hills, N.Y. 11375

My father, Paul M. Goldschmidt, born 1870 in Stuttgart, was active in several commercial enterprises. Among others, he owned a factory in Ludwigsburg. He perished in Poland in 1942.

My mother, Paula Goldschmidt, née Eltzbacher, born 1875, died 1941 in Stuttgart.

Concerning myself, I was born in 1900 in Amsterdam, Holland. Upon

73

the return of my parents to Stuttgart, I attended the Rodhertsche Maed-chenschule and later worked for several years as a secretary. Before emigrating to the United States, I was employed by Sapt A. G. in Unter-tuerkheim.

I arrived in New York in 1938 to join my brother Emil. After the arrival of my brother Julius shortly thereafter, my brothers and I lived together until Emil's marriage. From then on Julius and I maintained a household until his death in 1962.

During the first few years in New York I took care of children until I had the opportunity to make use of my German and English shorthand and finally worked for the URO for twenty years.

Since my retirement in 1975 I am a volunteer with Self-Help. I was never married.

JETTY GOLDSTEIN (née Fussmann)
6801 Indian Creek Drive #202
Miami Beach, Fla. 33141

I was born in 1909, the only child of my parents, Chaim and Rosa Fussmann, née Wassermann.

My grandfather, Mendel Fussmann, was the first *Ostjude* coming to Stuttgart in 1890 from Austria.

My uncle, Max Fussmann, youngest brother of my father, died in September 1914 as a soldier in the K.K. Army. His name is on the memorial for the fallen sons, members of the Jewish community of Stuttgart, located at Pragfriedhof, Stuttgart. My father also served in the K.K. Army during the First World War. He had a men's clothing store in Stuttgart, where we also lived.

I was educated at the Katharinenstift in Stuttgart. From 1928 to 1938 I was employed by Schocken Department Store and left as the last Jewish employee of the store in Stuttgart in March 1938.

I married Max Goldstein in 1938 and left Stuttgart shortly after that to emigrate to the United States.

We have one son, born in New York in 1941. His name is Joe H. Goldstein. He lives with his wife and three children in New Jersey. Joe graduated with a master's degree in business administration from New York University and served after graduation in the U.S. Air Force as a first lieutenant. My husband founded his own business in scrap metal in 1940 in New York.

We were active in Congregation Beth Hillel and Leo Baeck Lodge of B'nai B'rith. After retirement, we moved to Miami Beach, Florida, in 1975 and are still inactive members of the above-mentioned organizations.

BEATRICE GOTTFRIED (née Landauer)
32–45 88th Street
Jackson Heights, N.Y.

I was born in 1913, came over here in 1937, and married Victor Gottfried from Vienna, Austria. We are both retired and have two children.

My father, Nathan Landauer, came to the United States in November 1939, after having spent some time in Dachau and afterwards in Holland. He died in 1966. My mother, Mrs. Ricka Landauer, is ninety-six years old and lives in the Jewish Home and Hospital on Kingsbridge Road, Bronx.

My sister, Senta, born 1910, came to the United States in 1936 and is married to Wilhelm Stein from Crailsheim. They have two sons. She now lives in Meyerville, New Jersey.

My brother, Henri Landauer, born 1920, immigrated in 1938 to the United States. He is married with three sons and is living in Chicago, Illinois.

"SOPS" GOTTLIEB (née Sontheimer)
315 East 68th Street
New York, N.Y.

My name is "Sops" Gottlieb, my maiden name was Sontheimer. Like my parents, Carrie and Leo Sontheimer, I was born in Stuttgart. My father died there in 1930.

I married Berthold Gottlieb and we lived happily together with our daughter, Lilo. And then came 1933 and the turmoil started.

To help our people get out of Germany, we opened a travel agency. We ourselves intended not to leave "our Stuttgart" until all Jews had safely left the country. But the day we, too, had to abandon ship came earlier than we had anticipated, and by the middle of January 1939 we boarded a Swissair plane for Zurich, where we joined my mother and daughter, who had preceded us there. My dear mother died shortly thereafter; she could not master a new life and an uncertain future.

Three months in the beautiful Swiss Alps, and then the Swiss authorities kindly but firmly kicked us out of our mountain idyll and advised us to continue our pilgrimage elsewhere.

And so we came to Paris, where together with many of our compatriots we began to chase after the forever elusive *carte d'identité (Aufenthaltsgenehmigung)*, a chase that eventually led us to the provincial town of Angers on the banks of the River Loire. Our stay, however, was not quite as romantic as the surrounding countryside with its chateaux, and on top of the usual refugee problems we were now faced with the outbreak of war.

Internment camps sprung up overnight and all Jewish men of German descent were ordered to report to the camp nearest their domicile. Now we really had our fill of "good old Europe," and while my husband was behind barbed wire, my daughter and I were very fortunate to not only find an American consul to issue immigration visas to her and me, but who was not only willing, but actually anxious to travel the many miles to issue the visa to my husband in camp as well. What a wonderful omen of our future homeland this was, and so, with a lot of luck and God's help we set sail on the S.S. *De Grasse* on December 23, 1939.

Accompanied by escort vessels, we arrived in New York sixteen days later, on the coldest day ever recorded in this city.

We settled down in New York; my husband worked as a travel agent, and after his death in 1956, I took over his work and am, to this day, a travel agent myself.

It gives me great satisfaction to be able to send people all over the world for business and pleasure.

I have revisited Stuttgart many times, but although I cannot nor want to deny my "Schwaebisch," Stuttgart ceased being my hometown long, long ago, and I am now, like countless others, an American of German descent.

*EGON GOTTSCHALK

Born 1903 in Stuttgart, Dr. Egon Gottschalk was an attorney at the Landgericht in Stuttgart since 1923. In 1930 he resigned to enter the Civil Service. He was an assistant judge in Reutlingen and Stuttgart, and since 1931, district court judge in Reutlingen. In 1933 he had to resign in accordance with the Law for the Preservation of the Civil Service. But he was admitted as a lawyer in Reutlingen and Tübingen. However, after the judiciary became a matter of the Reich, this admission was revoked in 1937.

Dr. Gottschalk emigrated to São Paulo, Brazil, where he worked for an industrial firm until 1950. However, he succeeded in going back to his profession. By 1962 he was a lawyer in São Paulo and assistant professor at the Law School of the University of the State of São Paulo.

Dr. Gottschalk must have suffered especially under this fate, since he was close to the right-wing parties of the time. He belonged to the political right, was active in right-wing youth organizations, and published many essays and leading articles in right-wing newspapers.

His specialty was international law and the question of the war guilt, and shared the point of view of those Germans who condemned the war verdict of Versailles.

Last address known: Rua Boa Vista, Landac, Caixa Postal 150.

ALFRED GRAU (Widow Hilda Thalheimer Grau)
1500 Bay Road #937
Miami Beach, Fla. 33139

Alfred Grau, born 1898 in Stuttgart, Dannecker Strasse 15.

Alfred was the son of Wilhelm and Hedwig Grau (née Seeligman), and being the firstborn, he was considered a prodigy, especially when he picked as his constant play toy at the age of three, a small violin given to him by his grandfather Seeligman.

At the age of five he commenced violin lessons and was soon rated as a violinist of great potential. Alfred was well-known in the Stuttgart Jewish community, and he performed there in the Familienverein, Berthold Auerbachverein, Buergermuseum, and at charity benefits.

Alfred complied with his father's wishes to learn the latter's business and was delayed in his endeavor to become a professional artist. However, in Stuttgart lived the famous conductor Fritz Busch, who had listened to Alfred's music. Now came the highlight of Alfred's life when Mr. Busch requested Alfred to play with him. They played together in duos, and also in the Landestheater and the symphony orchestras. Joyfully proud was Alfred of this work.

When seventeen years old, Alfred joined the army and served at the front. After the war, all was well until Hitler came into power and we had to leave the country.

In 1937 we arrived in New York City, where we struggled to make a living, but Alfred did not neglect his music and became concertmaster of the New York Symphony Orchestra, although without pay. He played a great deal of chamber music, which included working with comedian Sam Levenson. Later Alfred attained a most successful contact as advertising manager at Rheingold Beer, with which firm he was held in the highest esteem.

In New York we had joined the Hebrew Tabernacle, where Alfred was honored with the position of vice-president and treasurer.

For twenty-five years Alfred played *Kol Nidre* by Bruch with organ accompaniment in the temple and for the memorial service it was *Largo* by Händel.

In 1974 we transferred our home to Miami Beach, Florida, where we had leased a spacious apartment overlooking the bay and lovely tropical gardens so picturesque that Alfred had phrased it "Like Paradise."

Here in Florida, Alfred met new musical associates with whom he resumed his music. Chamber music, duos, and practicing filled his days.

So on the 17th of October 1975 he played duos in the evening and arranged for his quartet to meet the next day at 6:00 P.M., but it was God's will for Alfred not to play anymore. On October 18, 1975, he passed away at 3:00 P.M.

Alfred's friends were granted permission to play at his funeral, it was the slow movement of a Beethoven Quartet.

And thus, my beloved husband of fifty-two beautiful years lived with—and died with—music.

BERTYL GROSS (née Kahn)
24 Springhaven Road
Wheeling, W. Va. 26003

My parents, Albert and Lotte Kahn, née Strauss, from Niederstetten, Wuerttemberg, were deported in 1941 and died in a concentration camp in 1943. Their family tree dates back to 1763 and some dates even in 1519 in Regensburg and include *Schutzbriefe* (letters of protection) from reigning Dukes in 1792.

My parents owned a drygoods wholesale and retail business, and they were well educated. They were highly respected by both the Christian and Jewish residents. There were about thirty-five Jewish families, belonging to most local German organizations. Their home life was strictly Orthodox Jewish, but they had friends in the non-Jewish community as well.

Father and uncles served in the First World War. Life was good until 1933. However, a postwar letter received from Christian neighbors describes the horror of their lives in Niederstetten, until 1941.

I was born in 1918, attended local schools, and later studied for one and one-half years in a convent high school for girls in Bad Mergentheim. When further studies were forbidden, I took jobs in Jewish firms in Stuttgart despite my very young age until the owners had to emigrate—only to be killed later by the Nazis. From 1935 to 1938 I lived in Stuttgart, Frankfurt, and Augsburg, became active in Jewish organizations—Aguda, R.J.F., Hakkoah. Some of the new friends survived, but many were never heard from and life became unbearable, with the fears and problems of where to go and who would want us.

I was young and strong, yet reluctant to leave my parents alone in Germany. My mother's sister in Philadelphia signed affidavits for my brother and myself, but not for the parents. Yet when I was fortunate to receive one of the last quota immigration numbers in 1938, I followed my brother to the United States, one week after the Kristallnacht, heartbroken to say goodbye to parents, family, and friends, never to be seen again.

I stayed with my aunt in Philadelphia for ten days, then became a governess in a Jewish family, but life in Philadelphia was lonely. Strangers were not easily accepted, so after improving my English and getting used to the customs of the new country, in 1939 I moved to Atlantic City, where my brother lived, where another kind Jewish family took me in, and I felt happy. Atlantic City was lovely. A Jewish Community Center provided friends and entertainment.

There I met my husband, Arthur Gross, a medical student. We married in 1941. While he was in the army in Louisiana, and while he was transferred to various army camps I held different jobs. It was a hard time. My parents were denied a U.S. visa due to father's poor health. We were helpless to bring them out. We were active in Jewish life in Alexandria, Virginia, New Orleans, Kentucky, and after my husband was sent overseas in 1943, I settled with my eight-month-old baby daughter in Pittsburgh, Pennsylvania, where uncle, aunt, and grandfather arrived from Germany.

My husband returned to the United States in 1945. A government job sent him to Wheeling, West Virginia. He could not complete his medical training despite five years study in Vienna. Wheeling, a town of about 50,000 inhabitants became our permanent home. We joined a Jewish Reform congregation and at the end of the government job my husband became a furniture merchant. Our son, Allen, was born in 1948.

My husband's family arrived from what was then Palestine. We became active in community life, served on the boards of the Sisterhood, Hadassah, art and music committees, PTA, Girl Scouts, Boy Scouts, and youth groups, and so did my children and my husband, serving also in the civil rights movement and human rights commission.

Our daughter, Barbara, graduated from Ohio State University, worked in New York, and married an attorney, Robert Shapiro. They live in Columbus, Ohio, and have two children. Our son, Allen, is an attorney in Philadelphia. Both children identify with our past. Allen went to Niederstetten as well as Vienna.

We are near retirement. We were interviewed locally when *Holocaust* was shown, and our life story appeared on the front page. We also were chosen "Religious Family of the Year." Several times my husband was president of our congregation.

About the past: We are not bitter but still hurt. I too went back to my hometown; it was a horrendous experience but I am glad I went.

We are in touch with many re-found former friends, and we are all young at heart and speak up for causes. We enjoy life and the fruit of our labor.

*MARTIN GRUENBERG

Attorney Dr. Martin Gruenberg was admitted to the bar in Stuttgart in 1932. He gave up the practice of law in 1933 and emigrated to the United States in 1938. Because of serious illness he was able to work only intermittently as a cashier in a restaurant and as an employee on a military base.

His mother, whom he had to leave behind in Stuttgart, died in Theresienstadt in 1942.

ELFRIEDE GRUENFELD (née Meth)
470 Third Street #219
St. Petersburg, Fla. 33701

I would like to tell you about my late husband, Max Gruenfeld, born in 1889.

He attended the teacher seminar in Esslingen and started in 1910 in Baden-Baden as cantor and teacher. He had this position until he was forced to give it up in 1938 by the Nazis. He naturally also had to give up his state office as rector, to which he was appointed. Released after being in Dachau concentration camp for ten weeks, he had to leave Germany, and parents and children were separated for seven years.

He found a small position in Gundershoffen, Alsace-Lorraine, spent some more time in France and also in Switzerland as a refugee with his wife. After the war ended, he was reunited with his children in England. In 1947 he was able to emigrate to the United States and was in charge of a refugee community in the Bronx, New York.

He died in 1973.

I myself, née Meth, lived in Schwaebisch Gmuend originally.

LEE GRUENFELD
140 South Middle Neck Road
Great Neck, N.Y. 11021

My name is Lee Gruenfeld, from Stuttgart. I was formerly a soccer-football player, member of the first team of the Stuttgarter Kickers.

My sister, Thea, lives at 21 Bond Street, Great Neck, New York 11021.

We emigrated to Argentina in 1935 and 1937 respectively, and since 1963, we live in the United States.

GERTRUD GRUENWALD
Altersheim Langnau
AG CH5426 Switzerland

When in November 1938, five men from our closest family were taken to the K.Z., one knew it was high time to leave Germany. I joined my brother Walter with wife and two children, and sailed to Chile, which we had never seen before, with the only legal visas supplied through a friend of my brother. I was lucky to get a job a week after our arrival as "English Miss" in the home of a lawyer in Vina del Mar, the famous resort on the ocean, near Valparaiso. The four girls, between seven and fourteen, should get a "European" education, and despite my meager English, I did all right. After a year, when my brother bought a store in nearby Villa Alemana, I quit and I worked with him and his wife in the store. After eleven years with them and their children, I moved to Valparaiso in the house of a friend who needed help with the sale of cards manufactured by her husband because her eyesight was in danger. I stayed with her until she died in 1970 after years of bad health. This was during the takeover by Allende.

Since 1972 I live happily on the beautiful island of Mallorca, close to my brother and sister-in-law.

HANS GRUENWALD
8 Mary Lane
Greenvale, N.Y.

I was born in Stuttgart in 1935 as the son of Walter and Lotte Gruenwald, amidst all the anxieties that those years encompassed. I have no direct personal memories of occurrences in Germany, except for individual, sketchy, photographic kind of memories and therefore cannot add anything, except to say that my first years of life must have been amidst a terribly anxious environment due to the uncertainties of the future at that time. Following my father's incarceration at Dachau, these anxieties became much more acute and the family finally emigrated in 1939, one and one-half months after initiation of World War II. We arrived in Chile in 1939 and lived for the first few months in a private boarding house in Vina del Mar. We settled in the small town of Villa Alemana in the early part of 1940, where my mother had obtained work in a boarding school. Her only compensation for this work was room and board for the rest of the family members. Even though I was only four and one-half years of age at the time, I did participate in quite a few of the scholastic activities in that school. This prepared me for the subsequent school experiences,

81

which were in the small town of Villa Alemana for the first five years and subsequently in Vina del Mar and Valparaiso until completion of high school. I entered medical school in Santiago and graduated with the M.D. degree in 1960. Immediately following graduation, I came to the United States since the postdoctoral training in Chile would have mandated a lengthy period of time of retributional services in the countryside. I did my internship and residency in internal medicine at Mount Sinai Hospital in Chicago and its various affiliates in the Chicago Medical School program, and subsequently took a two-year fellowship in clinical hematology at the Tufts New England Medical Center Hospital in Boston, Massachusetts.

I returned to Chile in 1965 with the expectation of participating in the training of new hematologists in the new medical school being established by the University of Chile in the city of Valparaiso, while at the same time performing duties as clinical and laboratory hematologist at the Carlos van Buren Hospital of the Chilean National Health Service. Since both university and National Health Service salaries at that time were very low, I had to supplement my income with the private practice of clinical hematology, which usually kept me busy until late hours of the night. These were extremely frustrating years due to the lack of support within the context of the medical school. Most of the people in power there felt threatened by young, well-trained physicians, of which there were a fairly good-size number making incredible sacrifices in order to try and teach modern approaches. This backward attitude of those physicians in leading positions finally led to the decision to return to the United States on a permanent basis, which I did in 1968.

Immediately upon my arrival in New York, and while preparing for the State Licensing Board Examination, I met my wife-to-be, Doris Heine, who at that time worked as a travel agent. We were married within six months of my return to the United States. My first position was as coordinator in the Department of Medicine at the Sisters of Charity Hospital in Buffalo, New York, and as clinical instructor in the Department of Medicine of the State University of New York at Buffalo. I held this position until 1972, at which time I accepted a position in the Division of Hematology of the Queens Hospital Center Affiliation of Long Island Jewish–Hillside Medical Center, a 700-bed municipal hospital of the City of New York. This position permitted a greater amount of clinical and experimental hematology research, which has nicely developed in the fields of bone marrow, cell culture, and the differentiation of myoblastic leukemia cells. Other areas of research interest have been the evaluation of mode of action and prediction of response to chemotherapeutic agents. Since our move to New York in 1972, we have lived in the village of Roslyn

Harbor. Michael was born in Buffalo in 1970. Judith was born in New York in 1973, and David was born in 1978. Professionally, I am at present chief of the Division of Hematology at Queens Hospital Center and associate professor of medicine at the State University of New York School of Medicine at Stony Brook. Thus, a very satisfactory position has been achieved both in my private and professional life.

In summary, the forced emigration from Germany and the Nazi persecutions did not impede the full development of my potential as a human being and as a professional. However, major difficulties suffered as a child belonging to a minority in a foreign, unfriendly country made this development unquestionably harder and required the overcoming of major psychological traumas which would not have occurred in a more stable and favorable environment.

WALTER AND LOTTE GRUENWALD
Edificio "La Colina" Ap. 2-B
Palma Nova (Mallorca) Spain

Unfortunately, we sold our business, the Shoe Wholesale firm of Neu & Gruenwald, very late, during the summer of 1938; therefore, we were still in Stuttgart during the Kristallnacht. During this action, I was sent to the Dachau concentration camp, and was released by the end of December. Thanks to the help of our friend, Walter Strauss, in New York, we obtained visas for Chile in the spring of 1939, but could leave only in October after the start of the war, together with our two children.

In Chile, my wife, due to her degree in linguistics, was able to get a position as teacher in an English school, while I started with a chemist from Yugoslavia a small business manufacturing a moth spray. At the end of 1940, the business was destroyed by a fire. We then took over a small store in Villa Alemana, a small place near Valparaiso, which we were able to enlarge to a good enterprise during the next thirty years.

In 1958 our older son, Rolf, a geologist, was killed in a mine accident. Just before, he had married a Chilean girl and become the father of a girl, Milena, who is now studying biochemistry in Valparaiso. Our second son, Hans, who established himself in Valparaiso as a medical doctor, emigrated to the United States in 1968. He has his practice now in New York, and a family with three children.

We ourselves left Chile in 1971 during the regime of Allende, and now live, retired, in Mallorca.

EDITH GUGGENHEIM-STRAUSS

Sal. Voegelinstr. 31
CH-8038 Zuerich
Switzerland

We left Heilbronn in 1937. My father (medical) Dr. Moses Strauss (unfortunately seriously ill at this writing) lived with us in a big house at Kilianstrasse 19, destroyed during the war. Father had a big practice as a family doctor; he was also president of the Orthodox Jewish community and of B'nai B'rith. He was forced by the S.A. and S.S. to sell his practice at a ridiculously small amount to a gentile doctor, was kept in their office until he agreed, and only after that he received his passport. As my mother, Elsy, née Wold, was born in 1897 in Switzerland, and her family lived there, we emigrated to Schaan in Liechtenstein, very near her family, because Switzerland did not issue a visa to us. "We" was my brother Walter, born 1922, now living at Haegelerstrasse 8, 5400 Baden, with his wife Margit, née Fein, from Stuttgart, and four children; my brother Dr. Ernst Strauss, born 1928, now at Kellariastrasse 33 8038 Zurich with wife Eva, née Loeser, from Stockholm, and four children; and myself, born 1926 and married to Werner Guggenheim—he is in the men's fashion business. We also have four children. Our eldest, Ralph, born 1952, is an M.D.; like his grandfather he is a family doctor in the United States. My daughter Evi, born 1955, is a social worker in Jerusalem; two boys Claude (1962) and Ron (1969).

I do not have many souvenirs of my early youth in Heilbronn, I was well protected, went to a small Jewish school. I have never encountered any anti-Semitism in Heilbronn, but experienced it during my school years in World War II, in Liechtenstein.

*SIEGFRIED GUMBEL

Lawyer Siegfried Gumbel, born 1874 in Heilbronn, practiced law there since 1900. He was for many years director of the Lawyers' Association in Heilbronn. Long before 1933, he found time to work for the Jewish community of Wuerttemberg.

In 1924 he was a member of the Constituent Assembly of Churches. He also was an elder of the Jewish religious community of Heilbronn and a member of the board of directors of the Centralverein Deutscher Staatsbuerger Juedischen Glaubens in Heilbronn.

The former constitution of the Jewish religious community of Wuerttemberg was, to a large extent, Dr. Gumbel's work. After 1933, he too lost his admission to the bar. In 1937 he moved to Stuttgart.

Having always been one of the most influential members of the Senate of the Jewish religious community of Wuerttemberg, he was elected acting legal counsel of this prestigious Jewish association. In 1936 he became president and judicial member of the Senate, and from then on headed the Jewish administration of Wuerttemberg.

In 1937 and 1938, Dr. Gumbel spent several weeks in Palestine. Despite his very clear idea of what awaited the Jews in Germany and despite the warnings of his colleague, Dr. Manfred Scheuer, who had settled in Palestine, Dr. Gumbel returned to Stuttgart because, as he said, he was needed there. He was, in fact, one of the main supports of the Jews in Wuerttemberg who had to remain there under increasingly intolerable conditions and with his energetic help pursued their ever-more-difficult emigration or hoped at least to stay alive in Germany. After the pogrom of November 1938, he was imprisoned in Stuttgart and Welzheim for ten days. He encouraged illegal emigration with the originally silent consent of the Gestapo. However, the Gestapo later dropped him and he consequently became entangled in criminal proceedings in connection with currency regulations and had to pay a heavy fine. After the wearing of the yellow star was decreed in 1941, he commented upon it to a seemingly reliable neighbor. This man, however, was a paid informer of the Gestapo. He was arrested and died or was murdered in the concentration camp Dachau in 1942. Today a street in Heilbronn is named after him.

*SIEGMUND GUMBEL

Attorney Dr. Siegmund Gumbel, born in Heilbronn in 1867, was admitted as attorney to the Landgericht Heilbronn in 1898. In 1913 he moved to Stuttgart. There he received his license as attorney in 1914 and was appointed public notary in July 1927. He lost his rights as public notary in 1933 on the basis of the Berufsbeamtengesetz. His attorney's license was revoked in 1938. He emigrated to England in 1939 and died in London in 1942.

*WALTER GUMBEL

Born in Heilbronn in 1903, was licensed as attorney in Stuttgart in 1929, and became a law partner of his father. His license was revoked, effective 1933. He left for England in 1933. There he succeeded rather quickly to gain command of the English language and to familiarize himself with English law, so that as early as 1935, he could resume his professional activities as an English barrister-at-law.

Last address known: 15 Ovington Square, London SW3, England.

*BENNO GUMP

Attorney Benno Gump, born in Ulm 1864, had practiced law in his hometown since 1901. He passed away in Ulm in 1936 and retained his license to the last. He witnessed the boycott of Streicher of 1933 and the infamous Reichsbuergergesetz of 1935, but was spared the harshest measures of persecution yet to come.

PETER GUNZ
136-60 71st Road
Flushing, N.Y. 11367

You know me as Albrecht Gunz from Stuttgart, but I adopted the name Peter in this country. Born in Stuttgart 1916. My father, Max Gunz, was born in Laupheim in 1878 and died in 1942 in Erie, Pennsylvania. My mother, Johanna Gunz, was born in 1887 in Stuttgart and died in 1960, also in Erie.

In Stuttgart I was a student at the Dillmann-Realgymnasium and then at the Staedt. Hoehere Handelsschule (Knospnasium) from where I graduated in 1933, just after Hitler's rise to power. The following two years I was an apprentice at Gerlach & Wiedenmann, a prestigious lingerie store in Stuttgart. After that contract's conclusion I worked for the Bettfedernfabrik Herz & Kops in their factory office as correspondent, etc. Then came the great and fateful day: my emigration to America in 1936. On the "boat" I met some nice acquaintances and friends, the families Richheimer and Grau and, of course, Walter Strauss, and also my good friend Theo Maier. I got adjusted in my new country rather well and was full of expectations and excitement for the future. For the first year I tried my luck at various jobs in and around New York, mostly as shipping and stock clerk. Then on recommendation of the Jewish Refugee Committee I ventured to Louisville, Kentucky. There I was warmly received by the Jewish Community Council and assisted in securing employment. During the summer months I worked as a waiter and bartender at a very prestigious country club, and during the winter months as stock and shipping clerk in a better men's-wear store. In 1939, my parents got out of Germany just in the nick of time, and they joined me in Louisville, where we settled for the next two years. Since my father was in the banking business in Germany, he naturally looked for work in the same or related fields. However, he was unable to find suitable employment. In 1941 we all moved to Erie, Pennsylvania where one of my father's brothers lived. Through the latter's initiative he found employment as a cost accountant in a manufacturing concern. By that time I was already pretty much at home in the men's-wear field as a salesman and later as department and assistant store manager. In 1958 I married. We have a son, Marvin Eli, now twenty-one.

My immediate family was very fortunate not having to endure the suffering of concentration camps for which we are ever so thankful.

*ALFRED GUNZENHAUSER (by his daughter, Lotte Steinthal.)

My father, Alfred Gunzenhauser, was born in Bad Mergentheim in 1869, the son of Rabbi Samson Gunzenhauser and his wife, Babette, née Hausmann. After attending the Humanistic Gymnasium in Schwaebisch Hall and Heilbronn, he studied law at the Universities of Berlin and Tuebingen.

In 1892 he started his law practice together with an older colleague, Dr. Loewenstein, and was a lawyer and later a notary until the Nazis forbade all Jewish lawyers to continue practicing.

Even though he was the son and grandson of a rabbi, my father was not a religious man, as far as practicing his religion goes. But he always was deeply interested in all Jewish affairs of the city and for some years, president of the Israelitische Oberkirchenbehoerde, later the Israelitische Oberrat. During these years he wrote *Sammlung der Gesetze, Verordnungen, Verfuegungen and Erlaesse betr. die Kirchenverfassung und die religioesen Einrichtungen der Israeliten in Wuerttemberg.*

He was one of the co-founders and a very interested member of the Stuttgart Lodge B'nai B'rith until its dissolution due to the Nazi laws. He was its president from 1902 through 1904. He also was a member of the Hilfsverein der Deutschen Juden, founded in 1900, and gave assistance— also as a lawyer—to the poor Jews arriving in Stuttgart from Poland, Russia, and other Eastern countries. My father also belonged to the Centralverein Deutscher Staatsbuerger Juedischen Glaubens. Closest to his heart, however, was the Juedische Schwesternheim, over which he presided for many years, and where he and my mother were allowed to spend their last few years in Germany, before emigrating to the United States.

In 1901 he married my mother, Martha. I was born in 1908.

Besides and in spite of all the above-mentioned activities and a very busy law practice, my father always found plenty of time to take care of my invalid mother as well as me and all my friends, who were very fond of him.

Like most of his fellow Jews in Stuttgart, my father considered himself a good German citizen. Unfortunately, therefore, he could not believe that anything might happen to the older generation of Jews in Germany. Only after the Kristallnacht in November 1938 he sent an urgent telegram to us in New York to provide affidavits for him and my mother, which at that late date proved to be very difficult.

Finally in 1941, after living through the first war years in Stuttgart, my parents succeeded in leaving Germany and came to the United States via Portugal. There they were held back for a few weeks due to my mother's physical condition, and only after receiving a much higher affidavit from my mother's American-born wealthy relatives, they arrived here in 1941—as father always said, "at the eleventh hour!"

Here the first years were very hard for my parents. They lived with us, first in the Bronx, where we barely made a living for ourselves due to the aftermath of the depression—then for two years in a small town in Connecticut, where my husband had finally landed a job in his own profession as a mechanical engineer. Unfortunately the people of Essex, Connecticut—a wealthy yachting place—did not make us feel at home there and considered us as "enemy aliens." They even suspected my father of being a German spy when they heard him talking German near the waterfront. The FBI then searched our whole house—Nazi fashion—and even took a booklet with all his addresses along, returning it to him a few days later.

As soon as possible we left this unfriendly atmosphere and settled down in Kew Gardens, New York. In spite of all the hardships and the difficult financial situation, my father never complained about their fate or ever mentioned how much better my parents had been off in years past. While I went to work he took my mother out in her wheelchair every day and tried to make life as comfortable for her as possible. At one time he took in homework, making soap bubble pipes for children from plastic thimbles. He prepared lunch and did the dishes for mother and our boy while we were at work and soon made many good friends in the new neighborhood. When the Leo Baeck Lodge was founded in New York he joined it and attended all their meetings. He read many English books and enjoyed reading his *New York Times* daily even though he barely knew a few words of English when arriving in the United States. English had not been taught in the Humanistic Gymnasiums of Germany while he attended them.

In 1948 my mother passed away after a two-months illness. He took that in stride courageously. At that time he taught himself to type in spite of his advanced age of eighty years and worked on restitution matters for many of his friends.

He was in remarkably good shape and quite vigorous until he had a stroke in 1955. He lived on for another five and one half years, first under my care in our apartment, then the last two years in a nursing home in our neighborhood. The stroke took a lot out of him, and in the end it was a blessing when he died in his sleep at the age of ninety-one in 1961, after a full life.

MARIE GUTMAN
525 Audubon Avenue, Apt. 1406
New York, N.Y. 10040

Born 1884, in Stuttgart. My husband, Sigmund Gutman, was born in Göppingen. He had spinning and weaving mills in Göppingen and Hechingen.

We left Germany in 1938. I had three sons. The eldest, Siegfried, came to the United States in 1937 via Palestine, as he had left Germany in 1933. After several undertakings, like working in a textile mill in Lawrence, Massachusetts, having a small business, and being a draftsman, since he had a German degree as mechanical engineer, he worked at MIT in Boston and there received a scholarship to Boston University, where he graduated in physics. He later moved to California and worked there in aerospace until his retirement. He is mentioned in *Who's Who* as a renowned physicist. He died two years ago of a brain tumor.

My second son, Otto, worked first as a dyer in a textile mill. When he was inducted into the army he went into OSS. After the war he worked in the financial department of the City of New York until his retirement.

The third son, Ralph, who was also in the American army, became a refrigeration mechanic and is working now in that capacity.

I am a member of Congregation Beth Hillel in Washington Heights and am now living in the Isabella House.

MARTHA HAARBURGER

Born 1898 in Stuttgart, chemist.

It is difficult for me to write about what happened to me in the years 1933 to 1945. In that difficult time I was not without help. My non-Jewish friends stood by me and often kept the connection with me, endangering their own lives. The management of the company I had worked for for many years, the Farbenfabriken G. Siegle & Co. in Feuerbach, Besigheim (at that time I was in Stuttgart), saw to it that my discharge was postponed as long as possible and helped me even thereafter. Most importantly I owe my life to Mr. Hans Walz, director of Robert Bosch in Stuttgart. Without his help I would not be alive. My Mr. Walz helped many Stuttgart Jews. He did not know me personally. I also did not know of the possibility of such help.

Mrs. Luzie Breitling, who always was good to me without consideration of her own danger, explained my difficult situation to Mr. Walz at the end of 1941 (I was sick with a high temperature and was due for transport to Riga in a short time). Mr. Walz acted at once. At that time I did not know that he had saved my life.

Mr. Walz got me a position in my field of color chemistry at his company with the greatest difficulty. As long as I worked at Bosch I was not transported to the East. When this was no longer possible and I was supposed to be transported to Auschwitz in June of 1943, Mr. Walz finally arranged that I was sent not to Auschwitz but to Theresienstadt. This saved me from being gassed immediately. The wearing of the yellow star, which made you appear like a criminal, was horrible for me. I had to fight for quietness and tranquility every day whenever I went into the street. In August 1942 more than a thousand old Jewish people, including my mother, Gertrude Haarburger, were deported to Theresienstadt and were collected in a big hall on the Killesberg. I could say goodbye to my mother, having after much difficulty been nominated as a helper. The old people were sitting miserably on the earth. Their faces were full of suffering but not one word of complaint was to be heard. Quietly and with dignity they accepted their fate.

ALICE HAAS (née Strauss, Hayum)
c/o Kurt Haas
121 Chestnut Ridge Road
Bethel, Conn. 06801

Born in Ulm in 1905. Daughter of Julius and Martha Strauss née Levi (from Cannstatt). Father, Julius, died in 1938 in Ulm. He was the owner and co-founder of Nathan Strauss Hüttenwerke (Foundry) in Ulm. Mother, Martha, née Levi, emigrated in 1939 to Israel (Nahariya) and died there in 1942.

I emigrated to the United States in 1938 and married in 1939 my present husband, Kurt Haas (originally from Munich). My husband was a partner of a hat factory in Danbury, Connecticut, until retirement in 1969.

I have two sons: Walter (Wolfgang) Hayum, born in Stuttgart in 1928. He has five children. Thomas J. Haas, born in Danbury, Connecticut, in 1940 (three children).

I have two brothers: Richard Strauss, who died in 1975 in Nahariya, Israel; his widow, Hilde, and a son, Michael, and a daughter, Raya, all of Nahariya. Rudi Strauss and wife Hilde (née Hamburger from Berlin). He has two sons, Joel of Haifa and Nathan of Tel Aviv.

My parents were forced to sell the foundry in Ulm under Nazi pressure after it had existed at the same location for almost seventy-five years.

I also had a sister, Lotte Strauss, who accidentally drowned in 1939 in Nahariya, Israel.

BERTE HALLE (née Kallmann)
440 East 79th Street
New York, N.Y. 10021

I was born in Stuttgart in 1900. My parents, Sigmund Kallmann, born 1867, and Ida (née Gailinger), born 1871, both in Stuttgart; they were the owners of the well-known *Metzgerei* (butcher store) L. Loew in Stuttgart, Nadlerstr. 17, which was held by many generations of Kallmann. My parents emigrated in 1939 to Rio de Janeiro, Brazil, where father died in 1956 and mother in 1943.

In 1921 I married Emil Halle of Heilbronn. His business was import of eggs and food. In 1937 we emigrated to Switzerland. My husband died there in 1946, and in 1949 I moved to Rio de Janeiro; in 1957 to the United States.

My three brothers: Mase, born in 1897, emigrated in 1939 with my parents to Rio de Janeiro, after he was several weeks in Dachau, and he died in Rio in 1958. My brother Eugene, born in 1899, died in 1965, emigrated to Rio de Janeiro in 1935, married there, and his two sons are living there. They are (1) Mario S. Kallmann, born in 1937, married 1964, has a daughter born 1967 and a son born 1963. (2) Renato C. Kallmann, born in 1940, married in 1977, has a daughter born in 1978. My youngest brother, Hans, born 1908, came to the United States, New York; died in New York 1969.

BERTHA HAMBURGER (née Rothschild)
Mill Road
Yaphank, New York 11980

I was born in Esslingen. My father, Theodor Rothschild, was the director of the Jewish Waisenhaus in Esslingen. I grew up there and later worked there until I got married in 1929.

My father was well known and respected among the Jews in Wuerttemberg. He was loved by the children who came to live with us. He was an excellent teacher, a man with an open mind and great understanding. I wish nothing more than he could have lived out his life doing the work he loved, staying in the country he always thought he was part of.

When we received the papers to go to the United States in 1938, we urged him for the last time to register with the American Consulate. He refused. He said he was warned if he would make the least move to leave the country, the Waisenhaus would be closed. He could not take the risk. There were too many children who had no place to go.

The Waisenhaus was closed after the Kristallnacht, opened for a short time later, and finally closed when the war started. Father was transported to Theresienstadt in August 1942 and died there in 1944.

Even before we left Germany, my husband, who always loved dogs, decided to do in this country the work he was interested in. Within weeks he found a job in a private dog kennel. I worked in the same family as lady's maid, but I learned enough about handling dogs so we could, after two years, find a job in another private kennel together. We did this for six years.

Then we had enough experience. We were fortunate to meet people who liked to raise dogs for showing and who were looking for a place to bring their animals. We opened our own kennel in Yaphank, Long Island, in 1946 (Country Club for Dogs). We operated this kennel for twenty-two years until our retirement. The dogs came from New York, New Jersey, and Connecticut. Often we had more than a hundred animals in the kennel. We boarded them and raised and showed dogs. It was a rich and interesting life. A new world opened, the world of animals.

Now we live in a small house among trees and birds and our own two dogs.

JULIE HANAUER (née Hirsch)
525 Audubon Avenue
Apt. 1204
New York, N.Y. 10040

I was born in 1898 in Goeppingen. My parents were Max and Ida Hirsch, née Bauland. My father was born in 1859 in Haigerloch, Hohenzollern. My mother was born in 1862 in Jebenhausen and died in 1934 in Goeppingen. My father died in Theresienstadt, as far as I could find out, in August 1945.

In Germany I worked in an office; in America I earned my money with machine-sewing.

My husband was Moritz Hanauer, who died in 1965. For many years I belong to Congregation Beth Hillel of Washington Heights. For more than two years I live in the Isabella House, 525 Audubon Avenue.

My eldest brother, Hermann, died after he came home from Dachau. My second brother, Karl Hirsch, was also in Dachau. He came to America, where he died in 1959. My oldest sister, Paula Mendle, and husband, Hermann, living in Stuttgart, perished in Theresienstadt; also my twin sister, Elsa Hirsch.

NELLY HANAUER (née Rosenberg)
2502 Canterburry Lane East
Seattle, Wash. 98112

My father's name was Ferdinand Rosenberg. He was born in 1872 and was a partner of Gebruder Bloch in Stuttgart. He passed away in 1961 in New York.

My mother was Martha, née Bloch. She was born in 1879 in Stuttgart and passed away in 1949 in New York.

I was born in 1900 in Stuttgart. My husband was Sigmund (Sidney J.) Hanauer. We married in 1923 in Stuttgart. He passed away in 1974 in Seattle, Washington. He was part-owner of the Pacific Coast Feather Company in Seattle. We had first emigrated to Lichtenstein, where we lived for about four years. My husband and Herman Schmidt founded and managed Hanauer and Schmidt, a feather plant.

We have one son, Terry Hanauer, who manages the Pacific Coast Feather Company, which he inherited from his father. I am part-owner.

I belong to Temple de Hirsch, Council of Jewish Women, ORT, Brandeis. I have always worked as a volunteer until about a year ago. My last job was with the Breast Cancer Detection Clinic, where I worked for about five years.

KENNETH S. HARPER (formerly Kurt S. Harburger)
48 Hilldale Road
Cheltenham, Pa. 19012

When I left Stuttgart in 1938 at age fifteen as Kurt S. Harburger with a children's transport for the South of England, I did not anticipate the sad fate in store for my mother and grandmother, who failed to escape Nazi atrocities, to which they lost their lives.

I spent the war years in England, mostly in London, and came to New York City in 1946, where I began to attend evening school at City College while working for a CPA firm during the day.

In 1951 I met and married Edith Block in Philadelphia, where I moved in 1952 after graduating from college. Although I received my CPA degree in 1953, I changed careers and joined my father-in-law's firm, principally as an outside salesman, a pursuit in which I am still active to this day.

Edith was fortunate enough to leave Goeppingen, where she was born, with her parents, Julius and Else Block, and her brother, Werner, in 1938. They made their home in Philadelphia, where a new life began. Her father started a wholesale jewelry business, a difficult task being new to the field and not knowing the territory or the language. Everyone pitched in, and the venture prospered. Werner joined the firm after his discharge from the Navy in 1946. We all mourned my father-in-law's death in 1974, but are carrying on the business bearing his name.

Edith and I moved to our present home in suburban Philadelphia, where we raised our three sons: Peter, born in 1955; Steven, born in 1957; Robert, born in 1960.

LOTTE HARTOG (née Moos)
74 Fox Meadow Road
Scarsdale, N.Y. 10583

My father was Max Moos, born 1881, and he was engaged in the manufacture of underwear. He died in Kew Gardens in 1945. My mother's maiden name is Paula Klein; she was born in 1885 and is still alive.

My father had two brothers, Ernst and Ludwig. Ernst died in Theresienstadt, and Ludwig in Israel. I was born in Ulm in 1913 and left Ulm in 1932. My sister, Ilse, was born in 1920 and lives in Florida.

ESTER HASGALL (née Kahn)
Bne Brak, Israel

My husband, Ezechiel Hasgall, Sr., born 1891, studied at the Rabbi Seminar Dr. Hildesheimer in Berlin. After the war, he studied in Wuerzburg, finishing as a doctor of economics, then worked as counsellor for Jewish councils in Karlsruhe, Hamburg.

In March 1936 we emigrated to Palestine with our two children, Abraham, then ten, and Miryam, four. After difficult years, my husband's workshop, specializing in rubber clichés, stamps, etc., began to provide for us. He was helped by Abraham since he was fourteen. The boy later spent two years in New York to study in this line. He married in 1955 a sabra, Tova. They have three boys, now twenty, seventeen, and seven.

Miryam obtained a B.A. degree in mathematics and statistics and married a lawyer, Ahren Freund. They have five children, twenty-three, twenty-one, nineteen, twelve, and eight years old.

My husband died eight years ago; we lived in Tel Aviv, but ten years ago we moved to Bne Brak near my daughter.

For the last five years I can walk only on two crutches, but my children and grandchildren, relatives, and friends care for me. To see my grandchildren grow up according to the religious upbringing, which my husband and I enjoyed, is a grace from the heavens just as the life in Israel, our promised homeland.

ABRAHAM HAVRON (Heilbronner)
Kibbutz Be'eri
Negev, Israel

My father, Dr. Edgar Heilbronner, lost his job at the Staedtische Krankenkasse of Stuttgart in 1933. The Nazis threw him out because he had not been a *Frontkaempfer* in World War I. They obviously blamed him for being only a surgeon at Cannstatt base hospital.

Undaunted, my mother, Dr. Anna Heilbronner, applied for the job, believing she was qualified. She was a doctor of medicine and had been an army nurse (voluntarily) in the terrible Galician campaign of 1916/17: A *Frontkaempfer*. The authorities took two weeks for deliberation. The reply was negative. They said Dr. Anna Heilbronner had not been a doctor of medicine at the time of her front-line service.

This incident, so typical of Nazi chicanery, baseness, and malevolence, righteously disguised, enabled my parents to see far into the future. By July my father was in Palestine, as a "tourist", and by December, mother and we three children had followed suit, after a heartbreaking departure.

My father started as an orthopedic surgeon in Jerusalem. First years were hard years, and his scant medical income had to be supplemented. With dexterous hands he plied the art of the orthopedic shoemaker, filling his own prescriptions. At this time my sister fell victim to brain cancer.

Later on Dr. Heilbronner became co-founder and medical director of the Society for Aid to Handicapped Children, a charitable-municipal hospital known today as Alyn. It became his life's work, and most fortunately it was just in time to intercept the crippling polio epidemic then sweeping the country. Dr. Anna Heilbronner was always at his side, volunteering in both medical and social capacities to the hospital and the society.

My brother Chanan and I both became kibbutzniks. He studied architecture at the Haifa Technicon and has been practicing his art for the kibbutz planning authority ever since.

I became a farmer, for many years in charge of the kibbutz dairy. Lately I became engaged in part-time research in the field of biological pest control at the Hebrew University, with the further aim of implementing practical projects in farming situations.

*HEINRICH (HEINZ) HAYUM

Attorney Dr. Heinrich (Heinz) Hayum, born in Tuebingen in 1904, was the son of attorney Dr. Simon Hayum (Dr. Hayum). He was admitted to the Landgericht Tuebingen in 1929 and practiced law together with his father. His admission, which was cancelled in 1933, was restored in 1934 because his father had yielded his own admission in favor of his son's. He left for the United States in 1938, started out by working on odd jobs, and finally found a modest position as a bookkeeper. Through private study in his spare time he managed to pass the examinations as a certified accountant and as a tax consultant. Within just a few years he became a partner of a prominent firm in his field. In addition to his regular work he taught his chosen specialty at several Western colleges. A serious illness shortened his promising career. He died in 1962.

*SIMON HAYUM

Attorney Dr. Simon Hayum, born in Hechingen in 1867, practiced law in Tuebingen from 1892 to 1934. At that time he yielded his admission in favor of his son. He left for Switzerland in 1939 and for the United States in 1941. He died in 1948. In Tuebingen he had been chairman of a citizens' committee and an alderman for many years. From 1930 to 1936 he presided over the Israelitische Landesversammlung.

W. WALTER HAYUM (formerly Wolfgang Adolph Hayum)
105 East 19th Street
New York, N.Y. 10003

Born: Stuttgart, 1927, son of Alfred Hayum (born 1898) and Alice Hayum (née Strauss, born Ulm, 1905). Father owned textile manufactory. Parents divorced 1937; mother went to America, father remarried and moved to St. Margarethen, Switzerland, 1938, where he had a women's clothing factory. He remarried in 1938 Anni Maisel, born 1900. He died in 1980.

The Hayum family left Switzerland in summer of 1941 via unoccupied France to Spain, then went to Havana, Cuba, on the infamous *Nave Mar*. Resided in Cuba until 1941, when they emigrated to America and resided in New York.

Wolfgang, now Walter Hayum, attended the Lake Grove School, Lake Grove Long Island, and then Albright College in Reading, Pennsylvania, for a B.A. degree in English and economics; also the New York University Radio Writer's Workshop, graduating June 1950 and M.B.A. C. W. Post College. Served in U.S. Army 1945–1947. September 1950, married Jane Reynolds of Alexandria, Virginia, and accepted a job as reporter, *Sydney Daily Telegraph,* Sydney, Australia. Subsequently started Diaphon Records in Festival Records in Australia. Son David Mark was born 1952.

Family returned to United States 1953. Walter worked for CBS Columbia Records Division and was instrumental with the start of Epic Records. Then went to Polaroid Corporation in sales and marketing. 1967 started Photo Media Ltd. a picture agency in New York.

The Hayums have five children: David, Amy, Susan, Andrew, and Brian. They live in New Paltz, New York, where he has a photography studio while his oldest son runs the New York City company. Walter Hayum is a member of the Overseas Press Club in New York.

HARRY HEILBRONNER
17 Watroug Street
Perry, N.Y. 14530

My father, Ludwig Heilbronner (1861–1923), was born in Hechingen and died in Stuttgart. He was a manufacturer with J. Heilbronner and Son. He married Selma Weiss (1873–1939), born and died in Stuttgart. My two brothers, Franz (1896–1956) and Ernst (1906–), were both born in Stuttgart and married Thilde Schmidt in 1924 and Miriam Hotkin, respectively. Frank died in Chicago. Ernst's wife died in 1973.

I was born in Stuttgart in 1900 and married Dora Loeb (1905–) in 1928. Her parents were Hermann Loeb (1878–1957), a partner of Gebrueder

Loeb in Stuttgart, and Mathilde née Straus (1881–1972). Her father was also born in Stuttgart. I was director of research and development of the Perry Knitting Company from 1939–1967 and a textile consultant from 1968 to 1975. Both of my parents-in-law came to the United States. My mother-in-law did knitting and mending after her arrival in the States. My father-in-law died in Perry.

We have two sons. Leslie L. was born in 1930 and owns the Hodges-Heilbronner Insurance in Perry. Warren H. (Werner) was born in 1932 and is married with three sons. He is an attorney. Both were born in Stuttgart.

ALMA HEIMANN
Rua Alenquer n. 97
San Paulo, Brazil

My husband was born in Oberdorf in 1913. He lost his father during the First World War, in the beginning of 1914. Then he returned to Creglingen with his mother, to live with his grandparents from his mother's side. His grandfather, Joseph Pressburger, was a schoolteacher in Creglingen.

My husband went to school first in Mergentheim and later in Frankfurt. In 1933 he tried to matriculate in a Berlin faculty to take a course in chemistry, and naturally one of the questions in the inscription form was if he was a Jew. He preferred not to fill out the form, but due to the fact that his father had died in the First World War, they decided to accept him. However, he preferred to leave Germany and went to France to study in Dijon.

Before leaving Creglingen, he saw a friend die at his side and he himself was hurt. He finished college in Dijon, as well as his chemistry doctorate.

He could have had good jobs in France, but instead he decided to immigrate to Brazil, where he started to work for an American firm, the Corn Products Refining. After some years, he opened a factory to produce chemical articles for foundries, which he administered until he became ill.

In 1979 he suffered an infarct and stroke. After a month he was discharged from the hospital and went home, but had another infarct, was removed to the hospital, but the heart did not resist anymore and he died.

We were married in 1942. We have a son and a daughter, both married. My son and his wife are physicians, and they have two daughters. My daughter is a teacher, and my son-in-law is a physician, and they have one daughter.

In 1939, my husband obtained a visa for his mother and his grand-mother to come to Brazil. Both enjoyed happy days in San Paulo, having met the grandson and great-grandson. His grandfather died in Germany.

*DAVID HEIMANN

Attorney David Heimann, born in Schwaebisch Gmuend in 1879, prac-ticed law in his hometown and was admitted to the Landgericht Ellwangen in 1908. He practiced his profession to the extent that this was possible under the boycott until his admission was voided on November 30, 1938. He moved to Stuttgart in 1939 and left for the United States in 1941.

In the course of the mass arrests of November 9, 1938 he was caught and imprisoned in the concentration camp Dachau, where he was held until 1939. He died in New York in 1947.

ELLA HEIMANN (née Moses)
154-55 24th Avenue
Whitestone, N.Y. 11357

I grew up in Esslingen as the youngest child (three other siblings) of parents who had both lived in northern Germany, and therefore, because of the dialect in Wuerttemberg, always seemed to me "different."

My father belonged to a Stammtisch, my mother had no real friends in the community, but was always held in very high esteem. My other siblings had many close friends. I could never manage that, but I never had the feeling that I was rejected because I was a Jew. Not ever was I made to feel that, neither by teachers nor by classmates.

I left Germany in 1939 together with my husband after he was released by the Nazis from Dachau. I first went to England for seven months, since I had no affidavit to immigrate to the United States, where my husband went. I never had to feel any financial hardship, though we started with exactly nothing, and it never seemed to matter that we had to count every penny. We were young, we did not need much to be content, and we brought up our children in the same spirit. During the first seven years my husband's father lived with us until his death, and I could take some jobs as a cleaning woman to make some extra money. When our youngest child started school, I took a job in a small manufacturing firm for lady's clothes, first as a finisher, later as a cutter. I have been there ever since.

Our children are a joy to us and have full, constructive lives. It is beautiful to see that they bring up their children with the same values that we tried to instill in them.

99

Our friends are practically all people that we met in the youth organization in Stuttgart (BDJJ). Somehow we had difficulty in making new ties with Jews and non-Jews, though we tried. But in the end we just felt more comfortable with our old "crowd."

KARL L. HEIMAN
2076 Central Drive North
East Meadow, N.Y. 11554

I was born in 1924. I am the son of David and Bertha Heimann. My father was partner in Gebrueder Heimann, a wholesale and retail textile business with branches in Stuttgart and Oberdorf. We had a fairly prosperous concern until the Nazis took over in Germany, and eventually we lost everything.

My older brother, Heinrich, left Germany in 1934 for Palestine. Since he was politically very active, it was imperative that he escape certain death and leave Germany as soon as feasible. My second brother, Martin U., left for Argentina in 1936. I came to the United States with my parents in 1939, two weeks before World War II broke out.

We survived Kristallnacht, even though my father wound up in Dachau. My experiences during the Nazi times left me with two conclusions: I have absolutely no use for the German political mentality, which throughout history has had a sense of wrong timing, is consistently pro-military, and made the twentieth century the bloodiest of all times. And secondly, if there is one lesson Hitler taught me, it is, even if I forget that I am a Jew, the outside world will always remind me that I am a Jew. So be it.

In Germany I was a student until all Jewish youngsters were thrown out of the Realschule during Kristallnacht. I was allowed to attend Realschule only because my father was a World War I veteran. In New York I attended James Monroe High School in the Bronx and then Point Pleasant Beach High School in New Jersey, after my parents moved to Lakewood, New Jersey, and became chicken farmers in 1940. I graduated in 1942 as shyest and also best student. After a short time as worker in a defense plant, I became a member of the U.S. Army. My unit was shipped to the Pacific, specifically Australia. I joined the 41st Infantry Division under General Douglas MacArthur. We eventually participated in landings, battles, and campaigns in New Guinea, Dutch East Indies, Philippines, and were the first troops in Japan after its surrender. As a combat infantryman, I was wounded, received battlefield promotions, and innumerable decorations. I was lucky to survive.

After the war I made use of the G.I. Bill of Rights, learned the sewing machine trade, became a serviceman, salesman, department manager for R. H. Macy, and later a division manager for Sears, Roebuck & Company. I am with Sears now since 1962 and am very happy. It had been a mutually very satisfactory relationship. I am a division manager in charge of sewing machines, vacuum cleaners, televisions, stereos, electronics, and related items.

Susanna E. Heiman, who comes from Archshofen, Wuerttemberg, is my wife. She is religious-school principal of the Suburban Temple in Wantagh, Long Island, New York, one of the largest schools of its type in the metropolitan area.

We have two children. Howard Steven, born 1955, after attending East Meadow High School with honors, graduated from Rensselaer Polytechnic Institute in Troy, New York, and is a doctor in the U.S. Army after last month's graduation in Bethesda, Maryland. He will do his residency at Walter Reed Hospital. Elisabeth T. is our daughter, born 1957. She also attended East Meadow High School and then Fashion Institute of Technology in New York. She is now a buyer for young men's clothing for the May Company. She was an assistant buyer at Sears at first.

Both of our children are happily married; Howard to Diane Marcus, a school friend from East Meadow. Elisabeth is married to Jonathan Prial, who is a computer expert with IBM. He too was a childhood acquaintance.

I keep active politically and socially. I speak to the younger generation about our history, its meanings and its lessons. Last year, we were honored by the Suburban Temple with a Generations Award—"In recognition of the mutuality and concern that has long given a special character to Jewish life and been transmitted from generation to generation, and for outstanding service to the Jewish people and to the nation of Israel."

MARTIN U. HEIMAN
58-37 186th Street
Flushing, N.Y. 11365

I was born in 1913 at Oberdorf, where my parents, David and Bertha Heiman, lived until their emigration in July 1939 to the United States. Since 1927 I lived in Stuttgart, first going to the Hoehere Handelsschule; later I was active in the family wholesale textile business.

In 1933, I read *Mein Kampf* and saw the complete blueprint for the rearmament of Germany and coming wars against France and the Soviet Union, as well as Hitler's mad hatred against Jews. During the pogrom, November 10, 1938, my father escaped certain assassination by the SS at Oberdorf only due to the fact that he was away in Stuttgart. The SS then arrested in the neighboring house Joseph Schuster and his father, took them to a nearby wood, and shot them. The father, however, survived.

In 1937 I left Germany for Buenos Aires, Argentina, where I spent four pleasant and interesting years. During the spring of 1941 I left for the United States to be close to the family. My parents, in partnership with Herman and Minnie Heiman, formerly of Stuttgart, had taken over a chicken farm near Lakewood, New Jersey, where they lived happily for many years.

At the beginning of 1944, I entered the U.S. Army. In the fall of 1944, I was transferred in France to the Military Intelligence Service and assigned to IPW-Team 168 (Interrogators for Prisoners-of-War) of the 42nd (Rainbow) Division in Alsace. During the advance in Southern Germany I was wounded in Nuernberg. Later I was busy in the province of Salzburg and Tyrol arresting SS men and Nazi big-wigs. Among the men arrested by our team were Matthias Greiser, Gauleiter from Danzig, and Bela Imredy, Hungary, both executed later.

After being discharged from the Army I returned to the First Spice Mixing Company, Inc., in New York, where I am still active now as inside manager. While in England, as a G.I., I met again my second cousin Ruth Heiman, and we were married in 1947. In 1949 our son, Michael, was born. He is now teaching biological and geographical environment at Berkeley, California. In 1952 Diane was born. She is now an office manager, advertising-publications firm in New York.

MINNIE HEIMAN
280-C Kingston Court
Lakewood, N.J. 08701

This is the story of our family in the old country and in our new homeland.

The Heimanns lived for more than two hundred years in Wuerttemberg; the family was large and branched out, but always kept in close contact. In 1832, Chaim Loeb Heimann founded a textile business in Oberdorf-Bopfingen, which was continued by the sons and grandsons till 1938, when the Nazis forced us to sell it.

In 1922 we were married; a son, Udo Guenther, and a daughter, Ursula Renate, grew up in Stuttgart. In 1939 we emigrated from Germany to the United States, where we tried our luck in New York. However, times were very hard and we were already over forty years old; thus finding suitable work was nearly impossible. So, why not consider a try in the country?

Fortunately, on our orientation trip through the well-known chicken-farming region of New Jersey, we found what seemed to be the right place for two families, as our brother, his wife, and son joined us in our new venture.

In spite of our lack of experience in agriculture and particularly in chicken farming, we learned quickly from good advice, by our own experience, and last but not least, from the chickens themselves. Those three thousand white-feathered "bosses" were very strict in their demands and kept us on our toes for long hours, leaving little free time for weekends or holidays. We took it all in stride—we liked our work and life in the country. Our daughter and the two sons, then teenagers, helped with the farm work while attending high school. Soon after graduation, the boys were drafted into the Army for duty in Europe and the Pacific during World War II. Fortunately, they returned safe and sound; they studied and pursued careers in the city. The children married German-Jewish spouses and they have children and grandchildren of their own.

In 1965, we sold the chickens but continued to live on the farm, enjoying our leisure years, traveling near and far to see America from coast to coast, and other countries and continents.

My husband passed away four years ago. I moved to a retirement village nearby.

RICHARD H. HEIMANN
154-55 24th Avenue
Flushing, N.Y. 11357

I grew up as the son of a lawyer in Schwaebisch Gmuend, a small town to which my grandfather had come from a nearby village. We were treated as a well-established family; however, during my years in elementary school I was subjected to name-calling as a Jew. I emigrated after thirteen years of high school (the customary preparation for an academic career), an apprenticeship as machinist, and some experience in mechanical drafting. I was kept in Dachau for seven weeks following the Kristallnacht.

In the United States I worked as a machinist for the first five years, then as a mechanical designer. In the evenings I went to various courses, which eventually led to an engineering degree. At the same time I raised a family. (I got married just before emigration, partly for legal reasons and partly because within a short time both our families would become scattered over several countries.)

I have lived in Queens, one of the greener boroughs of New York City, and worked in New York City or its vicinity. I love the cultural opportunities which this city provides. In my professional life I had to change employers a little more often than I liked, but I appreciate that in the New York area this is possible without changing one's domicile.

103

I have been a member of the originally all-German-Jewish congregation Habonim ever since its inception. My social contacts are mostly with other Jews who emigrated from Germany during Hitler's reign.

All my four children went through college; two have doctorates. Three of them are married and have children of their own.

I could now retire with an income which is adequate for ordinary living. However, a continued severe illness of me or my wife could wipe out our resources.

UDO G. (GUNTHER) HEIMAN
119 Forest Hill Road
West Orange, N.J. 07052

Even though I was born in Leipzig in 1924, I consider myself a "Schwab," and I still speak a good "Schwäbisch" with relatives and friends.

My father, Herman, was born in Oberdorf bei Bopfingen. In 1926 we moved with my younger sister, Ursula, to Stuttgart-Obertuerkheim. My father, together with his brothers, operated the Textilgrosshandlung Gebruder Heimann. Their store was located at Koenigstrasse 1 in Stuttgart. I attended the local grammar school in Obertuerkheim and then the Realschule in Unterturkheim until 1938. My father's and uncle's business having been sold, we emigrated to the United States in 1939. We lived in the Bronx for one year, and in 1940 my father and his brother David bought a poultry farm in Brick Town, New Jersey. I attended the high school in Point Pleasant Beach and graduated in 1942.

In 1943 I was drafted into the Army and trained in Texas and the Mojave Desert in California with a heavy-field-artillery battalion. In 1944 we were shipped to England, and in June we crossed the English Channel and landed in Normandy. My job with the artillery was as a computer, computing the fire settings for the crews at the 155-mm. guns. We followed the battle-lines across France, through Belgium, Holland, and Northern Germany to the Elbe at Magdeburg. The war was over then, and as part of the occupation army we were stationed in Hessen.

I wasn't a U.S. citizen yet and I finally became one in a courthouse in Bad Nauheim. I also had the opportunity to travel to Stuttgart and saw the devastation caused by the bombing, although in Obertürkheim not much was amiss.

We returned to the United States in 1945, and after my discharge I enrolled as an apprentice for a toolmaker. In 1952 I started to work for Proll Toy Company in Bloomfield, New Jersey, manufacturers of musical toys and Magnus organs. (The owner is Mr. Gustav Proll, formerly Prolsdorfer from Karlsruhe.) I am now tool-room manager and mold designer.

In 1950 I married my wife, Lore, née Blumenfeld. In 1952 we moved to West Orange, New Jersey. The same year our son Peter was born. Two years later our son Stephen was born. After attending local school, Peter graduated from Monmouth College and now works as territorial sales manager for Jockey International Company. Stephen received an engineering degree from Rutgers University and a master's degree from Stanford University. For the last three years he worked for Ford Motor Company in Dearborn, Michigan, and now is employed by Exxon Information Services. Both our sons are married.

With satisfaction I look back at the years since we arrived in the United States. Hard work and diligence put my family and myself on the road to success, and we are grateful for these blessings.

WOLFGANG HEIMANN
9 Bramhall Park Road,
Bramhall,
Stockport, Cheshire, SK7 3DQ
England

Your letter arrived on the eve of our departure for Württemberg with a party of twenty-two young people from three different schools in the area, plus an English woman colleague—a teacher of German like my wife and myself.

This will be our sixth series of exchange visits since we started the link with the Schiller-Gymnasium in Ludwigsburg in 1969, later transferred to a brand-new establishment, the Otto-Hahn-Gymnasium. It will also be my last visit, since, having reached the age of sixty-five, I shall be retiring in July, and it was only as a result of the urgent pleas of our friends in Ludwigsburg to have one more exchange before my retirement that I agreed to undertake once more the not inconsiderable amount of effort and organization involved.

Thus we are once again looking forward to a program, including a walk in the Urach area, a coach trip to Hohenzollern Castle and to Tübingen, as well as a civic reception by the Ludwigsburg authorities. We travel by train and boat, spending the night on the *Queen Juliana,* then on through Holland on the Rheinexpress to Cologne, from where we take the intercity train to Stuttgart. All our pupils have partners in Ludwigsburg, and they and their parents will have flocked to Stuttgart station to welcome us on our arrival.

Last night my daughter Cathy, a violinist with the Royal Liverpool

Philharmonic Orchestra, returned from an eleven-day tour of Germany. She played in the Frankfurt Jahrhunderthalle, the Stuttgart Liederhalle, the Nuernberg Meistersingerhalle (amongst a number of other places), and finished up at the Berlin Philharmonie.

My son Thomas is a lieutenant in the Royal Navy and a submariner. In August he is going to get married to a very nice (non-Jewish!) girl—a theatre sister at the naval hospital. It will be a formal naval wedding, with the couple walking out of church under the crossed swords of Tommy's brother officers.

My wife, Eva, and I got married about a month after the Queen and Prince Philip way back in 1947. Now our son will marry just about a month after their son, Prince Charles! A nice thought.

LOTTE HEINE (née Hirsch)
87 Intervale
Roslyn, N.Y.

Born 1909 in Cannstatt, Germany. Parents: Alfred Hirsch, born 1878; Meta Hirsch (née Metzger), born 1887.

I emigrated to the United States in 1936 and married Max Heine in 1938. My father passed away in 1961. My children are: Doris Gruenwald (wife of Dr. Hans Gruenwald), 8 Mary Lane, Greenvale, New York; Karen Heine, 2579 South York Street, Denver, Colorado 80210; Peggy Heine, 400 East Mexico Street, Denver, Colorado 80210. Doris and Hans have three children: Michael, Judith, and David.

My sister, Marian Perlman, lives at 45 Wingate Road, Yonkers, New York, and has a daughter, Claudia Humphrey. Claudia's daughter is Emily Humphrey.

MARION H. HELBING
167 East 67th Street
New York, N.Y. 10021

My father, Philipp Helbing, was director of the Dresdner Bank in Stuttgart. Born 1868, he died 1944 in a sanitorium in Central Valley, New York. My mother, Minnie, née Pappenheimer, was born 1879 in Fort Smith, Arkansas. She died in 1960 in New York.

My parents and I left Stuttgart for Zurich in 1933. This was possible because my father had reached retirement age. They stayed in Zurich until 1938. In the meantime my mother was able to regain her American citizenship.

In 1934 I emigrated to America and have been in New York since then, finishing my education ending with a bachelor's degree in dietetics and nutrition.

My brother, Robert Helbing, and his family had far sadder endings. He was born 1907 in Stuttgart, but was living in Köln and was able to join us in Zurich but soon thereafter went to Paris and finally established a toy business in Amsterdam, Holland in 1934. The same year he married. Their children were born in 1935 and 1936.

When the Nazis went into Holland, the entire family was put into Camp Westerbork. Then, in 1943, they all were taken to Auschwitz. The wife and both children were gassed in 1943. This information came to my mother and me only years later with the help of the Red Cross. We never could find out what had happened to my brother.

I was born in 1911.

FLORA HERZ (née Dittmann)
1201 Funston
San Francisco, Calif. 94122

I was born in 1895 and was married in Heilbronn. My husband passed away in 1929. I was a housewife. I emigrated with my two children, Lotte and Erich, in 1940 to Bogota, Colombia, South America, and in 1952 I emigrated to the United States. For some years I was working as a volunteer at the Jewish Home for the Aged in San Francisco.

FRANK L. HERZ
1022-A Heritage Village
Southbury, Conn. 06488

My family is deeply rooted in Wuerttemberg. My great-grandfather Lazarus Herz (1809–1881) moved to Heilbronn from Kochendorf, where at least two generations of his ancestors had been living. With his son Sigmund, my grandfather (1851–1921), he founded a piece-goods and clothing store under the name of L. Herz Sohn. My father, Hermann Herz (1879–1961), and his brother Otto (1877–1918) later joined the company, which flourished and became well known in Heilbronn and the surrounding countryside; in 1924 it celebrated its fiftieth anniversary "Zur Zierde deutschen Gewerbefleisses" (Handelskammer Heilbronn). My uncle Otto, however, had volunteered for the Army in 1914 and died for what he had considered his fatherland.

My mother's father, Jakob Levi (1845–1930), came from a large family in Muehlen (near Horb). He was educated to be a Hebrew teacher but instead settled in Hechingen, Hohenzollern, as manufacturer of knitted goods. (Factory Liebmann & Levi, founded in 1883.)

His daughter Jenny (1882–1961) married my father in 1907. I, their first child (born in 1908), studied law, and graduated in Tuebingen. I served my third year of apprenticeship (*Referendar*) in Heilbronn with the law firm Gumbel, Koch & Scheuer in 1933.

My brother Kurt, born in 1915, was an apprentice in an export firm in Frankfurt at that time; his firm had connections in many countries, especially the United States.

The political upheaval of 1933 hit my family like a thunderbolt, but it did not come as a complete surprise; they had not altogether disregarded the dark clouds in the political sky. My career in Germany was at an end. It was difficult for my father to realize that his standing in the community and his well-established ties with neighbors and customers, the "hero's death" of his brother, that none of these bonds would prove durable or even meaningful at this point.

The family decided, if we had to leave, it would be better to do so without delay. We spent the second half of 1933 and the year 1934 in France, where my brother had found temporary employment.

Since France did not grant permanent residence, the family prepared for a move to the United States. Fortunately, several nieces of my grandfather Levi had emigrated to this country around the turn of the century and had their own families in Brooklyn, New York. They now helped us get settled after our arrival in New York in 1935.

My brother began to work in his field and, after a number of years, established a company for the import and manufacture of leather goods and travel accessories; it is still active and respected in the trade. My father got involved in a small retail store in Jamaica, New York, which kept him busy until it was time for him to retire.

I myself did not care to start all over, learning the completely different procedure of the American judicial system. After trying several commercial employments, I joined my brother's company, with which I am still connected. During the war I was assigned to Army Intelligence.

The German background continued to play an overwhelming part in the life of my parents who never were anything but Swabians; the United States always remained a foreign country to them. My brother, during his yearly business trips to Germany, never fails to visit the grandparents' graves in Heilbronn and Hechingen; he also sees his old school friends in Heilbronn. My own son spoke only German to the age of five and shows interest in his background. But there it will end.

When I revisited Germany for the first time in 1960, Heilbronn did not seem to be the same city which I had known; I preferred to keep my memories intact and never returned there.

When visiting the Black Forest in 1978, however, I felt at home and enjoyed conversations in the native dialect. Even now my favorite occupation is the study of early-sixteenth-century German history, especially the life and works of Johannes Reuchlin, the Swabian humanist who risked his reputation and career to protect Jewish books from the fire, and their owners and defenders from the Inquisition.

ERNA HERZBERGER

My husband, Alfred, was born in 1896. Of the four children, two were killed by the Nazis. One brother survived and he lives in New Zealand. Also my husband's parents and all other relatives were killed. My parents were Siegfried and Berta Herzberger. My father passed away at an early age, and my mother moved with my sister to Stuttgart to make a new home and life for all of us, together with her brother. Her brother, my uncle Ludwig Grunwald, never married and took care of us as he had promised my dying father. My sister Elsa married Arthur Heidenheimer. They had one daughter and emigrated to São Paulo, Brazil, where her husband passed away at the age of eighty-four. Else lives here with Inga, who has two sons and four great-grandchildren. My husband, Fred, and myself were ten years in Zueiz, Switzerland. After the war we followed our only living son to the United States. My husband and myself worked very hard to help him finish his education. Today Ralph is a very well-known biochemist and works at the Scripps Laboratories in LaJolla, California. He is married and has two children. The boy is twenty-two and the girl twenty-one years of age.

BEATRICE S. HESS (née Spatz)
17 Fort George Hill
New York, N.Y. 10040

My parents were Samuel Spatz, teacher, born 1867 in Freudenthal, died in Stuttgart 1935, and Sophie, née Levi, born 1869 in Affaltrach, died in 1936 in Stuttgart. His personality and activities were such that I best repeat here the words from his last will, spoken at his funeral by Mr. Rothchild, director of the Jewish orphanage in Esslingen: "I beg you not to praise and thank me. I did what had been my duty, in school, congregation, and elsewhere, where I could fight for Judaism, went even to Koenig Wilhelm II, several times with success. I received the Distinguished Service Cross from the King for what I did for the Jews of Wuerttemberg." My father wrote many articles in the Hamburger Family Paper, the *Israelite*, the general teachers paper, and in the Wuerttembergische State Paper. He was a brilliant speaker, and his fight for Judaism and school was a holy task to him. My mother all her life was his partner, and as leader of the Sisterhood for twenty-seven years, her advice was sought by more than 260 members.

I was born 1895 in Affaltrach. We moved to Rexingen in 1904. I had one interest already then: music. I inherited this trait from mother's side. Her father, Hermann Levi, was a self-trained but spectacular pianist. After attending father's school to the seventh grade he took me to France to study voice. I lived in a *pension*, but had to return home when war threatened in the summer of 1914. I continued voice study with a famous opera singer, but he was not a teacher. I married after the war and my husband, Joseph Hess, helped me. After three years of intensive studies and contact with many singers, I became the singer for classics at the South German Radio Station. My programs and pictures were constantly in the press, and I was lucky to be accepted for further studies by the prima donna Rhoda von Glehn, of the State Opera. It was like a dream come true. The teacher told me that I would soon have a role with her in *Le Nozze di Figaro,* and in February 1933, the State Opera wrote that I would be hired for "Lola" in *Cavalleria* and that I should prepare for this (which I had done long before). But with Hitler's coming into power, I never heard from the opera house again. I had to wait six years before being able to emigrate to the United States. During that time, I could not even sing at home anymore, because my neighbor next-door was a Gestapo man!

In New York, without money, I became a nurse. As soon as I received the license, I left the hospital and did private nursing. I bought a grand piano. I loved it and it became my second profession. In the United States, I changed my first name from Brunhilde to Beatrice.

LIESEL B. HESS (née Mann)
3713 Menlo Drive
Baltimore, Md. 21215

I was born 1915 in Heilbronn. My father, David Mann, was killed in the Battle of Arras, 1917; my mother was Martha, née Rothschild. I have two sisters: Elfrieda Schwarzwalder 61–67 77th Place, Middle Village, New York, 11379, and Margaret Gutman, 300 Winston Drive, Cliffside Park, New Jersey, 07010. My father had a metal firm, founded by my grandfather, Max Mann. My mother remarried Ferdinand Levor in 1920; my stepfather died in 1934. My mother emigrated to the United States in 1941; died in 1969, aged eighty-two.

I graduated from the Jewish Teacher Seminar in Wuerzburg in 1936 and took a job at the Jewish Orphan Home in Fuerth, Bavaria; emigrated to the United States arriving 1938. I had a position in Cleveland, Ohio, at the Jewish Children Home, when I married in 1942. My husband, Kurt B. Hess, passed away in 1979.

Since we married, we lived in Baltimore, Maryland. I was the first teacher at the Bais Yaakov School for girls, and I am still active there now as a volunteer.

Our three children are all married. The oldest daughter lives in Monsey, New York, a son and youngest daughter live in Baltimore. I am also busy with Chevre Kadisha and with my grandchildren. I belong to the Shearith Israel Congregation; they have quite a few former German-Jews as members.

*LUDWIG HESS

Lawyer Ludwig Hess, born in 1864 in Ellwangen, was an attorney since 1890. Since 1912 he was also a notary public in Stuttgart. In 1935, the notary's office was taken away from him, and in 1938 his admission to the bar was revoked. As a man of seventy-eight—after he had first been evicted and had to find shelter in the so-called Home for Jews in Dellmendingen near Ulm, which was more like a workhouse (where one of his sisters died)—he had to set out on the journey without return to Theresienstadt, where he died in 1942. Another sister also died there.

WILLIAM W. HESS (formerly Werner Hess)
14303 Bauer Drive
Rockville, Md. 20853

I (originally Werner Hess), the son of William (Wilhelm) and Else Hess, emigrated by myself in 1937 at the age of fifteen and settled in Danville, Illinois, a town of 37,000, where I had a clerical job in the largest local department store. I was drafted in 1942, passed through Camp Ritchie, and spent the next three years in the Military Intelligence Service in the Washington, D.C., area. There I settled after my discharge, working first for the Army Map Service, Corps of Engineers, for sixteen years, then another sixteen years for the Defense Intelligence Agency as an intelligence specialist, reaching a fairly senior position before retiring early this year. The G.I. Bill enabled me to resume my interrupted education, and I attended George Washington University at night. Activities in the community included serving as an officer in the local citizens association and as its delegate to the Allied Civic Group, and teaching a religious school class at Temple Emanuel in Kensington for fourteen years. Shortly after VJ-Day I married the former Shirley Klein from Pittsburgh, Pennsylva-

111

nia. We have two daughters, Carole (Starkman), married to a New York neurologist whose parents had escaped the death camps of Poland, and Diane (Finder), married to a Brooklyn law student. We are now enjoying retirement, where my principal nonrecreational activities are working as a volunteer for Congressman Michael Barnes (D-Md.), and for our temple's Soviet Jewry Committee.

My parents had followed me to Danville after my father had spent five weeks in Dachau. He opened a small drygoods store in a nearby coal-mining community which he ran successfully despite wartime shortages and the initial suspicion the community had toward newcomers. He retired at age seventy-two and moved to this area with my mother. Both parents are now deceased.

I am most interested in your project, and hope you will be successful in your attempt to contact as many old Wuerttembergers as possible.

LOUISE HEUMANN (née Einstein)
1964 Compton Rd.
Cincinnati, Ohio 45231

My husband Richard Heumann, was a bank director in Laupheim. There he was jailed in 1933, released after resigning his job, then worked for Steiner Hops until threats on his life were made. We then moved with our son and daughter to Switzerland in 1934 and left for Paris in 1935, bought a small laundry business, and subsisted. My father, Emanuel joined us in Paris in 1938, after the death of his wife in 1937.

During the war and German invasion of France, my husband was interned by the French, as a German national, in several camps. He was temporarily released in 1942, then rearrested by the Nazis, put in a camp, then deported from France . . . and never heard from again!

Daughter Marianne emigrated to the United States in 1940; worked as a seamstress, returned to France in 1956, and works there in an art gallery.

Myself, my father, and son Frank fled Paris on foot in 1940, as the German armies overran France, returned to Paris, and stayed until 1942, when the Nazis rounded up refugees. Escaped this round-up with the help of friends, fled to the South of France, then still unoccupied. We were all three put in a camp by Vichy, but released, father and son on account of their age, I myself thanks to intervention by French friends. With the help of the underground, all three of us fled to Switzerland via Aix-les-Pains, stayed with Swiss sister-in-law till 1946, then emigrated to United States. Lived with brother Dr. H. Einstein in Washington D.C., and worked as his secretary.

Son Frank attended school in Washington, graduated from the University of Cincinnati as mechanical engineer, worked for General Electric Company in Cincinnati, currently as two system-manager for jet-engines. I moved to Cincinnati in 1965.

WERNER L. HEYMANN
554 Meryl Drive
Westbury, N.Y. 11590

My father, Julius Heymann, was born in Stuttgart in 1884 and died in New York in 1964. In Stuttgart he had been president of the Wuerttemberger Gardinen Weberei L Joseph, Co. A.G., a firm founded by his uncles in 1880.

My mother, Hanna Heymann, born 1896, died in New York in 1958.

We had left Germany for the United States in May 1937, and in New York my father established the firm of Julius Heymann Company, Inc., importer, wholesaler, and manufacturer of accessories, such as compacts, pillboxes, and novelties.

I was born in Mannheim in 1926 but lived in Stuttgart until we left for New York in 1937. There I went to schools including New York University and got my B.A. and M.B.A. degrees. The latter I received in 1953.

I married my wife Paula in 1951. We have three children: Gerard, age twenty-five, Jo-Ann, twenty-two, and Andrew, twenty-one. Gerard is a manufacturer's agent and the younger children are still in college.

I served in the U.S. Navy from 1943 to 1945 as aerial gunner on a torpedo bomber on an aircraft carrier in the Atlantic and in Europe.

My brother Gerard (Gerd) was born in Stuttgart in 1924, went to school there and in England from 1935 to 1938, and graduated from New York University. He was killed in Belgium during the Battle of the Bulge at the age of twenty, fighting with the U.S. Army (Infantry, 75th Division). He was posthumously awarded the Silver Star for bravery in action.

I am the president of Heyco Trading Corporation, importer of souvenir and gift items.

ADA C. HIRSCH
955 Park Avenue
New York, N.Y. 10028

Thank you for your letter. Since I worked as a manager of the Landesverband fuer Juedische Wohlfahrtspflege and for five years in the Kultusgemeinde, Hospitalstrasse, I feel like one of you.

I am eighty-four and still working to a moderate degree as a psychia-

113

trist. Thus I lack the time and the strength for detailed reports. Therefore, kindly accept a few data:

I was born in 1895. In Germany I trained and worked as a registered nurse and as a social worker. I studied medicine in Heidelberg. Having to leave in 1933, I was able to graduate from medical school in Vienna since I had studied and worked there in the past. Here I worked in hospitals, trained, and graduated in medicine, psychiatry, and psychoanalysis. I opened my office, and as I mentioned, I am still working with a few patients and also as a volunteer in Lenox Hill Hospital. I appreciate having found a new home and career in this country.

ELSIE HIRSCH (née Moos)
Norfolk, Va.

I was born in Ulm in 1921. My parents were Carl and Hilda Moos. I have an older brother, Heinz (Henry).

I left Germany with my parents in November 1939, having received affidavits from our relative, Professor Albert Einstein. We settled in Norfolk, Virginia, where my brother lived already. I met there my husband, Joachim Hirsch. We were married in 1944. Our daughter, Evelyn, was born in 1945, and our son, Steven, in 1949. Both children are now married. My daughter moved to San Diego; her two children are Carrie, born 1972, and Lisa, born 1976. My son lives in Virginia Beach. His child, Jessica, was born in 1978.

FANNY HIRSCH (née Wormser)
3601 Huntoon
Topeka, Kan. 66604

My husband, Eugene, born 1882, and myself, born 1890, both in Stuttgart, left our home in the Botnangerstrasse in 1933, with our sons Walter, fourteen, and Ernest Albert, nearly ten. One of the first emigrants. We arrived in the United States on the Hamburg-Amerika Line. To our great sorrow, my mother, Valentine Wormser, née Morgenthau, could not join us, but fortunately came to us in 1938, and lived with us for fifteen years until she passed away in our home in Jackson Heights, New York. I am still grateful that she could be with us, thanks to the efforts of our unforgettable cousin Otto Hirsch, and various Jewish organizations. She traveled at the age of seventy-five in cattle cars, via Russia, Japan, Honolulu, San Francisco, with us anxiously awaiting her at Grand Central Station in New York!

After a short stay in New York, we spent a year in Newton, Boston,

Massachusetts. It was personally a happy time, but uninteresting professionally, but my husband's family there made us feel very welcome.

A new phase in our lives started with the move back to Jackson Heights, New York, in 1935. Both boys attended good public schools, while my husband worked hard at a New York brokerage firm. Walter graduated from Queens College and Ernie attended night school at the City College; then both my sons went overseas in World War II, fortunately returning home safely. They finished their education, Ernie in psychology, and Walter taking graduate courses and teaching. Walter got married to Lotte Landman, from Mannheim. They live now in West Lafayette, Indiana; Walter teaching sociology at Purdue University, and Lotte teaching elementary school. They have four children.

After my husband and my mother died within a month in 1953, I became a baby nurse in New York. Twelve years later I moved to Topeka, Kansas, to be with my son Ernie, a clinical psychologist and research scientist with the Menninger Foundation. It was my privilege to share his life until he succumbed to a fatal attack of multiple sclerosis.

Now I live in our lovely home with a nice young companion, hoping to finish my last days peacefully.

HANS GEORGE HIRSCH
6513 Kenhowe Drive
Bethesda, Md. 20034

My father, Dr. jur. Otto Hirsch (born in Stuttgart 1885), served as a director of the Neckar-Aktien-Gesellschaft and as president of the Oberrat der Israelitischen Religionsgemeinschaft Wuerttembergs when the Nazis came to power in 1933. He was soon forced into retirement from his principal position. In the summer of 1933, the representatives of the Jewish communities in the German States and of the large Jewish national organizations elected him executive chairman of the newly created Reichsvertretung der deutschen Juden. Rabbi Leo Baeck was elected president. Thus father and, after some delay, also mother (Martha Loeb Hirsch, born in Stuttgart, 1891) moved to Berlin.

This is not the place to report on the far-reaching work of the Reichsvertretung. Father was arrested and sent to concentration camps three times, in 1935, 1938, and 1941. After his final arrest in Berlin, at the end of February 1941, he was shipped to Mauthausen Concentration Camp in Austria and was reported to have died there in 1941. Following this tragedy, mother received a U.S. immigration visa. However, her passport was taken away on order of the notorious Adolf Eichmann. She was deported from Berlin in 1942. Captured Gestapo documents listed her transport with "destination unknown."

My widowed grandfather Louis Hirsch (born in Stuttgart 1858) died on the high seas, three days before the arrival of his boat in New York, in 1941. My uncle Theodore C. Hirsch had succeeded in keeping the news of my father's death from him. Grandfather had been appointed a member of the Israelitische Oberkirchenbehörde, the predecessor organization of the Oberrat, by the King in 1912. After the separation of State and Church in 1924, he had been elected vice-president of the Oberrat for the term ending in 1930. Grandmother Helene Reis Hirsch was born in Niederstetten in 1860, and died in Stuttgart in 1939.

As indicated above, grandfather, at the time of his death, was in the company of his surviving son, Theodore C. Hirsch (born in Stuttgart, 1888; died in New York, 1965), his daughter-in-law, Minna Hirsch (born in Ulm, 1892 and now residing at Isabella House in New York), and the latter's mother, Friedericke Kiefe Hirsch (born in Baisingen, 1864, died in New Orleans soon after the end of World War II).

My uncle Theodore C. Hirsch, had been a director of the Salamander-Aktien-Gesellschaft (Germany's leading shoe factory). After his immigration into the United States, he found a modest job as a "girl Friday" for a well-to-do man of Rumanian-Jewish background. His wife worked as a practical nurse. They had an unusually hard and long beginning in this country. They lived in a single room without private bathroom and without separate kitchen for eight years. It was only then that my uncle could establish his export-import business and move into a real apartment.

I was the first member of the Louis Hirsch family to immigrate into the United States. (I was born in Stuttgart in 1916, graduated from the Eberhard-Ludwigs-Gymnasium in 1934, went to work on farms, first in Wuerttemberg, then in Bavaria and Silesia, and emigrated in 1938.) During my first year in America, I worked on farms in several states and I also had a factory job for a while. In 1940 I started studying agriculture at the University of Minnesota. In due time, I earned the degrees of B.S. with high distinction, M.S., and Ph.D. My studies were interrupted by army service (1943–1946). I came to Washington in 1947 and worked for the Food and Agriculture Organization of the United Nations for a short time. Since 1948 I have worked as an agricultural economist in the U.S. Department of Agriculture. From 1973 to 1977, I served as agricultural attaché on the U.S. Mission to the Organization for Economic Cooperation and Development in Paris.

I was active in my community and in my congregation in various ways. For over two years, I served as chairman of the executive committee of the

Government Division of the United Jewish Appeal. I also served as a member of the executive committee of the Jewish Community Council of Washington. I was recently elected to the board of the Leo Baeck Institute.

In 1941, I married Helen Strauss, a native of Nuernberg, whom I had met at the University of Minnesota. Our oldest daughter, Marga, a graduate of Radcliffe College, is the wife of Dr. Kenneth S. Kamm, a Dupont Company research chemist and the mother of our two granddaughters, Shira and Aviva. Our second daughter, Deborah, recently earned her master's degree in social work and vocational guidance at Washington University, St. Louis. Our son Daniel Otto is in his last year at Harvard Law School. Our youngest daughter, Naomi, is a sophomore at Brandeis University studying theatre.

My sisters Grete and Ursula and my cousins Trudy and Lotte (the daughters of Theodore and Minna Hirsch) all arrived in this country from England, where they had spent the war years, as helpers on a boat carrying "war brides" and their babies in April 1946. They left Germany in 1939. They were all born in Stuttgart. Grete (born 1921) earned degrees in piano and violin teaching from the Royal Academy of Music in London and later a master of music degree in New York. She is a violinist and violin teacher in New York. Ursula Joachim (born 1925) earned B.S. and M.S. degrees at the University of Vermont and at Cornell, respectively. For a number of years, she worked for the pharmaceutical firm of Lederle in Pearl River, New York; she is the co-patentee of some drugs. Since 1964 she has lived in White Plains, New York. Her daughter, Angela, is a high school student.

My cousin Trudy (born in Stuttgart, 1919) married Joseph Schwarz in 1952. Their sons, Peter and Thomas, are Ph.D. candidates, and their daughter, Peggy, is also doing graduate work. Trudy is a physical therapist and works for the New York City school system.

My cousin Lotte (born in Stuttgart, 1921) trained as a nurse and midwife in England and as a public health nurse in Colorado. She went to Alaska in 1954 and married Richard Bogard a few years later. Their son, Robin, attends college in Alaska. Their older daughter, Troya, studies at Carlton College, Northfield, and their younger daughter, Esther, lives in Arizona.

117

HERTA HIRSCH (née Erlebacher)
73–37 Austin Street
Forest Hills, N.Y. 11375

On April 4, 1938 my husband, Albert Hirsch (b. Horb a. Neckar), our daughter Lottie (b. Stuttgart), my mother Rosalie Erlebacher (b. Dettensee), and I, Herta Hirsch (b. Bretten, Baden) arrived in New York. Friends from Stuttgart met us and helped us get settled on 72nd Street, where we lived until September. Then we moved to Kew Gardens, Queens. After some time my husband bought a small embroidery factory which he ran successfully until he retired in 1959. He passed away in 1967.

Our daughter graduated from Queens College in June 1951 and married Henry Burger. My mother died two months before the wedding. Henry is a certified public accountant. Lottie is a reading coordinator in the New York City public school system. They have three children.

*LEOPOLD HIRSCH

Attorney Dr. Leopold Hirsch, born in Ulm in 1887, was admitted to the local Landgericht in 1919. At first he practiced law jointly with his father, Dr. Robert Hirsch. His admission was voided on October 29, 1938. He was allowed to continue working as a so-called legal counselor, but he left for the United States in March 1939.

(As reported by daughter, Susan Rosen, 1854 South Ivy Street, Denver, Colorado 80224:)

My father, Dr. Leopold Hirsch, died in New Orleans, Louisiana, in 1973. He had worked as a bookkeeper in New Orleans. My mother, Dora Elsas Hirsch, was born in 1905 in Ludwigsburg and is now living in New Orleans.

OTTO HIRSCH
Memories of Otto Hirsch by Theodor Heuss
From *Aufbau,* edited by Will Schaber

I met Leo Baeck in the house of my friend Dr. Otto Hirsch. Hirsch was, when the Nazis started to kill the Jews, absent from Stuttgart to become the president of Reichsvertretung der Deutschen Juden in Berlin. The sessions with Hirsch and Baeck were felt deeply tragic since both men had no illusions, and I would have lied if I could have dared, for I was standing before him ashamed to belittle the fate which threatened the Jews, but it was with deep sorrow that I heard from the wife of Otto Hirsch that they had murdered him in Mauthausen. I only heard about her similar fate after 1945. Leo Baeck would not have contradicted me when I said that the same love for Otto Hirsch and the same sorrow about his martyrdom was the common factor which gave our meetings in the last few years of our lives their real human character. We talked about history, politics, and religion, but Otto Hirsch was the silent inspiration of our conversations.

OTTO HIRSCH zum Gedächtnis

Der Freund ist tot . . . Das ewig Unfassbare,
das grosse Dunkel sog ihn in sich ein.
Was ist sein Los? Harrt neues Werden sein?
Wohnt ewige Ruhe hinterm Schmerz der Bahre?

Wir wissen's nicht . . . Wir wissen nur das Eine:
Er starb für uns,—für jeden, der entrann.
Er blieb und litt—ein Käpitän, ein Mann.
Mit unsern besten Namen lebt der seine.

Um sein erstarrtes Haupt schlingt ein Gewinde
als Totenkranz sich, wunderbar erblüht
aus grossem Herzen, schenkendem Gemüt,
dass kommender Geschlechter Blick ihn finde:—

Held ohne Schwert—Israel kennt die Art!
Sie ist's, die stets sein bröckelnd Haus gewahrt.

by Leopold Marx

*ROBERT HIRSCH

Lawyer Robert Hirsch, born 1857 in Tübingen, was an assistant judge in the Civil Service; from 1880 to 1881 he was an attorney at the District Court of Münsingen, from 1881 to 1883 acting district court judge in Aalen and Schorndorf, and from 1883 to 1886 acting district court judge and attorney in Backnang. In 1886 he was admitted to the bar at the District Court of Ulm; later he was also appointed notary public. He resigned this office in 1932 after his seventy-fifth birthday. He would have very much liked to be a regular judge, but before 1900, there was hardly any chance for a Jew. As a lawyer, he frequently represented the Kingdom of Wuerttemberg in connection with matters pertaining to railroad or postal matters. His criminal-law practice consisted mainly of cases in which he was the attorney for the defense in court-martials.

119

Since 1890 Robert Hirsch had been a member, and later acting chairman, of the Association of Jewish Elders in Ulm.

Although the law concerning lawyers would not yet have forced him to give up his profession, he resigned his admission under the changed circumstances in 1933, and moved in with his son-in-law in Stuttgart. The Reichsminister of Justice thought it necessary to twist the knife in the wound of the seventy-nine-year-old man by prohibiting him from using the title "Attorney, Ret.," in 1936. Dr. Robert Hirsch took this increasing pressure of persecution so much to heart that he committed suicide at his ripe old age in 1939 in Stuttgart.

RUTH HIRSCH (née Ottenheimer)
401 Evelyn Avenue Apt. #9
Albany, Calif.

My parents were alive in 1933. They were Adolf and Henriette Ottenheimer (née Eichengruen) Ludwigsburg. Father born 1870; mother, 1878. They were married in 1907 and died in 1943 or 1944 somewhere in a concentration camp in Poland. We had a Cuban visa for them to emigrate to the United States, but they could not get an exit visa from the Germans and were deported.

My name was Ruth Ottenheimer, born in 1908, and at one time I worked for Rechtsanwalt Schmal, Ludwigsburg, in his law office. I married Willie Hirsch in 1935. We came to America in August 1937. Very rich cousins of my husband sent us the affidavit. One of his cousins had a smoking-pipe factory and he became a salesman there. We were pretty lucky then.

We have a son, Ernest, who has a Ph.D. in physical chemistry. He went to California and got married. He has three girls. Upon retirement we also moved to California in 1968.

We had a good life, and I wish that my husband's health would be better; also the same goes for myself.

WALTER HIRSCH
514 Dodge Street
West Lafayette, Ind. 47906

My parents, Eugene and Fanny (Wormser) Hirsch, left Stuttgart with my brother Ernest A. and me in December 1933. We found our first home in Boston with my father's brother Siegfried, who had emigrated as a young man. After a year we moved to Jackson Heights, New York, since my father found employment in the Wall Street brokerage of his relatives.

My brother and I attended Flushing High School and Queens College. We were both staff sergeants during the World War, serving in the European Theatre. Our grandmother, Vally Wormser, finally joined us via Siberia and Japan. In 1947 I married Lotte Landman. That year we moved to West Lafayette, where I joined the staff of Purdue University, where I am professor of sociology. I received a Ph.D. from Northwestern University in 1957. Ernest received a Ph.D. in psychology from Kansas University and became senior psychologist at the Menninger Foundation. Both of us have published books and articles. After my father's death my mother made her home with Ernest. He died in 1977.

We have four children. My wife, Lotte, is an elementary school teacher (M.A., Purdue University).

We have been fortunate. Our parents left Germany early. We weathered the depression with the aid of relatives, and we found a new home where we and our children could live in freedom and could preserve some lasting aspects of our German-Jewish heritage. The only tragedy we experienced was the early death of my brother from multiple sclerosis.

MAX HIRSCHFELDER
408 West Second Street
Centralia, Ill. 62801

The roots of the Hirschfelder family are in the village of Rexingen. Our grandfather, Max Hirschfelder, had ten children. One, Dr. Isidor Hirschfelder, a prominent pediatrician and highly decorated in World War I, took his life in 1942 before the Nazis could deport him to a concentration camp. Another one, Moritz Hirschfelder, probably perished in a mental hospital during the Nazi regime.

The three children of Salo Hirschfelder—Gretel, Richard, and Victor—made their way to Chicago, Illinois, in the late thirties and eventually established a successful leather goods factory there which is still in existence. They as well as their children continue the business. The mother, Rosa (Loewengart), died in Chicago in 1946.

Irene Hirschfelder still lives in Chicago. She is the widow of Victor Hirschfelder. Her mother, a born Neckarsulmer of Rexingen, died a few years ago in Chicago. Richard's wife, Lise (Heuman), of Stuttgart, is well in the Chicago area.

Another son of Max was Heinrich, who settled in Munich in 1908 and established a textile business there. He died in 1929. His son Max (the undersigned) is an ophthalmologist in southern Illinois, having emigrated in the late thirties. Heinrich's wife was born Johanna Levy, a daughter of Sigmund and Frieda Levy (Lauchheimer) of Stuttgart.

121

Sigmund Levy had a sack-cloth business in Stuttgart, and he and his wife died before the Nazi time. The daughter Johanna was able to come to America to join her son in 1941, but her two sisters (Elsa and Hermine) as well as their husbands perished in Theresienstadt.

MR. & MRS. RICHARD HIRSCHFELDER
(née Lisa Heumann)
1750 Clavey Road
Highland Park, Ill. 60035

My father, Max Heumann, born in Rothenburg o.T. in 1883, and whose business in Stuttgart was Schuerzenfabrik Heumann & Brandt, and my mother, Hermine Heumann, née Rothschild, born in Nordstetten in 1891 came to Chicago in August 1939.

My father had spent some time in Dachau, and then both my parents went to England to stay for some months with my brother, Walter Heumann.

Shortly after coming to Chicago they learned from friends who had gone into the chicken-and-egg-farming business that a farm was for sale in Toms River, New Jersey. Since jobs were scarce my father was delighted to find an activity where he could be his own boss and where the chickens wouldn't mind the quality of his English. The next seventeen years were years of hard work but under pleasant conditions, as other German-Jewish friends were chicken-farming all around them. In 1957 Max Heumann, at age seventy-four, succumbed to a brain hemorrhage during a European vacation trip. His last days were spent in Stuttgart, and he is buried on the Pragfriedhof.

My mother Mrs. Hermine Heumann, then moved to Chicago, where she still resides—the past two years at Self-Help Center—as an alert and active senior citizen.

Turning now to ourselves: Richard Hirschfelder, born in Rexingen in 1905, and Lisa Hirschfelder, born in Stuttgart-Cannstatt in 1915. We were married in Stuttgart in 1936 and emigrated to Chicago in 1938.

After an initial stint for both of us in a department store, Richard and his brother, Victor Hirschfelder, went into the shoe-findings business, and after several years, joined by brother-in-law Kurt Loewenthal, they started the manufacture of some leather goods which later on expanded into importing and is known under the name of Rico Industries.

We raised two daughters and have six grandchildren.

We were both active at Temple Habonim and various charitable and service organizations in the Chicago area. Since retirement three years ago we spend the winter months in California.

122

AMALIE HOECHSTAEDTER (née Bach)
325 East 57th Street, Apt. 5A
New York, N.Y. 10022

Amalie Hoechstaedter, née Bach, born 1891 in Laupheim. Father: Heinrich Bach, born 1862 in Muehringen, died 1941 in Shanghai. Mother: Luise Bach, née Friedberger, born 1867, died 1934.

In 1913 I married Hermann Hoechstaedter, born 1879, died 1965 in New York.

Our son, Walter Hoechstaedter, born 1914, emigrated in 1934 to Shanghai, traveled through most of China, and is well known as an expert on Chinese art.

Our daughter, Trude, born 1915, married in 1938 Carl Nussbaum, born 1906. They emigrated to Rolandia, Brazil.

Our first granddaughter, Renate, was born in 1940; the second one, Marion, was born in 1944. Renate married in Rolandia. They adopted a little girl.

Marion married Wilson Zavinelli in Rolandia. Their daughter, Angelica, was born in 1965; their son, Fabio, was born in 1968.

The old-age home in Augsburg, known as the best one in Germany, was opened in October 1932, and I had the honorary post of being its head. In October 1938 the Gestapo ordered it closed.

1940 my husband and I, together with my father, emigrated to Shanghai and, in 1942, were interned in Hong Kong. In 1947 we left Shanghai for New York.

HAROLD HOLBURN (formerly Hans Heilbronner)
92–16 Whitney Avenue
Elmhurst, N.Y. 11373

My parents were Edward Heilbronner and Flory Heilbronner. My father was a wine merchant. I have a sister, Inge, whose last name is Chaskel and who lives in Bogota. She has two sons. I emigrated in 1938 to India and came from there in 1948 to the United States. I was formerly employed with Sapt in India and am, since 1965, working for S. S. Steiner, Inc., in New York. My mother is fortunately well and we live together at the above address.

*JULIUS HOMMEL
Zeppelinstrasse 37B
7000 Stuttgart 1
West Germany

Dr. Julius Hommel, born in Ichenhausen in 1897, managed to pass his second examination in the summer of 1933, but could no longer be placed as a legal intern. He found limited employment as a financial adviser. In 1935 he left for Switzerland, which offered shelter to immigrants but denied them a work permit. He was occasionally called upon as a language instructor. He returned in 1946 and was admitted to the practice of law. Since 1951 he served in Stuttgart as a public prosecutor and a judge.

His father, the highly regarded physician Dr. Max Hommel, who had also been prominent in Jewish affairs, died in Theresienstadt.

LISA HONIG (née Hirsch)
570 Fort Washington Avenue
New York, N.Y. 10033

Lisa Honig—born in Ulm a.D., 1911—elementary and Maedchenrealschule in Ulm—schools in Geneva, Switzerland; London, England; commercial schools in Ulm, Geneva, and London. Secretarial job in Stuttgart-Feuerbach from 1931 to 1936 for French and English correspondence.

Arrival in United States—1937. Worked as governess until 1942. Married Herbert Honig in 1937.

Various jobs—Comptometer operator, German and French censor for the Federal government; Varitype operator-typist. From 1948 to 1976 secretary to fund-raisers at the United Jewish Appeal of Greater New York. Volunteer work at Leo Baeck Institute. Member of Women's Auxiliary Board.

My husband, Herbert Honig—born 1902 in Prechlauermuehle, West Prussia. Veneer merchant in Germany. Emigrated from Stuttgart in 1938. Worked as furniture polisher in United States. Obtained a U.S. patent for a chemically treated furniture polishing cloth. Sold mutual funds. Died 1973.

My only sister, Edith, was born in Ulm a.D., in 1917. She had the same schooling as I in Ulm. She did office work. She also trained for baby nursing at Neu Isenburg until Kristallnacht. She arrived in the United States in 1939 and worked as a sewing machine operator—later office work—from 1957 to 1979; stock clerk for Loewenstein Textiles. She lived with parents at 11 Hillside Avenue, New York, N.Y. 10040.

Father—Otto Hirsch—born 1877 in Ulm. Co-owner of a wholesale and retail business for tailor accessories. He arrived in the United States in 1941 and did any kind of work he could get. He had a handicap—hearing problem. He died in 1967.

Mother—Helene Hirsch, née Neuberger—born 1887. Married my father in 1910 and they arrived in the United States in 1941. At present at the Jewish Home and Hospital for the Aged, University Avenue and Kingsbridge Road, Bronx.

MAX HORKHEIMER

1895	Born in Stuttgart, son of textile manufacturer Moritz Horkheimer
1911	Leaves the Gymnasium in *Under-secunda*, begins friendship with Friedrich Pollock
1912–14	Apprentice and volunteer in business abroad
1916	Called into the army
1919	Completes and graduates from gymnasium
1919–22	University studies in Munich, Frankfurt, and Freiburg, meeting with Husserl and Heidegger.
1922	Promoted with *summa cum laude* under Hans Cornelius in Frankfurt
1922–5	Assistant of Cornelius, friendship with Felix Weil and Theodor W. Adorno
1925	Habilitated at the University of Frankfurt
1926–30	Lecturer (assistant professor) in Frankfurt, married Rose Christine Riekher, 1926
1930	Appointment as full professor of social philosophy and named director of Institute for Social Research—Beginning of the *Civic Philosophy in History*
1931	Opening of branches of the Institute in Geneva and London
1932	The first edition of the *Journal for Social Research* published in Leipzig.
1933	Flight into Switzerland; deprived of the teaching chair, as well as of the Institute building and library; the journal publishes in Paris.
1934	Emigration to the United States, opening of Institute at Columbia University; *Dawn*, under pseudonym Heinrich Regius.
1936	*Authority and Family*
1937	*Traditional and Critical Theory;* trip to Europe, meeting with Walter Benjamin

1940	Moved from New York to California; Last year of *Journal for Social Research* published in New York
1943–44	Director of the scientific department of the American Jewish Committee
1947	*Eclipse of Reason.* Together with Adorno: *Dialectic of Aufklaerung*
1949	Research director and editor of five-volume *Studies in Prejudice*; return to Germany; call to the University of Frankfurt
1950	Institute for Social Research reopened in Frankfurt.
1951–53	Rector of the University; Goethe Medal of the City of Frankfurt
1954–59	Visiting Professor at the University of Chicago
1959	Retires
1960	Honorary citizen of Frankfurt
1969	Death of Maidon Horkheimer and Theodor W. Adorno
1970	Death of Friedrich Pollock
1971	Lessing Prize of the Hanse City of Hamburg
1973	Died in Nuernberg, July 7

MAGDA HULL (née Stern)
13 Cohawny Road
Scarsdale, N.Y.

Born in Stuttgart in 1911. Daughter of Ludwig Stern (1877–1967) and Friedel Stern, née Weil (1886–1970). My father had a knitting factory and was very active in the Democratic Party (Deutsche Demokratische Partei Staatspartei). He was one of the founders with Kurt Schumacher of the Reichsbanner in Wuerttemberg. On April 1, 1933, the wife of his friend Fischer (treasurer of the Democratic Party) called our house and advised my father to leave immediately. The Gestapo had just picked up her husband. This way he escaped the Gestapo which rang our doorbell a few hours later. My father took the night train to Zurich. The next morning it was announced over the radio: "The Jew Stern fled the country." His close friends, Friedrich Payer and the two Haussmann brothers, were indescribable in their help to us. My mother and I left a few days later for Zurich to the home of my mother before she got married.

In 1933–34 I studied in Paris and worked as a volunteer in the Club Henri Heine, founded by the Rothschilds for political refugees. An unbelievable experience. They served lunch and dinner—but realized also that these desperate people who could not work, needed spiritual motivation and support. Thomas Mann, Stefan Zweig, and many other famous writers went there and kept up their morale.

In 1935 I married Max Heilbronner, banker from Munich. He changed his name to Hull after our son was born. We moved to Geneva and in 1937 came to New York. Here I worked as a volunteer for Self-Help until my parents arrived in 1940. They were on a vacation in Vichy when the war broke out. They were both put in concentration camps. Mother was freed after a few weeks as she was able to prove that she was of French descent (letter from Herriot). Her diary about this experience is at the Leo Baeck Institute.

In 1942 our son Roger was born. He went to Yale Law School. He is the author of two books, *Law and Vietnam* and the *Irish Triangle*. In 1981 he became president of Beloit College in Wisconsin where he is professor of International Law.

My daughter Cathy was born in 1946. She is a well-known free-lance illustrator. The *New York Times, Daily News, Time* magazine, *Sports Illustrated, Business Week,* just to mention a few of her clients. She designs book covers, illustrates books; the last one published: *Social Psychology* by Goldstein.

Overseas her work is printed in *Graphic, Nebelspalter, Brigitte, Marie Claire, Realité,* etc.

I worked as a volunteer for many years for the Institute of International Education—fascinating work with foreign students.

Four years ago I decided to go back to Self-Help, which we supported all along and where my husband is on the board. I spend one day a week at Hillside, the day center for disabled people. Locally I taught for years in Woodland School (French) and one day at the Cornell University Hospital Psychiatric Department also as a volunteer.

HARRY HYMAN
4071 Broadway
Huntington Park, Calif. 90255

I was Bezirksrabbiner in Heilbronn from 1935–1938. On November 10, 1938, our synagogue there went up in flames like most other synagogues in Germany. I was arrested and dragged to the K.C. Dachau, from where I was released after seventeen days because I was able to prove that I could emigrate from Germany.

In 1938 my wife, Greta, née Steigerwald (from Heilbronn), and I immigrated into the United States, where after a few months I secured the position of rabbi in Nutley, New Jersey. After two years there I served for three years in Palisades Park, New Jersey, and then moved to California, where I was offered the pulpit of the Huntington Park Hebrew Congregation in the Los Angeles area. After having held this position for thirteen

127

years I became chaplaincy director for the entire Jewish community of Los Angeles in 1957, a position which I held for twenty years, until my retirement in 1977.

My wife's parents, Oscar and Alice Steigerwald, moved from Heilbronn to Berlin, from where they were deported in 1942. My father-in-law was killed in 1942 in the course of an "action" near Riga, Latvia; my mother-in-law survived until at least 1943 in the K.C. Stutthoff, near Danzig; after that no trace!

CHARLOTTE ISLER (née Nussbaum)
101 Station Road
Irvington-on-Hudson, N.Y. 10533

My parents, Claire Friedmann Nussbaum and Manfred Nussbaum, were married in Stuttgart in 1923. Claire was born in Stuttgart; Manfred was born in Hammelburg, Bavaria. Both were active musicians. Claire, a violinist, played with the Kulturbundorchestra, conducted by Karl Adler, and Manfred had been a well-known conductor with appointments in Zurich, Strassburg, various cities in North Germany, as well as giving piano performances in Stuttgart and elsewhere.

During the late twenties, Manfred Nussbaum became active in his father-in-law's clothing-manufacturing firm, which was closed by the Nazis during the thirties. Claire Nussbaum had studied physical therapy and medical massage, and practiced these while still in Stuttgart.

When they arrived in New York with their school-age children Charlotte and Ernest, the children went to live with relatives in upstate New York, while they tried to settle in Memphis, Tennessee. Unfortunately no professional opportunities were available there for either one, and so they returned to New York and took up permanent residence there. It was virtually impossible for Manfred to resume musical activity, and he had to find other employment in a variety of firms. Claire was successful in establishing a flourishing practice in physical therapy and medical massage, as she had done in Stuttgart.

Manfred and Claire Nussbaum were charter members of Congregation Habonim, attending services there. Chamber music was one of their principal enjoyments, and they frequently played trios, quartets, and other forms of music at their apartment and at the apartments of friends.

Their son, Ernest, attended Cooper Union College and became a civil engineer. He lives now in Bethesda, Maryland, with his wife, Patricia Pothier Nussbaum, a librarian.

The Nussbaums' daughter, Charlotte, graduated from the Mount Sinai Hospital School of Nursing in New York, practiced nursing for several years, and then continued her studies, becoming a journalist and writer in the health field. She is currently clinical editor of *RN* magazine, a journal for professional nurses, and has published several books for health-care professionals.

She is married to Werner Isler, who came with his parents from Berlin.

129

He is sales manager of the Rudd Plastic Fabrics Corporation. The Islers have two sons. Donald, a pianist who lives in New York, performed his début recital in 1980. Norman, his younger brother, lives in Brockport, New York, with his wife and infant son. He is employed by the Coca Cola Company of Rochester, New York.

Manfred Nussbaum died at the age of eighty-one in New York in 1965. His wife, Claire Friedmann Nussbaum, died at the age of seventy-two, also in New York, in 1973.

PAULA ISRAEL (née Kaufmann)
525 Audubon Avenue, Apt. 1002
New York, N.Y. 10040

We emigrated a week after the Kristallnacht from Karlsruhe, where we lived since my marriage in 1920. My parents, who lived in Cannstatt since 1896, were David Kaufmann (cattle dealer), born 1865 and died 1943 in London, and Mathilde Kaufmann, née Oppenheimer, born 1864 and died in London in 1949.

I, their daughter, was born in Leonberg (near Stuttgart) in 1895 and married Heinrich Israel in 1920. He died in 1962 in London. Our two daughters are Hannelore Graham, born in 1921 and living in New York, and Margot Hecht, born 1922 in New Jersey.

One year after my husband's death I moved to New York to be with my children.

RUTH JELLINEK (née Straus)
R.R. 2, May Road
Potsdam, N.Y. 13676

My father, Ernst Straus, was born in 1886 in Cannstatt/Stuttgart and died in 1952. My mother, Nellie, was born in 1888 and died in 1949. They owned Mechanische Tricot Fabrik, Stuttgart/Wangen. L. Maier and Sohn GMBH

Ruth Jellinek, born 1918, married H. H. G. Jellinek, D.Sc (Cantab), Ph.D. (Cantab), Ph.D. (LOND), D.I.C.. Anne Melitta Jellinek, daughter, M.S.W., B.A.

High school education in England: diploma special librarian (science). While in Australia with husband got diploma "Early Childhood Education." Since 1955 in the United States (husband, professor of chemistry). I taught school and preschool.

I am the great-great-granddaughter of Rabbi Dr. von Maier.

*SIEGFRIED JOSEF

Siegfried Josef was born in Stuttgart in 1906. He passed his first examination in the spring of 1931, was dismissed from his legal internship in 1933. In the spring of 1934 he was granted "special permission" to take the second and "higher" legal examination. Unable to practice law he engaged in some business activity until he left for Palestine in 1936. In 1937 he went to the United States, where he started out as a janitor. He studied accounting and has been working as a self-employed certified public accountant since 1945.

WILLY JOSEPH
by Erna Joseph
Avenida Paulista
2465-01311 São Paulo/SP
Brazil

My husband, Willy Joseph, was born in Stuttgart in 1892.

His parents were Lazar and Therese Joseph. Mr. Lazar Joseph, who was born in Stuttgart and died during the First World War, owned two factories. Mrs. Therese Joseph died in Theresienstadt.

131

Willy Joseph took care of his father's business and graduated from law school. Under Hitler he came to Brazil a few years before the war. In Brazil he tried several branches of business and after the war became the manager of Emerson in São Paulo. Later, with three other partners, he founded a loudspeaker factory, where he worked as one of the directors until his last days. He died in 1968, leaving no children. The family also includes a niece in America: Hilde Waring, 4675 Grosvenor Avenue, Riverdale, New York 10471.

I hope that these lines will help you and I'm ready to give you any other information you would wish. You can write either to Caixa Postal 7904 or to my home address given above.

GERTRUDE JUDELL
250 Cabrini Boulevard
New York, N.Y. 10033

My family moved to Stuttgart when I was one year old. From 1930 to 1936 I lived in Spain, went back to Stuttgart for three years, and in 1939 emigrated to the United States and live in New York.

My father, Joseph Judell, owned a lamp and appliance store on Ilgenplatz in Stuttgart. My mother died there in 1937.

My father and stepmother were later deported from Buttenhausen to Theresienstadt, where my father died of starvation. My stepmother was sent to Auschwitz.

I have one daughter, Ellen Strauss, who is living in Harrison, New York, with her husband and two children.

MAJA KAFFERMAN (née Freu)
1180 Midland Avenue
Bronxville, N.Y. 10708

My name is Maja Kafferman, née Freu, the only survivor of my immediate family. I was born in Stuttgart in 1924 and attended the Koenigin Olga Stift. I was a member of the RJF and very active in sports.

My father, Richard Freu, was born in Stuttgart in 1881. He was a textile merchant and owner of the firm of Jacob Kuhn.

My mother, Meta Freu, née Kuhn, born in Stuttgart in 1890, was an artist and a member of the Wuerttemberger Kunstverein. She studied under Professors Bayer and Hölzel and frequently exhibited in Stuttgart during 1930–1938. In the late 1950's, while living in the States, Meta Freu received an award from the Deutsche Rundfunk for her artistic accomplishments.

I had a sister, Ellen Perl, née Freu, born 1921. She was a student at the "Rodhert Schule" and later studied fashion design in Berlin, having inherited our mother's artistic talent. She emigrated to England in 1939 and joined our family in the United States late in 1940.

My sister, Ellen, had many talents and was involved in many crafts. She was a press agent and publicist, represented elegant dining spots in New York, held fashion shows, and presented many publicity stunts. She married Lothar Perl, who was a composer, conductor, arranger, and pianist. In Hollywood he worked for MGM and RKO. He wrote musical scores for pictures such as *Three Daring Daughters, Unfinished Dance, This Land Is Mine,* and many others. He wrote ballets for David Lichine and Ballet Russe and a complete ballet for Trudi Schoop. In New York, Lothar was with the "Show of Shows" and composer and musical director for the dance team of Mata and Hari. He performed at Carnegie Hall and has published various compositions. He was a member of ASCAP and the Composers Guild. He died in 1975. My sister, Ellen, passed away in 1976. They were members of Congregation Habonim.

In the United States my parents resided in Elmhurst, Queens. My father died in 1956, and my mother in 1978.

I completed my schooling in the United States and married a native American, Sy Kafferman, in 1947. Before my marriage and for some time after, I was in accounting and am now involved in the fashion industry. My husband is a dress manufacturer and shares my enthusiasm for sports and the outdoors.

133

*ALFRED KAHN

Attorney Dr. Alfred Kahn, born in Stuttgart in 1876, was admitted in 1904. He gave up his admission in 1933 and set out for Switzerland, where he could not establish himself since aliens were unable to obtain a work permit. His further course led him to Paris and London. He was last heard from in Abbazia, Yugoslavia, in 1936. Thereafter his trace vanished. Even his closest relatives do not know what fate befell him. He was declared dead in 1938.

ANNELIESE KAHN (née Loewengart)
Bolivia 269 4° A
1406 Buenos Aires
Argentina

Thank you for your kind letter, but I have to inform you that my father, Eduard Loewengart, passed away in 1973.

My parents and I went to Uruguay in 1938. My mother, Irma, was born in 1892. She died in 1965.

My father, Eduard Loewengart, was born in Heilbronn in 1887 and died in Montevideo in 1973. I was born in Heilbronn in 1919.

I left Germany in 1933 at the age of thirteen. My parents sent me to Paris, where I completed my education "Baccalaureat."

My husband, Herbert Kahn, was born in 1904. We have a son, Raul Andres Kahn, born in 1944, and another son, Tomas Simon Kahn, born in 1945. We also have a daughter, Graciela Eva Kahn, born in 1948.

My profession was Red Cross nurse. I worked at the Municipal Hospital from 1958 to 1976. I have been retired for three years, but I occasionally do some nursing, old people particularly.

FRED KAHN
2454 Benson Avenue
Brooklyn, N.Y. 11214

Father Jakob Kahn had a wholesale cigar business in Stuttgart together with his brother, Ludwig Kahn. He emigrated to the United States and arrived in New York in 1938.

Mother, Irma Kahn, born 1892, is living with my family at the above address. At the age of eighty-eight she is still very active in the Jewish Community House of Bensonhurst. She has been chairlady of the sewing committee for years and is also in charge of food at a senior citizens club. She participates in activities such as dancing, swimming, etc.

I was born 1924 in Stuttgart, where I went to school until my family's emigration to the United States in 1933. From 1944 until 1945 I served with the Third Army Armored Infantry in England, France, and Germany.

I attended Pace College in New York City. I worked for the Civil Services from 1949 to 1958. Army Base with Social Security Administration at North Eastern Program Center from 1958, where I am still employed.

I am a member of the Jewish Community House of Bensonhurst. My wife, Dora, and twins Jack and Barny are my family.

HARRY H. KAHN
University of Vermont
Department of German and Russian
Waterman Building
Burlington, Vt. 05401

Parents: Max Kahn, born in Baisingen, died 1918 in Baisingen; Johanna Kahn, née Stern, by decree of Amtsgerichts Horb was declared dead as of 1942.

I, Harry Helmuth Kahn, was born in 1912 in Baisingen and graduated Isr. Lehrerbildungsanstalt, Wuerzburg, 1931; Lehrer & Vorbeter, Isr. Gemeinde, Baisingen, 1931–1934; Lehrer & Vorbeter Isr. Gemeinde, Rexingen, 1934–1939.

I was active in the Jewish Youth Movement in southern Germany. I emigrated to England in 1939 and then to the United States in 1940. I did miscellaneous kinds of work. In 1944 I moved to Burlington, Vermont, where I was a Hebrew teacher until 1947. From 1947 to 1977 I was professor of German and Hebrew at the University of Vermont, Burlington. I was also director of the Hillel Foundation, B'nai B'rith, at the University of Vermont.

Spouse: Irene Kahn, née Levi, was born in Rexingen. She emigrated to England in 1939 and to the United States in 1940 where she was employed as a bookkeeper. In 1944 moved to Vermont, where she was a housewife and secretary at the University of Vermont. Her activities included Hadassah, Synagogue sisterhood, Red Cross volunteer, PTA.

Children: Hazel Greta (Kahn) Keimowitz, Washington, D.C. (born in 1943 in New York City). She married Dr. R. I. Keimowitz from Middletown, New York. They have two daughters, eight and five years old.

Activities: B'nai B'rith, Hillel Foundation, ZOA, Synagogue Fund.

HELEN KAHN (née Herta Kern)
61-36 82nd Place
Middle Village, N.Y. 11379

Thank you for your letter and inquiry. This is my first attempt at writing, although I have often thought of recording the past for the sake of my own children. I have met you several times, especially I remember one occasion at the Blue Ribbon, where my cousin Hermann Kern and I attended a pleasant evening meeting with Fritz Busch. How many years ago?

As for myself, I grew up in Heilbronn. My family had a furniture store and factory which was founded by my grandfather around 1880. It was taken over by the Nazis in 1937, or rather "bought" at a ridiculous price by the gauleiter of Heilbronn. My cousin Hermann Kern was in Dachau for a while but was freed after promising that he, his mother, and my mother, who was a widow by then, would leave Germany, which they did in 1938. I myself left in 1933 shortly after graduating from the Mädchen Real-schule. I went to England, and my sister followed me a little later. I spent the first two years as maid and nanny in private families until, with the help of the Jewish Refugee Committee, I was able to start nurses' training. My sister Edith became a baby nurse and was in charge of a day nursery during the war. I married an Englishman and when he joined the army, I was in charge of a first aid post in Manchester during the Blitz. Our first son was born in 1942. My husband was killed during the invasion of Normandy.

I then emigrated to the United States together with my little son and my sister. My mother, Hermann Kern, and his mother had arrived here after a year's stay in England and a risky journey on a boat during 1941. Here, we finally made our home. I got married again (to a German refugee) and we had another son. (They are both attorneys and have brightened our life.) I continued to work as a nurse.

We have been married for thirty-one years and we live in Queens in our own home.

Hermann died in 1951 of a heart attack after having established another furniture store together with my mother and sister. My mother died in 1957. Edith is happily married to an American, another furniture-store owner. (It seems to run in the family!) They have two lovely daughters.

Not a day has gone by without my being grateful about the way our lives have turned out—that we were able to come to this country. But I have not forgotten the millions who did not survive. We will always remember them.

SHLOMO KAHN
160 Wadsworth Avenue
New York, N.Y. 10033

I was born in 1926 in Stuttgart to Karl and Rahel (née Hirschberg) Kahn; father was Kaufmann (Spinnereivertreter). He was son of Siegfried Kahn, Kirchenvorsteher of the Gemeinde. Karl Kahn was a member of the Religionsgesellschaft and Vorstandsmitglied there.

I attended elementary school (Juedische Schule) until Kristallnacht (witnessed on the morning of November 10, 1938 the destruction of Jewish shops and of the Synagogue Hospitalstrasse).

Father with two small children (I was twelve and sister Sophie was nine—mother had died in 1937) emigrated to America in late February 1939 (affidavit provided by Henry Morgenthau, Sr., father of Secretary of the Treasury, a distant cousin).

Settled in Washington Heights, attended first public school, member of Rabbi Breuer's congregation (was their first Bar Mitzvah). Later studied at Yeshiva University, ordained as rabbi in 1952; rabbi of Congregation Beth Israel of Washington Heights since 1952.

In 1958 married Eva Gluck, born in Bratislava, Czechoslovakia. We have two children; instructor of Talmud and Bible at the Frisch School, Yeshiva High School of Northern New Jersey; chairman of the Washington Heights–Inwood Council for Soviet Jewry; active in Jewish Community Council of Washington Heights–Inwood; author of *Hoshanoth* (New York: Scribe, 1959), *From Twilight to Dawn* (New York: Scribe, 1960, 1969).

SIGMUND KAHN

Sigmund Kahn was born in 1872 in Kaiserlautern, Pfalz, into the family of a retail textile merchant. He was the youngest of eleven children. He was a good and ambitious student and attended school up to the Einjaehrige. There he was apprentice in Stuttgart with Hermann Stern, textile wholesalers. He remained there as one of the firm's traveling salesmen for Wuerttemberg and Alsace. Thus, he turned Swabian by choice!

In Alsace, he met Adrienne Woog, née Salomon, the sister of a customer. She was a young widow with a baby daughter, Andree. The wedding ceremony took place in one of the early years of the new century.

Kaiser Wilhelm's empire was a lucrative marketing place. Sigmund Kahn established himself in Strasbourg in the textile line. There in 1911, a second daughter, Simone, was born.

Upon the outbreak of World War I, Kahn took his family back to Stuttgart and was mobilized into the Degerloch Landsturm. After the war, he became a textile-factory representative in Stuttgart. He became a widower in 1928 and emigrated to New York in 1938. Here, at the age of seventy, he found employment in the warehouse of F. A. O. Schwarz Toy Company.

At the end of World War II, in August of 1946, Simone, her husband, Bernhard, and their daughter, Margot joined him in New York.

He devoted all of his spare time to helping Jewish refugees. He worked mainly for the Jews from Wuerttemberg. When necessary he was known to find ways to cut through the red tape and get help where it was needed. He was also a founding member of the Habonim.

He died in 1953 in New York.

[Sigmund Kahn saved the lives of many of our friends who were still in Germany at the critical time. He went to the respective American relatives and in most cases succeeded in getting the necessary affidavits of support by explaining the dangerous Jewish situation in Germany. One relative phoned us and said that he was finally signing the necessary papers just to get rid of Mr. Kahn and his daily visits! W.S.]

STEPHEN M. KAHN
118 Penn Road
Scarsdale, N.Y. 10583

Family: Kahn, Stephen (Stefan) M., born in Heilbronn in 1919. Married in 1950, to Eva, née Krafft, B.S., Bryn Mawr, M.S. Sarah Lawrence. Professionally employed as Genetic Counselor at Beth Israel Hospital in New York City.

Children: Wendy, born 1951; Jeffrey Paul, born 1953; James Gustave, born 1957.

Parents: Kahn, Anselm (father), born 1877; died in New York City 1957—cigar manufacturer. Emigrated from Germany in 1938 with wife to Amsterdam where he worked in leaf tobacco until German occupation of Holland in 1940. Arrived in the United States in June 1941. Worked for Hofor Tobacco Corporation (son's firm) almost until his death in 1957. Helene (mother) born 1888. Married Anselm in 1916. (Anselm had lost his first wife in 1914.) Raised three children by first wife (only one now survives, Hilde) and own son, myself. Chaired Committee of Home for the Aged in Sontheim for years.

Sister (half): Hilda Fuchs, now living in Mount Vernon, New York, born 1911. Married to Oscar Fuchs in 1934. Emigrated to the United States in 1939 (via Basel). Knitting and embroidery designer, published many books on these crafts. Knit shop in Mamaroneck, New York.

Her Children: Thea, Ph.D. Psychology, married to Richard Benenson, Evelyn, married to Dr. Sidney Starobin.

Myself: Untersekundareife, Realgymnasium, Heilbronn, 1935. Apprentice in Anselm's factory and office. Apprenticeship in leaf tobacco in Holland, Turkey, and Bulgaria. Emigrated to United States in March 1939. Worked in tobacco in North Carolina, Maryland, and Tennessee. With Hofor Tobacco Corporation from 1940 to date.

1943–1946: Army Service: Overseas with MIS late in 1943—specialized training by British MI—interrogator at Army Group level—promoted to second lieutenant in France in late 1944—moved to Berlin right after the Russians—lived in former Reichssicherheitshauptamt. Discharged as first lieutenant. Decorated with Bronze Star for valor. I was lucky to get exactly the kind of assignment in World War II which I would have picked myself, to make a contribution in the fight against Hitler, with whatever I was able to do well.

1946 to date: officer, then president of Hofor Tobacco Corporation. Director of several affiliated companies in Holland, Virginia, Colombia, Brazil, etc. Director and officer of Tobacco Merchants Association of the United States. Member of Jewish Community Center (liberal temple).

STEVEN SIGFRIED KAHN
69 Woodland Avenue
West Orange, N.J. 07052

I was born in 1914 in Niederstetten. My father, Albert Kahn, a drygoods wholesale merchant, was born in 1882 in Niederstetten. My mother, Charlotte (Lotte) Kahn, née Strauss, was born in 1887. My parents were married in 1913. Their home was in Niederstetten.

According to records from Stuttgart and Ludwigsburg, my family was deported in 1941. The particular annihilation of the remaining Jews in Wuerttemberg was classified by the Nazi regime as "Aktion Dünemünder Konservenfabriken (Riga)." They did not survive this action. In 1942 they perished in Riga, Lager Jungfernhof. Restitution for my parents' life was D.M. 1800 paid by the German Restitution Office and specified to go to charity.

My parents were very active in Jewish and town community life. My mother was also active in our business and she enjoyed writing articles and essays. The *Israelitische Familienblatt* awarded second prize for one of her essays when she had entered a nationwide contest.

According to our family tree, the Kahns relocated in 1519 in Berlichingen Adelsheim and Archsbofen. Specified in a Jundenschutzbrief still in my possession. Maier Hirsch Kahn, my great-grandfather moved to Niederstetten in 1799. The Kahn family remained there until their final deportation. All the Kahns, which included uncles, aunts, and cousins, perished during the Holocaust. The only survivors on my father's side were my sister and myself. All efforts to save their lives failed. A documented collection of their lives is the only leftover of a proud Jewish family. A plaque placed at the synagogue Ichud Shivat Zion in Tel Aviv represents their memorable past.

As had been the custom in my village, I matriculated the Real Schule (high school) in Bad Mergentheim. My parents arranged an apprenticeship for sales and bookkeeping in the city of Heilbronn for me. Late in 1934 I decided to learn a trade. The family agreed to that, and I went through a full apprenticeship to become a tanner for leather. I served this apprenticeship in Heilbronn and Pirmasens.

In 1937 I received a visa to the United States. It was very difficult and emotional for me to leave my family, especially my parents and sister. I had a foreboding I would never see them again, and except for my sister, this unfortunately came true. I started my journey via Paris (Exchange Place). It was truly the loneliest time of my life.

I arrived in the United States in 1937 (Columbus Day). My affidavit was sent by an aunt in Philadelphia. This aunt, my mother's sister Flora Strauss Elias, was sent to America at the age of nine as a foster-child to childless relatives. The purpose of this move was to give her a better life. The tragedy of this well-meant move is that it destroyed a great many family bonds. There was very little help given to the rest of our persecuted and desperate family.

I was able to stay only the first week at my aunt's house and then rented a room for $2 a week. I started working at a dog food factory in Philadelphia for $7 a week. I was on my own without the knowledge of the English language.

This job did not last long and I found employment in a tannery. This job was short-lived too. Even during 1938 and the tail-end of the depression it was barely possible to survive on $7 a week. I also tried, at this point, to find help for my parents. Few organizations listened to my problems. Neither the Council of Jewish Women or others who promised assistance worked fast enough.

I finally moved to Atlantic City, New Jersey, trying to earn more money so that I would be able to save some. I worked for the 1938–1939 season at the Knights of Columbus, first as a dishwasher and then as a short-order cook. This also was the year my sister arrived in the United States. We combined efforts to help our parents. Time was of the essence and the wheels of bureaucracy turned slowly.

Through a close friend I secured a position in the leather field. I moved to New York City. My new employer was helpful. He assisted us in obtaining an affidavit for our parents. They finally received a visa. Bookings were made. A family named Stern from Niederstetten was very helpful.

Shortly before the war broke out in Germany, my mother succeeded in getting my grandfather, Strauss, to America. My aunt in Philadelphia, his daughter, did help, and one night the HIAS office called to tell me of his arrival. It was a great day.

My parents' passage via Italy was canceled. It was late in 1939. Their visa expired but they received another one in early 1940. Due to the situation in Europe, arrangements had to be made from Germany. We paid passage via Russia to Japan but to no avail.

The draft had begun in America. In 1941 I was drafted into the U.S. Army. I was not a citizen yet. It became twice as difficult to be of effective help. My salary was then $21 a month. I was stationed at Fort Jackson, South Carolina. The local synagogue, Tree of Life, did their best to be of assistance.

In 1941 I was shipped to the Presidio in San Francisco, California, and a week after Pearl Harbor was attacked I arrived in Hawaii. I became a citizen by Army order in District Court of Honolulu. My army years were both good and bad. I stayed on Oahu for one year, then was shipped to Australia and from there to combat duty in Dutch New Guinea and the Bismarck Archipelago. I was overseas thirty-six months and finally arrived back in California in 1944. (My original entry to America was 1937.)

A long friendship and engagement and endless correspondence resulted in a wonderful marriage. Inge Schiff, the daughter of Isidor and Jenny Schiff, became my life's partner in 1944. We were blessed with three wonderful children and grandchildren.

Life was a struggle, but good. I found work in my field and in 1948 decided to enter the leather chemical business. In 1950 we started our own chemical plant in Carlstadt, New Jersey. We lived in the Pelham Park section of the Bronx for nine years. Through the enlightenment and psychology of the Lubavitcher movement, which organization I admire to this day, I reaffirmed an Orthodox Jewish way of life.

TILLY KAHN (née Speier)
111 Franklin Avenue
New Rochelle, N.Y. 10805

My husband, Rudolf Kahn, born 1884, did live in Stuttgart since 1900 and was employed by Gebr. Bloch, Tuchgrosshandlung. Afterwards he settled

141

in Stuttgart and started his own business—Tuchgrosshandlung—and was very successful.

I was born in 1906 and married in 1930. We have no children.

My parents were deported to Gurs, France, and with God's grace survived the concentration camp. They finally came here in 1947 and lived with us.

My father died in London, England, in 1966 at the age of nearly ninety. He had lived for one and one-half years with my sister who is married there. Mother died in 1965, close to eighty-three years of age.

We left Stuttgart in 1939 and waited in London, England, for our visa. We emigrated to the United States in 1940 and settled in New Rochelle, New York, living with my husband's brother, who was a doctor of medicine. We did any kind of work we could find. I myself worked in a defense factory. We finally both found employment at Sak's 34th Street, a New York department store—until my husband passed away in 1947. I held my job until the store closed down in 1965. I found new employment at Gimbel's department store in New York City until my retirement in 1978.

In Stuttgart we belonged to the Jewish Congregation. In New Rochelle, New York, we joined Temple Anshe Sholom, where I am a member. I belong to the sisterhood, joined B'nai B'rith, and contribute to different organizations.

In short, I gave you our lifelong struggle, the hardships we only carry in our hearts.

YOASH (HANS) KAHN
Rechov Kadish Luz,
Ramot Sharet 19/36
Jerusalem, Israel

I was born in 1930 in Heilbronn. My parents were Rita (née Meyer) and Karl Kahn, cantor and headmaster of Heilbronn's Synagogue and School. We emigrated to London, England, on May 4, 1939.

At the time of my emigration to England I was only nine years old. I left Germany with a children's transport under the auspices of the B'nai B'rith. In London I was received by an Anglo-Jewish family named Miriam and George Goodhardt, with those two sons and their families I still have the closest of ties.

With the outbreak of World War II the whole family was evacuated to several places before ending up at Woking, Surrey. The Goodhardts had still to run the family cleaning and tailoring business in London and could not cope with this and three "sons" also. I was sent to South Devon to *batim*, hostels, run by the Zionist Socialist Youth Movement—Habonim. Here I spent the war years in a Jewish atmosphere and kibbutz-style society. These early years were difficult ones in terms of social absorption but by the end of the war I was a convinced and active member of Habonim.

Upon my return to London at the end of the war, I spent a period in various hostels for German refugees run by the B'nai B'rith and on completing my schooling trained as an electrician at the London ORT School. In 1949 I went to Israel on a Habonim Youth Leaders' Course and on my return to the United Kingdom joined a Hachshara as an electrician to prepare for life on a kibbutz. The years 1951–1955 were spent, at Habonim's invitation, as a leader of the British movement at Habonim's headquarters in London. Prior to my aliyah I spent a year in Buenos Aires, Argentina, at the invitation of my uncle, who was my closest surviving relative. In place of going on aliyah on my return to England, I attended a Teachers' Training College for two years and qualified as a teacher in 1958.

Having taught for ten years in primary, secondary, grammar, and comprehensive schools, I was appointed director of one of England's first Teachers' Centers, that at Enfield, London, in 1968. Resulting from my successful work at this post I eventually became secretary of the National Conference of Teachers' Center Leaders (NCTCL) and of Wardens in the South East (WISE). Besides a number of lecture tours, including Canada and Barbados, I contribute extensively to the educational press on the subject of teachers' centers and in-service education for teachers in the United Kingdom and abroad. In 1974 I was awarded an M.A. in education by the University of Sussex.

In 1977 I finally emigrated to Israel. I am now settled in Jerusalem, still single, and employed in the Ministry of Education and Civil Service Commission.

My parents perished in the concentration camps, but the family from my mother's side, apart from my uncle in Argentina, lives in Israel and the United States. On my father's side, after twenty-five years without contact, in 1973 relatives living in New York "discovered" me in London and have since reestablished close contacts.

MARGARET KANDLER (formerly Kahn, née Loeb)
Bromley House Apt. 311C
6901 Old York Road
Philadelphia, Pa. 19126

Graves
Later generations will not know why the grave of my father, Martin Loeb, born 1874 in Stuttgart and died 1942, is in Haigerloch, Hohenzollern.

His grave is at the Jewish cemetery in Haigerloch—downhill in the first row all to the left. A plaque with my mother's name—"Laura Diana Loeb-Schweizer 1880–1943, deported by the Nazis to a concentration camp and killed"—is attached to his grave.

My parents, Martin and Laura, known as Lolo, were born in Stuttgart and lived there until 1942, when all Jews from Stuttgart were evacuated to small places in South Germany. They had to leave all their belongings in their apartments in Stuttgart and were only allowed to take the most urgent things along. In 1943 all Jews over sixty-five years of age were shipped to Theresienstadt. My mother, who was not yet sixty-five years old, had to join a transport to Poland and was killed there.

History of the Family: The parents of my father are buried in Stuttgart, Jewish Cemetery Abt., and the parents of my mother had a findling stone at the Urnen Hain in Stuttgart. After World War II the city took this part of the cemetery over and the grave is not there anymore.

The Family Kahn: Paul Kahn, father of my husband, Dr. Rudolf Alfred Kahn (changed our name in 1941 upon arriving in the United States to Kandler), was deported to Theresienstadt, where he died (1869–1943). The family grave is at the Jewish cemetery in Stuttgart. His wife, Rosa, (1876–1940) and a son are buried there and a plaque attached which says: "Paul Kahn, deported by the Nazis to Theresienstadt, where he died."

My husband, Alfred Rudolf Kandler, was born in Stuttgart in 1900 and died, 1974 in Philadelphia. His ashes were destroyed.

We arrived in 1941 in the United States. Our two sons were in England (1939–1944). We worked hard to give them a good education. Professor Dr. Henry O. Kandler, born in 1929 in Stuttgart, is a psychiatrist, teaches at the Yeshiva University, Albert Einstein Hospital, Bronx, New York. He also has his own practice. Gerald E. Kandler, born in 1932 in Stuttgart, is professor of international law and teaches at Widner University. He is employed at Du Pont in Wilmington. Both sons are married, and each family has three children—two girls and one boy.

*JULIUS KATZ

Attorney Dr. Julius Katz, born in Tuebingen in 1887, was admitted to the bar in 1913. After giving up his admission his name was taken off the list of lawyers at Landgericht Tuebingen in 1935. In 1935 he left for Switzerland and proceeded to the United States in April 1941. In Switzerland he had taken up the study of law once again and had succeeded in being admitted to the bar in April 1938. He was able to practice law until he continued on his journey. In the United States, after acquiring the necessary language facility, he was able to hold a modest position as a bookkeeper. In 1947 he had to give up his job on account of ill health. He died in 1948.

FRITZ KAUFFMANN
Horizon Towers South, Apt. 1609
Fort Lee, N.J. 07024

Parents: Father: Dr. Eugen Kauffmann, born in Stuttgart 1872 and died in Theresienstadt 1943. He practiced as eye specialist in Cannstatt. Stepmother: Elsa Kauffmann, née Neuburger, born in Stuttgart, 1886 and died in Auschwitz 1944.

About Myself: Born in Cannstatt 1904, matriculated from the Humanistischen Gymnasium in Cannstatt in 1922. Completed two years apprenticeship with the Darmstaedter and National Bank, studied law for one semester. Inflation forced me to stop and I took a job with Stettiner & Co., Stuttgart.

In 1927 I went to Australia as representative of a number of Wuerttemberg firms (Junghans, Jetter & Scherer, Dornier Flugzeugwerke, and others).

In 1931 I went to Shanghai, China, as the agent of Australian firms and settled there. At first I was employed as department manager by a German firm. Upon the outbreak of the war in 1939 I left them and started my own business under the name Merchants & Traders as importers and exporters. I stayed in Shanghai during the war, little molested by the Japanese, and was for a time vice-chairman of the Gemeinde for Central European Jews.

I married an English girl in 1941. We left Shanghai in 1949 just before the arrival of the Communists. We went at first to the British West Indies and opened Merchant & Traders offices in Jamaica, Trinidad, and Guyana. In 1951 we came to the United States and continued to run the West Indian business from here until I sold it in 1963 and retired.

THEKLA KAUFFMANN

Thekla Kauffmann was born in 1883 in Stuttgart, the daughter of Hermann Kauffmann and Rosalie Hirsch Kauffmann. She died in the Isabella Nursing Home in 1980, shortly before her ninety-eighth birthday.

Thekla Kauffmann was active in the women's-liberation movement and in the political life of Germany long before German women engaged in public life. After World War I she became a member of the Constitutional Assembly of Wuerttemberg. Thereafter she was a member of the Wuerttemberg Legislature for many years. As a member of the German Demo-

145

cratic Party, she was one of the few successful women in the parliamentary life of Wuerttemberg and was the only Jewish woman among them. Her profession was that of a social worker in the Stuttgart State Employment Office, and when she had to leave that office following the takeover by the Nazis, she was active in many Jewish organizations and head of the Stuttgart Immigration Organization, which worked closely with the American Consulate to obtain visas for the Jews from South Germany, who were forced to leave their native country. Many of the Jews from South Germany owe it to her that they were able to leave Germany in time. She was one of the last ones to escape Stuttgart with her eighty-five-year-old mother before the deportations to the East started.

When she arrived in the United States in 1941, she settled first in Chicago, where the rest of her immediate family lived at that time. In Chicago she became the head of a large home for working mothers, and after she had attained retirement age she worked in the Chicago Public Library. In 1960 she came to New York, where she lived for many years together with her sister, Alice Uhlman.

BRUNO KAUFMAN
10 Willow Street
Wellesley Hills, Mass. 02181

My parents, Jakob and Klara Kaufman (née Rosenfeld), lived in Bad Cannstatt. They were married in 1913. My father had his own business as a cattle dealer. My parents were always very active in our synagogue in Bad Cannstatt (Chevra, Fauenverein, services).

I was born in 1916, and my sister, Hanna, in 1923, in Bad Cannstatt, where we attended elementary and high school. I started to work in 1933 in Cannstatt at the Mech. Zwirnerei and for Gutman & Marx in Neuffen. My sister just finished school and had no other opportunities but to work for Jewish organizations.

My father died in 1940 in Bad Cannstatt. My mother had to go to Haigerloch, and in 1942 she was deported to Theresienstadt and Auschwitz and did not return. My sister, Hanna, was deported in 1943 and did not return. In 1939 I was fortunate enough as the only member of my family to emigrate to the United States and to Boston, where I now live. I found a job and new friends. In 1944 I was drafted and served with the army in the Philippines. That same year I married. We have a son, Ronald, who was born in 1951. At the present time we are still working, are members of B'nai B'rith and the Immigrants Mutual Aid Society.

*OTTO KAULLA

Otto Kaulla, born 1866 in Stuttgart, came from an old and well-known family. Since 1894 he served the judiciary of Wuerttemberg; 1898 he became a district court judge; and in 1928, he received the title Landgerichtsdirektor. Since he retired in 1933, he was spared being discriminated against, but in 1933, he was badly mistreated by a group of SS-men in Metzingen. It was an act of personal vengeance, because in 1932 one of them had been convicted and sent to jail in criminal proceedings in which Otto Kaulla took part. Dr. Kaulla died in the United States in 1955.

*HUGO KERN

Attorney Dr. Hugo Kern, born in 1896, initially entered the Civil Service and worked as a magistrate at the Oberamt Heilbronn until the end of 1925. From 1926 he worked as a lawyer in Heilbronn. During the November pogrom of 1938 his home furnishings were wrecked. He himself was dragged off to Dachau in 1938.

On December 1, 1938, he was stripped of his license to practice law. For a while he was permitted to serve as a legal counselor for Jewish clients. In January 1939 he left for Switzerland and went on to Palestine in March 1939. In the beginning he joined a law firm. He worked as a bookkeeper, an accountant, and as a tax consultant. Both his parents became victims of persecution in Theresienstadt.

*ADOLF KIEFE II

Attorney Dr. Adolf Kiefe II, born in Baisingen in 1876, was admitted in Stuttgart in 1902. His admission was annulled in 1938. He emigrated to Portugal and died in Porto in 1940.

*ALFRED KIEFE III

Dr. Alfred Kiefe III, born in Stuttgart in 1907, was admitted to the Landgericht and Oberlandergericht Stuttgart in 1932. He was able to join his father's law firm for a short time only as his admission was canceled in 1933. He left for Portugal in 1933 and was able to work as a legal counsel and as a business representative of Swedish and even German companies. For daring to handle legal affairs of German firms he was reviled in an article which appeared in the *Nuernberger Beobachter* in 1933. These very same activities caused him trouble at the end of the war, when the

147

Portuguese authorities denied him a passport which would have enabled him to return to Germany. This incident gnawed at him so persistently that he took his own life in 1951.

*WILHELM KIEFE I

Attorney Dr. Wilhelm Kiefe I, born in Baisingen in 1875, was another lawyer of the Kiefe family, which had been settled in Wuerttemberg for four hundred years. He had been admitted in Stuttgart in 1902 and also became a public notary at a later date. When he was stripped of his license as a public notary in 1934, he left for Switzerland in 1936 where he could no longer obtain a work permit. He died in Zollikon, Switzerland, in 1946.

ALICE KION (née Adler)
Nahariya, Israel

I was born in 1896 in Heilbronn, daughter of Ludwig and Johanna Adler. In 1921 I married Arnold Kion, lawyer in Rastatt; he was, together with Professor Stein, a member of the Oberrat besides his honorary offices in the city of Rastatt. As a Zionist he went to Palestine in 1935 to buy land, and by the end of that year we finally got permission to emigrate. We moved on our own land in 1936, working hard under difficult conditions. We had chickens, cows, lots of vegetables. Whatever money we saw went into the farm. We did everything alone, together with our two boys. In 1969, long after my husband's death, we gave it up; I was too old. My younger son was always working in agriculture as manager of a department; since a year he started a banana and avocado plantation on our land.

My mother, unfortunately, could not emigrate and died in Auschwitz after first being transported to Theresienstadt. My sister, Nellie Riechheimer, lives in Chicago; my brother, Robert, was badly hurt in Dachau, had to emigrate immediately, and died a few years later in El Paso. My mother's name is entered in Yad Vashem in Jerusalem. Shalom!

BETTY KLEEMAN (née Gideon)
67-01 Maurleen Street
Baltimore, Md. 21209

My parents were Sigmund and Bertha Gideon, née Schwartz. My father was born in Rexingen in 1875. My mother was born there in 1880. My father was a cattle dealer until his deportation in 1941. I am not sure if my parents were deported to Theresienstadt, but I know they were on the last transport from Rexingen.

I was born in 1918 in Rexingen. I went to the Realschule in Horb, and then as an apprentice I learned the manufacturing business. I became a salesgirl. In 1940 I married Sigi Kleeman, who brought me to the United States. I have two sons, both married. One lives in Chicago and has two children, and the other one lives here in Baltimore.

I am very busy with social activities. I am a past-president of the Chevra Ahavas Chesed Organization of the Ladies Auxiliary. Also I was president of the Beth Tfiloh Sisterhood (Beth Tfiloh Congregation), which has about seven hundred members. My husband and I will soon be installed at our Club Jubilee (also a division of our congregation) as president of this big group.

MAX KOCHMAN
25 Westfield Drive
Centerport, N.Y. 11721

I was born in Stuttgart in 1895. From the age of three until eight, I was brought up in Ludwigsburg, but Stuttgart remained a center because my grandparents Bodenheimer lived there. My grandfather came from Nochberg in Schwarzwald, a town of weavers. It seems that he established a wholesale business of fabrics in Stuttgart and was successful enough to retire before his age of fifty, bought real estate, and lived with his family, consisting of his wife and eight children, from his rental income.

One of his sons, Dr. Max I. Bodenheimer, became a Zionist leader in Germany (Cologne), who promoted the idea of a Palestine homeland for the Jews, particularly of Eastern Europe, several years before Theodor Herzl's *Judenstaat*. He was one of the Herzl party in 1901 visiting the Sultan in Constantinople and meeting the German Kaiser in Jerusalem, in the cause of securing Palestine for the Jews. He came from Wuerttemberg.

As a child of six I knew Oberkirchenrat Kroner and Rabbi Dr. Stoessel from the synagogue on holidays and as attendants to one of my aunt's wedding. Once, my grandfather sent me with a message to Dr. Kroner's house, where Mrs. Kroner treated me with the most delicious marzipan cake. It must have been on Pesach.

I remember the Wilhelmplatz with its fountain, the Konsumverein, and the store in the Wilhelmstrasse, where I bought the newspaper for my grandfather. I remember the Weinsteige with its vineyards, the Hasenberg and Schloss Solitude, the Royal Schloss in the city, which was bombed out and restored, the Koenigstrasse and the Koenigsbau, the Neckarstrasse and Cannstatt, where we had relatives.

In Ludwigsburg, the Salonwaeldle, where the fall leaves made it an attractive playing ground, the Schlosspark and Monrepos and Marbach, where Schiller was born, hiking to Neckarvaihingen for a swim in the Neckar, school years with the kind teacher Loebich (who smelled of tobacco) and the more severe Sauer, religious school with Dr. Schmal, the synagogue on Saturdays, where every time I got a headache from the dim light since I am shy of synagogues.

The *Seiltaenzer* (high-rope dancer) coming to town, my eldest brother wanting to be a *Seiltaenzer* (he became a doctor). "Seiltaenzer Knie, wenn er runterfaellt, ist er hi (n)." Military parades, helping ring the church bell and being pulled upward quite a bit. January 1, 1900, the turn of the century.

All these memories from my childhood form the roots of my mind. They are in Wuerttemberg, where I have been speaking the Schwaebisch dialect in recent years better than all the inhabitants whom I met in Stuttgart.

Alfred Auerbach, who had lived with his parents in my grandfather's house, had become the dramaturgist of the Frankfurter Schauspielhaus. He visited us in New York, also spoke once in the Habonim, related enjoyable stories in his Schwaebische Geschichten. His uncle, Berthold Auerbach, had written a well-known book about Spinoza.

In Berlin since 1903, I visited the Realgymnasium, started to study law in 1914. Finished my studies after various war activities, became a doctor juris in Goettingen, and worked in business as an accountant. In 1933 I became a Wirtschaftspruefer and Steuerberater. On account of the Nazi pressures I lost most of my clients and emigrated in 1937 to the United States with my wife and two children. I became a CPA in New York and retired in 1973.

HANNA AND EDWARD J. KOHL (née Gundelfinger)
27725 Via Granados
Mission Viejo, Calif. 92692

My father: Rudolf Gundelfinger, born in Stuttgart, 1873, died in Stuttgart 1924 due to illness; married to Recha Schiff, 1910, died 1971 in Los Angeles; one daughter, Hanna, born 1912. Married to Edward J. Kohl (born in 1908) 1934; immigrated to Los Angeles in 1936.

My mother left Stuttgart in 1941 with the last train to Spain and came then to Los Angeles through a special act of Congress in 1943. I worked in Stuttgart for the Juedische Gemeinde from 1931 to 1936 (you most likely will remember me). My husband worked in the men's clothing retail business eight years in Stuttgart for Glass & Wels, starting as stockboy and ending as vice-president; twenty-four years with one company and eighteen years with another company, he retired in 1977.

I worked twenty-five years with one company and sixteen years as secretary for a plumbing contractor. In 1980, we moved to Mission Viejo to retire, but I still drive to Los Angeles each month-end to work for my firm.

NATHAN KOHN
1125 Grand Concourse
Bronx, N.Y.

I was born in Crailsheim in 1891 and married Ida, née Goldstein, in 1921. We immigrated to the United States in 1937 and started a hardware store in Womelsdorf, Pennsylvania. My wife died in 1952. Our son, Martin, studied psychiatry at Yale and has a Ph.D. I am presently living in the old-age Freedom Home at the above address.

CARRIE KROFF
1400 Geary Boulevard
San Francisco, Calif. 94109

I was Felix Kroff's second wife and did not know him in Germany. His parents, Simon and Paula Krautkopf, left Stuttgart in 1939; his father died on his way to the United States in Lisbon and is buried there. Simon Krautkopf and his two sons, Siegfried and Felix, owned Strickwaren Fabrik Krautkopf in Stuttgart until it was taken away in 1938 by the Nazi government. Paula Krautkopf-Kroff died in San Francisco in 1973 at the age of eighty-nine.

My husband, whom I married in 1947, started here as a Fuller Brush salesman; later on he became salesman in janitorial supplies—wholesale houses as for twenty-five years was an associate of Tamaras Supply Company, office manager, etc. He worked, although he suffered from circulatory disease until two months before he died in 1978. I must say, he was very popular and well liked by all people who came in contact with him. He was a member of the Jewish Council of 1933, membership chairman for some years, member of Golden Gate B'nai B'rith lodge, Temple Bnai Emunah, and affiliated with different business clubs.

My husband has a son from his first marriage who is a successful CPA and tax lawyer in Palo Alto. There is one daughter of Steven who is now twenty years old and goes to the University of Colorado in Boulder, Colorado.

151

KURT KRONER
610 West 196th Street
New York, N.Y. 10040

In 1933 my mother, Sophie Kroner, born in Fuerth in 1876, was still alive. The date of her death, however, is unknown.

I am Kurt Kroner, traveling salesman, son of the late Rabbi Dr. Hermann Kroner, Oberdorf, and grandson of Oberkirchenrat Dr. Theodor Kroner, Stuttgart. My wife Flora, née Seligman, and I have one married daughter. We belong to the Congregation Ohav Scholaum, 4624 Broadway, New York.

My brother was the late Dr. Jacques Kroner of New York. My sister was the late Nelly Meyerstein of New York. Another sister, Bella Reutlinger, is still living in New York.

RUDOLPH KURZ
123 Longview Avenue
Leonia, N.J. 07605

Rudolph Kurz, born 1904 in Laupheim, Wuerttemberg.

Parents: Siegfried Kurz, born 1877 in Gailingen Baden, married 1903 in Laupheim to Laura Hirschfeld, born 1880 in Laupheim. One son—Rudolph Kurz—married to Irma Schwarz, born in Horb.

Her Parents: Rubin Schwarz, born 1865 in Rexingen, Wuerttemberg, married 1898 to Melanie Schwarz, née Kurz, born 1875 in Gailingen, Baden. They lived in Horb. Three children: Simon Schwarz, died 1925 in Horb; Ludwig Schwarz, died under Nazi persecution 1934 in Horb; and Irma Schwarz, married to Rudolf Kurz.

Siegfried Kurz died as victim of Dachau concentration camp, 1939, in Laupheim.

Laura Kurz deported from Laupheim in 1940 and murdered in Riga in 1941.

Rubin Schwarz deported from Laupheim to Theresienstadt in 1942 and died in Theresienstadt in 1943.

Melanie Schwarz deported from Laupheim to Theresienstadt in 1942 and died in the Auschwitz gas chambers in 1944.

Rudolf Kurz, Irma Kurz, and daughter Beatrice (Beate) emigrated through the intervention of Otto Hirsch to Palestine in 1938 and have lived since 1940 in the United States; first in New York City and since 1950 in Leonia, New Jersey. Beatrice is married to Kurt S. Adler in New York.

Regarding social activities in Germany I was active in the Deutsch-Juedischen Jugend-Bewegung and den Kameraden in Mannheim. Here in the United States we belong to the Freedom Lodge—Sons of Israel and the B'nai B'rith lodge.

BELLA LAMM
45 Fairview Avenue
New York, N.Y.

Born in 1920 in Bad Mergentheim. Immigrated to the United States in 1939 with parents and brother. In 1944 married Hans Lamm. I then started working as a maid. We have two children, born in 1951 and 1965.

MR. & MRS. L. K. LAND (formerly Landauer)
770 El Camino Del Mar
San Francisco, Calif. 14121

Having lived in freedom before Hitler, it was clear to me that he would succeed in doing what he proposed to do in his book. When I saw the *Schupo* march fully armed across the Rhine bridge in Koeln in February 1933, I decided to leave a fine job and gave six days notice to uncle Louis, the head of our large family, and left. First I went to France, then to England, and eventually to America.

Luck has smiled on me and I am duly grateful, never proud for my achievements and success which is only possible in America. However, I feel there is a recent decline in economical and political circumstances which benefits none and may lead to Statism.

Fortunately all members of my close family escaped the Hitler period and are living abroad. Knowing that time spares none, I semi-retired at about sixty and became interested in mineralogy and pre-Columbian art. In both I have sizable collections. Many of the first are now at the Smithsonian Institute and the local Academy of Science. Having this what is erroneously called a "hobby," I derive daily a stimulation of interest. I also receive a goodly amount of visits from academicians who know so much more than I, who write books but often are only slightly acquainted with the actual specimens.

Do come and visit some day and see for yourself.

META LANDAUER (née Marx)
118-17 Union Turnpike #16F
Forest Hills, N.Y. 11375

My parents were still living in 1933. Jakob Marx, born 1875 in Baisingen, Horb. Auguste Marx, née Weil, born 1880 in Hechingen.

153

My father was a cattle dealer. Both my parents were deported in March 1942 by the Nazis to Izbica, Poland. There has never been any news from anybody in this transport.

As for myself—I was born in 1906, married in 1931, and have one son, Jerry. I lost my first husband in 1951 and have been married twice more and am a widow since 1974. I have worked as a diamond cutter for six years, as a saleslady for six years, and in an office for nine years.

I am a member of Congregation Habonim and of the Council of Jewish Women of America, Mogen David, and HIAS.

FRED LANDON (formerly Levi)
5921 Norway Road
Dallas, Texas 75230

My two sisters, Lore and Ilse, asked me to answer for them.

Lore is retired and lives in a suburban part of Fort Lauderdale. You might know that she is a widow since a good many years. Ilse (Joan), also widowed, is working but has two of her three boys very close to her in the West Palm Beach area. Both want to be remembered to you.

I am sad to have to report our dear mother's passing. She died peacefully in 1979 after her ninety-third birthday. Mama was fairly well and mentally clear to her last day, when she had to be brought to a local Dallas hospital. Her last eighteen months were spent in my home and then later on at the Golden Acres, a real good Jewish home for the aged. She was a very positive, very fine lady who had won the hearts of everybody who became acquainted with her here in Dallas. Here she had the love and affection of our large family and our friends for which she was so very grateful. We all miss her and are glad that she had enjoyed such a good life in old Stuttgart where we were neighbors in the Dannelkerstrasse and in the States since 1939.

Since Lore was only in her early twenties when she left Stuttgart, and Ilse was just in her teens, they have very little recollection of people there. As to myself I was sixteen only when I left, came back for two years, only to leave again for good early in 1933. Sorry to say that my roots with Stuttgart are very shallow. My wife, Joan and I took one trip back three years ago and found an entirely strange city. After some forty-three years and all the rebuilding done after World War II not much else could be expected.

Sorry, neither one of us has much to add to your efforts concerning the Research Foundation.

As the executor of Carola Landon's last will and testament, I am enclosing a check for the Foundation as discussed with Lore and Ilse in our mother's memory. She was always proud of her friends from Stuttgart and loved many of them very dearly.

KURT LANG
Food Broker
83 Roberts Road
Englewood Cliffs, N.J. 07632

Kurt Lang—born 1924 in Suessen, Wuerttemberg, survived Riga transport. Emigrated 1946. Now vice-president of large food import firm. Four children.

Louis Lang (father)—born 1893 in Ernsback, Kreis Ohringen—killed in Riga Kaiserwald, 1944.

Pauline Lang (mother), died of natural causes—1935.

Ingeborg (Teddy) Long (sister), born 1921 in Suessen, Wuerttemberg. Emigrated in 1939 to the United States. Died of cancer July 1973—no children.

Henny Lang Gutenstein (sister), born 1922 in Suessen. Emigrated in 1939 to the United States. Now living in Florida (three children).

Siegi (Siegfried) Lang, born 1925 in Suessen, survived Riga transport. Emigrated to United States, 1946. Now retired because of health problems in Florida (two children).

Below is my father's brother and his family, also from Suessen.

Leopold Lang (uncle), born in Kreis Ohringen—killed in Riga, 1941.

Eva Lang (aunt), born in 1896 in Mönchen/Glatterbach—killed in Riga, 1941.

Fred Lang (son of Leopold), born 1921 in Suessen. Emigrated in 1939 to England, then in 1942 to the United States. Now living in Brunswick, New Jersey (two children).

Hugo Lang (son of Leopold), born 1923 in Suessen. Emigrated in 1940 to United States via Portugal. Now living in Union, New Jersey (two children).

Ruth Lang-Lemberger (daughter of Leopold), born 1925 in Suessen—survived Riga transport. Emigrated to United States in 1946. Now living in Baltimore, Maryland (two children).

ERIC LAUB
756-A Heritage Village
Southbury, Conn. 06488

My father Samuel Laub died in 1934 still in Stuttgart. My mother was a Philippino. She emigrated to Israel in 1939. After a one year stay in Italy she returned to Munich in 1953 and then moved to Wuerzburg, where she died in 1961 at the age of eighty-five.

I came to New York in 1938, worked at a few odd jobs and then started with F. Jacobson and Sons, shirt manufacturers, where I remained for forty years until 1978 when I retired as product manager. I spent thirty-eight months in the army. I saw overseas service from Normandy to the Elbe, in the Intelligence Section of an infantry battalion. Prior to going overseas I attended Hamilton College in Clinton, New York for a S.T.P. course in French. After returning to civilian life I continued to go to college at New York University.

In 1942 I married Gertrude Jelinek who came from Vienna and recently retired as vice-president of Rizzoli International Bookstores in New York.

Sister Carla came to the United States in 1939, married Eric Sander (later Sanders) from Rottweil. He was drafted in 1942 and after the war decided to stay in the army. He retired in 1963 as a major, and is still living in Frankfurt. Carla died in 1962 in Dugway, Utah.

Sister Else emigrated in 1936 to Karlsbad with her husband David Rimpel. From there they moved to Brno from which they and their newborn daughter were first sent to Theresienstadt and from there transported to Auschwitz where they perished sometime in 1944.

JOSEPH LAUFER
1255 Peppertree Drive, Apt. 603
Sarasota, Fl. 33581

I was born in 1909, the second of five children of Baruch and Erta Laufer, née Fussmann Mohr. My parents had emigrated at the turn of the century to Germany from Galicia, then part of the Austro-Hungarian Empire. Together, they had established a men's clothing store in the "old city" of Stuttgart. They and their children were granted German citizenship in 1931 but lost it by a Nazi decree a few years later. In keeping with Jewish tradition my parents were deeply concerned with our education. Thus, after completing elementary school, I entered the Karlsgymnasium in Stuttgart in 1919 and graduated in 1927. I then studied law at the Universities of Heidelburg, Berlin, and Tuebingen, where I passed the "first" state bar examination and thereupon was appointed "Referendar" (law clerk in training) in 1932.

When the Nazis seized power in 1933, I was dismissed. Three months later I left Germany and went as a tourist to Palestine, where I found work first in a kibbutz, then as a laborer in a tile factory, as a hotel clerk, as a bookkeeper, and eventually as an apprentice journalist in the Jerusalem branch of *Haaretz*, a Hebrew daily. I decided to return to law; then I realized that it would take at least four years of night school to qualify for an examination.

I applied in 1935 for a visa to the United States, where I arrived in 1937. Almost at once, I entered Duke Law School in Durham, North Carolina. Upon graduation in 1940, I received a scholarship to Harvard Law School, where, after one year, I received a master's degree in law. I then returned to Duke Law School to teach for one semester. All teaching, however, ended with the entry of the United States into war against Germany and Japan.

When I could not qualify for military service because of an eye defect, I joined a law firm in Charlotte, as a law clerk. A year later I became an American citizen; I joined the United States Department of Labor after I was admitted to the bar of the District of Columbia. In 1944, I was transferred to the Department of Justice, where I specialized in litigation involving alien property.

In 1952, I returned to the Harvard Law School as a research associate in law and as the first director of the Harvard-Brandeis-Israel Cooperative Research for Israel's Legal Development. This program provided Israel's Ministry of Justice, between 1952 and 1970, with various legislative services, including comments on Israeli draft bills, prepared in light of comparative law.

In 1957, I was appointed lecturer in comparative law at Harvard. Later that year, I accepted a professorship at the Buffalo Law School (since 1963 part of the State University of New York), where I taught law until I retired in 1979. I also served from 1963–64 as a Harvard fellow at the Hebrew University School of Law in Jerusalem, and from 1967–68, as visiting professor at the Law School of McGill University at Montreal.

While still a student at Harvard Law School in 1940, I married Lily Loewy, a native of Vienna whom I met in San Francisco. I never knew my parents-in-law. They were deported from Vienna to Poland in 1942 and perished in one of the smaller extermination camps. We have two sons, aged thirty-six and thirty-three. The older is a corporation counsel in Los Angeles, the younger is a partner in a law firm in Concord, New Hampshire. We now live in retirement in Sarasota, on the Gulf coast of Florida, where I am active in Jewish community affairs and the resettlement of Southeast Asian refugees in this area.

I appreciate your great efforts to research the history of our emigration. I remember you, but whether we will recognize each other after half a century is something else again.

*MANFRED LAUPHEIMER

The youngest jurist in Wuerttemberg they murdered was Manfred Laupheimer, born 1910 in Stuttgart. He became a Referendar in 1932. In 1933, he was dismissed in accordance with the Law for the Preservation of the Civil Service. In 1934 he emigrated to Holland. There he worked as a gardener.

After the German troops invaded Holland, he probably was taken first to Westerbork, which was mainly a transit camp. Manfred Laupheimer then went on the journey-without-return to Auschwitz.

SIMON LAUPHEIMER
5021 34th Street N.W.
Washington, D.C. 20008

I was born in 1909 in Laupheim. My father, Sigfried Laupheimer, was born in 1882 and was a butcher in Laupheim. My father died in New York in 1955. My mother is living at 701 West 180th Street in New York City. My wife was born in 1908. We were married in 1940 and have no children.

I was originally a merchant in Laupheim. Later I became a butcher and owned a restaurant in Washington, D.C., for twenty years. We are living in Washington, D.C., and are active in Adas Israel Synagogue and the Achduth organization in Washington; a member of both organizations. My wife is also very active in the Senior Citizens Hadassah organization.

(Part of this information was given over the telephone.)

CURT M. LEBRECHT
314-89100 Blumenau
S.C., Brasil

I was born in Ulm in 1911, as son of Wilhelm and Rosa Lebrecht. My father together with two of his brothers owned the leather factory Gabriel Lebrecht. This firm was founded by my great-grandfather as a tannery in 1827. I studied at the Realgymnasium in Ulm, started to work for three years as an apprentice in factory, worked from 1929 to 1935 as a volunteer in leather factories in Finland, Austria, Sweden, and Spain, and took a one-year course at the technical school for tanning located in Freiberg, Saxonia. In 1935 I entered the factory as a junior partner but accepted a position as a leather technician in a factory in Turkey. Half a year later, and not seeing any real chances there, I returned to Germany and worked in the family factory but prepared for my emigration to South America. In 1938 I had a chance to take over a tannery in Chile, but until all the

158

necessary papers were ready, November 9 arrived and I was taken out of bed by a group of SA men who brought me in front of the synagogue. I tried to escape but was caught and beaten up several times by the mob and again later in prison, whereto I was taken together with about forty other Jewish men, mostly business and factory owners. The next day we were put into a bus headed for Dachau, where I stayed due to my wounds received during that night of November 9 until the middle of January of 1939.

A few days after my return from Dachau, there arrived in Ulm a German resident of Blumenau, owner of a small chocolate factory, who had the intention to return to Germany and tried to sell his factory in Reichsmark. As my family was meanwhile forced to sell our leather plant, we tried through special channels to put through this transaction, which at that time was very difficult. But within two months the transaction was completed. My father, Mr. Loeffler from Munich, and myself were owners of a chocolate factory in Brazil. We started to get busy on receiving our immigration visa, for which we paid exorbitantly. As time passed by I left Germany for relatives in Lichtenstein in order to prepare another emigration to the United States.

The Brazilian visa never came through; therefore, I left in early 1940 for New York, where I found employment as an assistant technician in a leather factory in Hoboken, New Jersey. In 1942 I was married to Lottie Metzger from Stuttgart and was drafted into the Army in early 1943. I went through basic training with the Engineers in Fort Belvoir, Virginia, and later on I was transferred to an Army Intelligence camp in Ritchie, Maryland. I was lucky enough to have my parents join me first in the United States in 1941 and later on in Blumenau, where both of them passed away after reaching a high age.

After finishing special courses as interrogator of prisoners-of-war, I was sent to an IPW-team with the 79th Infantry Division. After a training period in the California desert and in England, our division made the landing on Utah Beach in 1944 and went straight on to take part in the capture of the port of Cherbourg. Suddenly my IPW-team of four men had to take care of about three thousand German prisoners. Our division continued head-on through France to Belgium, making the first crossing of the River Seine near Paris. Then we took part in the conquest of France, and in October reached Lorraine, near Lunéville, where we stayed for a few weeks in and around this city. On November 13 we started out again for Strassburg and in the general direction of the West Wall. But during this campaign I was badly hit by mortar shrapnel fire on November 15; the impact smashing two bones and severing nerves and muscles of my right arm and thus the war was over for me. I was shipped through several Army hospitals in France, England, Scotland, finally back to hospitals in the United States, had all in all eight operations on my arm, and was dismissed from the Army in 1946.

As I had become a naturalized American citizen, I encountered no more difficulties in obtaining a visa to Brazil, to which my wife and I embarked in June of the same year in order to have a look at our chocolate factory. In the meantime, this plant had been rented, but as we—the owners—were considered German citizens, and Brazil being at war with Germany, the payment of rent had been frozen into a special enemy bank account. Thus we arrived in Brazil and Blumenau. We liked the place at first sight, and as the two gentlemen who had rented the plant made me an offer of equal partnership and I smelled chances for a development, I accepted.

I worked in this factory as a sales and production manager until my retirement in 1976, when I reached sixty-five. When I started the plant employed thirty workers. When I left there were more than two hundred. I sold because neither my son, Franklin Paul, who works for the Siemens Organization as an electronics engineer, nor my daughter, Barbara, who married into the family of one of the biggest textile mills of Brazil, were interested in taking over my share of the factory. I therefore sold my part and got myself a sales representation, with which I keep myself now occupied and which brings in some money.

Besides these commercial activities, for some years I was president of the most traditional sports club of this town, which maintained at that time a professional soccer team. I was member and counselor of the Chamber of Commerce and Industry, and together with the help of some friends, we reopened fifteen years ago the local Boy Scout group, which had then been out of action for a few years. I was elected president of this group, an office which I held for close to five years, but since then I have become their financial manager and also president of the Parents' Council. Last year our Boy Scout group managed to receive the highest efficiency marks in the entire country—Brazil. I am thankful to my wife, Lottie, who gave me permission to exercise all these activities. She herself is known as one of the best English teachers in town and exercises her profession in giving private lessons and with the local American-Brazilian Cultural Center, whose president I have been from 1974 to 1978, and whose finances I still care for.

FRITZ LEBRECHT
5850 207th Street
Bayside, N.Y. 11364

I was born in Ulm in 1906. My father was a leather manufacturer. My mother came from a wealthy Munich family. Both parents, while nominally Jewish, were trying to be assimilated with liberal views.

I had a happy childhood followed by fruitful years as a chemistry student. While anti-Semitism was existing, it did not seriously disturb me. So much greater was the shock with the advent of the Hitler regime. I had just gotten married and found stores displaying signs: "Dogs and Jews not allowed"! I knew we had to leave.

After an exploratory visit to America in 1935, we came with our baby daughter in 1936 as immigrants to the New World. We started poor but were saved.

Fortunately, despite the depression, I found employment in an important leather firm in New York and worked myself up to export manager. This employment ended in 1970 when the firm decided to move out of New York.

It gave us great satisfaction that we were able to help several family members to obtain visas for immigration and thus save them too.

My wife, Lilli, helped from the start in earning a living, and to this day she is active in her field of physical fitness and relaxation.

We live in modest comfort in our own home with our younger daughter, born here. Both girls became registered nurses. The older girl got married, and we have three grandchildren.

We have made a few trips back to Europe, but our roots are now here and we are grateful that the United States gave us a new chance for life when the hour was dark.

We are proud to be American citizens.

HANS LEBRECHT
P.O. Box 6322
61062 Tel-Aviv
Israel

No Hatred Toward Germans—Hatred Towards Fascists

Ulm—I look back to the first twenty-three years of my life, it seems like life on an alien star, the life of a different person! The home of the parents, school, and the way to school, friends, the first young loves.

Then, the Nazis appeared in my life. They grew like weeds, in the school, and in related activities. Discussions, "Jews—that does not mean

161

you, it means only the Eastern Jews." I read Hitler's *Mein Kampf*. But that referred to me too! Then Hitler came into power. Educated completely stupid by a father who was typically bourgeois, believed in Jewish assimilation and was German-nationalistic, I was so enthusiastic at first about the "Deutschland Erwache" (Awake, Germany) slogan, that I hung a Hitler-painting over my bed!

But first the lie about the burning of the Reichstag (Parliament building) and the consequent terror—the father of a friend of mine was one of the victims—and then the elections in March 1933 opened my eyes. The Hitler picture was burnt, just like the good books on the bonfires of the SA (storm-troopers). My brothers and myself got empty trunks from the attic and marched into our living room: "It's time for us to bolt!" Our father thundered: "A good German does not leave his country . . ." April first and the boycott came. My brother Curt went with me to police headquarters—to see the new chief of police in Ulm, an old Nazi named Dreher: "Where is the police? Why do they not keep order?" He laughed (it could have had worse consequences): "I can't place a policeman in front of every Jewish store." That is how naive we were. We thought we could get rid of the Nazis with stupid jokes and ridicule.

In 1934, the director of my school, Weller, called me. I had to disappear from the Realgymnasium (high school), I wrote an undesirable essay, ridiculing the Nazi hordes, glorifying war. Then, I heard from a police sergeant reports about his three weeks service in the concentration camp Heuberg, and why he refused service after that. At home, I related only a small part of the tortures which the prisoners there had to suffer. This earned me the last slap in the face from father, accompanied by: "Horror propaganda—Germans don't do things like that."

At night, we—a few Jewish boys—followed the Hitler youths and tore down their anti-Semitic posters, and had brawls with them. Then, in 1935, I was thrown out as a member of the Sports-Club, "with full honors." In the fall of that year I had to give up my first apprenticeship after one and a half years.

I continued my apprentice years to become a machinist in a factory. I came in contact for the first time with real upright workers, people who developed illegal anti-Nazi activities—fliers, information, etc., but I myself did not at that time participate actively. I completed my apprenticeship, and—after I met and learned to love my life-companion, Tosca, the daughter of Ulm's last cantor—I began to work underground. A connection with the Zionist Organization (the Nazis at that time showed weakness toward them, because they advocated emigration to Palestine) served as cover, besides milking cows, to smuggle a number of good comrades and money across the border, near Lake Constance; some of them were

162

escapees from jail and concentration camps. Their goal was the defense of the Spanish Republic. This lasted nine months, when I had to disappear as quickly as possible from the farm. After two weeks in Ulm, I received a warning again to flee. My connection gave me permission to emigrate. Not to Spain, because the fight there was over. I was really quite happy that I could fly from Munich in a three-day flight as a "tourist" to Palestine. This type emigration at the time was so rare that the borders at the airport were not yet so hermetically sealed, as it was customary, to detect the "criminals" on the Nazi wanted list elsewhere.

In Palestine—years of poverty and hard work—but happiness in love, family, in harmony with Tosca and the two daughters.

Toward the end of 1940, I learned about the British colonial jail Akko from the inside as "illegal overstayed tourist" or as a "political undesirable" (the Communists at that time were underground, and I did not hide my convictions, although I was not yet a party member). In jail, I made some acquaintances, which had a deep influence in the future course of my life. I learned some truth about Palestine and recognized that Jews and Arabs should not fight each other, but together should get rid of the British colonial power and construct a free Palestine State. 1942—I was active in the union and led a strike. Later I became a member of the Palestine Communist Party (from 1948 CP Israel). I was wounded in the war of 1948. After two operations and recovery I was discharged from the army service, and was for a few years a taxi-driver, since 1955 a journalist, and from 1965 until today member of the Communist Party Central Committee.

Israel became my homeland. Tosca and I participated in the political struggle for another Israel, an Israel which shall live with good-neighborly relations in peaceful coexistence and mutual respect with the Palestine people, the folk which has his home in Palestine, and which has to have, just like the Israelis, his right of self-determination, so that finally peace may come.

I have no hatred towards the Germans or Germany—only towards the Fascists and the Nazis, the former and the new ones. I remained faithful in the fight against Fascists. (By the way, I am a member of the General Council of the International Federation of Resistance-Fighters and was awarded a honor-medal of this all-European organization located in Vienna.)

At my repeated visits to Ulm in the postwar time, I found only few friends. (I refused all contact with "friends" who did not know me any more after 1933.) I have no special feelings or love for my old hometown. I am Israeli, and the old times are on a different planet. I am often in Germany as a tourist and guest. I have innumerable friends there, people

163

who spent the Nazi years in jails, concentration camps, or underground, or who had to go in the emigration, like myself; younger and older Germans, who go in the streets and fight again the reawakening Neo-Nazis, hopefully more successfully than formerly.

RICHARD LEBRECHT
801 Spring Street, Apt. 907
Seattle, Wash. 98104

I was born 1909 in Ulm. My father was partner of a tannery, a firm founded by my great-grandfather in 1827. I attended the Realgymnasium until 1925. I then took my apprenticeship at a bank. I was then groomed to learn the various phases of the leather business, both in our own and in other firms. In 1931, I was sent out as a salesman for our firm and from 1932 to 1933 I was co-manager of our sales branch in Frankfurt/Main.

I had followed with growing apprehension the political evolution in Germany and become fearful and utterly opposed to Nazism. The Nazi victory made me conscious of being a Jew. And I felt already in 1933 that I would not want to stay in Germany. Thus I went to France, a country which had always interested me. However, it was impossible for a foreigner to get a job. The only way to make a living was to invest money in a partnership. This I did, but, unfortunately, the small metal firm was not successful and had to be liquidated in 1936. Having lost most of my money I went to the United States, where a cousin of my mother employed me in his lace mill in Patchogue, Long Island. I worked there from early 1937, at first as stock clerk, later as bookkeeper.

I was in the Army from 1941 to 1945. After my discharge I settled in Washington, D.C., and worked in the Library of Congress, first as clerk, then as map cataloger from 1945 to 1951. Afterwards I was a research analyst in the Army Map Service until 1962. From 1946 to 1953 I went in the evening to the George Washington University, getting my B.A. in history in 1950 and my M.A. in 1953. From early 1963 I was an economic analyst at the Economic Development Administration of the U.S. Department of Commerce, and from 1967 a project officer in the Appalachian Regional Commission. In 1970 I took early retirement to pursue my many interests, particularly in history and geography, and in 1974 I moved from Washington, D.C., to Seattle, Washington.

WALTER LEBRECHT
Casilla 588
Contulmo, Chile

My parents: Wilhelm Lebrecht, leather manufacturer in Ulm; born 1880 in Ulm; emigrated to United States in 1942; moved in 1947 to Blumenau, Brazil; died there 1974. Rosa, née Kohn, born Nuernberg 1887; died 1971 in Blumenau.

My brothers: Curt, born Ulm 1911; emigrated to United States in 1938; then moved after war to Blumenau; chocolate specialist. Hans: born 1915 in Ulm; emigrated about 1937 to Israel. Heinrich: born 1919 in Ulm; came to Contulmo in 1941; died December 1941.

I was born in Ulm in 1913, attended the Gymnasium in Ulm, studied law for five semesters, and could not continue after 1933. Changed to learn agriculture with various practice in teaching-farms (Gross Breese, etc.) and peasant farms. Emigrated to Contulmo, Chile, in 1937, where I was promised land, a promise of which nobody knew anything after my arrival. Therefore: businessman (very poor); traveling salesman (a little later); finally studied to be a certified bookkeeper, this is my occupation now. Since Contulmo is very small—although very pretty—by the way a former German settlement—I travel every week 100 kilometers to the provincial capital Lebu, where I maintain also an office.

My wife: Raquel, née Diaz-Pinto, born in Contulmo 1918.

My children: Rolando, born 1939, married Eliana, née Sperberg; they have three children. Edmundo, born 1943, married Gilda, née Bettai, two children, lives in Berlin, theater specialist. Guillermo (Wilhelm), born 1946, married to Norma, née Saez, lives in W. Germany, electric technician. Anemaria, born 1948, married to Jaime Exert, three children. Walter Enrique, born 1960.

Contulmo has a beautiful location. I have around the house about one hectare land, with vegetable, flower and fruit gardens (especially lemons); besides my wife takes care of about 150 chickens. About 5 kilometers from here I own about 180 hectares land on the completely unspoiled lake of Lanalhue, a beautiful beach, a few cows, but no house (my wife says, so as not to have visitors; but if we have, they have to sleep like we do, in a tent).

As a "side-line" I am in Lebu member of the Rotary International and of the Masons, while here in Contulmo I am the superintendent of the Voluntary Fire Department. Luckily this is just a honorary job. Incidentally in all Chile there are no professional fire-fighters, only volunteers. This gives an idea about the Chileans, the land of the biggest middle class. They are hardworking people, maybe in this different from other South American states. The climate is perfect, not too hot nor too cold, no poisonous animals, hardly poisonous plants. I am very happy here, even though I had—after 40 years plus here—to discard some of my former habits.

ERICH M. LEHMANN
Post Office Box 34
Nahariya 34, Israel

Born in Stuttgart in 1912, the son of Hermann Lehmann, businessman, and his wife, Sofie, née Dreifus. I never knew my paternal grandparents, only my mother's parents. My grandfather was Moritz Dreifus, teacher and cantor in Heilbronn, where he had this position from 1874 until 1924. My father was killed in Auschwitz.

After years at the Karls Gymnasium and the School of Commerce, I finished a business apprenticeship and found employment with the firm of Tiefenthal & Halle in the Spitzenhaus on the Wilhelmsbau. Looking back, I must say that the years I spent in the Jewish Wanderbund Kameraden (later, Werkleute) formed my character to a great extent.

In 1936 I emigrated to Palestine with a fictitious "capitalist" certificate. I worked as an agricultural worker, salesman in a store, waiter, milkman, and hairdresser. In short, I was typical of those years, an *Umschlichtler*. Only after the foundation of the State of Israel in 1948 did I get administrative positions, by far more suitable for me. Looking back on fifty years of work, the last ten were undoubtedly the most interesting ones, in the export division of a large industrial firm (Iscar Ltd.). I was in charge of the German desk.

Through the decades my journalistic activities were apparent. I have been living for more than forty-three years in Nahariya, a community founded by Jews from Germany in the north of Israel. Life in the village, which developed into a town, life in the province of West Galilēe was and is an inexhaustible source of social, sociological, and economic observations. These appear in articles in the German-language newspaper *Chadaschot Israel (Israel Nachrichten)*. I wrote the book *Nahariya: A Contribution of the Middle European Immigration to the Construction of the Land of Israel*, which appeared in 1960.

In 1938 I married Vera Rosenheimer. My wife passed away in 1976. We have two children, Ruthie and Gideon. Both are married and living in Nahariya. So far I have four grandchildren.

My second marriage is to Margot Meyer from Heidelberg.

IRMA LEIB (née Rothschild)
818 Boulevard
New Milford, N.J. 07646

Parents: Louis Rothschild and Mina Marx. Settled and married in 1905 in Buttenhausen. Children: Born in 1906, Hanna Rothschild, married Manfred Metzger (deceased), native of Crailsheim. Born in 1908, Irma Rothschild, married Otto Leib, native of Konstanz. Born in 1909, Eugen Rothschild, married Edith Katz, native of Schenklengsfeld. Born in 1911, Siegfried Rothschild (deceased), married Mia Levy, native of Mühringen.

Irma Rothschild, born in 1908 in Buttenhausen. Moved with entire family to Schwäbisch Hall in 1912, where father, Louis, worked in the Schwäbisch house of his father-in-law, Raphael Marx, master butcher. (Emigrated to Holland where SS men killed him.)

Apprenticeship: Alzenau, 1929–1930. Cashier and secretary: Schwäbisch Hall 1931–1932. Jobless due to discrimination. Emigration to New York City, 1933–1934, household helper. Reemigrated to Palestine in order to marry Otto Leib in 1935. Household helper, cashier in open-air swimming pool, where husband was pool supervisor (bath-master, lifeguard, first-aid attendant). Born to both, Daniel Jochanan in 1936 at place of residence, Bat Galim, Haifa.

Reemigrated to the United States with husband and son in 1937 and lived in the Bronx for three months. In 1937 moved to Chicago, Illinois. Worked as homeworker for knitted-cap manufacturer because of skill with needle, thread, knitting needle, and took care of my infant son at home.

In the fall of 1938 moved back to New York City. Employed by costume jewelry manufacturer as assembler, which occupation I was engaged in until 1948. Born to the parents of Daniel J., a daughter Helen Francis in 1948.

In 1939 parents joined all children who had assembled in New York; Hanna in 1928, Irma in 1937, Eugen in 1938, and Siegfried in 1939.

At first, Hanna and Manfred, Irma and Otto lived together with the parents as dependents; monetary supplements contributed by all children for the maintenance of parents, who took over caring for Daniel Jochanan and the household, while the children and in-laws were at work—1939 to 1940.

Later in 1940 arrangements had to be changed. Since Manfred was working at night for Swift and Company, daytime activities in the house became difficult. Parents, Louis and Mina, moved with Irma and Otto to separate quarters but still in the Bronx.

After birth of daughter Helen Francis, Irma took in homework from a

167

distant cousin of husband, knitting valuable dresses on order until 1955.

Louis Rothschild suffered from arteriosclerosis in one leg, which had to be amputated. He died in 1952.

Mina Rothschild, née Marx, died in 1954. She and husband were active members of the German-Jewish Synagogue Community of the West Bronx.

In 1955 we bought a house in New Milford, New Jersey, despite the wishes of Otto's parents, who felt that the substantial amount of money would be put to better use in a business enterprise with a partner. Son, Daniel, commuted to New York to attend CCNY to study engineering. Later he changed to Fairleigh Dickinson University in Teaneck, New Jersey. Daughter, Helen, began school already in the Bronx and continued from second-grade public school onward. Daniel is now an engineer in electronics with a master's degree, heading his own distributing-representation in Leonia, New Jersey. He lives in Paramus, New Jersey, with his wife and their two sons and a daughter.

Life of Irma Rothschild Leib after 1955: 1955 to 1957, babysitting in neighbors' houses. One job is five days weekly while the lady of the house helped her husband run their business. 1955 to 1974–taking the place of the above-mentioned businesswoman who was badly needed at home to bring up her children. Cashier and saleslady in a houseware store in the Bronx five days weekly. 1974–to present: housewife, retired, pensioned by U.S. and German Social Security systems.

Activities: Work for the Hospital for the Jewish Chronic Sick, in the Bronx, through the Bertha Busch Anna Sommerfeld Society, composed mainly of German-Jewish former refugees.

Works, as a favor to her former employer in the Bronx, once weekly in his newly opened shop in Nanuet, New York.

Life of Otto Leib after 1955: Worked in New York in a sheet metal factory. In Chicago worked in tool and gear factory, later in a paper company owned by an early German-Jewish immigrant, a native of Gailingen, from where Otto's grandparents originated (on both sides, Bloch). Continued to work for the same company in Long Island City, New York, but went to school to learn how to weld. Advanced from beginner to New York licensed structural welder in the Iron Workers Union, working in shops and on job sites under the union's jurisdiction. Assistant shop steward. Retired in 1974. Pensioned by U.S. and German Social Security systems and Iron Workers pension.

Activities: In the Bronx, New York, squad leader of the civilian defense on his block. In New Milford joined auxiliary police in 1957, advanced to lieutenant and squad leader. Requested restricted duties after age seventy was attained in 1979. Stamp collector and philatelist since age nine.

Member of the APS. Wrote historical articles, referring to postage stamps for stamp periodicals in the U.S. and in Germany (after 1946). Amateur historian, specializing in German history. Teaches a course in welding at the local Technical and Vocational High School, Evening Division, since 1972.

SOL AND RUTH LEMBERGER (née Lang)
5823 Gist Avenue
Baltimore, Md. 21215

Sol: Father Isidor L., born in Rexingen in 1892. Cattle dealer. Deported to Jungfernhof Riga K.Z. in 1941. Died in 1943 in Auschwitz.

Mother: Rosa L., née Gideon, born in Rexingen in 1900. Deported with father to Riga. Died in Latvia in 1942.

Three brothers: Sigwart, born 1927 in Rexingen, died 1944, KZ; Lothar, born 1933 in Rexingen, died 1942, KZ; Erich, born 1935 in Rexingen, died 1942, KZ.

Sol was born in Rexingen in 1923 and deported to Jungfernhof, Riga, from 1941 to 1945. Has been in the United States since 1946. Is a butcher by profession, married to Ruth, née Lang. Two married sons, five grandchildren. We belong to Shearith Israel and Chevra Ahavas Chesed and are active in schools and Yeshivas.

Ruth: Father Leopold, born in Ernstbach Wuerttemberg in 1895. Cattle dealer in Suessen Wuerttemberg. Deported to Jungernhof, Riga K.Z. in 1941 and died in Latvia in March 42.

Mother: Eva Lang, née Liffman, born in Odenkirchen Rhld in 1896. Deported to Jungfernhof Riga KZ in 1941 and died in Latvia.

Two brothers: Fred and Hugo Lang, both living in United States.

Ruth Lemberger was born in Suessen, in 1925 and deported to Jungfernhof, Riga KZ from 1941 to 1945. Married Sol Lemberger.

HERBERT H. LENK (formerly Hans Herbert)
8919 Eldora Drive
Cincinnati, Ohio 45236

My compliments for starting work on a history of the Jews from Wuerttemberg and thank you for wanting to include me. It is indeed an idea for which the time has come.

Having left Stuttgart in 1936, my sixteen years in Germany now appear like another life. It was a good life and I suffered little other than insults at school. My parents had the foresight and the means to send me to school in Lausanne, Switzerland, and later to London, England. There I became an electronics engineer (then known as radio engineer.) Always short of money, with almost a year of internment as an "enemy alien" in 1940, and living with bombs and the V-1 and V-2 rockets, still I was among the lucky ones. In 1946 I crossed the Atlantic. Eighteen days on a Norwegian freighter. I rejoined my family in New York. My father Richard, co-owner with his brother Erich of the publishing house Herold-Verlag Levy & Mueller (founded by my grandfather in 1871), had to "sell" the business. After some time at Dachau, he and my mother escaped to New York at the eleventh hour, in 1941. My sister Olga, who had also spent the war years in England, reached New York a year earlier. Between my mother's sewing and my father's applying gold lettering on wallets, they managed to live simply but not uncomfortably. I had a hard time getting started. After work in a Brooklyn toy factory, then dishwashing in Catskill resorts, I finally got back into the radio and television industry. In 1952 I received an offer from the Electronics Division of Avco, now Cincinnati Electronics Corporation, in Cincinnati, where I have been employed ever since. Cincinnati, my adopted hometown for twenty-seven years, has been good to me.

Happily married—my wife, Ellen, also of German-Jewish background—with a fine son and daughter, I am thankful for my good fortune.

Parents: Father: Richard Lenk, born in Stuttgart, 1880; died in Kew Gardens, New York, 1972. Co-owner of Publishing Company Herold-Verlag, Levy & Mueller, Stuttgart (children's books), until forced sale and emigration to New York in 1941. Mother: Martha (Hirsch) Lenk, born 1892; died in Kew Gardens, New York, 1967.

Myself: Born in Stuttgart, 1919. Student at Reform Realgymnasium, Stuttgart, until 1936. Then Lausanne, Switzerland, and London, England. In United States since 1946; in Cincinnati, Ohio, since 1952. Electronics engineer in Cincinnati.

Wife: Ellen (Schurgast) Lenk.

Children: Ronald J. Lenk, born 1958. Anita R. Lenk, born 1962.

Social/Congregational Activities: Members of Temple Sholom (Reform), Cincinnati. Ellen is treasurer and bookkeeper. Herbert is member of school committee. Also, both are active on local board committees.

HILDE LENNENBERG (née Hilb)
67-40 Booth Street
Forest Hills, N.Y. 11375

My father, Leopold Hilb, was born 1880 in Buttenhausen. He had a haberdashery store in Ulm. This business was dissolved in 1935. In 1939 my father came to the United States; and he passed away in 1960.

His children are: Claire Fay, Hilde Lennenberg, and Fred (Fritz) Hilb.

Fred Hilb married Hannah Fleischman in 1944. Came to this country in 1939. He worked here as a tool and die worker and has his residence in Bridgewater, Connecticut.

Claire Fay married Herbert Fay (Feigenbaum) in 1937. He had studied law in Germany before coming to the United States in 1936. He worked in this country in the field of industrial instruments. He passed away in 1975. His mother, Rosa Fay, is ninety-four years old. There are two children, Frederick S. Fay, professor at the medical school in Worcester, Massachusetts. He has two children, Andrew and Nicholas. Louise married Andrew Bergman in 1973. She is a social worker and therapist. Andrew Bergman is an author and scriptwriter. They have a son, Jacob.

Hilde married Carl Werner Lennenberg in 1940. He was a passenger on the S.S. *St. Louis.* In this country he was a diamond-cutter and labor supervisor at a manufacturing plant of fine instruments. He passed away in 1976. They have a son.

JELLA LEPMAN (née Lehman)
(as reported orally by sister Clara Bloch)

Born 1891 in Stuttgart. Parents Joseph and Flora Lehman. Married Gustav Lepman. Very active in Democratic Party. Children: Annemarie, born in 1918, and Gunther, born in 1921.

Husband died in 1922. She went to Katharinenstift. Was editor of the *Frauenzeitung* at the *Stuttgarter Tagblatt.* She emigrated in 1936 to Florence, Italy, and from there to England, where she was during the war. Finally, in 1970 she retired and passed away.

After the war she founded in Munich the International Youth Library; she also received the Hans Christian Andersen Award.

*ERNST LEVI LERSE

Attorney Ernst Levi Lerse, born in Stuttgart in 1875, was admitted as an attorney in 1900 and became a public notary in 1925. He lost his license as a public notary in 1935 and died in Stuttgart in 1937.

*RUDOLF LERSE

His son, Rudolf Lerse, born in Stuttgart in 1908 and admitted as an attorney in 1933, lost his admission soon after, in 1933. He emigrated to England in October 1933 and began to study law once again. He was able, interrupted only by military service in 1939, to pursue his profession and has been licensed as a solicitor since 1946.

Last address known: 53 Oakley Gardens, London S.W. 3, England.

ARI LEVI
2502 Kenook Road
Baltimore, Md. 21215

We lived in Niederstetten (Wuerttemberg) and my parents died in Auschwitz.

I was born 1918 and learned my trade in Germany as a machinist. When I arrived in this country I went into the printing-machine repair business.

My wife's name is Charlotte. We have two children, Fred and Elaine. Both are married now, and Fred has four children and is executive director of the Family and Children Service in Baltimore. My daughter is married to Dr. Bodenheimer and has three children. They live in Philadelphia.

I belong to the Chevra Ahavas Chesed, Inc., International Typographical Union (ITU), and the Lubavitch Congregation.

ERIC LEVI
3105 Labyrinth Road
Baltimore, Md. 21208

I. *Parents*

Father Berthold Levi, born 1877, died Stuttgart 1941. Graduated from Teacher's Seminary in Esslingen in 1897, officiated as teacher, cantor, and shochet in Ulm, Heilbronn, Horb, Oehringen, and Goeppingen until retirement in 1936. Lived in Stuttgart until his death.

Mother Paula Levi, born 1884, died Baltimore, Maryland 1974. (Note: my mother's father, Ruben Gummersheimer, served as teacher, cantor, and shochet in Lehren-Steinsfeld, near Heilbronn, for fifty-two years, from 1858 until 1910.)

II. *Self*

Born Oehringen 1916. Graduated Jewish Teachers' Seminary in Wuerzburg 1937. Emigrated to the United States 1938, settling in Baltimore, Maryland. Continued studies at Ner Israel Rabbinical College, University of Maryland, and Loyola College, all Baltimore. Master's degree in education, Loyola College, 1973.

Taught at the Jüdische Bezirksschule in Bad Nauheim 1937–1938. Teacher and then principal, Beth Tfiloh Hebrew and Day Schools in Baltimore, 1938–1968. Since 1968 director of Continuing Education Center, Social Security Administration Headquarters in Baltimore.

Board member of Religious Zionists (Mizrachi) of Baltimore, Chevra Ahavas Chesed, Suburban Orthodox Congregation. Active member of

172

scholarship, membership, and school committees of Beth Tfiloh Congregation. Member of campaign committee of the Associated Jewish Charities and Welfare Fund in Baltimore.

Editor of *ILBA Wuerzburg Newsletter* (published semi-annually by the Alumni Association of the former Teachers' Seminary in Wuerzburg). Editorial board member and contributing editor to a forthcoming book, *History of ILBA Wuerzburg 1864–1938*. Co-editor of forthcoming book, *Chronicles of Beth Tfiloh* (a sixty-year history of Baltimore's foremost Orthodox congregation, 1921–1981).

Received the Jewish Education Award for three decades of dedication and devotion to Jewish education, presented by Beth Tfiloh Community Day School, 1972.

Married Ruth Goldsmith in 1948. Three children, three grandchildren.

HANS LEVI
230 Ridge Road
Highland Park, Ill. 60035

Thank you so much for your letter regarding the Jews from Wuerttemberg and I appreciate hearing from you.

My name is Hans Levi, and I was born in Stuttgart in 1908 and lived there at Gerokstrasse 4. My father was Carl Levi, a partner in Julius Schmidt & Cie. a *Trikotagenfabrik,* and I worked as a salesman for this firm from 1929 to 1933 after graduating from Technische Hochschule in Reutlingen.

I married Elsa Kienzle, born in Levuka, Fiji, a British subject, who visited her relatives in Stuttgart in 1934. Her grandfather was Gustav Kienzle, also from Stuttgart.

We have a daughter who is married. Her husband is president of Ford of Spain and they live in Madrid. He is American-born and his name happens also to be Carl Levy (spelled with a "y"). They have two girls, one born in Oslo and the other in Paris, twelve and nine years old respectively.

We left Stuttgart in February 1934 and I worked as a salesman, both in retail stores and on the road. I also was assistant buyer for a Chicago department store for five years and operated my own retail store from 1941 to 1952. Since then I have been a manufacturer's representative, selling hosiery, sportswear, and related items, and am still at it.

173

LOTHAR LEVI
61-81 79th Street
Middle Village, N.Y. 11379

My parents lived in Rexingen. My father, Adolph, was born in 1879. My mother, Sophie, was born in 1885.

I was born in 1911.

My wife's name is Hilde. We have a son born in 1935. I was in the meat business until 1974, when I retired. I belong to the Jewish Center of Forest Hills West.

MARTHA LEVI
30 Seaman Avenue
New York, N.Y. 10034

My parents, Emanuel and Julie Levi (née Loewenberg), were born in Buttenhausen, and lived there until their deportation to Theresienstadt and Auschwitz. My father was born 1871; my mother was born 1878. I have never been able to find out the date of their death.

My brother, Karl Levi, was born 1900 in Buttenhausen, lived in Munich, and was deported from there to Riga.

I was born 1904 in Buttenhausen and went to the Jewish Public School there, and later on to the Commercial School in Ulm. Thereafter I had several office positions until I was dismissed, being Jewish.

In April 1933 I moved to Stuttgart, where I had positions in the Jewish Community, as assistant teacher at the Jewish Domestic School, supervisor at the Jewish Lehrhaus, the Jewish Art Community, and the Office of Immigration. I finally emigrated to the United States in 1940. My boss in Stuttgart was Karl Adler.

In New York I had a position as housekeeper in a motherless household with full responsibilities for twenty-nine years. I am retired now and am a member of the Y Senior Center, 54 Nagle Avenue, New York 10040.

LILO LEVINE (née Guggenheim)
16 Cove Lane
Port Jefferson, N.Y. 11777

I was born in Goeppingen in 1921, daughter of Julius and Lini Guggenheim. I went to school in Goeppingen for nine years, and during the last year there I was the only Jewish girl. We moved to Stuttgart in 1937. After one more year in Stuttgart, studying sewing, beauty culture, massage, and cooking, I emigrated to the Isle of Wight in England as a domestic servant and stayed with travel acquaintances of my parents until the Isle of Wight became restricted area. I went to a hostel in London and then to another domestic job for six months, where I cooked, took care of the house and the three children. I then entered nurse's training in May 1940 and was honored together with some other County Council nurses at County Hall. I took six months midwivery training and then came here. I worked at New York Hospital, where four weeks after my arrival Lotte Hirsch from Stuttgart arrived. I went back to high school during the evenings and took some more courses; Lotte and I were the first British-trained nurses at New York Hospital after the war. I got my RN in 1945 while working as a graduate nurse. I contracted tuberculosis. I was sent to Trudeau Sanatorium in the Adirondacks, where I recovered and then worked as a nurse. I met my husband there, who was there as a patient. After he recovered he continued his studies in physics at the University of Virginia and received his Ph.D. My husband has been working with reactor safety since his graduation in 1955. He is now an authority on reactor safety and has been much in the news since the Three Mile Island accident. Since 1959 my husband is working at Brookhaven National Lab in Upton, Long Island, and we live in Port Jefferson.

All my life I have been interested in dance. It started in Goeppingen with lessons in rythmic gymnastics. I continued in Stuttgart at Mrs. Nussbaum. I stopped in England during the hectic war years. I started again when our son was two years old. I have been a dance teacher for the past sixteen years; I teach ballet, tap, jazz, aerobic, and creative dancing. I used to be affiliated with the Royal Academy of dancing and my students took exams. I studied at the Royal Academy when our family spent a year in England 1969–1970. I am a member of Dance Educators of America since 1966. Every year I stage performances with my students; also during the year in England I wrote a children's book, *Elsamae,* about dance with cut-out paper dolls and created a doll who goes with the story. I am very interested in children's choreography; I think it started in Goeppingen because of Trude and Siegfried Rohrbach, who staged performances with us in Dettelbacher every Chanukah. I teach aerobic dancing for Port Jefferson at our local high school. I started the program here last fall.

I found a chronicle my father wrote in 1940; it is about his life in prison in Stuttgart. He and my mother had hidden some silver in the lift and it was discovered. My dad was imprisoned; fearing the worst, my mother committed suicide. I also have her suicide note. I have the report of my dad's fair trial at Stuttgart. Dr. Angress from Stony Brook University told me it was well written and a document. I gave it to the archives of the Leo Baeck Institute. The whole report is sixty pages long in German and I translated it.

My oldest brother, Emil, emigrated to South Africa in 1936 and lives 1 Cross Terrace, 20 Cross Road, 2192 Glenhazel, Johannesburg, South Africa.

My younger brother, Poldi, left Germany early 1939 and went to good friends in England. He stayed there until early 1940 and came to New York. My brother started his own jewelry business when he came here. He is married to Gretel "Margie" Rosenfeld from Gablenberg. Together they have built up their thriving business. Their address is Leo Guggenheim, 15 Maiden Lane, New York, N.Y. 10038.

The following is an exerpt from my Dad's document:

> It is mentionable, especially in respect to the present circumstances, that I was treated well in every way. I didn't hear a nasty word from the lowest to the highest. They concluded the case with a matter-of-fact tone and to the point. This fact I acknowledged with thanks, especially to the officials from the customs service, who led the search. The case remains a tragedy because of the death of my beloved wife, who sacrificed herself. The case ended the way I had felt and the way I had told my wife shortly before we parted. Much of life depends on chance. I might find good judges and maybe through other events my actions wont be judged so harshly.

I would like to add: My dad undertook his own defense, even though he had good lawyers, especially Dr. Mainzer and Dr. Ostertag. My dad had the talent to be able to express his true feelings in words. I believe it was his bearing, his honest, clear description of the situation, which touched the compassion of the officials. Compassion and positive human emotions, these were feelings many Germans felt for Jews. So much has been written about the persecution, somehow I would like to show with this writing that even as a Jew sometimes you had a chance.

LOTHAR LEWIN
680 West 204th Street
New York, N.Y. 10034

My mother, Bella Lewin, née Hirschfeld, was a war widow. Born 1889 in Laupheim, she came with me to the United States in 1941. In the United States she supported herself by working as a baby nurse. Passed away in 1964.

My wife's mother was Rosa Weil, née Marx, born in 1884. She was also a widow and lived in Buchau am Federsee. The end of 1941 she was transported to Riga, from where she did not return.

I, Lothar Lewin, was born 1915 in Stuttgart-Feuerbach. Emigrated to the United States in 1941. Married Susi Lewin, née Weil, in 1943. Daughter Linda was born 1950 and is married, living in Leonia, New Jersey.

176

I served in the U.S. Army (South Pacific) from 1943 to 1946. Joined the Interstate Chemical Corporation in Fort Lee, New Jersey, in 1952 as sales manager and later on was executive vice-president of same company until August, 1978. Active in Congregation Chav Sholaum, Washington Heights, as president of men's club for the past twelve years.

*KARL LIEBLICH
Danneckerstr. 4
7000 Stuttgart 1

Attorney Dr. Karl Lieblich, born in Stuttgart in 1895, was admitted there in 1923. He gave up his admission in late 1935 and emigrated to Brazil in 1937.

In 1933 he was prohibited from continuing his work as a writer who had already gained renown and remarkable success through his historical novels: *The Dream Travelers (Die Traumfahrer, Thomas Muenzer und sein Krieg)* and *The Children's Crusade (Der Kinder Kreuzzug)*. Among his other books are: *The Roaring World (Die Welt Erbraust)* and *The Proletarian Couple (Das Proletarische Brautpaar)*. He also dealt with Jewish problems in his publications *We Young Jews* (1931) and *What Is Going to Happen to the Jews?* (1932).

In Brazil, as the owner of a printing shop and later as an importer of graphic material, he was able to retain his ties to at least the technical aspects of literature. At the end of the war he returned to Stuttgart and is now the owner of an industrial enterprise which was previously owned by his family. He is still writing and giving speeches.

KAETE LINDAUER (née Levi)
8150 Lake Shore Drive
Chicago, Ill. 60657

My father, Joseph Levi, was born 1863 in Haigerboch, died 1937.

My mother, Miranda Levi, née Rosenfeld, born 1869 in Muehringen, died 1934.

I was born in 1905 and married Dr. Fritz Lindauer in 1932. We emigrated to the United States in 1936, and after a year of internship my husband started his own practice in internal medicine in the fall of 1937.

He became a fellow of the American College of Cardiology as well as of the American College of Chest Physicians. He died in 1963 after a coronary attack.

We belonged to the Chicago Sinai Congregation, of which I am still a member. I am also on the women's board of the Louis A. Weiss Memorial

Hospital since 1953, as well as on the board of Self-Help, Inc. I am also active in numerous philanthropic and social organizations, and for twenty-eight years I do some voluntary work in hospitals.

GRETA LINDAUER (née Wolf)
5 via da Bissone
Ch. 6900 Lugano, Switzerland

I cannot tell you too much about my husband's family, as we only met in New York. We got married in 1946. My husband, Erwin Lindauer, lived in Barcelona from 1921 to 1941 and then came to New York. His wife, Trude, née Judell, had left Spain with their daughter, Ellen, because of the Civil War and settled in New York, while Erwin had stayed behind. In 1939 mother and daughter had emigrated from Stuttgart and had stayed with Erwin's uncle.

My mother-in-law, Jette Lindauer, came to the States on the last boat via Barcelona.

I arrived in New York in 1939 and got my first job in a household which paid $30 a month. One year later I got my first office job, $12 a week, and a month later another one where I earned $14. Steady raises followed. In 1941 I was able to get my brother, Otto Wolf, and his wife Hilda, out of Stuttgart to the States and was at that time earning $18. Since I had to provide a trust fund of $1,000 and only had $550, the director of the company gave me the balance and dictated a letter to the company stating that in case I could not repay the loan he would be responsible for it.

Otto and Hilda arrived and, after a short time, started work as a couple in a household. After three years in my office job, earning $35, I resigned, finding it no longer interesting. I found at once another one. Instead of buying gifts for friends, I had always made them myself. The lady who employed my brother actually pushed me into business. At first I made laundry bags and, in 1944, soft handbags. Erwin, whom I knew through my brother, came to see my work. After we got married I persuaded him to give up his job and we both struggled to build up our firm, Greta Originals, or as the fashion magazines called it later, Bags by Greta. In 1957 I received awards from *Glamour* and, in 1966, the Designer Award of the Leather Industry of America. The thrilling part of our success was the fact that I had never learned how to make bags and had never before seen a factory.

We made many personal appearances all over the States and never had to pay for advertising in the leading fashion magazines. We were on television and radio in New York, Dallas, Cleveland, Oklahoma, Detroit, and many other cities.

In 1972 we sold the factory and moved to Lugano, where Erwin passed away in 1977. The years of retirement, which we had wanted to enjoy, were interrupted by sickness. The most rewarding time was the thirty-three years we had worked together.

My brother, Otto, and sister-in-law were spared internment. He passed away in 1977 and Hilde in 1979. They had moved to Florida in 1974.

Erwin's daughter, Ellen, is married to Martin Strauss. She was born in 1930. They have two children, a son, twenty-seven, and a daughter, twenty-four. They live in Harrison, New York.

Erwin was born in 1901, and I was born in 1906.

My sister, Meta, was sent to Izbica, Poland, and did not return. Her son, Otto, left on the Kristallnacht with a transport to England, worked on a farm there, and was later interned on the Isle of Man. Here again he was transferred—to Canada, where he was also interned. He was placed on various farms and was, after a certain time, allowed to immigrate legally to Canada. He has his own farm now in Rockland, Ontario, where he lives with his wife and son.

My oldest brother, Ernst Wolf, was helped by non-Jews to escape to Holland and went from there to Antwerp. He was sent to Perpignan and died when the Germans came. My mother passed away in 1940 after she had heard about the death of my brother Ernst. Otto and Hilde said goodbye to her before leaving for the United States and mother closed her eyes the next night.

The only close relative of my large family left is my nephew in Canada, Arthur Wallace.

LIESE B. LISSNER (née Shomberg)
112-31 69th Avenue
Forest Hills, N.Y. 11375

Father: Dr. Ernest Schaumberger (Shomberg), born 1890, died in New York 1972. He practiced dermatology in Stuttgart until 1938.

Mother: Aenne, née Kaufman, born in 1891. Married in 1921.

Brother: Gert (name changed to Gerald Shomberg when he became a citizen in the Army at the suggestion of the Army since he was sent to the European theater of war). He was born 1922 in Stuttgart.

I was born 1926 in Stuttgart. I attended Hoehere Toechterinstitute (later called Moerike Schule) until 1938, when I was expelled. I belonged to Dr. Rieger's congregation and sang in the choir, which took place on high holiday services at the Gustav Siegle Haus.

I arrived in New York City in 1939. From September 1939 until 1941 I attended Junior High School 73; from 1941–1944, George Washington

High; 1944–1948 Hunter College. While attending school, I had various jobs.

I joined B'nai B'rith Leo Baeck Chapter Youth Group in 1946 or 1947. I met Jerry Lissner in that group and married in 1949. Jerry was born 1925.

I continued to work until 1953. Daughter Michelle was born 1953, and son Michael was born 1957. We joined Congregation Habonim.

ANNELISE LOESER (née Levi)
2059 East Huber Street
Mesa, Ariz. 85203

I am Annelise Levi, born 1917 in Stuttgart, the daughter of Arthur and Rosa Levi, née Bernheim.

I have one brother, Richard R. Levi, born 1907, now in Boston, Massachusetts.

My father was born 1876 in Heslach (suburb of Stuttgart) into a family of ten children. He died in 1963 in Boston. He married my mother in 1906, and she passed away shortly after their fiftieth wedding anniversary, also in Boston. My father owned the Lederfabrik Zuffenhausen, Siehler & Company, one of the largest tanneries for both upper and sole leather. His brother, Max Levi, was the founder of the Salamander Shoe Factory, which, in turn, became the largest shoe factory in Germany and at one time of Europe. His partner was Jakob Siegle. As the factory grew, others of the family joined them. My father was on the board. His brother, Sem Levi, was the general manager for Salamander in the northern part of Germany and lived in Berlin. Then there was another brother, Siegfried Levi, who also had a shoe factory and, as a side attraction, owned the Castle Schloss Stettenfels, close to Heilbronn. Then there was a sister, Bertha Rothschild, and her husband, Isidore Rothschild, who also were connected with Salamander.

I attended the Maedchen Real Schule in Stuttgart until 1935 and then studied farming—much to the distress of my father at that time—for two years before I married my husband, Heinz Loeser, born 1914 and passed away 1980 in Mesa, Arizona. Due to the fact that we both had studied farming and had the sponsorship of the Ochs family from the *New York Times*, we were able to leave in 1938 and come to the States, where, for the next five years, we farmed in Pennsylvania, Ohio, and then finally settled in Decatur, Michigan on a 70-acre farm. There we became the parents of a daughter, Marjorie Rose, born 1943 and a son, Kenneth Louis, born 1953. The next thirty-five years the farm was our home, but our business developed into three large shopping centers located in Dowagiac and

Niles, Michigan, and also one in South Bend, Indiana, before we decided to sell and spend our time in the Valley of the Sun here in Mesa, Arizona.

My parents were able to leave Stuttgart in 1939 after my father had spent a few weeks in prison, and we were fortunate to get another sponsor to get them out safely. Since by that time the war broke out, they, together with my father's sister, Bertha Rothschild, spent the war years in Lausanne, Switzerland, and then in 1945 came to join us. They lived in Decatur until about 1950 and then divided their time between us and my brother in Boston.

Fortunately, my side of the family was spared the concentration camps, but we are scattered all over the world if we think in terms of uncles, aunts, cousins, and friends. My husband's family suffered much more, and we lost many dear ones in camps or we never heard of them.

Our daughter, Marjorie, and her husband, Gary G. Gaynor, gave us two grandsons: Gregory L. Gaynor, born 1971, and Mark G. Gaynor, born 1972. Gary has his own CPA firm, and both are very active in civic and Jewish activities.

Our son very recently moved to us in Mesa and therefore his future is not quite determined yet.

In his latter years my husband became an avid ballroom dancer, and he and his partner attended many competitions with great success. I too got involved in it but then decided to go into volunteer work and I joined the auxiliary at the local hospital, where I am working presently four days a week and sometimes even more. I feel I am doing something worthwhile for my country that gave me a new chance in life.

Thank you for giving me the chance to write these lines in the memory of my immediate family and I am looking forward to the memoirs as soon as it is printed.

ARTHUR LOEWENGART
By daughter Mimi Schwartz
4 Evelyn Place
Princeton, N.J. 08540

As the first Yankee of the family (born in New York, 1940), I remember well the childhood gatherings in Forest Hills, New York, when my parents, uncles, aunts, and cousins on both sides would hold parlays over *flanken, berches,* and *linzertorte* to discuss how to assimilate their past lives in Rexingen, Frankfurt (the Loewengarts), and Stuttgart (the Tiefenthals) to this new American land.

My father, Arthur Loewengart, was born in Rexingen in 1899, the second child of Rubin and Anna (née Tannhauser). He had two brothers,

Sol and Julius, and a sister, Kaethe, who later married Max James. At seventeen, Arthur ran away from this Orthodox Jewish farm community and joined the German Army to fight on the Russian front in World War I. It was here that he became aware that unlike his liberalized German-Jewish experience, Eastern Jewry lived in poverty and persecution. When a "Jew count" was made to see how many Jews were fighting on the front lines (and there were embarrassingly many, it was found out), Arthur Loewengart, angry and disillusioned, became an ardent Zionist. His commitment continued throughout the rest of his seventy-four years, first in Zionist youth groups in Frankfurt (1919–37) and then in the United States and in Israel (1938–73).

In 1931, he married Gerda (née Tiefenthal) of Stuttgart, the youngest child of Joseph and Helene (née Jacob). They lived those early years in Frankfurt, where Arthur was a leather wholesaler, first with his uncle, Emil Tannhauser, and then on his own. Joined by his brothers, Sol and Julius, the three built up a successful firm until, 1937, when it became clear that to survive, they must leave Nazi Germany. Because of the international nature of the firm, they were able to get enough money out of Germany so that Arthur could emigrate to the United States (1937) and then sponsor the others—both Loewengart and Tiefental families—to come here as well.

In 1938, the brothers joined commercial forces again and started Loewengart & Company, a leather-manufacturing company which began with one tannery in Mercersburg, Pennsylvania, and expanded to include eight tanneries in the United States and in Puerto Rico by 1969, when Arthur retired as president of the firm. His dedication to Zionism and Israel continued throughout these years and he served both on government committees and in Jewish philanthropic groups. He was a member of the War Production Board and Office of Price Administration (1942); chairman of Hides Division of the UJA (1945–46, 1957); board member of the UJA of Greater New York; co-chairman of the Federation of Jewish Charities (1946); vice-chairman of the Committee for a Jewish Brigade. He also was active in Self-Help and a regular member of UJA Study Missions to Israel.

In 1963, he built a house in Israel, near Shavei Zion, a moshav near Nahariya that had been settled by former "Rexingers" who had relocated as a unity from the Black Forest to the Mediterranean in the wake of Hitler's power (1937). When, in the early sixties, the German government offered Arthur and his brothers restitution, Arthur decided, with his brothers' support, to create two Shavei Zion–based community projects in Israel. He built the Loewengart Hall, a cultural center for people of the *moshav*, which also contained a Memorial Room for victims of Rexingen who died in the Holocaust. And he started the Loewengart Scholarship Fund, a grants-in-aid program for disadvantaged youth from Western Galilee to pursue a higher education. Since its inception in 1964, 705 students, largely from North Africa, Yemen, and Iraq, have attended high schools and universities in Israel and become teachers, engineers, social workers, and managers in their respective hometowns.

Arthur Loewengart died in New York in 1973 and is buried in Shavei Zion. He is survived by his wife, Gerda, and his two daughters, Ruth and Miriam. Ruth, who married Edgar Goldmuntz, has three children, David, Michael, and Susan, and lives in New York City. Miriam, who married Stuart Schwartz, has two children, Julie and Alan, and lives in Princeton, New Jersey.

KURT M. LOEWENGART
1857 Bluefield Place
Cincinnati, Ohio 45237

My father, Rubin Veit Loewengart, born 1874 in Rexingen, entered his father's livestock business and continued after his father's death with his brother. They had stables in Calw. He died in 1934. My mother, Betti, was born in 1879. She was deported to Theresienstadt concentration camp.

I was born in Tuebingen in 1917 and attended Hebrew school in Rexingen and public school in Horb. I then entered my father's business, but in 1932 I started as apprentice in the cigar factory, Heinrich Jacoby in Mannheim, becoming a salesman, but had to quit in 1938 when the firm was taken over by the Nazis.

I came to the United States in 1939. In New York City I worked as a janitor, in a laundry, and in a home for Jewish infants. Finally, after a year as a Fuller Brush salesman, in 1941, I entered the U.S. Army. I then volunteered for parachute school but was injured on a jump and instead graduated from the cook and baker school, going to the Pacific as a mess sergeant in 1944. I was hurt in Okinawa and spent about a year in hospitals. During the recuperation I married Lenore Stern. In 1946 I became a salesman in the food field and finally wound up in meat-packing, becoming a night-shift supervisor with Kahn Company. Now I am manager of all night operations and have eighteen supervisors and about five hundred workers under me.

We had two sons. Michael was a lawyer, graduated with highest honors, developed cancer, and died in 1974. Steven, now twenty-seven, is a baritone at the opera in Regensburg, Germany, moving to Karlsruhe for a two-year contract with the opera there.

For thirty-five years we belong to the Rockdale Temple (Reformed). I have been a Mason for thirty years.

I love my work and family. We visit our son in Germany every year to hear him sing.

*WALTER LOEWENSTEIN

Attorney Walter Loewenstein, born in Stuttgart in 1880, was admitted there in 1908. He left for Milan in 1934 and while in Italy made a living as a sales representative for welding equipment. In 1939 he proceeded to Argentina, where he founded a small manufacturing plant which was taken over by his son in 1950. He died in 1957.

GRETL LOEWENTHAL (née Hirschfelder)
1680 Clavey Road
Highland Park, Ill. 60035

This is a short account of my life between childhood and now, senior years.

The fears, disappointments, and heartaches I cannot put into words. The hope to live in the United States of America and to be free of despair proved to be the answer to my prayers.

My two brothers Victor, Richard, and I were born in Rexingen Wuerttemberg. Children of Salo and Rosa Hirschfelder.

In 1925 we moved to Stuttgart. I attended the Olgastift and finished my education at the Froebel Seminar in Stuttgart with a degree in nursery school teaching. My father passed away in 1927.

In 1936 I was married to Kurt Loewenthal of Munich. He was a partner in Gebrueder Loewenthal, a millinery store.

During the Crystal Night, November 1938, our store was demolished by the Nazis and my husband had to spend six weeks in the concentration camp Dachau. After his return we left for Chicago, United States, in 1939. Within a short time we were all reunited in Chicago, my two brothers, their wives, and a little niece. Our mother arrived in 1940, traveling from Sweden through Siberia, China, Japan, to America. She passed on in 1946. Fortunately all our parents arrived here safely.

After several years of hard labor, my husband and brothers founded Rico Leather Specialty, Inc., in 1943, which is still in existence under the name Rico Industries, Inc.

Brother Victor passed away in 1960, my husband in 1970.

Our son, Steve, was born in 1945, and our daughter, Lynn, in 1947. Both are married and have families of their own.

I am enjoying a comfortable life and being grandmother to five young-sters. To anyone who remembers me, my greetings.

BERNHARD LOWENTHAL
1751 N.W. 75th Avenue
Plantation, Fla. 33323

The patriarch of the Lowenthal family was Moriz Lowenthal, who had married Caroline Jakobi from Mannheim in 1868. He operated a success-ful winery in Stuttgart. They had two daughters and three sons. Emma married Moses Flegenheimer. Hermine married Leopold Kahn. Their son, Hermann, became a well-known Israeli artist under the name of Kahana. The sons were Heinrich, an opera singer, and Karl, who went to live in the United States and married an American girl. Otto, Bernhard's father, was active in the winery and married Selma Uhlfelder. Bernhard was their only son, born in 1914. They also had two daughters, Hermine and Matilda.

Bernhard emigrated to New York and married Ruth Hofmann in 1938. He was a sales administrator for import/export and is now retired in Florida. Bernhard and Ruth have two sons, Richard, who is an insurance broker, and John, who is a sales administrator.

Hermine died in 1954 in the United States. Tilda lives in Riverside, California, near her son, Avram.

FELIXDAN MAAS
Kibbutz Ma'abarot
Israel

Father: Simon Maas, born 1878.
Mother: Else, born 1890.

My parents married in 1911 and moved to Stuttgart, where my father acted as independent salesman of textiles. My father participated in World War I until 1919. After his return he reopened his business. During the 1929 crisis, he lost his money and worked as sales representative for various textile factories.

In 1939 my mother opened a sewing salon and contributed to the necessary income for the family. My parents were deported in 1941 to Riga and were killed by the Nazis.

I was born in 1916. I attended the Grundschule for three years, and four years I spent at the Gymnasium. For two years after that I studied at the Hoehere Handelsschule, Knospstr. In 1931 I started to work at the SAAT A.G. in order to prepare myself as a textile merchant with this company. With the rise of the Nazis I decided to be a Zionist together with my friends from the Werkleute in order to join a kibbutz in Erez Israel.

From 1933 until 1935 I worked as a laborer at the Oscar Rothschild Textile Factory and from 1935 until my aliyah in 1937 I served on the post of secretary of the Zionist movement, the Keren Havessed and Karen Kavemet. I was also responsible for the leadership of the regional Werkleute movement.

In the spring of 1937 I went to Italy for agricultural Hachshara, and in July of that year I went, together with my wife, Trudel Maas-Loewenstein, to Kibbutz Mishmar Hadarom (Hasorea B) at Gan Yavneh. The kibbutz was not vital and therefore in 1939 I joined Kibbutz Ma'abarot.

During the years 1939 until 1948 I worked in the agricultural branches of the kibbutz. I was arrested three times by the British Army.

In the summer of 1948 I joined the Ministry of Agriculture of the State of Israel as adviser for field crops. During 1953–1955 I was responsible for the successful conduct of 2,500 acres of field crops of my kibbutz in the Negev.

1955: Secretary-general of the Field Crops Growers Association. 1956: Treasurer of the kibbutz. 1957–58: Head of the agricultural team to Burma. 1959–60: Secretary-general of the Field Crops Growers Association. 1961–63: Adviser to Haile Selassie. 1963–68: Head of the Extension Services of the Ministry of Agriculture. Since 1968: Adviser of the Minister of Agriculture of the State of Israel. 1967–76: Member of the Executive Committee of the FAO and 1974 to 1976 its chairman.

I served on many agricultural missions for the State of Israel and international organizations.

We have three children and five grandchildren, all at Kibbutz Ma'abarot.

Since 1974 I have been chairman of GIFRID (German-Israel Fund for International Research and Cooperation).

*ERWIN MAINZER
Last known address:
14 Corringham Road
London N.W. 11 England

Attorney Dr. Erwin Mainzer, born in Stuttgart in 1908 was admitted to the Landgericht and Oberlandesgericht Stuttgart in 1924. His admission was annulled in 1938. For a while he was able to continue working as a legal counselor. At that time Nazi policy had as its aim the emigration of Jews, and since Dr. Erwin Mainzer dealt mainly with matters of emigration, the authorities did not want him to leave and, therefore, invalidated his passport. But in 1939, on the eve of the war, he managed to get to England with just the clothes on his back.

He would have had to serve as an unpaid apprentice to a British lawyer for three years as a prerequisite for admission to the bar, but could simply not afford this. Thus, this outstanding jurist had to confine himself to the private study of English law in his spare time and earn his living as a businessman. The brown-shirted criminals' reign of terror had robbed him of his parents, attorney Dr. Robert Mainzer and wife, and of his in-laws, attorney Dr. Heinrich Wolf and his wife.

FRANZISKA MAINZER (née Gruenwald)
908 West Argyle Street
Chicago, Ill. 60640

Born in Stuttgart in 1890. *Father:* Rudolf Gruenwald from Nordstetten. *Mother:* née Weilmann from Stuttgart. They had seven children, one died early.

We had a happy youth. After high school, I went with younger sister Adele to a *pension* in the French part of Switzerland to improve our foreign languages. Home again we studied housekeeping, cooking, sewing, etc.

In 1914 I married Albert Mainzer, a lawyer. At the outbreak of World War I he tried hard to enlist, but was refuseed due to some kidney troubles. (I was glad.) But in 1915 he succeeded to be accepted for garrison service. A year later he was accepted for the front and sent to the Balkans. Shortly after, a serious internal disease brought him back home, but again by April 1918 he was sent to the Western front and was gravely wounded by a bullet in his head. His service was rewarded with the Iron Cross, first and second class. (The thanks of the Fatherland is assured!)

After a few quiet postwar years, the latent anti-Semitism came into the open and culminated with the beginning of the Hitler regime. It is impossible to mention all the discriminations to which the Jews were subjected. I am grateful that I forgot much of the humiliations. The world learned all, if too late, of the happenings during the Crystal Night, the concentration camps where the Jewish men were sent. My husband, after being arrested at five in the morning, was luckily released due to the intervention of the state attorney in Stuttgart, a friend of my husband. Our luck, however, caused my husband not to try to emigrate, and soon all Jews not yet deported had their homes confiscated and restricted to one store for shopping. When our house was taken, we had to move to relatives, but when they were deported, we were forced into a smaller place, in the former office of my husband. If it were not for good German friends, we might have starved to death already then in Stuttgart.

Easter, 1943, we were sent to Theresienstadt with a transort of twenty people, where we were housed in a dark cellar. The camp commandant greeted us with the threat that everyone found with money, cigarettes, etc., will be punished by death. Then men and women were separated.

A very nice woman took over, and she helped me to dispose of the small amount of money which I had hidden. Another prisoner promised us food for it, but we never got it, as he was transported to another camp. Nevertheless, I was glad to have gotten rid of the money.

My husband had to live with about three hundred men, overrun with lice and bedbugs. I was with one hundred women in bunks three feet high. My husband's work was with the mail, and I had to work with forty other women, filling small bags with a blue substance. We never knew what it was, presumably ammunition. A Stuttgart friend succeeded to find work for me in a hospital, to do repair work with thread and needle, and we were not much bothered there by the Gestapo. While we suffered from lack of food and from lice, it is remarkable what the Jewish leadership produced for entertainment, with outstanding contributions by the Czechoslovak Jews.

Constantly further transports arrived from all over Europe. Many people were of mixed Jewish-Gentile origin. Constantly transports were leaving into an uncertain future. One spoke of work-camps but nobody knew anything. My husband was taken on one of the last transports, as well as all the women in my sewing room, but I, against my will, was transferred to a military tailoring establishment, where no one was sent on a transport. I had to promise my husband never to voluntarily go on a transport. His last words were: "We meet again in Stuttgart." Did he really believe that?

After that I had to work hard, with little food, and no word from my husband. Toward the end of the war endless columns arrived of nearly starved people in tatters, most without shoes. They were released by the Germans before the Russians and Americans occupied Germany. Doctors told us later that most of these people could not survive as they were exposed to contagious diseases. To see these refugees was simply heart-breaking.

Finally one morning the news came that the Russians are arriving. They treated us well, but since the Germans stole nearly all our foodstuffs before they left, for weeks we were on short rations. Because of the danger of contagious diseases we were not allowed to leave before the middle of June, but then about forty people left, first to Dresden by railroad, then to several other places by any available vehicle. We arrived about a week later in Stuttgart. Our food, which was given to us by the Russians, was used up and nowhere could we buy anything on the way. A faithful helper in my parents' home, Miss Hartmann, was the only one who was close to me and she was sick in a Tuebingen hospital. I finally got a room in my parents' house, but I realized that I could not stay in Stuttgart. I quickly contacted my family in the United States and Chile, resulting in my emigration to Chicago.

The first religious service on the boat, the *Marine Flasher,* was a cry of thanks to God from people, finally safe and hopeful for a new life. Then came the reunion with my family and afterwards a few months rest. Where could this be done better than in the United States?

I began working in a shirt factory, as I always liked sewing. It was the best medicine to get over the terrible happenings, including the gas chambers, which ended my husband's life. I could live nicely and earn extra money as a babysitter, always treated as a lady.

After I became a citizen and saved some money, I took a trip to Chile to see my family there. Back in Chicago the first restitution payments were received. After five more years on a sales job, I moved to Chile and was never sorry I did. But when Allende took over, I returned to Chicago and took a nice apartment in Evanston. For five years I have been living in an old-age home; well taken care of and spoiled by my nieces and nephews.

*ROBERT MAINZER

Lawyer Dr. Robert Mainzer, born 1864 in Weinsberg, settled in Stuttgart after he had passed both exams with high marks. Already in 1886 he received a prize from the Law School of the University of Leipzig. The notary office that had been given to him in 1923 was taken away from him in 1933. From 1912 to 1933 he was a member of the board of the Bar Association of Wuerttemberg, from 1929 to 1931 its acting director, and from 1931 to 1933 its director.

His two children were able to emigrate. He and his wife, Helene, née Heilmann, were deported to Theresienstadt in 1942. He and his wife died there.

*ERNEST MANN
Last address known:
High Elms, 33
Lye Green Road
Chesham/Bucks
England

Ernest Mann, born in Ulm in 1910, passed his examination in late 1932 and was dismissed from preparatory service in 1933. He left for England in 1934. For several years he worked there as a gardener and later on as a business employee.

*SIEGFRIED MANN

Attorney Siegfried Mann, born in Ulm in 1877, had practiced law there since 1905. He served on the board of the Bar Association and was president of the Lawyers Association in Ulm from 1924 to 1933. During the later part of that period he also was a member of the Court of Honor. His admission was annulled in 1938. During the November pogrom the sixty-one-year-old was brutally beaten. He left for England in 1939 and proceeded to the United States in 1940.

ISABELLE MARGON (née Weinschel)
4450 South Park Avenue, Apt. 619
Chevy Chase, Md. 20815

My parents, Oscar and Sina Weinschel, together with my brother, Bruno, emigrated to New York in 1939. My father had been consul of Panama in Stuttgart, and in New York became the owner of the Weinschel Company (brokers and rating engineers).

My brother, Dr. Bruno Weinschel, is president of the Weinschel Engineering Company in Gaithersburg. He has five children.

My father passed away in 1949, and my mother moved to San Francisco to make her home with my husband and me. My husband, Eric Margon, formerly Margoninsky, had been a partner in the Heralco Company, Ltd., in Stuttgart. He passed away in 1963. My brother Bruno, sister Addy, and I were born in Stuttgart. Adelina and her husband, Kurt Meyer, also born in Stuttgart, emigrated to Peru in 1938, where he was professor of pharmacology and later founded the Wilson Pharmacy in Lima. After his death in 1970, my sister took over the business. She has two children. Son Roland Margon is employed by the Inter-America Development Bank in Washington. Daughter Susy is living in Peru.

In 1967 my mother and I moved to Maryland where she passed away in 1978.

Addy's address is: Dr. Addy Meyer, Farmacia Wilson, Wilson Avenue 1066, Lima, Peru.

*ALFRED MARX

Alfred Marx, born 1899 in Cannstatt, was, since 1929, district court judge in Waiblingen and at the Regional Court of Stuttgart. Dismissed from the Civil Service in 1936. During the pogrom of November 1938 he was arrested and spent five weeks in Dachau. He was arrested again in 1939 and as late as 1945, he was deported to Theresienstadt, where his mother had died in 1942.

Since 1939 he was active in the Jewish Emigration Office for Wuerttemberg-Hohenzollern and at the Jewish Relief Office in Stuttgart. There he held the difficult position of head of the organization until 1940. When the courts reopened in 1945, he was able to resume his profession.

ERIC L. MARX
120 Bennett Avenue
New York, N.Y. 10033

My father, Ernst Marx, was born in 1865 and died in New York City in 1949. My mother, Hedwig, was born in 1881 and died in New York City in 1971. As an Ausserordentlicher Professor, my father taught history at the Technische Hochschule in Stuttgart.

I was born in Stuttgart in 1905. Several years before my emigration to the United States, I was active as a manager of retail shoe stores. I continued to stay in the retail end of the shoe business in various capacities in the new country. My wife's name is Margot. We belong to Freedom Lodge 182, an affiliate of the Free Sons of Israel.

HANNELORE MARX (formerly Kahn)
600 Fort Washington Avenue
New York, N.Y.

I was born 1922 in Stuttgart, and my parents were Max Kahn of Gemmingen (Baden) and Hilda, née Pick, of Bad Cannstatt. My maternal grandparents were Ernst and Anna Pick, née Ostertag, of Bad Cannstatt.

Both my brother Heinz Kahn, born 1921 in Stuttgart, and I spent a normal and beautiful childhood and were showered with love and understanding by our parents. We lived near the Bopser in Stitzenburgstrasse and attended good schools until Hitler came into power. Our parents had a housewear store on Marktplatz. In 1935, my brother had to give up his studies at Wilhelms Oberrealschule as he was repeatedly beaten up by a teacher and by classmates. In 1936, I was forced out of Eberhard Mittelschule, to cleanse the school from the last Jewess. For a while, I worked as a cutter for Krautkopf, a well-known factory for machine-knitted dresses. When this business was sold, once more all Jewish employees had to leave.

In 1939, my brother Heinz had the opportunity to emigrate to England. There, he spent five years in the English army and changed then his name to Harry Kennedy for safety reasons. After the war, he settled in Kenton, Harrow, and married a lovely English girl. They have two children and three grandchildren.

When most of our friends and relatives had a chance to leave Germany, my parents and I stayed behind, as our affidavits for the United States were not enough to get a visa. In 1941, we were forced to wear the *Judenstern*, a yellow Star of David with Hebrew-like letters spelling out *Jude*. This had to be worn on the left side of your clothing for everybody to see. We also had to buy all groceries, vegetables, fruit, and the small portion of meats at one store. Our ration-cards had small *J*'s printed all over to make it impossible to redeem them somewhere else. Shopping time was restricted. All over Stuttgart's butchershops there was no pork available; only the Jewish store had mainly pork for sale. Since we had no other choice, we bought it and exchanged it later with friends, gentile people. Life was made harder and harder for us. On Yom Kippur, we had to bring all the radios, we owned to the Gestapo. In 1941, my parents and I, together with 1,050 Jewish people from all over Wuerttemberg, had to assemble at the Reichsgartenschau near the Weissenhof. We were allowed personal clothing and also some tools to take with us. Our apartment with all our belongings was sealed behind us by the SS. All our identifications like passport or *Kennkarte* was taken from us, and, of course, all the money we still had in our possession. When we arrived in Riga, Latvia, and saw what lay in store for us, we knew if any, only a handful of us would survive. My beloved parents were killed, slaughtered together with thousands of others by the Nazis. Three and one-half years as an inmate in several concentration camps, in Riga, nearby, in Stutthof, and others, going through hell, I survived with a handful of Jews and was liberated by the Russian army in 1945. Instead of freedom, I was given another six months of hard labor and great misery by the Russians, until finally I could return to Stuttgart.

I was the very last of the Jews of Wuerttemberg to return. By that time they had opened up two camps for displaced persons; one was in the upper Reinsburgstrasse not far from Westbahnhof, and the other was in Degerloch near the tennis courts. I was in Degerloch. In 1945, I married Victor Marx, formerly of Tuebingen, who like me spent the years in Riga and other camps. He had lost his wife and daughter, an adorable girl eight years old in Riga.

Our wedding took place in Stuttgart at the so-called Eskin Haus. This was a floor in an apartment building, partly as an office and partly as a prayer room. Rabbi Eskin, a chaplin in the American Army, founded and organized this little shul and every Shabbos, all of us went there to attend services. The ceremony of our wedding was performed by another chaplin, who was stationed in Stuttgart at the time.

In 1946, we emigrated to the United States. We left Germany on the very first boat taking Jews to America. In 1947 our son, Larry, was born. His birth gave our lives meaning again. He is long since married to a lovely Jewish-American girl. My husband and I built a new life together in New York City. We are grateful and happy for every day we can spend together, and we try awfully hard to forget the horrible past.

HUGH M. MARX (formerly Hugo)
1561 Southland Circle, NW
Atlanta, Ga. 30318

I, Hugh M. Marx, formally Hugo, was born in Buttenhausen in 1898. I emigrated to this country in November 1938, a few days before the infamous Kristallnacht, with my wife, Paula, and two children, Inge and Albert, at that time nine and five respectively. We settled in Little Rock, Arkansas, where I was employed as a sales representative working the local trade. In a short time I advanced to assistant manager and, in May 1945, to manager of the Little Rock Paper Company. In 1948, I was promoted to manager of the Jobbing Division of the Atlanta Paper Company, the parent company. This division was dissolved in 1950, at which time I started my own company under the name of Piedmont Paper Company in Atlanta, Georgia. I was originally a one-man operation doing everything: selling, buying, billing, delivering, etc. We changed our name to Piedmont National Corporation and we employ now about fifty-five people. Since my start, I outgrew five locations, and in 1957 I put up my own warehouse of 27,000 square feet. However, this location soon proved to be inadequate, so I built another warehouse of 55,000 square feet, which we presently occupy. We are considered one of the leading distributors of packing material and machinery in Atlanta, and have plans for additional expansion.

Here are some dates of our families: My wife's father's name was Max Hartstein, born 1873. My wife's mother's name was Blanka, born Rosenstiel from Rottweil, Germany. Mr. Hartstein had a men's clothing store in Stuttgart. Both perished in Theresienstadt in 1944. My father's name was Max, born 1863, in Buttenhausen. He died there in 1938. My mother's name was Emma, born Liebman. She was born 1872, in Tuebingen. In 1940, she left for the United States via Spain and lived with my sister in Cincinnati, Ohio, until her death in 1962.

My wife was born 1904, in Stuttgart.

Our daughter, Inge, is married to George Robbins, and they have two daughters.

Our son, Albert, is married to Ethel, born Bartell. They have three children.

JULIUS MARX
419 Woodland Place
Leonia, N.J. 07605

My mother, Babette Marx, née Rothschild, and both of her brothers were deported to Theresienstadt in 1942, and all died shortly thereafter from illness and deprivation. My wife's father, Wilhelm Rothschild was deported to Theresienstadt in 1942. Upon arrival there his group was put on an open truck which started to move before the elderly passengers could even settle down, causing him to fall out and to suffer fatal injuries.

I was born in Cannstatt in 1893, the second of four children, and was married to Liddy (née Rothschild), who was born in Cannstatt in 1902. Immediately after our marriage we moved to Neuffen. Our family business—Mechanische Gurten und Bandweberei B. Gutmann und Marx—was established in 1875 and consisted of plants in Cannstatt and Neuffen. I shared the management of the business with my brother Leopold.

In the small town of Neuffen we were the only Jewish family. As important employers, we enjoyed a very good reputation and full acceptance there. Our lives began to be affected from time to time when Hitler came to power, and particularly after the passage of the Nuremberg Racial Laws.

Our two oldest children, Sofie and Walter, attended the Volksschule in

Neuffen and later the Realschule there. While at first they had no problems, this changed when their classmates became old enough to join the Hitler Youth. From that time on they were both completely ostracized. For this reason we made use of an opportunity in 1937 to send Sofie to a boarding school in England, and Walter entered the Juedische Landschulheim Herrlingen in 1938.

While we had tried for a long while to sell our family business, we were only able to do so in 1938. The sales contract required me to stay on for at least six months longer to help work out an orderly transfer of the business. So I was still in Neuffen in November 1938, where I was fortunately saved when most adult Jewish males elsewhere were arrested.

We moved to Cannstatt in 1939 into the family home. Soon after the outbreak of the war the authorities built an air raid shelter in the form of a concrete tower in our garden without even asking our permission. Ironically, during air raid warnings we, as Jews, were prohibited from using it.

We received our visas to emigrate to the United States in 1941. At this time, in the midst of the war, the possibilities for travel to the United States were, of course, very limited. Several scheduled departures were canceled. But in 1941 we were finally able to leave on a special train from Berlin with many other emigrants, traveling under heavy guard through occupied France. We could take with us only fifty pounds of baggage and 10 D.M. (worth about $2.50 then) per person. Still there was at least some small satisfaction when the Nazi customs inspector at the Spanish border managed to soil his new uniform with ink on examining my fountain pen. This caused him to lose all interest in checking our luggage any further.

We embarked from Seville on the Guadalquivir River on the infamous vessel *Navemar,* a freighter crudely converted to hold more than 1,100 passengers. Already on the first day at sea there was a serious outbreak of illness from food poisoning made even worse by the effects of seasickness. By the time we reached Lisbon, the Portuguese authorities would not allow the ship to proceed without extensive repairs and sanitary improvements.

During the voyage, daylight hours were spent on the open deck, which we had to share with the slaughtered cattle hung up there waiting to serve as our main source of nourishment. The conditions on the boat were directly responsible for a number of deaths and many serious cases of illness. Those too sick to continue were removed from the vessel in Bermuda. There again continuation of the voyage was delayed by the British authorities, who insisted on further improvements. The ill fame of the *Navemar* had preceded its arrival in Bermuda, where even the impoverished native population was moved by pity to contribute clothing to the passengers.

Our first home was the small apartment of my sister Grete and her

195

husband Karl Adler on Waldo Avenue in Riverdale. My wife soon found work as a housekeeper. It took me several weeks longer until I landed my first job as a weaver in Philadelphia.

After a short time I accepted a similar position in Buffalo, New York, which seemed to offer more of an opportunity for the future. But these hopes were dashed when I suffered a work accident which eventually caused an 80 percent loss of the use of my left hand.

After a lengthy recovery period, I found work as a lens polisher in a large optical-equipment factory. This job lasted until the end of the war, when I was replaced by returning veterans who naturally had to be rehired by my employers. While I was offered reemployment a few months later, by then I had already accepted a position with an export company in New York.

After working there for two years, I started an export business of my own. My wife, who had helped to supplement the family income to a large extent, first through various housekeeping jobs, and later working as a masseuse, eventually joined me in my new business.

We had moved our permanent residence from Buffalo to Leonia, New Jersey, in 1947, first renting a house, and then purchasing our own home, with a large garden, in 1949.

After having commuted to New York for twenty years, my wife and I retired from work in 1967. We spent the subsequent years keeping up our home and garden. Our summers were spent traveling either to California to visit our son, Michael, and his family, or to Europe to see our daughter, Sofie, in London, and my brother Alfred and his wife in Stuttgart. There were also a few visits with my brother Leopold in Shave Zion, Israel.

On our trips to Europe we also returned to Neuffen. We were always very warmly received by some of our former employees and other old acquaintances, who had stood by us in friendship during the Nazi years and reestablished their contact with us soon after the war had ended.

My wife died of heart disease in 1980. She had stood loyally at my side during the good and especially also the difficult times through which we lived. The example set by her life and character contributed greatly to the development of our children into responsible, respected, and useful members of society.

In spite of being severely handicapped by failing eyesight, I am managing to keep up my home and garden. This is made possible by the great assistance from my sister, Grete Adler, who lives nearby, from my son Walter and his wife, from my wife's sister, Else Rothschild, and also from kind neighbors.

Ours was a closely knit family in Germany when we all lived in close proximity to each other. It has remained this way even though the surviving members are now spread far apart. It is my hope that this closeness continues into the future.

LEOPOLD MARX
Shave Zion
Israel

Born 1889 in Stuttgart-Cannstatt. Father's death forced him to leave school. Instead he had to prepare himself with technical and business training in Germany, England, and France so that he could take charge of the family firm, the Mechanische Gurten-und Bandweberei Gutmann und Marx (1909). In 1916 he married Ida (later called Judith) Hartog. Shortly thereafter military service on the Western Front ending in capture by the French. As prisoner-of-war, despite hard labor, he founded the prison library with the assistance of Hermann Hesse, then working for the Deutsche Kriegsgefangenenfürsorge, Bern (resulted in lifelong friendship with Hesse). After successful escape to Spain in 1919 and return home, he resumed management of the weaving factory until 1938.

Two sons were born: Erich Jehoshua in 1921 and Eduard (later Ephraim) in 1923. In 1926 Leopold Marx with Otto Hirsch founded the Stuttgarter Judische Lehrhaus at suggestion of Martin Buber, a frequent guest at his home. Planning possible later emigration, he visited Palestine in 1936.

In November 1938 he was arrested and sent to Dachau for two weeks. Later, a short prison term in Stuttgart for failure to report at Gestapo. Both times released through efforts by brother-in-law, Karl Adler. Having sent their sons to schools in Palestine—Jehoshua for an agricultural career, Ephraim to become a building expert—he and Judith left Germany in 1939 to join the cooperative settlement of the Jews from Rexingen, Shave Zion, both doing farm work.

Mother, Babette Marx and her brothers (Max and Martin Rothschild) died in concentration camp Theresienstadt 1942–1943. The older son, Jehoshua, was killed in 1948 defending an isolated Jewish settlement near Hebron. In his memory Leopold Marx dedicated Beth Jehoshua, a social center in Shave Zion, as he had some years before initiated an Otto Hirsch memorial, built with contributions from Wuerttemberg Jews, the City of Stuttgart, and Theodor Heuss.

Besides his daily farm work he became involved in the local landscaping project. Shave Zion, in the beginning "a waste land in Western Galilee without a single tree or bush," today has become an outstanding vacation resort "with well-designed private and public gardens, a village almost hidden in greenery."

His wife, Judith, became a consultant in all local educational matters until she died in 1972.

Poetry and philosophy were always part of Leopold Marx's life. His writings include poems and essays in magazines and newspapers such as *Jugend, Berliner Tagblatt, Jüdische Rundschau,* etc. Unpublished works include a drama and two comedies.

1941   *Hachscharah,* poems, publisher Peter Freund, Jerusalem.

1960   Booklet about Shave Zion, German and English.

1963   *Otto Hirsch—Ein Lebensbild,* publisher Leo Baeck Institute.

1964   *Song of Songs,* translation from Hebrew into German (annotated), publisher Reclam, Stuttgart, U.B. No. 8896, set to music by Georg von Albrecht and performed by Suddeutsche Rundfunk Stuttgart.

1976   *Es Führt Eine Lange Strasse,* poems, Publisher Friedr. Nolte Berlin

1979   Contributions to *Stimmen aus Israel,* anthology Deutsch-sprachiger Literatur in Israel. Edit. Meir Faerber. Bleicher Verlag.

1979   *Jehoshua, Mein Sohn, Lebensbild Eines Früh Gereiften* publisher Bleicher Verlag, Stuttgart-Gerlingen.

LOTTIE MARX (née Wolf)
8518 Old Bonhomme Road
St. Louis, Mo. 63132

My name is Lottie Marx, née Wolf. I married Ludwig Marx from Stuttgart in 1936. We emigrated to St. Louis, Missouri, in 1938 and I am still living there.

My husband passed away in 1978 after a battle with cancer. I have a daughter, Peggy, and two grandchildren, Alan, ten years old, and Todd, eight years old.

My husband had worked as an insurance agent and I as a saleslady for many, many years. We had our own house, but I sold it and am now living in a small apartment. I have a brother-in-law Marx and wife also from Stuttgart, another brother-in-law, Edgar Marx and wife, and a sister-in-law Florence Mainzer, née Marx, who is a widow and is living here. We are very thankful to have come to the United States in time and hope for peace in the entire world.

TRUDE MARX (née Gailinger)
28-22 156th Street
Flushing, N.Y. 11354

I was born in Stuttgart in 1922 and went to school there until 1938. In September of that year I went to the Haushaltungsschule in Frankfurt for three months until the Kristallnacht closed the school. Until my parents and I emigrated to the United States via London, England, I took a course in Health Swedish Massage and private lessons to study English. The same relatives who had helped my sister Ilse, born in 1915, to escape from Germany also provided us with the necessary documents, and so we arrived in New York in 1940. My sister was already settled in Chicago, where, after a short period of marriage, she was divorced and worked as a private secretary until her death in 1969.

My father found work in the business of my mother's cousin and so was able to allow me to enter a secretarial school after a short interlude of six months when I was working as a maid and baby nurse. Before I married Walter Marx in 1949 I worked for G. Schirmer, the music publishers, and a photo-finishing firm. We have three children, two boys and one girl, and all three are professionally active. After I went back to work, having stopped to rear the family, I am now working part-time as a doctor's assistant and have acquired a college degree in my spare time.

My life is spent with the knowledge that I owe a great deal to the many who were less fortunate than I was, and I hope to devote some of my time "giving back" in the near future when my present commitments have been met.

VICTOR MARX
680 Fort Washington Avenue
New York, N.Y.

Victor Marx born 1903 in Baisingen. My parents were Liebman Marx of Baisingen and Blanda Marx, née Schwarz, of Rexingen. My brother, Egon Marx, was born 1904. When I was three years old, my parents moved to Tuebingen, where my father had his business as a cattle dealer.

In 1933, I married Marga Rosenfeld. We had a little girl, Ruth, and she was a real sunshine for the entire family. My brother left Germany in 1933 and settled in France. My mother followed him there in 1935. My brother married a French-Jewish girl and they had two sons, both of them now married with children. When Hitler marched into France, my brother hid his family in the South of France; he himself was drafted into the Foreign Legion in Africa. My mother was deported to Poland and killed there. My brother died in 1972.

During the Hitler regime, I moved to Stuttgart with my family, as there were no Jews left in Tuebingen and also no jobs available. I worked for a construction firm until our deportation to Riga. In 1941, we were taken to Killesberg near Weissenhof to assemble 1,050 Jews from all over Wuerttemberg. From there, we went by train three days and three nights to Riga. At no time were we permitted to leave the train. Only one person per car was allowed, on the very few stops we made, to get water for everyone. Once arriving at our destination, we found out quickly that this was sheer hell. It was so much colder there than we were used to. Food was very scarce. Our daily ration consisted of very thin malt coffee with one slice of bread for breakfast. Dinner was a watery soup with the taste of horsemeat, one or two pieces of potatoes swimming in it. With this, we worked outdoors all day. People died like flies. Thousands were killed by firing squads. My wife and my child were killed that way, in 1942, in an action called "Duenamuende." The SS had told everyone that they would be sent to Duenamuende to work there indoors in factories and for the children to attend school. All this was lies, horrible lies. I was shipped to several camps around Riga. When the Russian Army came closer, we were taken by boat over the Ostsee to Stutthof near Danzig. Later, I came to Buchenwald, to Zeiss in Thueringia, and in the very end, after a march that lasted many days, I came to Theresienstadt. Soon after, I was liberated by the Russians. The City of Stuttgart sent buses to pick up the very few Jews of Wuerttemberg. They took us to an UNRA camp to feed and clothe us and to give us shelter. Slowly our strength returned and we no longer looked like "Mussulmen," but like normal, civilized human beings. In 1945, I married Hannelore Kahn, formerly of Stuttgart, who also found her way back from the hell of Riga. We emigrated to the United States in 1946 where our only son, Larry, was born. Together, we built a new life. Our son is married to a Jewish-American girl. My wife and I are retired now, enjoying each day together and trying to forget the years that lie behind us.

WALTER E. MARX
34-30 78th Street
Jackson Heights, N.Y. 11372

I was born in Stuttgart, Germany, in 1925, the second child of Julius and Liddy Marx, née Rothschild, both of whom were born and grew up in Cannstatt.

An older sister, Sofie, was born in 1923, and a brother, Michael, in 1933.

The first years of my life were spent in Neuffen, where my father managed a family-owned weaving mill. We were the only Jewish family there, and until 1933 participated fully in the town's social and club activities.

In early 1939 my parents, after the family business had been sold, moved to Cannstatt. I joined them there after the Herrlingen School closed down, and for half a year attended the Jewish school in Stuttgart. From this period one day in particular stands out. This was Yom Kippur of 1939. The diminished Jewish community of Cannstatt held its services in our family home at Seelbergstrasse 1, when suddenly an official order was announced requiring all Jews to immediately turn in their radios to police headquarters in Stuttgart. I recall the long trek through the streets, pulling our radio on a small hand-cart on this sacred holiday.

In 1940 I left Germany and came to the United States through the intermediary of the Jewish Children's Bureau. My parents and brother were to follow only late in 1941 on one of the last vessels able to bring over refugees to this country.

I spent two years in Chicago, living in foster homes under less than ideal circumstances. In 1942 I rejoined my parents in Buffalo, New York. In 1944 I entered the U.S. Army after having completed my freshman year at the University of Buffalo. I served in the Infantry and was wounded during the Battle of the Bulge in the Ardennes. Subsequently I was assigned to military-government duties in Bavaria and Austria, and became a civilian again in 1946.

I continued my studies at the University of Buffalo for a year and then joined my family again, who had in the meantime moved to Leonia, New Jersey. I then entered New York University to complete my college work.

It had been my intention to go into social work; and I worked for a while in a position related to this field. But I found my experiences disappointing and unsatisfactory enough to persuade me to look elsewhere for my future. I then joined my parents in an export business which they had started and have continued in this line of work ever since.

In 1954 I married Charlotte, née Andelman. We had first met as members of a choral group conducted by my uncle, Karl Adler, as part of the New York City College Adult Education Program. Our son Geoffrey, was born in 1959.

I started to get involved in community and political activities after a few years and am still spending much of my spare time with this. In 1972 I was the Democratic (losing) candidate for the State Assembly in the 35th Assembly District. I served for four years as chairman of the Community Planning Board #3, Queens, and am at present president of the Jackson Heights Community Development Corporation.

HERBERT M. MAUTNER
6507 Longridge Avenue
Van Nuys, California 91401

Herbert M. Mautner: Profession, industrial engineer; born 1923 in Stuttgart; attended Heidehof Real Gymnasium until 1935, then attended Jüdische Schule until emigration in 1937. Lived in New York till 1947. Served in France with U.S. 2nd Infantry Division in World War II. Married Marianne Dina Lilienthal, in 1948. She is an electro-encephalograph technician by profession. We have two children: son, David Arnold Mautner, born in 1951, profession: senior buyer; daughter, Vivian Julie Mautner, born in 1952, profession: nursery school teacher, married Yitzchak Lay in 1971, living in Kibbutz Hazorea (near Haifa), Israel, with daughter Noah, born in 1974, and son, Ilan, born in 1975.

Parents: Fred (Fritz) Mautner, manufacturer's representative, born 1891, died 1966 New York City. Else Mautner, née Wolff, born 1891, died 1979 New York; occupation: travel agent.

Sister: Alice Mautner, born 1919, occupation: travel agent. Lives in Jackson Heights, New York.

[*Editor's note:* Fred and Else were members of the first Committee of the Jews from Wuerttemberg, and we will always be grateful for this service.]

HENRY MAY (Heinrich Mai)

Henry May (1882–1954), his family, and fourteen other Jews from Heilbronn were picked up in a police wagon on the first day of World War II, September 1, 1939, and taken to the Rhine bridge in Kehl. The Jewish men and boys were thoroughly beaten up on the bridge and everyone was told to cross it and go to "Jew Blum," the French Premier. All were penniless. This whole episode was staged for the benefit of the Nazis. It was arranged, executed, and paid for by Robert Bosch, A.G. in Stuttgart under the direct supervision of Hans Walz. After the termination of the war, the May family was influential in obtaining a special honor for Mr. Hans Walz, the second German to be so honored by Israel after Konrad Adenauer. The May family arrived on the S.S. *Washington* in October 1939 and settled in Elmhurst, Long Island. Henry, formerly a merchant and owner of Hugo J. Saenger Textiles in Heilbronn, became a butter printer, a blue-collar worker, and a union man. He was most grateful to have found refuge for himself and his family and never complained about his difficult beginnings in his adopted country. He volunteered as an air raid warden during the war and sold United States War Bonds in his spare time. Henry May is the sole survivor of the Holocaust, having lost brother Louis and sister Lina in the concentration camps in Poland. Henry May, until his death, assisted his wife in her extensive activities to build bridges between the Jewish and German communities both in the United States and abroad.

[For further information about his family, see: wife Thekla MAY, son James MAY, daughter Ellen WEITZEN, and mother-in-law Emma SAENGER.]

JAMES MAY (Julius Mai)
137 East 36th Street
New York, N.Y. 10063

James May (Julius Mai) arrived alone in the United States at the age of fifteen. His first job was as an assistant laborer in the Bronx on a construction site. The job paid a dollar a day plus tips. Being underage and working illegally, jobs had to be changed often and included work in a radio shop, a hat factory, a wire manufacturer, a sporting goods house, a delicatessen, and finally his first permanent job, with the Benrus Watch Company at $12 a week. To learn English, American history, and bookkeeping, he attended George Washington High School in Manhattan. He volunteered after the war broke out and was promptly put in the Infantry as a private stationed in Oregon. He was accepted in Officer's Candidate School, graduated, became a second lieutenant in the U.S. Signal Corps, and was assigned as a cryptographer at the Pentagon in Washington. James May decoded the message from General Omar Bradley to General George C. Marshall advising the Chief of Staff that Pierre Lavalle was captured and asking for further instructions. It was 3 A.M. and James May had to awaken the general. After three years of honorable service, he was discharged as a captain. He studied with fashion designer Frederick Karoly and, in 1949, opened his first design studio. Today, thirty years later, he is one of the foremost floor-covering stylists in the world, with clients on four continents. His work has been shown at international fairs in Frankfurt, Paris, Harrogate, Johannesburg, and Moscow. James May has lectured in many universities in the United States and abroad, was the guest of honor at the Spanish Furniture Fair in Valencia, and presently is on the Advisory Board for Home Furnishings appointed by the mayor of New York City, Edward Koch. He previously volunteered his services in the refurbishing of the White House under Mrs. Kennedy and assisted Mrs. Johnson in her program "Make America Beautiful." Mr. May authored a book, *Carpet Printing*; was elected to the board of his professional association for three terms; and is listed in *Who's Who in the East*. He has a daughter, Vicki Barbara. [For information on the rest of his family, see entry for his sister Ellen WEITZEN, father Henry MAY, mother Thekla MAY, grandmother Emma SAENGER.]

THEKLA MAY (née Saenger)

Thekla May (1893–1961) liked to write poetry, act in the theatre, and write serious and humorous articles. She had been a founder of the German *Textil* newspaper in Chemnitz and reported on fashion and allied subjects. She continued her writing after her arrival in the United States in 1939 and had many articles published in the *New Yorker Staats Zeitung & Herold* and in *Aufbau,* and was well-known on the German-language broadcasts in the New York metropolitan area. Shortly after her arrival, she founded the Heilbronner Nachmittage, a get-together of the German-Jewish refugees of the Swabian *Unterland,* an organization of several hundred persons at one time but now, long after her death, a trickle of a few dozen members. After the termination of World War II, she founded the Meinungsaustausch Klub as a bridge between German-Jews and German-speaking Christians both in the United States and abroad. In Stuttgart, she was a charter member of the Swabian-American Friendship Table at the Stuttgarter Rathskeller. In the devastation in Wuerttemberg after the war, Mrs. May organized a group of Jewish women within the Organization of the Jews from Wuerttemberg which collected, packed, and shipped clothes and food packages to Wuerttemberg. She opened her home to German dignitaries, and Mayor Paul Meyle from Heilbronn stayed in her house during his official U.S. visit. So did Interiorminister Fritz Ulrich and many others. German President Theodor Heuss, a friend of her father, Hugo J. Saenger, in Heilbronn, invited her to the official U.S. reception upon his arrival and corresponded with her until his death. Her letters out of Nazi Germany, written between 1933 and 1939, are published in the official documentation by Hans Franke, *Geschichte und Schicksal der Juden in Heilbronn* (Stadtarchiv, 1963).

[For information on the rest of her family see: husband Henry MAY, son James MAY, daughter Ellen WEITZEN, and mother Emma SAENGER.]

*ALFRED MAYER
Last address known: Olivos, Prov. Buenos Aires, Argentina

Attorney Alfred Mayer, born in Ulm in 1889, was admitted in Stuttgart in 1920. During World War I he served as an officer at the front. He emigrated to Argentina in 1935, where he found employment in a textile mill.

IRMA MAYER (née Sicherer)
100 Overlook Terrace
New York, N.Y. 10040

My parents emigrated to the United States in 1939. My father, Nathan Sicherer, was born in 1874 in Oberdorf and passed away in 1963. My mother, Emma Sicherer, née Einstein, was born in 1878 in Laupheim and passed away in 1968.

I was born in 1906 in Oberdorf Bopfingen. I belong to the HIAS, the Y.M. and the Y.W.H.A., the B'nai B'rith, and to the congregation Fort Tryon Jewish Center on Fort Washington Avenue in New York City.

IRMA MAYER (née Loeb)
82-25 Grenfell Street
Kew Gardens, N.Y. 11415

I was born in Stuttgart in 1892. We were three sisters; I was the youngest. After finishing high school, I wanted to study to become a social worker; this was opposed strongly by my father. At that time not many women studied and became professionals. My father was not only strictly opposed to one of his daughters studying, he felt it would be out of the question that one of them would ever accept a position paying any salary. My father acted equally towards my second sister, Marta, who intended to become a teacher. She consoled herself by studying piano, not to become a professional musician, but she was talented and loved music.

I myself did not entirely give up the wish to do social work, and therefore I worked several days a week without remuneration in a child-care agency. When World War I broke out in 1914, I was asked to work at a city agency that dealt with families whose husbands and sons were at war. Also here my father gave his veto, but my brother-in-law, Otto Hirsch, tried to explain to my father that as he had no son who could be called to war duties, one of his daughters had to be asked to work for the war effort at home. Finally my father gave in, and I worked full-time for four years at Hilfsausschuss of the City of Stuttgart. I dealt with wives, children, and often with mothers of the soldiers, with the landlords, religious advisors, etc. I learned more than I could have learned through lectures and books.

In 1918 I married Paul Mayer. I found it hard to move to Mannheim and to give up my various social positions in Stuttgart, but my two children, Ruth and Peter, made the separation easier. I was on the board of various social agencies.

In 1938 I emigrated to America and I became gradually a Self-Help volunteer. Fred Borchardt came from the Reichsvertretung in Berlin to the Joint in New York. Mr. Borchardt felt that I should work with Self-

Help and introduced me to Professor Paul Tillich, the president, and other executive members. First I became a volunteer in charge of the Employment and Service Department. I loved what Self-Help stood for and what it had already accomplished. I was working for Self-Help as a volunteer, but when in 1938 my husband and my older sisters and their spouses came to this country I had to accept being paid by Self-Help to be able to assist them. All together, I was with Self-Help for over thirty-five years. The last years, again as a volunteer, because I had passed the retirement age—even for a voluntary agency. These thirty-five years were, I believe, almost the greatest fulfillment of my life. I have the great pleasure and honor of working with understanding board members.

In 1939 Rabbi Hugo Hahn called me and told me that Congregation Habonim was about to be founded. He suggested that I become the president of the sisterhood. I first did not want to accept, but when Dr. Hahn said that he felt my brother-in-law, Otto Hirsch, would be so pleased if he knew I had joined to work for the German-Jewish congregation, I accepted, and later not only my children were serving as board members but my teen-age granddaughter, Nancy, took charge of the youth group. My youngest granddaughter, Susan, now serves on the Camp Shalom Committee.

For years now I go, once a week, to the Margaret Tietz Center for Nursing Care. The home is being run by United Help. I go there as a volunteer and visit sixteen or eighteen people whom I met during my Self-Help years. Of my seven grandchildren, two granddaughters are social workers, one granddaughter is a lawyer, one teaches and works in public relations. One grandson is a professor of English literature. One is a medical doctor, and another one is studying to become an art teacher.

And I would not like to omit my daughter, Ruth. She is a very brave and lovely person, and although she has multiple sclerosis, she is still capable of helping and caring for other handicapped and ailing persons. She is a professional painter; she loves and understands plants; she works with the Jewish Community Services of Long Island and belongs to the Quality-of-Life-Programs. This is a service for chronically ill, shut-in people. The Society sends volunteers to her, and she gives them cuttings, soil, and pots as well as instructions, which the volunteers take to the handicapped. She also writes a column on indoor gardening for the monthly bulletin of the agency. In this way she helps many unhappy people to enjoy a hobby. She and her husband, Carl, are also very much interested in music, art, and traveling. Carl makes it possible to take her, in a wheelchair, to many places of interest.

My son, Peter, is on the board of the Margaret Tietz Home, and his wife is an executive member on the board of Self-Help. They are both active in Habonim and serve on various committees.

MAX MAYER

Max Mayer (1873–1962) formerly of Stuttgart, and his wife, Olga, née Nördlinger, born in 1884 in Stuttgart and died in 1960 in New York. Experienced both protective custody (1933) and Dachau (1938) prior to their spontaneous flight to Switzerland a day or two before the outbreak of World War II. After their arrival in New York via Portugal in 1941, Olga took in sewing piece-work for a brassiere manufacturer, while Max became a messenger for a photostat firm. This proved too much for him. As he had always aspired to music (he played the glockenspiel in World War I) beyond the wholesale leather business he had inherited, he applied his knowledge and skills to the layout and calligraphic execution of orchestral scores and individual instrumental parts, a task rewarded with minimal pay. Max and Olga's infinite patience and modesty were exemplary. After Olga's sudden death in 1960, Max was persuaded to retire to Freiburg and live in a home run by Roman Catholic sisters, in order to be close to the family of his daughter, Lotte Paepcke (born 1910), née Mayer, who had survived the war in a Black Forest monastery.

Dr. Hans Mayer (born 1911), son of Max and Olga, was the first in the family to leave Germany via Italy. He came to New York in 1938 and found work as a trained optician. During World War II he served in the 10th (Mountain) Division, being an expert skier, and saw action in Italy. After his discharge he earned a doctorate in optometry at Columbia University. He is married to Eva, née Elkuss.

MAX MAYER
60 Donna Road
Framingham, Mass. 01701

My parents: Gustav Mayer, born: 1867; died 1954 in Lynn, Massachusetts. Emma Mayer (née Gruensfelder), born: 1872, Crailsheim, Wuerttemberg; died 1960 in Lynn, Massachusetts.

Wife: Joanne Mayer (née Bauer), born: 1907, emigrated to United States in 1925; married Max Mayer, 1930.

Myself: Max Mayer, born: 1900, Schwaebisch Gmuend, Wuerttemberg, emigrated to United States in 1923.

Our son: Robert James Mayer, born: 1932, Lynn, Massachusetts.

I am a member of B'nai B'rith since 1923. Member of Temple Beth Am, Framingham, Massachusetts. Retired. Living in Framingham at above address.

*OSCAR MAYER

Attorney Dr. Oscar Mayer, born in Heilbronn in 1893, served as a lawyer there since 1922. In 1927 he wrote a *History of the Jews in Heilbronn.* In 1935 he surrendered his license and went to Palestine. There he was among the founders of Nahariya in the northern coastal plain which by 1963 had grown into a town of 20,000. In 1936 he became chairman of the local agricultural cooperative, and in 1941 he was elected mayor. In 1947 Dr. Mayer left for California. There he took a scholarly interest in graphology and wrote a book on this subject. He died in Los Angeles in 1964.

RUDY J. MAYER
3197 Mark Alan Drive
Wantagh, N.Y. 11793

I was born in Stuttgart in 1920, the only child of Max Mayer and Ida, née Weiner.

My father was a manufacturer's representative in textile goods. After I left, my parents had to move to smaller quarters before they were shipped to Theresienstadt on their way to Maly Trostinec, where they perished in 1942.

I attended school from 1927 until 1935 and became an apprentice with Neu & Grunwald, Friedrichstrasse 4. My apprenticeship ended in 1938, and I was able to stay on at Neu & Grunwald until their *Arisierung,* and with their successors A & F Hetzel until December 1938. Early in 1939 I was working to clean up the rubble from the burned-out synagogue. After I hurt my foot I was out of work until a friend of my father (Gentile) offered to teach me a trade in his leather-goods factory in Zuffenhausen. In 1939 I received my visa to go to the United States. I was able to leave Stuttgart by way of Holland and Belgium, arriving here in November.

I worked in the leather-goods line until I was drafted into the Army in 1943, serving until 1948. I saw combat in Italy with the 34th Infantry Division from 1943 until 1945 and stayed on in Italy until 1946. After returning to the United States I was stationed in Fort Riley, Kansas, until my discharge, when I received a direct commission in the Reserves. I stayed in the Reserves until 1970 and retired as a major.

In civilian life I was married to Freda Gropper in 1946. We have two sons, thirty and twenty-eight, one of whom is an electronics engineer working for the government and the other an attorney-at-law.

My civilian occupation has been in the accounting field after the war and I am presently working for a manufacturer in Brentwood, Long Island.

We have been residing at the present address for nearly twenty-six years.

When I became a citizen of the United States I changed the spelling of my first name from Rudi to Rudy. No other change was made.

I omitted additional schooling of myself. While I was an apprentice at Neu & Grunwald I attended the Stadtische Handelsschule.

I am a member of the following organizations: Union Lodge #7, A.F.&A.M., National Sojourners, Reserve Officers Association of the United States, Military Order of the World Wars, Disabled American Veterans, American Security Council, American Association of Retired Persons, Anzio Beachhead Veterans of World War II, and Gesellschaft fur Christlich-Judische Zusammenarbeit.

RICHARD MAX MAYER-MORGENTHAU
Guzman El Bueno 2
Madrid, Spain, 15

I was born in Heilbronn in 1912. My father, Joseph, was born there too, and my mother, Rosa, née Morgenthau, was born in Mainz. All the Morgenthaus came from Hessen, including the family of Henry Morgenthau. The Mayer family came from Horkheim, near Heilbronn.

In 1933, against the will of my family (my father passed away in 1921), I went to France, on a bicycle, and was naturalized there in 1939. I married Madeleine Schwartz in 1941; she was born in Paris in 1921. We have six children, three boys and three girls; two girls and the oldest boy are married in Israel and have eight children between them. The three younger children are unmarried and live in Madrid, where we, too, moved in 1956.

I worked in Madrid until 1979 as co-owner of various firms, (trading firms, building contractors, etc.). Until the end of 1979 I was vice-president of the B'nai B'rith Lodge Maimonides in Madrid, also president of Keren Kayemeth, of which I am now the latest honorary president. Besides I am an honorary representative here of the HIAS in New York, since over twenty years.

*HERMANN MERZBACHER

Attorney Dr. Hermann Merzbacher was born in Oehringen in 1892. In 1921, while still an assessor, he served as an assistant judge at the Landgericht Heilbronn. In 1924 he left the Civil Service and went into private practice in Heilbronn. In 1927 he was admitted as an attorney in Stuttgart. He practiced law together with his brother, Siegfried Merzbacher. Since he left for Brazil in 1936, his admission was annulled in 1938. After having been in Brazil for a number of years, he finally found a position as a broker. He died in 1957.

*SIEGFRIED MERZBACHER

His brother, Dr. Siegfried Merzbacher, born in Oehringen in 1898, became an attorney in Stuttgart in 1924. He published various studies on real estate. He was also a founder of the national association of German real estate agents, mortgage brokers, and loan officers in Berlin. In 1933 he had to resign from his position as the association's legal representative. He left for the United States in 1937. In the United States he worked in a movie house until 1939 and since 1940 as an insurance agent. He died in that year.

ERICH METZGER
282 Highland Avenue
Tenafly, N.J. 07670
(by Else Metzger Cosman
#2604 Point of Americas II
2200 South Ocean Lane
Fort Lauderdale, Fla. 33316)

Family of Julius and Gertrude Metzger, née Schwarzschild

Mr. Julius Metzger was born in 1877. Mrs. Gertrude Metzger, née Schwarzschild, was born in 1884. They were married in Stuttgart in 1908 and lived there during the entire period of their marriage until the death of Mr. Julius Metzger in 1933 from a heart attack, the direct result of his shock when Jewish attorneys were no longer permitted to practice law.

They had three children: Else, born in 1909; Lotte, born in 1911; Erich, born in 1920.

In 1938 Lotte emigrated with her husband, Alfred Landauer from Creglingen, to Israel. Both had been members of the Werkleute, a Zionist group, and wanted to dedicate their lives to Israel. They now live in Kibbutz Hazore'a in Israel with their large family: five children, four of whom are married, and nine grandchildren.

Also in 1938 Else, her mother, Gertrude Metzger, and Eric emigrated to the United States with the help of American cousins of Mrs. Metzger, the family Mendelson. After several years of real struggle and Eric's Army career, discharged as a first lieutenant, with a battlefield promotion, both Eric and Else had successful business careers in New York. He is married to his childhood sweetheart, Jeanette, née Bendheim. They have two daughters, Diane and Sandra. Else became a vice-president of a shoe company and later on had her own consultant business in the footwear and leather industry. She is married to Claus Cosman, born in Wuppertal in 1909.

Mrs. Gertrude Metzger passed away in New York at the age of eighty-seven in 1971.

The family is closely knit and keeps up the traditions established by their parents. Both Eric and his family, and Else are members of Reformed congregations.

*EMIL MEYER

Attorney Dr. Emil Meyer, born in Heilbronn in 1889, was admitted there in 1915. In 1933 his licence was revoked. In 1939 he emigrated to England and went on to the United States in 1940. There he barely supported himself as a sales representative for a textile firm. He died in Los Angeles in 1961.

KURT MEYER (widow Addy Meyer, née Weinschel)
Phamarcia Wilson, Ava Wilson
1066 Lima, Peru

Born in Stuttgart 1905. Parents: Estella, née Haas (1880–1942); Dr. Phil. Adolph Meyer (1868–1912).

Studied pharmacy at Tübingen and Frankfurt. Married Addy Weinschel in 1928. Emigrated to Peru in 1939. He was professor of pharmacy at the University of Trujillo, where he taught many young future South American pharmacists. Later, with the help of his wife, he established an outstanding pharmacy in Lima.

He had two children and five grandchildren. Died 1969.

LEO MEYER
184-14 Henley Road
Jamaica, N.Y. 11432

I was born in 1913, in Oberdorf-Bopfingen, the son of Herman and Claire Meyer (née Karlebach). There were two more children in the family—my older brother, Ernst (David), born in 1907, and my younger sister, Lisl, born in 1916. My father was a horse and cattle dealer, born in Oberdorf-Bopfingen in 1876; my mother was born in Untergrombach, Baden, in 1887. My mother's maternal family was also from Oberdorf; as a matter of fact, my great-grandparents (Schwabacher) were buried at the Jewish cemetery in Oberdorf.

My schooling was in Oberdorf-Bopfingen, until I went to Stuttgart from 1927 to 1929, for further education.

From 1929 to 1936 I lived in Mannheim, where I had my *Lehrzeit* and two more years with the firm of Heinrich Jacobi, cigar manufacturers.

I was the first in my family to emigrate to the United States in 1936. (Six months later I was joined by my sister, and another six months later by my brother.) Six weeks after I arrived in New York, I started to work for J. Aron & Company, Inc., coffee importers (in the meantime we added precious metals), and I have been with this firm to this date.

In November 1938 (Kristallnacht), my father, like all other Jewish men in Oberdorf, was taken to Dachau, but was fortunate enough to be released four weeks later. In 1939, my parents and even my mother's eighty-year-old mother arrived in New York. We settled in Washington Heights until 1941, when we moved to Jackson Heights. My mother, at the time, was active with Dr. Jacques Kroner in the Oberdorf-Bopfinger Group, a subgroup of the Organization of the Jews from Wuerttemberg.

I served in the U.S. Army during World War II, from 1943 until 1946; part of my Army time was spent in India.

In 1947 I married Hilde Alexander. In 1949 our first daughter, Janice, was born. She is married and she and her husband live in New Jersey. Our second daughter, Carin, was born in 1952. She is a teacher and lives in Arizona.

For the last twenty-five years we have lived at our present address in Jamaica, New York. Shortly after moving there, we joined Temple Israel of Jamaica, where both my wife and I have been and still are active. I have been on the board of trustees for many years and am a past-president of the temple. I am also on the board of the New York Federation of Reform Synagogues and on the advisory committee of the Margaret Tietz Center for Nursing Care. My wife and I are active in our Civic Association (Jamaica Estates Association).

My mother died in 1951. My father, after the death of my mother, moved to Florida, where he lived with my brother Ernst and family until his death in 1966, shortly before his ninetieth birthday.

My brother, Ernst Meyer, came to the United States in 1937. After a short stay in New York, he moved to Miami Beach, Florida, where he lives to this day. He is married to a former Boston girl; they have one daughter and two granddaughters. He is retired.

My sister, Lisl, came to the United States in the fall of 1936, after having spent a few years in England, studying to be a baby nurse. She worked at her profession for a few years in New York. She is married to Sig Burg, and they live in Jackson Heights, New York. They have two daughters, (both married) and three grandsons.

MARGARETE MEYER (née Landauer)
Apartado Aereo 4328
Cali, Colombia

I was born in Ravensburg. My father, born in 1872, grandfather, and great-grandfather were born in Buchau, but my father moved, as a child, to Ravensburg, since his father started a department store there. The store, Kaufhaus Landauer, was in the family for over fifty years, continued by my father and uncle after my grandfather passed away.

My husband and our seven-year-old daughter emigrated in 1938 to Cali, Colombia. My two sisters live in Melbourne, Australia, and Cape Town, South Africa. Unfortunately we could not save our parents, and they perished.

In Cali there are practically no Wuerttembergers, but there are a few families in the capital, Bogatá.

ALFRED MOOS
Kauteraeckerweg 18
7900 Ulm-Seeflingen
West Germany

I will try to explain the reasons for my return, and will try to find understanding, without too much emotional involvement.

Born in Ulm in 1913, I graduated from the Humanistic Gymnasium in 1931, studied law in Heidelberg and Berlin, but quit in 1933 after Hitler took power, tried to go abroad, not seeing any chance for a life in Germany.

I became a member of the Reichsbanner Schwarz-Rot-Geld already as a high school student. Although I attended Jewish religion classes, my feelings got away from the thinking of the majority of the Jewish community, but were attracted by the German workers' movements. At the University I joined the Socialist Student Group, as well as the Social Democratic Party; later, however, I severed this connection and in 1932/3 joined the Red Student Group in Berlin. I believed there was either Fascism or a takeover by the revolutionary workers in store for Germany. (The Jews from Ulm did not even support the Social Democratic Reichsbanner!)

My father, Hugo, born 1877 in Ulm, was an exception, was one of the Reichsbanner founders; as a veteran of World War I, he supported the expropriation of the former German kings and dukes. He owned a wholesale and retail textile store, with his father and a brother; it was dissolved in 1938.

Although he had no illusions, he waited too long to emigrate (not even his cousin, Professor Albert Einstein, was able to help any more), and after deportation to Theresienstadt in 1942, he died there a few months later from a bladder tumor. I heard this from the only Ulmer Jewish family, Weglein, who survived Theresienstadt to return to Ulm after the war.

My mother, Ida, née Herzfelder, was born 1886; her father, Isaak, by profession a lawyer, was a poet, translator, and Goethe researcher. My mother died in 1932, at least did not live through the Nazi terror. While the paternal roots (Moos and Einstein) went to Buchau and Kappel in Wuerttemberg, mother's family originated in Bavaria; one was certified as a jeweler in Munich by royal edict. There was, therefore, a mixed background, not exclusively tradespeople only.

With the help of a relative in Ulm, I got a volunteer job at Landauer and Company, in London, 1933, and got there my business training. I joined there the Socialist Workers Party. (Willy Brandt was a prominent member later.) However, when my working permit, after one and one-half years, ran out, I applied for a Palestine Certificate in early 1935. I cannot state for sure whether it was lust for adventure or consciousness of being Jewish after 1933. Anyway, I arrived in Tel-Aviv in May 1935, looking for work. At this time I married Erna Adler, born 1916 from Ulm too; her father, Isaak, born 1877 and his wife, Frieda, née Obernauer, were from Laupheim; he was a cattle dealer. They came to Palestine only in 1939; my father-in-law, who had a serious operation just before emigration, committed suicide shortly afterwards "because he did not want to be a burden to his family." His wife lived with us, returning to Ulm in 1952, and died there in 1956. I got a job with the German Levante Line, in Jaffa; however, at the start of the war, the British Administration closed the firm, and I—with the help of my former London firm—established myself as agent for foods and foodstuffs, but when shipping space became scarce I worked for the American firm of Johnson, Drake and Piper, Inc., and later to the U.S. Army (called USAFIME). When the war ended, many of my colleagues went to Aramco in Saudi Arabia, but Jews were not hired. I resumed work as an agent, but by 1948 the young State of Israel had no foreign currency for my imports.

January 1953 we sailed to Genoa, my wife, myself, and our son, Michael, born 1947 in Tel-Aviv, and settled again in Ulm. Why?

Already in 1935 I thought that there were great problems settling in Israel, contrary to our original beliefs. Also tension between Arabs and

214

Jews was obvious, and I felt that, with the exception of the Left groups, the Zionist organizations lacked understanding of the needs of the Arab majority, who in turn followed blindly the line of people like the Grand Mufti of Jerusalem. I realized, that I, a non-Zionist, erred in going to Palestine. When I came to Palestine I joined again the same group of Socialist Workers Party, which I directed until the Nazis marched into France in 1940 and the group ended its activity.

Already during the war, I had contacts with other German-Jews, who intended to return home after the overthrow of the Nazis. Prominent among these was the writer Arnold Zweig and the painter and later president of the Art Academy in Dresden, Lea Grundig. Therefore the decision to return went already back to this time, although we, or most of us, were comfortable in Palestine/Israel. But we believed in a new democratic and socialistic Germany, and thought it was our duty to carry on part of the task awaiting us there. When right after the war unrest increased, and the radical Jewish organizations committed acts of terror against Arabs and Englishmen, our decision to go back was made easier.

In Germany I quickly became active again in the SPD, peace movement, anti-Vietnam fight, etc. but despite some positive experiences, there were bitter disappointments too, especially in trying to find a new existence again. I found that most of the people, despite all terror of the war, did not change basically, and that the old social and economic classes, with the help of the Americans mainly, were soon reestablished, with many former Nazis in leading positions in administration, politics, and justice. The anti-Communism is the predominant ideology of the state, which bars any attempt at real democracy. Even anti-Semitism, even if not important now, still exists.

But just because these things exist, the presence of active Jewish citizens is useful. Much has been done to spread the truth in schools, etc., and especially after the showing of the *Holocaust* film the demand for Jewish speakers grew enormously.

In 1956 a second son, Peter, was born in Ulm. Both sons, the older a lawyer in Freiburg, the younger studying electroengineering, feel at home in the Bundersrepublik. May the development of Germany be such that it will remain that way.

*ERNST MOOS

Lawyer Ernst Moos was born in 1884 in Ulm, where he practiced law since 1912. His admission to the bar was revoked in 1938. He was permitted to act as consultant for Jews. In this capacity and also as member of the board of the Jewish Religious Association in Wuerttemberg from 1940 on, as

215

acting and managing director since 1941, and finally, after Dr. Gumbel was arrested that same year, as its director, he managed to alleviate the most difficult living conditions of his fellow sufferers as much as was humanly possible under the circumstances.

Ernst Moos was a personality who was respected even by the Gestapo officers whom he had to deal with daily. His cheerful nature and indestructible optimism simply did not let him believe that people could be capable of what they obviously were capable of. When the Jewish Religious Association was dissolved in 1943, he spent several days in a Stuttgart jail, from which he returned, bitten by vermin, but only to be deported to Theresienstadt, and from there, in 1944, he started on his last journey, death in Auschwitz.

FELIX MOOS
149 Seal Rock Drive
San Francisco, Calif. 94121

Born in Ulm, I came to the United States in April 1941 at the age of fifty-four years after having stayed in Belgium, England, and for a short time in Mexico. Very fast, I found out, that in the United States my former positions as commercial and administrative director of the Motoren Fabrik Oberusel, A.G. (later merged with Deutz Motorenwerke), and of the Sewing Machine Works of Haid & Neu A.G. in Karlsruhe were not helpful in finding an executive or other acceptable job. I decided to live in semi-retirement, adding to my investment income some earnings as public accountant and tax consultant. Socially I am nearly exclusively together with Jewish emigrants from Germany, especially with members of the Berkeley Jewisher Kreis, which I joined as a member. My life in this country was, therefore, essentially a continuation of my life in Germany.

*FRANZ RUDOLF MOOS

Franz Rudolf Moss, born in Ulm in, 1910, passed his first examination in the spring of 1932, was discharged from preparatory service in 1933, and left for Brazil in December 1938. Prior to his emigration he worked as a business employee in Goeppingen. Since late in 1939 he has been working as an independent agent in Brazil.

216

GERHARD G. MOOS
2310 N. E. 193rd Street
North Miami Beach, Fla. 33180

I was born in Ulm in 1922, son of Carl Julius Moos and Grete, née Lebrecht, and I have a younger sister, Gabriele, now Mrs. Ernest Gatzert, living in Chicago.

Our world collapsed during the Kristallnacht in 1938. My father, gravely wounded in the First World War, was nevertheless beaten up during the round-up of Jews in Ulm and sent to Dachau. Our rabbi, Dr. Cohn, died later as a result of this action. I myself was arrested in Munich and met my father in the camps. I was one of the youngest inmates. My sister was able to go to a home for children in New Herrlingen in England, which was set up by friends of my parents formerly having such a home in Herrlingen near Ulm.

I went to Luxembourg immediately upon my release from the camp, and my parents joined me there in 1939. Early in 1940 I was able to escape to Haifa in Palestine and became a machinist. In 1941 my parents were caught again in Luxembourg by the German occupiers but managed to escape, practically with the last transport, via Spain and Portugal and finally wound up in Rochester, New York.

I volunteered in the British Army and served with the Royal Engineers in the Middle East and Greece for five years. I was reunited with my family in Rochester after the war and worked in a machine shop, starting at $1 per hour. I met and married my late wife, Ruth Zeitlin. We moved to Tulsa, Oklahoma, where my daughter, Judy, was born. I studied in night school and became a CPA in 1955 as well as treasurer in an oil-well supply company. In 1958 we moved to North Miami, Florida, where Laura arrived in 1961. That year I opened my own firm of certified public accountants, and now I am the oldest firm there, in our own building. I served as president of the Chamber of Commerce and was active in our Temple Sinai of North Dade (Rabbi Kingsley) and other organizations.

Our temple was good to me. Through it, I met my wife, Miriam, who was also widowed. Between us we have five children. Judy is already happily married in New York. We are most fortunate to be happy and healthy, and both of us are working. My wife is a nursing teacher. I feel that life has been good to us.

GRETE MOOS (née Lebrecht)
Collegium Augustinum, Apt. 6112
7 Stuttgart 75 Florentinerstr. 20

Born 1896 in Ulm. Daughter of leather manufacturer Gustav Lebrecht. Liberal home, celebrated Christmas. Attended Girls High School then one year boarding school in Folkestone, England, returning home into newly built villa in 1914.

Next attended women's schools for social work, first in Berlin under Alice Salomon, then in Stuttgart, followed by a practical year at the Youth Office in Ulm. Received Charlotte Cross for voluntary work during First World War.

Married Karl Julius Moos, owned a textile wholesale business in Ulm. Later he founded the manufacture of electric heating pads.

First child, a son, Gerhard. Four years later a daughter, Gabriele. Both are now living in the United States. Gabriele was able to go to children's home New Herrlingen in England. Boy first went to Italy, but returning to Munich was arrested during Kristallnacht.

Husband in Ulm, too, was thrown into a fountain, although he was wounded in the First World War. Father and son met in Dachau concentration camp. Later, both emigrated first to Luxembourg. I followed later. My son emigrated to Israel. We escaped via Spain and Portugal. For several months we were stuck at the border village until the United States visas were available. We resettled in Rochester, New York, in 1942. My husband worked in factories. I helped with household service, children's care, piano lessons.

After twenty years in Rochester, we returned to Ulm, where my husband died in 1967, eighty-one years old. In 1971 I moved into a home in Stuttgart.

Gerhard is a CPA and has his own business in North Miami. Gabriele is married to an engineer with GTE in Chicago of German-Jewish background. I have four grandchildren. I also have two brothers; three and ten years younger; Otto in Zurich and Fritz in New York.

HENRY MOOS
330 W. Brambleton Avenue, Apt. 903
Norfolk, Va. 23510

Parents: Carl Moos, born 1880, Ulm. Co-owner Fa. Adolph Moos in Ulm. Died 1959 in Norfolk, Virginia. Hilda Moos, née Hirsch, born 1892, Ulm. Died 1973 in Norfolk, Virginia.

Myself: Henry Moos, born 1912, Ulm. Active in parents' business. Came to United States 1938, Norfolk, Virginia where I was employed in retail, first as salesman, then manager, and buyer for a chain of forty stores (men's clothing and furnishings) until my retirement in 1979.

Wife: Charlotte, née Wiener, born 1914. Married 1950.
No children.

Sister: Elsie Hirsch, née Moos, born Ulm, 1921. Married to Jerry Hirsch, born in Vienna, Austria, 1916. Two children. Evelyn Schwimmer, née Hirsch, San Diego, California, born, 1945, Norfolk, Virginia. Married, two daughters, Carrie and Lisa, ages eight and four. Steven Hirsch, born 1949, Norfolk, Virginia. Married to Pamela Cox. One daughter, Jessica, age two years.

RUDOLF MOOS
Rua 9 de Julhe, 445-Santo Amaro
04739 Sao Paulo, Brazil

My mother, Selma Moos, née Gutmann, born in 1877, was deported in the fall of 1940, together with all Jews of that area, to the Camps de Gurs (France), and in 1942, being sent from there to the East, she died in the transit camp of Drancy. She took the deportation and concentration camp with dignity, even heroism, but her weakened body ended her life, thus sparing her death in the gas chamber.

My Personal Life: Rudolf Moos, born 1910 in Ulm a.D. Studied law in Munich, Heidelberg, Berlin, and Tuebingen. I served as referendar in Ulm, discharged forcefully from this preparative law service in mid-1933. Then was employed by Carl Veit in Goeppingen, a relative, manufacturing felt cloth until mid-1938. I was, with other Jews from Goeppingen, arrested and sent to Dachau concentration camp. In December 1938 I emigrated to Brazil with my first wife, Ellen, née Heinemann.

Arriving at our final destination, São Paulo, in 1939; two weeks later I found satisfactory employment as German correspondent, while my wife worked at first as a modiste, and later as governess.

In 1939 I started with various firms as their sales agent, working with them for thirty-six years. In 1975 I gave it up and started to give private German lessons, which I still do today.

My wife Ruth Rosenthal, née Schnitzer, arrived in England with a children's transport at age fourteen and emigrated two years later to Brazil to her parents. She devoted a large part of her time directing social work in the shelter workshop of the League of Jewish Women in São Paulo, which is a member of the International Council of Jewish Women.

My daughter, Claudia Metzler, born in Brazil, lives in São Paulo. I have three grandchildren; Catarina, Robert, and Jacqueline Metzler.

We are attached to Brazil and its people and love to live here, especially as our offspring are deeply rooted here.

*SALOMON MOOS I

Attorney Salomon Moos I, born in Buchau 1862, was admitted in Ulm in 1889. From 1919 to 1922 he served as a member of Ulm's City Council. He tendered his written resignation from the bar in 1933 and emigrated to France in 1940. He died in 1944.

URSULA MORGAN (née Mayer)
Hadley Wood, Barnet
Herts, EN4 ONU
England

My father was Hans Mayer, born 1897, died in London 1980, married to Mathilde Luise, née Kahn, born 1895, died 1975.

My parents were very active in Jewish life in Stuttgart before 1939, my father being at one time leading violinist in Karl Adler's orchestra.

Since that time we all have lived fairly uneventful lives, filled with love for the family, which includes three granddaughters. They passed on to them and shared with them their enthusiasm for life and especially for music. They have put down quite deep roots in this country, having lived here, after all, almost half of their lives, and making new and close friends right up to the end of their lives.

My mother had a sister, Rosa Schwarz, and a brother, Hermann Kahn; both emigrated from Stuttgart to Israel between 1936 and 1938. My uncle, under the name of Aharon Kahana, built up quite a reputation as an artist and ceramicist. My aunt, after her daughter's marriage to an Englishman, moved later to London.

GABRIELE BEN MOSCHE (née Michelbacher)
Beerseba
Israel

My parents, brother, and I moved to Stuttgart in 1933; my parents started a laundry. I first attended a public girls' school, but already a year later, with the anti-Semitism increasing, I was enrolled in the Jewish school. My brother was an apprentice with Mr. Davids. He died in 1945 in Dachau; Mr. Davids and his entire family committed suicide in 1938.

In 1939 I was sent to Holland with a children's transport and lived with a Dutch family. My parents, believing that the Hitler rule would soon be over, stayed in Germany, where my father died in 1944. When I was sixteen, I was sent to Westerbork, but with fictitious papers, I was freed and returned to Germany as non-Jewish. I worked in a printing house until the end of the war.

In 1947 I tried to enter Palestine illegally with a group, but we were caught by the British and had to spend five months in Cyprus, arriving in Israel in 1948. I started in a nursing school in Jerusalem, working a few years after training in the same hospital. I met my husband in 1954, studying at a teacher's seminar. He was Alfred Moses, from Landsberg, changing his name to Ben Mosche.

After his studies we returned to his kibbutz, Mazzuvah, where in 1957 our son Ohad was born. Three years later came our son Alon. We decided at that time to leave the kibbutz and moved to Beerseba, capital of the Negev, where my husband works in a school for problem children, and I—after my mother moved to us for good from Stuttgart in 1963—started work in the hospital here, until this day. My mother passed away 1970 at age eighty.

We took or sons, now grown, to Stuttgart, to see the grave of their grandfather, and to show them our former home-city. Unfortunately, we could not go to Landsberg, since this city is now Polish. Our oldest finished his military service and will study; the younger one is still a soldier. My husband and I continue to work, hoping for peace in our country.

BERNARD MOSS
660 Fort Washington Avenue
New York, N.Y. 10040

My father, Salomon Moos, was born in Buchau, died 1972. My mother, Theresa Moos, was born in Gailingen, died 1977.

I was born in 1921, was an apprentice in Stuttgart. In the United States I am assistant traffic manager in chemicals.

My wife is Rita Moss; my son is Marc Moss.

We belong to an Orthodox synagogue.

THOMAS NAEGELE
285 Central Park West
New York, N.Y.

The Naegeles and the Mayers were able to enter the United States thanks to affidavits of support furnished by Olga Mayer's and Alice Naegele's American-born first cousins, the three brothers Arthur, Lester, and Edward Nördlinger of New York. Their father, Emil Nördlinger, was the second of the three Nördlinger brothers of Stuttgart, the other two being Dr. Karl Nördlinger (1867–1931), president of the Israelitschen Oberrats 1924–1930, and Sigmund Nördlinger (1855–1928), the father of Olga and Alice.

Emil had come to New York in the 1880's where in time he founded the partnership Steinhardter and Nördlinger, Food Brokers, a firm still thriving today under the management of Lewis Nördlinger, Emil's grandson.

The Nördlingers spoke only English, but responded with family concern when Arthur's daughter, Helen Nördlinger-Cohen, an executive secretary with the American Council of Jewish Women, alerted her father and uncles to reach out to their cousins in Germany and offer them asylum.

Alice Naegele, M.D., née Noerdlinger (1890–1961), and her husband, Reinhold Naegele (1884–1972), whose paintings and etchings typify the Swabian scene in more ways than one, arrived in New York with their two younger sons, Thomas, born 1924, and Philipp, born 1928, with the cello of their oldest son, Kaspar (1923–1965), and little else, by way of embattled England in 1940. They had left behind in Stuttgart Alice's mother, Helene Nördlinger (1862–1942), who was to join the family as soon as they had found their bearings in America. Instead, she was transported to Theresienstadt, where she could not long survive.

Predictably, Reinhold Naegele had a difficult time in New York. Most of his paintings were bartered or exchanged for kindness and hospitality. To earn a living he became adept at various fine-art reproduction techniques. Alice, at first confined to nursing terminal cases at night and piece-work in the daytime, was ultimately permitted to practice medicine again. She took over as house physician for the United States Committee for the Care of European Children, which operated a reception and processing center for young people en route from DP camps to adoptive families across America. Subsequently, until her death in 1961, she served as a dedicated school doctor for the New York City Department of Health in the poorest sections of the Bronx, where schools had indeed become the surrogates of last resort.

In 1954, thanks to the efforts of Bürgermeister Joseffirn and Dr. Josef Eberle, co-publisher of the *Stuttgarter Zeitung*, a comprehensive retrospective exhibition of Reinhold Naegele's work was mounted in Stuttgart, including works on loan from American collectors. President Theodor Heuss was among the thousands of visitors who came to see the staggering display of lovingly executed detail.

After the death of Alice, Reinhold returned to his Häusle in Murrhardt, where he resumed his favorite technique of reverse-glass painting (*Hinterglasmalevei*). In the course of the remaining years he created an astonishing collection of fragile little pictures, at least fifty of which have been deeded to the Schiller National Museum at Marbach am Neckar. About a hundred more paintings are now in the possession of the Staatsgalerie, the Galerie of Stuttgart, and the Stadtische Kunstsammlung Murrhardt. A monograph is in preparation to be published in 1984, the hundredth anniversary of Reinhold Naegele's birth.

Kaspar David Naegele, born in Stuttgart in 1923 and died in Vancouver, British Columbia, in 1965, was interned in England after Dunkirk like his father, but was shipped ahead to Canada as a "prisoner-of-war" instead of being set free as a "friendly enemy alien." Conditionally released after eighteen months behind barbed wire, he continued his studies at McGill University (B.A.), Columbia (M.A.) and Harvard (Ph.D.), the recipient of various prestigious fellowships and grants in recognition of his pioneering work in sociology. A highly regarded lecturer and consultant, a tireless researcher into the human condition, with emphasis on intrafamily relations and suicide, and last but not least a loyal Canadian in spite of the haphazard circumstances of his immigration, he became dean of the Faculty of Arts at the University of British Columbia. In a state of deep depression he tragically ended his own life, leaving an ailing wife, two daughters, and a son.

Thomas Ferdinand Naegele (born 1924). Followed the family tradition of skilled craftsmanship in the applied arts. Graduated from the New York School of Industrial Art in 1942; he became an assistant to art editor of *Glamour, Vogue,* and *House and Garden.* Drafted in the spring of 1944, he served Uncle Sam in various capacities, notably as a sergeant in the Military Police, looking after German prisoners-of-war. Three hundred fifty thousand *Wehrmachtsangehorige* had been brought to the United States for safekeeping. The efforts made by various groups and units under the direct command of the Provost Marshal General's Office to

223

classify, instruct, and prepare for repatriation those men who could be counted on not merely to follow orders but to listen to their own civic conscience, played an important and as yet little-known role in the restoration of a democratic Germany. Coincidentally, there were many bizarre and comical meetings between refugee GIs and their former classmates, neighbors, teachers, and colleagues.

In 1946 Tom Naegele was engaged by CBS Television as graphic designer. Later he moved to Channels 13 and 9, designing station breaks, program titles, and commercials, and in 1953 he became art director for television at the J. Walter Thompson Company, supplying story-boards and visual devices for thousands of television commercials in the course of fifteen years of greatest growth in programming. Over the years, he contributed close to two hundred paintings and designs to the American Artists Group, which were published as Christmas cards. Between 1964 and 1966 the U.S. Post Office Department issued six stamps designed by Thomas F. Naegele. Today his working is divided between teaching, advertising design and the extension of a series of allegorical illustrations. Married to Rosemary, née Hurst, daughter of the late Sir Arthur Hurst, FRCP, founder of the British Gastroenterological Society and discoverer of certain connections between emotional stress and digestive malfunction. Rosemary Naegle is a painter in her own right and style. A number of New York exhibitions have produced a growing following. There are three sons and a daughter; not very surprisingly, all are active in or preparing themselves for the communications arts and media.

Philipp Otto Naegele, born in Stuttgart in 1928. Started playing the violin in Stuttgart in 1936. He is a graduate of the High School of Music and Art, Queens College (B.A.), did graduate work at Yale and Princeton (M.S. and Ph.D.), has toured with the Salzburg Camerata Academica and the Heidelberg Chamber Orchestra. He was first violinist of the Seventh Army Symphony, has been playing at the Marlboro, Vermont, Music Festival since its founding by Adolf Busch and Rudolf Serkin in 1950, played in the Cleveland Orchestra under George Szell, in the Vegh String Quartet throughout Europe, has participated in many "Music from Marlboro" concert tours across the United States, and returns between concerts to his chair in music at Smith College, Massachusetts. Over the years, many recordings of solo and chamber music on both violin and viola have been released. Among these are six discs of the violin music of Max Reger. Philipp Naegele is also a regular member of the Cantilena Players and the Boccherini Ensemble. Philipp's son, Matthias, is a full-time cellist. Philipp's former wife, Susanne, owns and runs the famous Laugenbretzel Bakery in North Hampton.

224

ALEXANDER NATHAN
rua Santo Antonio, 505 apto. 102,
Caixa Postal, 1887
90.000 Porto Allegre, RS Brazil

I was born in Laupheim in 1905; from 1930 until I emigrated, I lived partly in Laupheim and partly in Berlin.

Since 1930 I was active in the Lichtspielbetriebs Gesellschaft (cinema), domiciled in Laupheim. (Carl Laemmle and Max Friedheim were associates.) In the course of elimination of Jewish firms, I was transferred by the director of the German Universal Film, Inc., in Berlin, Mr. Ruediger von Etzdorf, to his office, in order to wind down the business from there.

I emigrated in 1938, married Susanne Ruth Singer in 1939, and then went to Brazil. Arriving with a tourist visa, we did not get a work permit and unlimited resident privileges due to the Germanophile attitude of the Vargas government, until Brazil entered the war against Germany. Since 1940 I have been in this city. The first years were not easy for us. I started as an importing agent; in 1958, due to the lack of foreign currency, I changed to exporting. This is my field still today.

*AUGUST NATHAN

Attorney Dr. August Nathan, born in Laupheim in 1884 was admitted in Ulm in 1911. His admission was canceled in 1938. He was imprisoned in the Dachau concentration camp briefly in 1938. He left for England in 1939. From 1940 to 1941 he was interned as an ex-officer of the German Army. In late 1941 he succeeded in resuming his legal activities as an associate of a number of English advocates and as a legal adviser in matters of German and international law. In 1957, he left for Basel, where he died in 1962. He was the brother of Paul Nathan, a public accountant, who was deported to Theresienstadt, where he died.

MARGRET REGINA NATHANSON (née Maier)
1 Pebble Lane
Roslyn Heights, N.Y.

My grandfather, Ferdinand Hanauer (1869–1955), founded the Canstatter Bettfedernfabrik in 1884. It was completely destroyed in 1944 but was subsequently rebuilt and the business was carried on by my uncle, Frederick F. Hanauer (1901–1980), who was its president and chief executive officer until it was sold in 1974. Besides being a leading industrialist, my grandfather was the German consul to Rumania until Hitler. Both he and my uncle were imprisoned in Stuttgart. They were released in 1938 and emigrated to the United States, where my grandparents joined my parents in Hempstead, Long Island. My uncle soon established a down feather business in Seattle, Washington.

My grandfather, Ferdinand, was born in Bad Cannstatt. His wife, Selma (1878–1957), died in Hempstead, Long Island. My mother, Marie Hanauer, was born in Bad Cannstatt in 1899. My uncle Frederick died in Switzerland. My father, Marcus Maier (1889–1963), was born in Muellheim and died in Hempstead. My parents were married in 1920. My brother Hans and I were both born in Stuttgart in 1923 and 1926 respectively.

HERTHA NATHORFF
30 West 70th Street
New York, N.Y. 10023

Born 1895, Laupheim. Married to Dr. Erich Nathorff, 1923. Son, Heinz Henry, born 1925, Berlin. Senior examiner of engineering, Albany, New York.

Chief physician of the Women's and Babies' Hospital of the Red Cross in Berlin and of the Family and Marriage Consultation Center of the City of Berlin-Charlottenburg.

Emigration from Berlin after husband returned from Sachsenhausen concentration camp, 1939, to England and, 1940, to United States.

At first odd jobs, kitchen help, housekeeper, nurse. After husband passed medical examination and started his own practice, was his "office help" until his death 1954.

I received my license as psychologist, State of New York, and have practiced psychotherapy since 1955, staff-member of the Alfred Adler Mental Hygiene Clinic, member of the Society for the Advancement of Psychotherapy. Since 1942, for about twenty five years, weekly broadcasts over German radio stations. Topics: medicine, psychology, poetry, short stories. In 1941 started voluntary work for immigrants as a board member (now honorary board member for lifetime) of the New World Club, founded the women's group, and the group for nursing and baby care, whose president I was; gave advice and help to immigrants and helped them to find work (voluntary work) as the president of the women's group. Arranged lectures, concerts, and other performances. Lectures in many clubs, congregations, especially in the "Open House" of the New World Club (my "favorite child"), the first club for the elderly immigrants. Member, board member, and for many years vice-president of the Social Scientific Society for Intercultural Relations, Inc. Wrote poetry (book

Stimmen der Stille published 1966); prize from Harvard University for manuscript *Life in Germany,* especially during the Nazi regime; will be published in the near future. Award from German American Studies Society (Cleveland, Ohio) for poetry. Many poems and short stories published in German-American papers and magazines regularly for at least thirty years in Nebraska, California, Ohio, and other states.

ANNE NEUBAUER (née Dreifus)
67 South Wyant Avenue
Columbus, Ohio 43213

My parents: Max Dreifus, born, 1891 in Stuttgart, was with Dreifus & Lehmann and retired from his Dr. Scholl Foot Comfort Shop in Columbus at age sixty-five. Lives actively in Columbus. Else, née Loewenstein, born, 1893 in Stuttgart, died 1930 in Stuttgart. (She was a childhood friend of Irene Einstein, as I was of Gudula.)

Myself: Born, 1920, graduated from Rhoderths Maedchenrealschule in 1937, spent one year in Lausanne, left Stuttgart 1938 with my father and sister, Helga.

Spouse: Otto Neubauer, born, 1907. Came to Columbus in 1938 and began to work as a hand-shoe cutter. He continued this employment till his retirement in 1970. Has been a participant in Program 65 at the Ohio State University since its inception and is very active in an Orthodox congregation, Ahavath Sholom.

We were married in 1948 and the following are our children: David, born 1950, graduate of Ohio State University and Boston University Law School. He is an assistant attorney general for the State of Ohio. Carol, born 1953, graduate of Earlham College and Queen Mary College of London University, about to complete her dissertation at Indiana University for her Ph.D. in English literature. Adlai, born in 1956, graduated from Ohio State University and has worked in the fields of alcoholism and retardation. Agnes, born in 1961 is completing her freshman year at Stern College for Women. She intends to continue her studies at City College, if she can find suitable housing.

Last, not least, I became a full-time student ten years ago and earned a B.S. in social welfare in 1972. Recently, I completed my seventh year with the County Welfare Department in case management.

Columbus is a rather pleasant town to live in, without the hustle and bustle of New York. Unfortunately there are no other Stuttgarters or Wuerttembergers of my age-range or immigration here.

Wishing you success with your project.

*ALFRED NEUBURGER

Lawyer Alfred Neuburger, born 1883 in Ulm practiced law there since 1925. From 1938 on, he was no longer admitted to the bar, but because of the boycott measures he had stopped practicing law at the end of 1936. Since then, until its destruction on November 9, 1938, he was superintendent of the synagogue and active in the Jewish community. In connection with the November pogrom he was arrested and was in Dachau until 1939. In 1944 he received his deportation order. In a farewell letter to his son, dated January 11, 1944, he still hoped for a "not-too-distant, happy and healthy reunion. But he did not return from Theresienstadt, where he was taken on January 13, 1944, because in October 1944 he was further deported to the death camp Auschwitz.

*EUGEN NEUBURGER

Attorney Dr. Eugen Neuburger, born in Stuttgart in 1877, was admitted there in late 1903. As an attorney he specialized in the representation of theatres. His admission to practice law was annulled in 1938. During the November pogrom of 1938 he was thrown into the Welzheim police prison. In 1939 he managed to get to England by the skin of his teeth. He was unable to find a job. Although seriously ill, he left for New York and died there two months later in 1947.

His nephew Helmut Hirsch, a former student of Stuttgart's Karlsgymnasium, had emigrated to Prague. Equipped with weapons, he returned to Germany for the purpose of assassinating Julius Streicher. He was caught and put to death.

HUGO NEUHAUS
(by Gottfried Neuhaus
376 Highland Avenue
Upper Montclair, N.J. 07043)

Dr. Hugo Neuhaus, born Ellwangen, 1885, died Freeport, Long Island, New York, 1959. Married 1920, in Laupheim, to Marie Roeschen, born 1890, and died in Yonkers, New York, 1974. He practiced pediatrics in Ulm, 1919–1936, and on Long Island from 1936 until his death in 1959. Marie Roeschen, until her husband's death, served as his pediatric office assistant and nurse.

Children of Hugo and Marie: Gottfried Neuhaus, born Ulm 1926, and Barbara Eva Neuhaus, born Ulm, 1928.

Hugo, Marie, and the two children emigrated from Germany by way of Antwerp, Belgium, in 1936.

Son Gottfried Neuhaus is a graduate of Harvard College and has taught school and served in various commercial and administrative functions at Schering-Plough International, Kenilworth, New Jersey, a manufacturer of pharmaceuticals and health-care products, where he has been employed since 1953. He is married to the former Helen Bull, born, 1928, who received her A.B. from Cornell and her M.A. from Harvard, and who has taught English at the college, high school, and elementary levels. Their children are: John Gottfried, born, 1953; Barbara Gifford, born, 1955; Joseph Emanuel, born, 1957; Elizabeth Marie, born, 1959; Susanna Margaret, born, 1961.

Professor Barbara Eva Neuhaus is a faculty member of the School of Occupational Therapy at the College of Physicians and Surgeons, Columbia University, and is currently acting director of the school. She received her bachelor's degree from Keuka College, Keuka, New York, and her master's degree and doctorate from Columbia. She has served in many different clinical, teaching, and administrative positions in occupational therapy since 1952.

MARTA NEUHAUS (née Goldschmidt)
Rua Eliseu Viconti, 120-c/I
Rio de Janeiro
Brazil

I emigrated with my parents to Brazil in 1936. My father, Walter Goldschmidt, born 1882, was one of the sons of Rabbi Israel Goldschmidt, who officiated in Weilburg from 1860 to 1889, and then until his retirement in 1919 in Offenbach. My father lived since his marriage in 1914 in Esslingen and was a partner with my uncle in the firm of Leopold Moses, producers of gelatine, and later cellophane prints and packing materials.

In 1936 my father, together with Mr. Lothar Neckarsulmer—who, I believe, came from Rexingen—founded the firm of Walter Goldschmidt, later changed the name to Grafica Goldschmidt. This firm, whose technical director was my husband Kurt Neuhaus (born in Westerburg), was the first and for many years one of the leading firms specializing in cellophane printing and packaging. My father died in 1953 a few months after his retirement; my husband, due to failing health, had to give up his business activity in 1954, and the firm, after being continued a few years by the new owners, is no longer in existence. Mr. Lothar Neckarsulmer also passed away since.

My mother, Thekla, née Neumann, came from Friedland, born in 1885. She was the sister of Fraenze Moses. She died 1966 in Rio de Janeiro.

My brother, Leopold Goldschmidt, born in Esslingen 1915, emigrated already in 1933, shortly before finishing high school, and went to Pernambuco, in the north of Brazil, where a brother of my father lived already prior to World War I; he was later a few years with my father and now has his own business and lives also in Rio de Janeiro.

I was born 1918 in Esslingen and went to the Gymnasium till November 1935. After the Nuernberg Racial Laws were announced, I was taken out of the school and worked in my father's business until we emigrated in 1936. The business was sold to a Mr. Bayer in Esslingen, and my father always states that the buyer, known as an "Ober-Nazi," acted very correctly towards him.

In Rio I worked in my father's business nearly up to the time of birth of my oldest son, Luiz, in 1941; he studied sociology and business administration and works now in the Tax Department of the State of Rio de Janeiro, married, has two children. Ruth, born 1943, works as a secretary for German and English correspondence, and finally Paul, born 1946, studied economy; works since 1965 with the Brazilian Central Bank; at this time he is with the International Monetary Fund in Washington, married, one daughter.

We are all members of Associaco Religiosa Israelita; also members of Jewish old-age homes, children's homes, and of the Jewish Hospital.

MARGARET NEUMANN (née Thalheimer)
Miami Beach, Fla.

I remember you and your parents very well. My mother, Auguste Thalheimer, née Eppstein, was born in Mühringen, and when my husband and I emigrated in 1938, we took her with us. In New York she lived with my sister and brother-in-law, Alfred and Hilde Grau. Mother died in 1956.

My husband, Justin Neumann, and myself had a shoe store in Stuttgart called the Edox Shoe Company. My husband belonged to the B'nai Brith and for quite some time was its treasurer. Shortly after our arrival in New York, we opened a little factory and fabricated braided shoe vamps with the name Edox Vamp Company. We employed homeworkers. We loved it here and America was good to us.

We retired in 1960 and my husband passed away in 1961. I lived in the same house as the Graus, and they were a big help and assistance to me.

In 1974 the Graus and I moved to Miami Beach. We enjoyed it very much here, but only six months after our arrival my brother-in-law, Fred Grau, passed away. Hilde and I made the best of it. We both belong to B'nai B'rith, ORT, and Hadassah, and enjoy the concerts and operas in Miami Beach.

IRMA NEUMETZGER (née Mendel)
B-16 Roman Gardens
Newburgh, N.Y. 12550

Parents: Louis Mendel, born 1869 in Aufhausen, near Bopfingen am Ipf.
Rosa Mendel, née Gumperz, born in 1873 and killed in Theresienstadt.

I am Irma Neumetzger, née Mendel, born in Bopfingen in 1903. I married Otto Neumetzger, born 1899 in Oberdorf. He died in Newburgh, N.Y. in 1957.

Son, Lothar, born in Noerdlingen in 1930. He married Beverly, née Weiner.

Two grandchildren: Cheryl Ruth, born 1960; Douglas A., born 1962.

I am retired now and belong, together with my family, to the Reformed Temple Beth Jacob, the Hadassah, B'nai B'rith, and the Senior Club. My son is in business, an agent for the North American Van Lines.

We are living in Newburgh, New York. My daughter-in-law is an English teacher at the high school here.

MARTIN NEUSTAEDTER
Ave. Madero No. 402, Habitacion 311
Cuernavaca, Morelos
Mexico

My wife Jenny, née Haimann, from Stuttgart, was born in 1897, the daughter of the late Bernhard and Sophie Haimann, née Haas. She was a co-owner of the Cafe & Bakery Haimann, destroyed by the Nazis in 1938. Her two partners, Hedwig and Emma Haimann, died in Mexico City.

I was born in 1898. After World War I, I was employed by the Darmstädter & Nationalbank, later by the private banking firm of Dreyfuss & Co. in Frankfurt. In 1929 I moved to Stuttgart and assumed a leading position in the firm of Hirsch & Lichter, distillers and vinegar manufacturers. Taken to the Welzheim concentration camp in 1938, I emigrated to Mexico in 1939 via New York, where I stayed for a year.

From the end of 1940 I worked in the machinery branch. For many years I was president of Hatikvah Menorah, an organization of German-speaking Jews active all over Mexico.

Since 1974 we have lived here in the Jewish old-age home, since we are both in very ill health and the clean air here helps us.

ARTHUR NEY
"Sumter"
44 Sandilands
Croydon CRO SDB
England

My mother, Luise Ney, née Moos, was born in Ulm in 1872, lived in Ulm and Stuttgart, came to England in 1939, died in London 1959.

I was born in Stuttgart in 1902, educated at Reform-Real Gymnasium in Stuttgart, became a partner in Gustav Ney Company, Stuttgart.

Came to England in 1936, co-founder and part-owner of Londex, Ltd., manufacturers of electric and electronic controls. Retired 1968 from Londex, joined Clark Clutch Company, manufacturers of electromagnetic clutches and brakes, in 1968. Retired from Clark in 1975.

I am married since 1939 to Lotte, née Friedlander; she was a trained nurse and acting operating-theatre sister, when she left the hospital to marry. We have two children: Mrs. M. A. Harris, married 1965 to David Harris; they live at 48 Erskine Hill, London N.W. 11; they have two children, Caroline Louise and Matthew Frederick. Miss A. R. Ney, lives at Rechov Ha-Tibenim 10, Rechaviah, Jerusalem. Angela was born in England, is a speech therapist.

We are very active in B'nai B'rith, are founder members of the Surrey Lodges, belong (Mrs. Ney) and belonged (myself) to the Leo Baeck Lodges. We are both past-presidents of the Surrey Lodges, and Mrs. Ney is a past-national vice-president of the United Kingdom District of B'nai B'rith #15. We also belong to the Streetham Liberal Synagogue in South London.

CLARE NEY
Kfar Hanassi 12305
Israel

Your circular reached me very late. I have been living on the kibbutz since my husband's death several months ago. I gave your first circular of September 1979 to my brother-in-law, Arthur Ney, and asked him to answer for the whole family [see ARTHUR NEY].

By the way, we know each other from Stuttgart. I remember a very lively evening at my cousin, Otto Hirsch's house.

ELIZABETH NEY
14 Cromwell Close
London N2 OLL
England

My father died in Stuttgart in 1920. My mother, Louise Ney, née Moos, was born in Ulm in 1872 and came to London from Stuttgart in 1939. My brother Arthur provided for her; she died in London in 1959.

I was born in Stuttgart in 1911, went to school at the Kathrinenstift, took secretarial training in Berlin, returning to Stuttgart to work in my father's business, Gustav Ney, together with my brothers. In 1933 I went to Florence, Italy, at first with the family of an attorney, teaching their twelve-year-old son German. I attended university classes in arts and history to learn Italian. Later I changed my position and worked in the household of a prince, teaching the eight-year-old daughter. After a year I went to Juan-les-Pins as a companion for a Berlin refugee lady, to perfect my French, taking lessons from an old actress daily.

In 1936 I came to England, worked first as a domestic. With the help of the Refugee Committee I got a year's secretarial training, and after a few jobs ended up to work for the committee first as a secretary, later in charge of the children's section. I obtained professional standing in evening classes, and about ten years later, with financing from the Home Office, I studied at the London School of Economics and received a Child Care Certificate. From 1949 I worked for various local authorities, ending up in charge of a children's section in the East End of London. I retired in 1976.

I am a member of B'nai B'rith, also a member of the British Association of Social Workers.

OTTO NEY

Otto Ney's father, Gustav, died before 1933. His mother, Luise, née Moos, was born in 1872 in Ulm and died in London in 1959.

Otto Ney had four brothers and sisters. Richard was born in 1897 in Stuttgart and died in 1970 in Gowanda, New York, where his widow, Annie, still lives. Marie was born in 1899 in Stuttgart, married Notar Alfred Gutman, and died in 1949 in Philadelphia. Her only son lives in Pittsburgh, Pennsylvania. Arthur was born in 1902 in Stuttgart. He married Lotte Friedlaender, has two daughters, and lives in London. Elisabet was born in 1911 in Stuttgart. She was a child-welfare officer and lives in London.

Otto himself was born in 1899 in Stuttgart and died on a visit to Kfar

233

Hanassi, Israel, in 1972. He took over his father's business as an agent for clothes mills in Stuttgart. In Germany he worked mainly for the Central Verein Deutscher Staatsbuerger Juedischen Glaubens, last as chairman for the Stuttgart branch. In England he had a small engineering works, manufacturing bimetal thermometers, which did very well after a struggle. He was very active in the B'nai B'rith Lodge, mainly as treasurer and in welfare.

In Stuttgart, in 1932, he married Claire Reis, who had been born there in 1900. She was a chemotechnician loosely active in Germany in the Zionist Movement; in England in B'nai B'rith, in all capacities up to president, and WIZO.

Otto had three children. Eva Karoline was born in Stuttgart in 1933. She studied pure mathematics in London and reached a First Class Honors Degree. She married Peter John Lawrence. They have two daughters and live in St. Albans, England. Johanna was born in 1934 in Stuttgart and studied French and German in London. She married Yitzhak Potasz in Kibbutz Kfar Hanassi. She has three daughters. George Gustav was born in Stuttgart in 1935, studied Hebrew and Arabic at Oxford, and has a degree in English from the Jerusalem University. He married Ruth Anders in England and worked as a youth leader. He has lived in Kfar Hanassi since 1961. He has two daughters and one son.

MRS. RICHARD NEY
184 West Main Street
Gowanda, N.Y. 14070

My husband was born in 1897 in Stuttgart, where, after graduation from medical school, he practiced until 1934. We got married in 1928. Since I was born in Baden, I am not going to talk about myself.

Our son Robert, was born in Stuttgart in 1930. He got his education in England from 1937 until 1944, when he came to America. My husband and I had emigrated in 1941 and lived in New York, where he was an intern and later resident in several hospitals. He received his State Board [certification] in 1943. Due to the war and a shortage of doctors, we moved to a village in western New York known as South Dayton, where he opened his own office in 1944. As we had never lived in the country before, our start was a very difficult one, the more so as the winter in this region usually lasts into May.

After four years at the University of Michigan our son got his medical degree from the University of Buffalo and is now a specialist in allergies in Jamestown, New York.

My husband died in 1970.

234

META NOVECK (née Meyer)
2621 Palisade Avenue
Riverdale, N.Y. 10463

Both my parents were still alive in 1933. My father, Aron Meyer, was born in 1871 in Oberdorf Bopfingen. He was the owner and operator of a cattle ranch. He passed away in 1937. My mother Gidella, born in 1881 in Pflaumloch, was the mother of five children. She died in 1940.

I was born in 1915 in Oberdorf. I had been a dressmaker before being taken to a concentration camp. I work as a tailor in this country too.

My husband is Leon Noveck. We have two children, Adrian and Milton.

I belong to the Hebrew Association of the Deaf, as I have been deaf since childhood.

EUGENE E. NOYMER (Neumetzger)
Noymer Manufacturing Company
430 Summer Street
Boston, Mass. 02210

I was born Eugene Emanuel Neumetzger in 1896 in Oberdorf. In 1938 I changed my name to Noymer.

Our family tree begins with Ben Jacob, cantor and merchant in 1691 in Pflaumloch, Oberamt Neresheim. His descendants moved to Oberdorf near Neresheim between 1770 and 1780, where my great-great-grandfather started a butcher shop. It was called Neue Metzgerei, and in 1810, under Napoleon, it became Neumetzger. I kept this name until 1937, when I emigrated with my family to the United States.

I had one brother, who was killed in 1917 in the First World War. My mother died in 1918, and my father, Sigmund Neumetzger, in 1932. Our rabbi, Dr. Herman Kroner, Oberdorf, told me that he could trace our family tree 200–250 years more in Kleinerdlingen, near Noerdlingen. I told him, however, when I married in 1920, that the year 1691 was early enough.

The company in Oberdorf was Gebrueder Neumetzger, horse and cattle dealers. It was well known in Bavaria, Wuerttemberg, Baden, and Platina.

A cousin of mine, Sigfried Neumetzger, together with his wife and children, was shot to death near Wilna in 1942.

LOTTE NOYMER (née Goldschmidt)
249–24 Cambria Avenue
Little Neck, N.Y. 11362

Born in Stuttgart in 1921 as Lotte Goldschmidt. Upon graduation from the Private Rodertsche Maedchen Realschule in Stuttgart in 1937, emigrated to England and attended nursery-training school there. During World War II volunteered for service in ATS (Auxiliary Territorial Service) of British Army in 1942 and served for four years. In 1946 emigrated to United States and, in 1948, married Ernest Noymer (formerly Neumetzger, originally from Nuernberg). Two daughters: Carol, born 1950, single, lawyer for J. C. Penny Company in New York City; Sandy, born 1952, single, systems analyst for Bank Leumi in Tel Aviv. I am presently working full-time with husband in wholesale trimming business in New York City.

*ERNEST OETTINGER
Last known address:
Berlinerstr. 6
6000 Frankfurt, West Germany

Ernest Oettinger, born in Riedlingen in 1911, was able to pass his examination as a referendar in late 1933, but was denied access to an assessorship. He left for North America in 1937. There he entered government service in 1946. He returned to Germany and made the transition to the private sector. In the years to come he shuttled between Germany and the United States on behalf of an American company in Germany.

GERTRUDE OETTINGER
22 Sterot Hayeled
Ramat Gan 52444
Israel

I have read your letter with a great deal of interest. Mazel Tov with the project.

I was born in 1904 in Buttenhausen. I spent my adolescent years in Stuttgart and eventually moved to Ulm A.D., where I became manager of the fashion department at L. M. Bernheimer Company.

As a result of the Nazi boycott of Jewish businessess, in 1933 I emigrated to Palestine, carrying only my personal belongings and P 50 Sterling. After many difficult weeks, I found work in a fashion salon. Eventually I founded my own business, where my customers consisted of women of all nationalities, including princesses and a queen. During World War II, I was, in fact, invited to Baghdad for three weeks to conduct a fashion show benefiting the Red Cross and under the sponsorship of the Queen of Iraq. In the course of this visit, I was several times invited to tea at the Royal Palace and at the Prime Minister's residence.

The name of my boutique was Carina, in which I had a silent partner who was a Moslem Arab. Unfortunately we had to dissolve the business because of the riots prior to, and the fighting during, the Israel War of Independence.

In 1948, I moved to the United States. Since I did not like New York City, I made my residence in Des Plaines, Illinois, where I worked as a nurse in a psychiatric hospital for fifteen years. In 1968 I was awarded a commendation as "Nurse of the Year" and a vacation trip to Arizona. At the age of sixty-five I retired and returned to Israel, where I now reside at Ramat Gan.

LARRY OETTINGER
805 East Macy Street
Los Angeles, Calif. 90012

My parents, Tekla and Herbert, were married in Buttenhausen in 1923 and lived for a short time in Ulm a.D., where Herbert was employed at the grocery firm of Gaissmaier and Company, and Tekla worked for relatives at the Hotel Zum Mohren.

They returned to Buttenhausen for several years, where Herbert operated a family-owned haberdashery store. Subsequently they moved to Riedlingen a.D., where Herbert managed the local Gaissmaier branch. By this time they had three sons. Due to Nazi pressures, which resulted in Herbert's dismissal from his position and the expulsion of their oldest son from Realschule, the family moved to Stuttgart in 1935.

Their oldest son, Larry (Lothar), left for England in 1937 through the Kindertransport, and the rest of the family for the United States in 1941, having received their visas two days before the United States severed diplomatic relations with the Third Reich. Larry rejoined the family in the United States in 1943.

Larry was born in Ulm in 1924. He served in the United States Navy Seabees from 1943–1946 and was graduated from George Washington High School, New York City, and Woodbury University, Los Angeles. He and his wife currently reside in Sherman Oaks, California. They have a son and two daughters. Larry is an executive with a scrap-metal processing firm.

Their second son, Ernst, was born in Buttenhausen in 1926 and also served in the United States Navy from 1944–1946. He and his wife reside in Somers, Westchester County, New York. They have three sons and a daughter. Ernst is a part-owner of a precision-machinery firm.

John (Hans), the youngest son, was born in Ulm in 1930. He graduated from Samuel Gompers High School and City College of New York, both in New York City. He and his wife Janet, née Freeman, presently reside in Verona, New Jersey. They have three sons. John is an executive in the metal-smelting business.

Herbert died in 1965, and Tekla in 1969.

JOSEPH OPPENHEIMER
25, rue du Chateau
92200 Neuily-sur-Seine
France

I was born in Stuttgart in 1906. I was an agent for a textile firm. In 1935 I emigrated to France and went to Paris after several months in Strassbourg.

Since my family, on mother's side, lived in Alsace before the war of 1870/71 and therefore had French nationality, I had the option, under a paragraph of the Versailles Treaty, to again choose French nationality. I had prepared for this option for some time before I came to France and received my French passport in 1935. This gave me the same rights and duties as any French citizen, and consequently I served in the French Army from 1936 to 1938. I got married in 1939 when my wife, also from Stuttgart, came to Paris. Immediately upon the outbreak of war in 1939 I was mobilized and sent to the front. Later, due to sickness, I was sent back from time to time, and returned to Paris the same year working in the Renault auto factory there until 1940 as a mechanic. I left Paris in June with my wife and mother. My brother, who also lived with us in Paris and was in the army, was taken prisoner by the Germans, returning safely in 1945.

We found a place to stay in then-occupied France in a small house in the middle of France, without water or sanitary installations. We were glad to find a haven after nine days of exodus. We stayed there nearly four years. We gradually started a garden and worked in the field and raised chickens. In early 1945 it became too dangerous since by then the Germans were also in the unoccupied zone and were heavily attacked by resistance groups. The German punishment expeditions were horrible, also for the French population. Many Jews were shot, thirteen behind our farmhouse! I fled alone to Paris and went underground there. My wife came a little later; my mother stayed in the country and had a difficult time, as we had, too, in Paris. We were there at the liberation, and a little later my mother came to us in Paris.

After the war I had various occupations, but in 1947 I joined a metal firm, obtaining power-of-attorney after some years and then becoming a director. I was there until 1980 and I am now retired. My wife started her own business in 1947, designing fur models. She had a few employees and worked in France and with many foreign countries. She had this business for twenty years.

My mother came from Freiburg and died five years ago in Strassbourg. My father, also born in Stuttgart, died there in 1927. My brother, Jules W.Oppenheimer, lives at 26, rue de Bruxelles, 67000 Strassbourg.

MRS. MAX OPPENHEIMER (née Levi)
1616 East 50th Place
Chicago, Ill. 60615

My father, Carl Levi, born in Freudenthal in 1872, moved (with his family) to Stuttgart at the age of one. He married Friedericke Rosenberger, born 1884, of Nördlingen, in 1906. He, with his brother-in-law Julius Schmidt, owned and ran Julius Schmidt and Company, Trikotagen, and later with Mr. Veder as partner, a factory in Amsterdam, Holland, as well. He was the president of the Jewish community also.

I was lucky to get them over here on the second-last ship in 1939. He founded the Self-Help here and shortly afterwards, the Chewra Kadischa. He was busy in both until he got sick and died of cancer in 1952.

My mother, who became an invalid in 1941, passed away in 1971.

I, whom you knew as Gretel Levi, of course, was born in 1908, came to the United States the first time in 1936, but had to return to Stuttgart five months later. Father had asked for passports for himself, mother, and my brother, Kurt, and was told, "Nothing doing—but if your daughter is not back within four weeks we will pick you up, etc., etc."—so after his phone call to me and learning that he could send me a ticket to come back, I came back, of course, in 1936. It took until 1938, until Kurt and I left for the United States, again as far as I was concerned. My first job was as a teacher, having a French and English degree. But needing one more year of college to get the equivalent of an American degree and trying to get my parents out, I went to work at Michael Reese Hospital, first in the hospital record room, then as secretary in pathology. After getting my parents adjusted here—switching to a half-day job and being a trouble-shooter, I worked in auditing, ending up as being in charge of bookkeeping, payroll, etc., in the serum center, having married Max Oppenheimer in 1945. Max died in 1970, and I am now a volunteer at the Self-Help home, aside from being a board member and on various committees, and am also on the board of the Jewish Elderly and one of the other committees.

My brother, Kurt, has been very successful. He was born in 1915. In 1938 he started as a busboy for Mr. Eitel, also from Stuttgart, who gave a great many refugees a job. Kurt then became a salesman in a department store, switched to work in an air-conditioning plant, then worked his way up from shipping clerk to production manager at Revere Camera Company. He went to Miles City, Montana, for a few years, where his father-in-law had a ladies ready-to-wear business, but came back to Revere in Chicago as customer-relations man and then started his own company as manufacturer's representative.

240

RUTH OPPENHEIMER
15 Stoneridge Court
Baltimore, Md.

I am the youngest child of Ludwig and Else Oppenheimer, née Grunwald. My father was the senior partner of the shoe business Neu and Grunwald in Stuttgart, which was founded by my grandfather.

Originally my parents did not want to leave Germany, as my father had been in poor health since 1935. My older brothers, Erwin and Kurt, went to live in Lima, Peru, and Buenos Aires, Argentina, in 1935 and 1936 respectively. My youngest brother, Helmut, went to Israel, where he died in 1966 from heart trouble.

My father was unable to get an immigration visa for South America due to bad health. He died in Stuttgart in 1940, and my mother managed to get out of Germany in 1941 for Lima to join my brother there. Subsequently she moved to Buenos Aires, where she died in 1970 at the age of eighty-one.

I went to England in 1939 at the age of nineteen. I did a nurses' training, but subsequently worked in a Quaker boarding school until 1947. By this time I had become very interested in working with difficult children and studied at the University of London in the evenings in order to get accepted for training at the Hampstead Child Therapy Course, directed by Miss Anna Freud. During these years I was working in nursery and elementary schools as a teacher.

I started to train as a child analyst with Miss Freud in 1953 and graduated in 1957. For three years I remained on the staff of her clinic and also treated children in child-guidance clinics in and around London. This work finally brought me to the States, where at that time more interest in child analysis was shown than in England. I first came to Cleveland and have been in Baltimore since 1965. I am presently working in a private psychiatric hospital and doing part-time teaching at the University of Maryland and Johns Hopkins University.

I live in a small condominium townhouse and have good friends living nearby.

WILHELM OPPENHEIMER
rua Gorceix 11/102
Rio de Janiero
Brazil

My father, Josef Oppenheimer (1879–1952), was owner of the firm Christian Kuenzlen, Sulzbach. He was born in Schwabisch Hall. We were living in Stuttgart. I went to school in the Dillmann Realgymnasium, where I graduated in 1928. I studied chemistry in Heidelberg, where I joined the fraternity Bavaria, then in Munich, and finally in Stuttgart, where I graduated as an engineer in 1932. I then started on my doctoral thesis and got my Ph.D. in 1933 despite the advent of Nazism. I left Germany for Brazil in 1934. After a month there I got a job in the lab of a ceramics factory. I stayed with the company and in due time became its technical director. I am retired now but still active as a consultant.

After a year I felt secure enough to send for my fiancée, Hilde Katzenstein (born 1910) from Bielefeld, and the day after she arrived we got married. We have two daughters, Eva Dorit, born 1941, and Marli, born 1944, both in Rio. Eve is an English teacher and married to an American, William Haas (born 1940), at the present working in the marketing department of Fleischmann. They have two children, Andre, born in 1968, and Eric, born in 1971. Marli is single and is a systems analyst with Petrobras, the state petroleum company. My father was able to hold his business until 1938, when he was forced to sell. My parents had played with the idea of emigrating, but as many of the older people, not too seriously. Besides, my brother Hans, born in Stuttgart in 1915, was also there. He and some of his friends had the romantic idea of staying in Germany at all costs. The consequence was that he as well as my father were sent to Dachau after the assasination of von Rath in Paris. My father got out after I sent the immigration permit to Brazil for my parents. I could not do the same for my brother, as permits were only granted to relatives of the first degree, but he was lucky enough to get a visa as a student to England, so he could wait there till his number for the United States came up. My parents arrived here in 1939, two months after my parents-in-law. My salary at that time was relatively small, and we all lived together in one apartment and had a pretty rough time, especially as my mother became fatally ill four weeks after her arrival.

My father also died in Rio. My brother Hans married Hilde Fleischer and died in 1972. They had two children, Joan, born in 1954, now married, and John, born in 1955. So far there is one grandchild.

Of relatives in Stuttgart there was a brother of my father, Max Oppenheimer, who died several years before the advent of Hitler. His daughter, Erna, was married to Dr. Arnold Eppinghausen, a gynecologist. They lived in Stuttgart until they emigrated to Cali, Colombia. Erna moved to New York after her husband's death, and she herself died about six years ago. There were no children. A brother of my mother, Dr. Ernst Shomberg (Schaumberger), went to New York with his family. His widow and children still live there.

LOTTE OREN (formerly Landauer) (née Metzger)
Kibbutz Hazore'a 30060
Israel

My father, Julius Metzger, died in 1933 in Stuttgart. He was born in Berlichingen in 1877 and owned a shoe business (wholesale) together with Moritz Glueck. The firm was named Glueck & Metzger.

My mother, Gertrud Metzger, née Schwarzschild, was born in Stuttgart in 1884. She left Stuttgart in 1938 and went to New York with my sister, Else Metzger, and my brother, Erich Metzger. She passed away in New York in 1971.

I was born in Stuttgart in 1911. I worked as a secretary.

When I came to Israel I joined Kibbutz Hazore'a in 1938. I worked as a shoemaker for thirty-eight years besides doing several different jobs in the children's houses.

I am married to Alfred Landauer (now Oren, as our Hebrew name) from Creglingen. He was born in 1914. We got married in Stuttgart and have five children: Shulamith, born 1939, is married to her second husband, Dani Samir. They live in Kibbutz Mishmar Ha'emek. Amos, born 1942, is married to Ziona, née Schoental. They live in Hazore'a. Avital, born 1945, is married to Ejtan Shapira. They live in Hazore'a. Jehuda, born 1951, is married to Gale Adler. They live in Hazore'a. Aja, born 1955, unmarried. We have nine grandchildren; six in Hazore'a.

As to my social activities, I have been active all the time on different committes as kibbutz life brings with it.

*BENNO OSTERTAG

Born in Goeppingen in 1892, he was admitted in Stuttgart in 1921. He lost his admission in 1938. Thereafter he could only work as a counselor for Jews.

After the war he became a leading attorney in matters of claims for restitution, with a reputation reaching far beyond the borders of Wuerttemberg. He had a decisive influence on restitution legislation, and he was in the forefront of efforts to rebuild Jewish organizations. He died in 1956.

JULIUS G. OTTENHEIMER
111 East 85th Street, Apt. 3F
New York, N.Y. 10028
Residence:
160 E. 84 Street
New York, N.Y. 10028

We—my wife and I—met while we were both resident physicians at the Municipal Hospital Stuttgart-Cannstatt and married in Stuttgart in 1928. I was the chief medical adviser of the Wuerttembergischen Landesverband of Farmers and Bauern and also Vertrauensarzt of the Stuttgarter Ortskrankenkasse. After the Nazis took over I became, together with the late Dr. Otto Einstein, the physician for the Judenbehandlung in Stuttgart.

Up to the Nazis we had a good life in Stuttgart, with a lovely circle of friends with interest in the arts and community causes.

After trouble with the Gestapo we left without any money, and as we had a high number at the American Consulate, we were able, through the kindness of a relative, to emigrate first to England (London), where we stayed until our number was called by the American Consulate to our final settlement in New York in 1940.

As we were without financial support, we spent one week with relatives of my wife and then set out on our own. To make a new life we started in a cheap furnished room, and my wife got employed as a practical nurse (with sleep-in in Brooklyn). Her income was the only livelihood we had. We had decided on this plan because I devoted my full-time to prepare for my language and medical examinations, which I passed immediately in 1940. After I opened my office here, my wife followed with her own preparation for her medical and speciality boards.

As soon as I could hang my shingle out our worries were over, because many of my patients from Stuttgart and Wuerttemberg were already here and stayed faithfully with me, some of them to this very day.

My wife embarked on her career as psychiatrist. After a thorough training (four years resident in the very well known Bellevue Hospital in New York City) she immediately became a member of the Faculty of New York University Department of Psychiatry, and also was called to the faculty of the New York Medical College as an associate professor of psychiatry and training analyst of the Psychoanalytic Division.

She was a past-president of the Society of Medical Psychoanalysts and a charter fellow and twice councillor of the American Academy of Psychoanalysis. She is a life fellow of the American Psychiatric Association and a fellow of the Royal Society of Health. She still has a full-time psychiatric private practice.

I can add for myself that I was one of the three physicians who chartered, with Dr. Franz Groedel (formerly Nauheim), the American College of Cardiology in New York (1952), which is today the greatest national and international college of cardiology in the world.

*LUDWIG OTTENHEIMER

Attorney Dr. Ludwig Ottenheimer, born in Goeppingen in 1881, was admitted in Stuttgart in 1909. In 1938 he emigrated to England, left in 1941 for Venezuela, and in 1946 for the United States. In Venezuela and later in the United States he represented British and German companies. He died in 1958.

MINNA OTTENHEIMER (née Mezger)
Morton Towers, Apt. 1244
1500 Bay Road
Miami Beach, Fla. 33139

My father's name was David Mezger. He was born in 1872 in Crailsheim. He was the owner of a wine store and died in Crailsheim. When I came to the United States I brought my mother with me to New York, where she died in 1946. I was a secretary in Crailsheim until I married Isaac Ottenheimer, a cattle dealer. In the United States we had a delicatessen store in Baltimore.

Our only daughter was born in 1929 and is a teacher. Her husband is Robert Wagner, professor at Sarah Lawrence College, Bronxville, New York.

We have been active in New York in the Cancer Society and belong to the Congregation Sherah Tefilloh.

RICHARD J. OTTENHEIMER
179 Yankee Peddler Path
Madison, Conn. 06443

Father: Max Ottenheimer of Ludwigsburg. Mother: Else Moos, daughter of Richard and Julie Hirsch Moos of Buchau am Federsee (Trikotfabriken Hermann Moos), served in the Red Cross as a nurse in her hometown hospital. They married in 1920. Max was a Kaufmann partner in a dress-shirt factory, Vertreter. Two children were born, Anneliese in 1922 and Richard in 1926.

In 1935, my parents, Max and Elsie Ottenheimer, moved from Ludwigsburg to Stuttgart. Richard attended the Jewish Day School, Anneliese a Realschule. In 1938, the family emigrated to the United States.

Our sponsors were the Frank family of Pittsburgh, and they settled us in Altoona, Pennsylvania, where Max worked for Puritan Sportswear, first sweeping the factory, then in the cutting room. All four of us worked there off and on. We joined the Reform temple since the refugee committee all belonged there.

Anneliese became a legal secretary and moved to Philadelphia during World War II to work for OPA. Richard attended junior high and high school and entered the Navy in 1944 before graduation. He became a radioman second-class in the Pacific Theater. He used the G.I. Bill to obtain a mechanical engineering degree from Penn State in 1950. He has lived and worked in Zanesville, Ohio, from 1950–1957; Visalia, California, from 1957–1969; Madison, Connecticut, from 1969 to the present. He is director of engineering at the Armstrong Rubber Company, New Haven, Connecticut.

In 1960 the parents, Max and Else, moved to California to be near Richard and family and to retire to a warm climate. Max retired from Puritan in 1960 at the age of seventy-eight. In 1969 Richard was promoted and transferred to Connecticut. Max died in San Francisco in 1971 at the age of eighty-nine. Else remained there until 1976, when we persuaded her to move closer as she was eighty-one years of age. She lived in New Haven in her own apartment until 1979, when age and its effects forced her to move into a home.

Richard's sister, Anneliese (Ann) Bartell, was born in Stuttgart in 1922, is widowed, and now lives in Cherry Hill, New Jersey. She operates a tax service. Her children are Elaine Crown Friedman, born in 1950, who married Howard Friedman, and Jeffrey K. Bartell, born in 1961.

His own children are Susan E. Ottenheimer, born in 1955, and Robert W. Ottenheimer, born in 1957.

MAX OTTENSOSER
157 Lincoln Avenue
Elizabeth, N.J. 07208

My name is Max Ottensoser and I was born in 1915 in Markelsheim. I am the second son of the Lehrer Sally Ottensoser and his wife Ricka, née Strauss. My father was a teacher, cantor, and shochet in many communities, starting in Nordstetten, later in Markelsheim, Weikersheim, Edelfingen, and Mergentheim. He died in a tragic motorcycle accident on the eve of the Succoth festival in 1927 while on the way to officiate for the holidays.

As for myself, I attended the Progymnasium in Bad Mergentheim from

1925–1931, getting my Abitur at the Gymnasium in Wuerzburg in 1934. As at that time Jews no longer could attend German universities, I entered the Juedische Lehrer Seminar in Wuerzburg, from which I graduated in 1936.

My first job, like my father's, was in Mergentheim, but soon after I was called to Karlsruhe, where I taught at the Jewish Elementary School until November 10, 1938 (that infamous date), when I was arrested in front of my children and sent to Dachau. Luckily I was set free after one week and left Germany shortly thereafter, going to Trinidad, British West Indies, via Holland. There I again set up a religious school for Jewish children who had fled to Port-of-Spain with their parents from all over Europe.

I got married there to Ruth Israel of Karlsruhe, who had come to Trinidad via New York. In 1940 we left for New York, since all the refugees from Germany and Austria were interned in a camp on a deserted island in the Caribbean.

In the United States we settled in Washington Heights and later in Elizabeth, New Jersey. I never again became a teacher, but went into business for myself and later worked as a social worker for the City of New York. We are the parents of two sons and a daughter; all three of our children are practicing attorneys. They have presented us with seven grandchildren.

Our children had a Yeshiva education from kindergarten through college; all our grandchildren are attending Jewish day schools. Thus the heritage which we brought with us from Germany we hope will be preserved for many generations to come.

*ROBERT PERLEN

Born in Esslingen in 1884, was admitted in Stuttgart in 1912. After losing his admission at the end of 1938, there remained for him only the possibility to act as a legal counselor. From 1941 on, he became a target of the ever-increasing persecutions which were aimed at people identified by it as Jews.

In 1945 he made the transition to serving as a judge. He started out as chairman of the Senate at the Oberlandesgericht Stuttgart, that very same year became president of the Landgericht, and in 1950 Oberlandesgericht Stuttgart. In the Juedische Kultusvereinigung of Wuerttemberg and Hohenzollern he held a leading position from 1954 on. He died in 1961.

WALTER PERRY (formerly Peiser)
8 Weizmann Street
Rehovot 76280
Israel

Parents: Eugen and Lucie Peiser (née Danziger). My father died of illness in Munich in 1918 when I was only three. We moved to Heilbronn and lived there with my grandparents (mother's side), Isidor and Regina Danziger. In 1936 my mother—at the urging of my grandparents—managed to leave for Israel, where she lived with me until her death in 1956.

Grandparents: Isidor and Regina Danziger (née Baumann). Both were prominent citizens of Heilbronn, grandfather being among the leaders of the local Jewish community and one time president of the local B'nai B'rith. He also had various honorary jobs in the city at various periods. During the Nazi regime, about 1938, they were evicted from their six-room apartment in Heilbronn and had to live in one room at an old-age home in Stuttgart, after refusing to leave the country at their high age. Grandfather died soon after his eightieth birthday, but soon afterwards grandmother Regina, then also eighty, was taken to the concentration camp of Theresienstadt and, as we heard later, perished there under the most inhuman conditions.

It is worthwhile to record at this stage that apart from my mother they had another daughter—my aunt Grete—and also a son, Walter Danziger, who was killed in World War I. I do remember to this day that my

248

grandparents cherished an official certificate they had received at the time of his death from the then German government. Part of the text read: "The thanks of the Fatherland are always with you." Unfortunately the Nazis thought otherwise . . . and the "thanks" were that grandmother had to die in a German concentration camp.

My aunt: Grete Klopstock (née Danziger). Very early after her marriage, she too became a widow and lived with her only daughter, Suse, in Pforzheim. The latter married a doctor and they went to Buenos Aires. Aunt Grete left Germany for Holland to escape the Nazis but was caught by them near Amsterdam and sent to the concentration camp of Auschwitz. We never heard of her again.

My uncle: Dr. Martin Peiser, M.D., specialist in skin diseases in Stuttgart. From my father's side there was really only my uncle Martin, my father's only bachelor brother, with whom we were in very close relationship and contact.

As already mentioned, he was not married and carried out "fatherstead" to me owing to the early death of my father. He wanted me to study medicine eventually and take over his practice one day, which, by the way, was one of the best-known and most reputable in Stuttgart and frequented by Jews and non-Jews alike.

Dr. Peiser made his decision to leave Germany too late and as a result of this mistake was not able to leave. Consequently his practice was taken from him, he was evicted from his apartment and had to move to one room on the outskirts of Stuttgart. Forbidden to practice, he was left without livelihood and eventually shipped to a concentration camp near Riga from which he did not return.

Walter Perry (formerly Peiser), since 1934 in Israel (Palestine). I managed to leave Germany in 1934 after a serious illness caused by former schoolmates who had become overnight little "generals" in the Nazi SA. As at the time there was no medical faculty at the nearby Hebrew University in Jerusalem, medical study was out for me, and after doing all kinds of physical work I found a job with the British American Tobacco Company and so supported myself and my mother, who had arrived in 1936. During World War II, I volunteered for the British Royal Air Force and served with them in the intelligence department until 1946. After the establishment of the State of Israel in 1948, and also in the interim years before, I was a member of the Haganah, and later amongst the first to join the new Israeli Air Force from the very beginning.

In 1958, during the government under Ben-Gurion, I was asked to head an official delegation of the newly founded Office of Israel Bonds in Germany and was director of Bonds in the three German-speaking countries in Europe until 1962. Thereafter I had an official assignment in the

United States on behalf of the Israel Museum in New York and later with the Israel Government Tourist Office in Florida. During that time I met with the Bronfman family both in New York and Montreal and in 1965 became their worldwide export manager and in 1970 the managing director of their Israeli distillery. I served with them until my retirement in 1978.

I married in 1942 and have a married daughter and at present two grandsons.

MARGARET PICK
860 West 181 Street
New York, N.Y. 10033

I Margaret (Grete) Pick came to the United States in August 1939. I worked for a while as a lady's companion but went back to my old position as a bookkeeper in 1942. I worked for one firm until my retirement in 1972. I was not married.

My family lived in Stuttgart–Bad Cannstatt. My parents, Ernst and Anna Pick, née Ostertag, had eight children. One brother, Emil, was killed in the First World War. Manfred, who was a dentist surgeon in Stuttgart, went with his wife and son to Wellington, New Zealand, in 1937. He died in Canada (where he lived with his son the last few years, after his wife had died). Hilda was married to Max Kahn. They both were killed in Riga. Julius is still living in Buffalo, New York. Ellen (Ella) was married to James Strauss. She suffered for many years with multiple sclerosis and passed away in 1979. She was not working. Bernard lived with his wife, Else, née Richheimer (who also came from Stuttgart, Bad Cannstatt) and lived for sixteen years in Israel. He passed away three years ago. Erna lived in Panama but passed away also.

RICHARD L. PICK
Sierra Leona 770
Mexico 10, D.F.

Parents: Paul Pick, born in Freudenstadt in 1894; owned a small department store; was murdered in 1944 in the KZ Riga. Emma Pick, née Baum, born in Stuttgart in 1896; she was murdered in 1944 in the KZ Stutthof.

Spouse: Lore Pick, née Steiner, born in Stuttgart in 1923; worked until recently as a designer and patternmaker in our own business.

Myself: Richard L. Pick, born in Sollingen in 1921; worked at the Auswandererstelle fur Wuerttemberg und Hohenzollern prior to emigration in 1941; three years U.S. Army during World War II; since 1947 in Mexico City manufacturing ladies' garments; now this business is being handled by son-in-law while I am being active in the investment field, dabbling in the construction business, and teaching economics at the university. I am also a member of the board of the Beth Israel Community Center in Mexico City.

Children: Susan, born in Mexico City in 1952; she has a Ph.D. in psychology from the London School of Economics. Sylvia, born in Mexico City in 1954; she is an M.D., National University of Mexico City.

SUSI PLAWNER
860 West 181st Street
New York, N.Y. 10033

I, Susanna Plawner, was born in 1913. My parents were born in Poland and came to Germany in 1909. I have two sisters, Hilda Josef and Paula Salzman. In 1934 my parents emigrated from Germany to Palestine with my two sisters. Both my parents died in Israel. My sisters are now living in the United States.

I married Josef Plawner in 1934. He was born in Stuttgart in 1907 and was finishing his schooling at the Reform Real Gymnasium there. He was connected for many years with the firm of S. Krautkopf, manufacturer of knitted garments. We left Germany in 1938 with our first son, who was born in Stuttgart in 1938, for England. One year later we immigrated to the United States. We lost our first son in 1941. He had been born in the Marien Hospital. Through neglect of the nurses at that time he was burned on both legs a few days after his birth. Then we became the parents of my daughter Elaine Sulkes, née Plawner, and my son Morton, who is married to Marylin, née Haller. Both my children reside in New Jersey. My daughter has two children, and my son has three children.

We lived in New York and made our living manufacturing leather gloves. My husband passed away in 1969.

CARLOTTA POLLOCK
Via Gaggini da Bissone
6900 Lugano
Italy

Professor Friedrich Pollock was born in 1894 in Freiburg, the son of a merchant. A few years later the family moved to Stuttgart, and during dancing classes he met Max Horkheimer. This developed into a rare friendship, since that time the two men deliberated and decided nearly everything together. After the First World War their fathers gave permission to attend the university: Horkheimer studied philosophy, Pollock sociology and economics.

For this reason, Pollock assumed the task of administering the Institute for Social Research. Unfortunately this has deprived him to a great degree of the time for his own work. His last book, *Automation: Materials for the Judgement of Its Economic and Social Consequences,* was especially successful and was translated into eight languages. A further book of my husband's, *Planned Economic Trials in the Soviet Union,* was widely noted, and for that reason a new edition was published by New Kritik K.G. in Frankfurt in 1971.

SELLY AND LENA PRESSBURGER
200 Vandelinda Avenue
Teaneck, N.J. 07666

In answer to your inquiry, we are glad to submit the following summary since we both are Schwaben.

Selly Pressburger (Sally), born 1909 in Rexingen to Max and Pauline Pressburger. My father died in Rexingen in 1938, and my mother was deported to Theresienstadt. We were seven children, most of whom came to the United States.

I was educated in Rexingen, was active as shoe salesman, and in the late 1930's was a cattle dealer for a short time.

Visited Palestine in 1935 with the intention to settle there but contracted a type of malaria and had to return to Germany. In 1937, I emigrated to the United States, was employed in the meat industry till 1943, when I was drafted into the U.S. Army. After the physical discharge from the Army, I started my own retail business, and after three years founded Bergen Wholesale Meats in Hackensack, New Jersey, of which I am still president.

In 1938 was married to Lena Lang from Suessen near Goeppingen. We lived in New York City till 1940 and then moved to New Jersey. In 1943, we bought a home in Teaneck, New Jersey, where we are still residing. Teaneck had a very small Jewish population in 1943, and I was responsible for furthering Jewish religious activities at the Jewish Center of Teaneck, which today has a membership of a thousand families. We both have worked and are still active in UJA, Bonds for Israel, ZOA, Lubavitch, and Yeshivoth.

We have a son, Mark, and grandchildren.

For recreation we travel. Our cultural pleasures are reading and music.

Lena (Lang) Pressburger, born in Suessen near Goeppingen to Jacob and Fanny Lang. My father died in 1918 and is buried in Goeppingen. My

252

mother emigrated to the United States in 1937, where she died in 1953 in New York.

I was educated at the Realschule in Goeppingen, and we were active members of the Goeppinger Jewish community.

During my early teens I lived with my relatives and guardians Sigmund and Millie Victor in Heilbronn, where I continued my education. Later I worked for the Seidenpapier-Fabrik Eislingen for two years and came to the United States in 1929 as a visitor when circumstances led me to remain here. Had a secretarial job at New York University at the beginning and held positions with two more firms till I retired when my husband was released from the army.

Have been active in the family business, as mother, grandmother, housewife, and in organization work.

WOLF AND IRMA RABINOWITSCH (née Selz)
Haifa 34, Nordau Street
Israel

Irma: I was born 1905 in Weikersheim. My father, Ferdinand Selz, came from Laudenbach, Wuerttemberg, and was born in 1877. Mother Mina, née Stein, was born in 1870 in Nesselhausen, Baden. My father founded in Welkersheim a department store, and in 1933 the Nazis forced him to give it up.

We are five children; three emigrated to America since my mother had two brothers here. My oldest brother lives in the United States since 1928. My younger brother, Walter, lives in Israel since 1934 and is a farmer in Beer Tuviyah.

I studied medicine in Germany and worked as a doctor in hospitals in Wuerzburg, Stuttgart (Katharinen-Spital), and later in the Jewish Hospital in Berlin. Emigrating to Israel in 1933 I worked at Hadassah Hospitals in Jerusalem and then Haifa.

I married Dr. Wolf Rabinowitsch in 1934. We have two sons, Schaul and David, and six grandchildren. One son lives in the Kibbutz Chazerim in the Negev, the other in Haifa.

I worked together with my husband, who is a surgeon and urologist in private practice, until now.

My oldest brother, Arthur Selz, lived in Beechhurst, Long Island, New York, married Martha Kahn from Bad Mergentheim, and moved to Florida. His address is 600 NE 14th Avenue, Hallandale, Florida 33009. My sister Meta married Carl Mann. They had a chicken farm in Berlin, New Jersey. They also moved to Florida, and their address is 8220 Byron Avenue, Miami, Florida 33141. My sister Senta Mayr is a widow and moved from Jamaica Estates to Miami Beach. Her address is 7900 Tatum Waterway Drive.

LEA RAFFAELI, (formerly Lieselotte Goldschmidt)
Kibbutz Hazore'a 30060
Israel.

Parents: Josef Goldschmidt and Auguste, née Weil. My father was born in 1880 in Vacha, Thuringia. My mother was born in 1882 in Waldorf/Baden. Both were deported to Theresienstadt from Stuttgart. My mother died there in 1943. My father was sent to Auschwitz in 1944 and perished there.

I was born in 1917 in Stuttgart, attended secondary school until 1934. To prepare for Aliyah I worked for one year with the family of Franz Wolf in Frankfurt (now in Washington, D.C.) and subsequently for another year doing agricultural training (Hachshara) in Northern Italy, where I was sent by the German Hechalutz. I went on Aliyah in 1937 and joined Kibbutz Mishmar Hadarom, the second kibbutz of the Werkleute, which eventually—in 1942—merged with Kibbutz Hazore'a, where I have been living ever since.

I have lived at Kibbutz Hazore'a since 1937. Since 1933 I belonged to the youth group Werkleute. I finished Katharinastift in 1934. My husband Moshe Rafaelli (Manfred Vogel) died in 1971. My children, Omri, Boas, and Dochai, live here in the kibbutz. My social activities are limited to the kibbutz. I would like to keep the connection with your organization if this is possible.

*JOSEPH REIF

Judge in Stuttgart, died during the years of persecution, but it cannot be determined whether his death was due to persecution. Born 1864, had been a district court judge in Stuttgart since 1897. Before that he had been an acting district court judge in Biberach. In 1902 he became an assistant judge at the Regional Court in Stuttgart, later Regional Court judge in Heilbronn. He retired in 1907. He died in 1942, after having been exposed to all the mean indignities invented by that time; such as, to name only the principal ones, the capital levy imposed on Jews, additional first name, Star of David, restricted living quarters, short rations, being forced to buy in Jewish stores only. Shortly after his death, his widow Marie, née Hausmeister, was deported to Theresienstadt, where she died in 1942.

WALTER REIF
75 Wimpole
London W. 1
England

Father: Eugen Reif, M.D., born 1868 in Stuttgart, died there 1933.

Mother: Hedwig, née Hellmann, born 1881 in Ulm, died in London 1972.

Myself: Born 1905 in Stuttgart, Eberhard Ludwig Gymnasium, Universities of Munich and Bonn. Assistant in Bonn and Hamburg from 1928 to

1930, practiced dentistry in Stuttgart from 1930 to 1935, in London from 1935 until now.

I married in 1941 and became a British citizen in 1947. We have one son, Alan, born in 1948.

ALICE REIS
5, Vallance Road
London N22 4UD
England

I have not answered your letter of September 1979 because I assumed that the fortunately uneventful life of a single person would not contribute anything of interest to the purpose of your research, which would be mainly concerned with the question: What has become of the children? Still, whenever it came into my hands I had a bad conscience, and I therefore give you now some details.

We left Germany in 1939; i.e., my mother, Selma Reis, née Gutmann, of Goeppingen, born 1877, who died in London in 1956; my sister, Claire Ney, with husband, Otto, and three children between six-and-one-half and three-and-one-half, myself, born 1901 in Stuttgart. I was secretary of the Centralverein.

I went on domestic permit; my mother had a guarantee. I had two household jobs in refugee households, with the advantage of missing the sometimes funny and sometimes very unfunny experiences of domestics in British households. Eventually I slipped into office work on special permit (during the war) at a salary at which no other staff was obtainable. It was work for a junior and I was forty by then, but in sixteen years I gradually elbowed my way up. After my mother's death, when job security was no longer of prime importance, I left. I had, in all, four office jobs over thirty-six years. The best of them I obtained at the age of sixty-four and kept until seventy-five. Only the last two jobs were the ones for which I was trained and best suited. I am now retired.

*ELLA KESSLER-REIS

Lawyer Ella Kessler-Reis, born in Stuttgart in 1899, was the daughter of Lawyer and Notary Dr. Richard Reis. In 1932 she was admitted to the bar in Stuttgart, but she had to resign as early as Spring 1933. After that she held an executive position in the Jewish Relief Organization in Stuttgart.

Her own fate was sealed when, in the second half of 1941, emigration was prohibited. When, in 1942, her mother was deported to Theresienstadt, she voluntarily joined that transport in order to help her mother. In

256

1945 her old mother was liberated. Before that, however, she had to live through the experience of seeing her daughter, Ella, deported further to Auschwitz, where she was murdered.

*RICHARD REIS

Attorney Dr. Richard Reis, born in Stuttgart in 1864, served as an attorney from 1891 on and later also as a public notary. He died in Stuttgart in 1938.

His widow, Auguste Reis, and his daughter, attorney Ella Kessler-Reis, were dragged to Theresienstadt in 1942. While the daughter was hauled to Auschwitz and murdered there, his widow, Mrs. Auguste Reis, survived Theresienstadt and died in Switzerland.

ERNA REISFELD (née Herzberger)
6455 La Jolla Boulevard, #247
La Jolla, Calif. 92037

Alfred was born in 1896, the oldest son of Lalo and Gusti Reisfeld. There were four children in the family—a sister and the youngest brother were killed by the Nazis—one brother survived—he lives in New Zealand and comes to visit us every five years. Fred's parents and all his other relatives in Austria were killed. My parents were Siegfried and Berta Herzberger. My father passed away when he was thirty-nine years old, and my mother moved with my sister Ilse and myself to Stuttgart to make a new home and life for all of us with her brother. My uncle Ludwig Grunwald never married and took care of us as he had promised my dying father! My sister Ilse married Arthur Heidenheimer. They had one daughter, Inge, and emigrated to São Paulo, Brazil, where he passed away at the age of eighty-four. Ilse lives here with Inge (she has two sons) and four great-grandchildren. Fred and I were in Zurich, Switzerland, for ten years. After the war, we followed our only son, Ralph, to America. We both worked hard here to help Ralph as good as we could to finish his education. Today he is a well-known biochemist working at the famous Scripps Laboratory in La Jolla. He is married and has two lovely children—Dan is twenty-two, and Debbie is twenty-one. Ralph and the children are the pride and happiness of my life.

If you ever come here, please visit me. It feels good to see old friends! Best wishes to you and all who remember me.

ELLY REUTLINGER
7900A Stenton Avenue, Apt. 308
Philadelphia, Pa. 19118

My husband, Gustav Reutlinger, was born in Haigerloch in 1897 and died in Philadelphia in 1979. He was the son of Jacob Reutlinger and Ida, née Schmal, from Buchau. He went to the Jewish school in Haigerloch until he reached the age of nine. Then his parents moved to Kirchheim-Teck, where he finished the Realgymnasium. In 1920 he started his own dry goods business in Kirchheim-Teck, which he continued till the end of 1938. We had gotten married in 1929, and have one daughter.

When we were forced to leave Germany, my husband went to Cuba in 1939 with the intention of going to the United States. I myself and my daughter, Renate, tried to follow him two months later and were on the infamous ship *St. Louis*. We were forced to go back to Holland, where we were interned in a Dutch camp. Late in 1939 we were able to leave Holland and were united with my husband in Philadelphia.

My husband opened a ladies' apparel shop in Philadelphia, which we kept until we retired in 1970.

OTTO RICHHEIMER
75 Radnor Street
Great Neck, N.Y. 11023

Myself: I am the son of Mr. and Mrs. Walter Richheimer. I was born in 1924. I received a B.S. in pharmacy at St. John's University. I am the owner of Independent Merchandise Company, distributors of drug sundries.

Wife: Grace—she received a B.A. degree at Wellesley College and is employed as an administrative assistant for a cosmetic firm.

Daughters: Lynne, twenty, and Cindy, seventeen.

*WALTER RICHHEIMER
8326 Lefferts Boulevard
Kew Gardens, N.Y. 11415

Born 1889 in Stuttgart. Came in 1916 to the District Attorney Office in Stuttgart, and was promoted in 1925 to a district attorney. In 1930 was appointed a judge of the court and had been working in this capacity until he was removed in 1933 through the Civil Service Law. Later admitted to the bar. He lost the admission in 1938. During the pogrom of November 1938 he was sent to the concentration camp Dachau, but had been dismissed after a short time under the following conditions: (1) to leave Germany as soon as possible, (2) never to return to Germany, and (3) not to speak about what he had seen in Dachau.

Politically Richheimer belonged until 1918 to the National Liberal Party and to the board of the Youth Group of this party. After this was dissolved, he was a co-founder of the German Volkspartei Landesgrou Wuerttemberg.

In the United States, where he went in 1939, he started as a "porter for heavy load," in order to learn from the bottom American business life, and later was a representative of a large wholesale house, until he retired at the age of eighty-four. He died in 1981, and Walter Strauss spoke words of thanks in the name of the Wuerttemberg Jews at his funeral.

KARL RICHTER
800 Benjamin Franklin Drive, Apt. 305
Sarasota, Fla. 33577

I was born in 1910 at Schlosserstrasse 5 in Stuttgart, as the son of Samuel and Josephine Richter, née Pick. From 1916 to 1928 I attended the Karlsgymnasium, from which I received the Abitur in 1928.

I was a member of the Blau/Weiss, later the Kameraden, and attended the lectures of the Berthold/Auerbach Verein. Our family attended the Hauptsynagoge, where I celebrated my Bar Mitzvah in 1923. I was a student of Lehrer Jaffe and Cantor Adler, later of Rabbis Dr. Paul Rieger and Dr. Julius Cohn.

My sisters were Ruth (born 1915), now Mrs. Jack Fox, 600 Parkside Avenue, Buffalo, New York 14216, and Edith (born 1920), who was killed in an accident on her way home from school in 1927.

Dr. Rieger prepared me for entry into the Jewish Theological Seminary of Breslau, where I matriculated in 1928. I also attended the Friedrich Wilhelm University in Breslau until 1933. In 1935, I was ordained as rabbi. I served as district rabbi in Schivelbein, Pomerania, 1935–36 (for fourteen congregations); as communal rabbi in Stettin, (1936–38); and as city rabbi *(Stadtrabbiner)* of Mannheim, 1938/39.

I married Lina Ruth May in 1935. Our children are Esther, born in 1936 (now Mrs. Warren Blumenfeld of Atlanta, Georgia), and David (born in Sioux Falls, South Dakota in 1945), now Dr. David Richter of Tampa, Florida.

We left for the United States in 1939.

My father was Samuel Richter (born 1879), came to Stuttgart in 1905, and worked as a salesman for the Jacob Music House. My mother, Josephine Pick, (born 1882), married my father in 1910. My parents left for Tel-Aviv in February of 1939.

My father was an early Zionist (delegate to the Zionist Congress of 1903) and was always interested in Jewish sports. After 1933, he was chairman of the Hakoah football club in Stuttgart, and his home became a center for Jewish young people.

He was severely wounded in an Italian air raid on Tel-Aviv in 1940. We brought our parents to the United States in 1947. They lived with my sister and her family (my father worked till his eighty-first year) in Buffalo, New York. My mother died in 1961, at the age of seventy-nine, and my father in 1960, at the age of ninety-one.

As a young student at the Karlsgymnasium I was deeply impressed by your performance as Varus in Kleist's *Hermannsschlacht* in 1923. I still see you in my mind's eye strutting in your toga and Roman helmet. I also remember the blond fellow who played Arminius der Cherusker, your adversary, but I don't remember his name. [It was Egon Braun who not only was very active in drama but was a colleague of Hans Walz in helping the Jews to emigrate. *Editor.*]

I was a very impressionable, stage-struck post–Bar Mitzvah (Dr. Paul Rieger was my rabbi) and played the violin in the school orchestra during the performances. This brought me very close to the stage. I remember a particular scene where a girl was led in after having been raped by Roman soldiers, and the Germans vowed bloody vengeance. Not knowing at my age what rape was all about, I was frightened and had nightmares for some time. You were a good Varus indeed.

Served congregations: District rabbi of Eastern Pomerania (1935–36); Communal rabbi of Stettin (1936–38) and of Mannheim (1938–39). Emigrated to the United States after the destruction of the synagogues in Germany by the Nazis. Served as rabbi of Temple Israel, Springfield, Missouri (1939–42); Mt. Zion Temple, Sioux Falls, South Dakota (1942–50); Sinai Temple, Michigan City, Indiana, (1950–76), elected Rabbi Emeritus (1976).

College teacher: Language departments of Drury College, Springfield, Missouri, Augustana College, Sioux Falls, South Dakota; lecturer in philosophy, North Central Campus of Purdue University (1965–71).

Served as chaplain: U.S. Medical Center (Federal Prison) and O'Reilly General Hospital, Springfield, Missouri (1940–42); Sioux Falls Army Air Base and military installations at South Dakota State College in Brookings (1942–46); Sioux Falls Veterans' Hospital (1948–50); South Dakota State Prison (1943–50); Indiana State Prison (1950–76); Beatty Memorial Hospital for the Mentally Ill, Westville, Indiana (1955–70).

Past president: Chicago Association of Reform Rabbis, 1969–71 (treasurer 1961–64; vice-president 1964–69). Knife and Fork Lecture Club, Sioux Falls, South Dakota; Marshall Kottler Lodge of B'nai B'rith, Michigan City (1957–58); Michigan City Ministerial Association (1966–67) (Secretary, 1963–65); Community Service Council (1952–54); Michigan City Rotary Club (1970–71); La Porte County Commission on Aging (1961–62).

Retirement activities: In Sarasota, Florida since 1976. Lecturer, Institute on Judaism of Temple Emanu-El; member of Sarasota Ministerial Association (member of the Chaplaincy Committee); participant in monthly Interfaith Dialogues, sponsored by the National Conference of Christians and Jews; taught at the religious school of Temple Emanu-El; speaker before civic and church groups; contact person for Common Cause; director of Condominium Association.

EMILIE RIEGER
Palisades Gardens
Oak Tree Road
Palisades, N.Y. 10964

My husband, Rabbi Dr. Paul Rieger, suffered immensely and passed away in 1939 after an operation in the Marien Hospital.

Our son emigrated in 1938 from Switzerland to America and married in 1943. He served in the United States Army from 1942 until 1946. Martin has two children and two grandchildren, and I have two great-grandchildren.

MARTIN M. RIEGER
704 Mountain Way
Morris Plains, N.J. 07950

I was born in 1920. We moved to Stuttgart in 1921. I have two children; Pamela Sherman lives in Tinton Falls, New Jersey, and has two children, ages four and two. She is a high school teacher. Dr. Dean Rieger, M.D., lives in Ann Arbor, Michigan, and is unmarried.

I am not active socially but participate in professional and administrative activities of technical societies.

ALEXANDER ROBERG
13128 Wales
Huntington Woods, Mich. 48070

I was born in 1914 in Berlichingen, the youngest son of Feodor and Ernestine Roberg, née Hanauer. Here I received a very intensive Jewish education from Rabbi Moses Berlinger, a descendant of the famous rabbinical family who resided in Berlichingen for centuries. In 1927 I entered the Israelitische Lehrerbildungsanstalt in Hoechberg-Wuerzberg and graduated in 1933.

My first assignment as a teacher was in Niederstetten in 1933. Only a short time before the terrible pogroms had taken place in Niederstetten and Creglingen. But I recall with admiration the high caliber of devoted members of that community who retained their dignity as human beings and remained faithful to their Jewish traditions. Through my friendly relationship with the Protestant and Catholic ministers, I was able to prevent some planned attacks on Jewish individuals. In fact Pfarrer Umfrid became a victim of his courageous stand, and only recently fifteen former members of the K'hillah planted a garden in his memory in the Martyr's Forest in Israel.

From 1937 to 1940 I was a teacher at the Juedische Volksschule in Stuttgart and cantor and religious teacher at the Religiousgesellschaft. After the tragic death of Felix David, I also taught the Jewish subjects at the Bloch's Sportschule. My friend the late Ludwig Aaron and I spent the terrible days of the 9th of November 1938 in the forest and thus were saved from concentration camp. In August 1939 my wife, Ilse, née Hertz, and I received certificates to emigrate to England, but since there was no teacher replacement we were prevented from leaving at that time.

In 1940 Director Rothschild from Esslingen and Adolf Zucker, who was released from concentration camp, took our places and thus we were able to come to the United States. Since our arrival we have lived in Detroit. I received a position as principal of the United Hebrew Schools, a very large citywide school system. In 1941 I organized a German-Jewish self-help organization, Chevrah Gemiluth Chassodim. The purpose of this organization was to assist new immigrants to adjust to this new environment and to provide help overseas. The Chevrah later on developed into Congregation Gemiluth Chassodim, which existed for twenty-two years until it joined an American congregation, Beth Abraham. During the existence of the congregation I served as executive director and cantor.

Since my retirement in 1977, I do volunteer work as chairman of the Detroit Friends of Sha'arei Zedek Hospital in Jerusalem. I am also participating in the publication of a history of the *Israelitische Lehrerbildungsanstalt in Wuerzburg.*

ILSE ROBERG (formerly "Fraulein Herz")
13128 Wales
Huntington Woods, Mich. 48070

Born in 1915 in Beuel near Bonn, Rhineland, I am kind of reluctant to write my story as a "Wuerttemberger," for to this day I cannot *schwäbele* nor make *Spätzle*. However, to tell the truth I loved to live in Wuerttemberg and am happy to have married my own "Goetz von Berlichingen," namely, Alex Roberg. After my Abitur in the Oberlyzeum in Juelich Bezirk Aachen, there was in 1934 no chance for me to study at any university. Therefore I had to bury the dream of my youth: to become a physician. the only possibility to continue any kind of studies was then a few Jewish seminaries, which trained Jewish teachers. In Cologne, only 50 kilometers away from home, I could have trained as teacher for "Religionsschulen," while Wuerzburg offered full training of elementary school teachers and simultaneously training in the teaching of religious subjects.

In 1936 I graduated from the Israelitische Lehrerbildungsanstalt, Wuerzburg, and was ready for employment. Director Karl Adler, our beloved friend "Karolus Magnus" of blessed memory, came to our school to give us a course in how to teach singing, and immediately detecting my voice, he wanted me in Stuttgart to take over *his* job as music teacher at the Juedische Schule in Stuttgart. In fact, when I first came to Stuttgart there was no regular class available; however, it was decided that I should teach *Handarbeit, Zeichnen,* and *Werkarbeit* in addition to eight music lessons per week. This way I got to meet all the students in our school; indeed it was a strenuous assignment. Needless to say that more than once I was ready to go home to Mama. Things became easier when my dear colleague Shmuel, at that time called Siegfried, Hopfer decided to leave our school and go to Yeshivath Mir in Lithuania. That gave me an opportunity to take over as *Klassenlehrerin* of our fourth grade, and we became dear friends. In fact some of these my "little friends" are close to us still today. Our school was more than a place of learning. It was an island where young children could forget their troubles, for cheerful homes had turned into depressing places of worries and anxieties, where fathers had no work nor income and often disappeared into concentration camps. In school we could talk and laugh and do nice things, sing, and feel good with each other, and the sun would shine for all of us. The late Julius Baumann, our gym teacher, provided the children with sports activities of all kinds, indoors and outdoors. Combined efforts of teachers, students, and appreciative parents made Sunday afternoon performances in the gym hall events which could never be forgotten.

The enormous pressures from the outside made the relationship between teachers and students an unbelievably close one. We gave of ourselves and received a thousandfold in return. I loved "my" children so much that I would never have left them, had my dear husband not been able to convince me that that would have been actual suicide.

In March 1940 we were able to go to America, and when I heard that we were called "refugees" I acknowledged that with gratitude rather than as a stigma. With the help of God we had found "refuge." Four years of teaching in Stuttgart, plus thirty-seven years of teaching at the United Hebrew Schools of Detroit, enriched my life in a most beautiful way. They gave me a chance to see our own children Esther, Leah, and Ezra in the right perspective. In retirement since 1977 I keep busy with Hebrew and English calligraphy, needlepoint of all kinds, good books, and travels. The crown of our lives, however, are our twenty grandchildren and my ninety-four-year-old mother, who has been making her home with us for the thirty-two years (till 120).

HOWARD G. ROSEN
1854 South Ivy Street
Denver, Col. 80224

I was Hans Gustav Rosenfeld, son of Dr. Fritz Rosenfeld. I was born in Stuttgart in 1921, the last of four children. My three older siblings left Germany prior to mine and my parents' emigration. We arrived in New York City in 1937. I was then almost seventeen.

I found a job in a knitting mill in New York and at night went to an evening high school. I graduated in 1943 and soon thereafter was drafted. I became a citizen of this country prior to being shipped overseas.

I stayed with the 36th Infantry Division through battles in Italy. We invaded Southern France, crossed the river, liberated Stuttgart, and when we reached Austria the war in Europe had ended. I was wounded twice and received one Bronze Star medal.

Following my return to this country, I settled in New Orleans and attended Tulane University, care of the G.I. Bill. In 1948 I received a B.A. and in 1950 got my master's in social work. For one year I worked at a teaching hospital in New Orleans. Then I was recalled to active duty, this time as a social work officer. Eighteen months later I was released and attended the University of Pittsburgh for one additional year.

In the meantime I had married and eventually became the father of three children, Deborah Lynn in 1952, Gregory F. in 1954, and Mark in 1960. My wife Susan, née Hirsch, was born in Ulm.

In 1953 I became director of the Child Guidance Clinic of the Tacoma–Pierce County Health Department. The program grew and developed into a mental health division of the department. In 1966 we left Tacoma and I became regional director for developmental disabilities of Region VIII of the Department of Health, Education and Welfare, located in Denver. In 1971 I received the Mary E. Switzer Award from HEW for outstanding services.

SUSAN ROSEN (née Hirsch)
1854 South Joy Street
Denver, Col. 80224

I, too, am very interested that my children and future family have an understanding about me and my background, as it concerns the Jews from Wuerttemberg.

I was born Susan Hirsch, daughter of Dr. Leopold Hirsch of Ulm, in 1926, the oldest of two girls. My sister, Irene, lives at 3820 St. Charles Avenue, Apt. A, New Orleans, Louisiana 70115.

I emigrated with my family in 1939. We stayed in New York City for two weeks and then went to New Orleans. We joined my mother's brother, Walter Elsas from Ludwigsburg, who had been living there for several years and combined our households. In the fall of 1939 we were joined by another of my mother's brothers, Henry, (Hans), my maternal grandmother, Frieda Elsas (both from Ludwigsburg), and my paternal grandmother, Friederiche Hirsch, from Ulm-Stuttgart.

I completed elementary and high school in New Orleans and graduated *cum laude*. I then entered Tomo Infirmary School of Nursing, since lack of funds prevented me from attending medical school. Upon graduation I worked in public health for the City of New Orleans and later on for an industrial firm.

In 1946 I married Howard Rosen (Hans Gustav Rosenfeld) from Stuttgart. Upon his graduation from graduate school we taught together and led many group-therapy sessions on a voluntary basis. We were also very active in organizations promoting human relations.

We have three children. Our oldest, Deborah Lynn, lives on the big island of Hawaii, working for a large resort hotel. Greg lives in Denver and is presently in his last year of medical school. Mark is attending college and is working for a degree in hotel and restaurant management and wants to become a Continental chef.

Since our arrival in Denver in 1966, I have received a B.S. and consequently an M.S. I work as a consultant in early-childhood handicap. I am also on several boards, an appointee to the Governor's Commission for Children and Their Families, and am an advocate for children.

We have been active in the Reform synagogues and are now active members of the Reconstructionist Federation.

For recreation I garden, grow house plants, read, and travel in pursuit of anthropology and archaeology. I am also active politically—the only way another Holocaust can be prevented.

JULIE (SHULA) ROSENBAUM (née Oettinger)
22 Sterot Hayeled
Ramat Gan 52444
Israel

I was born in 1893 in Buttenhausen, the oldest of nine children. After completion of elementary and high school (Realschule), I entered into an apprenticeship in Augsburg and Frankfurt in order to learn the business of women's high-fashion design and tailoring. After this learning period, I worked in the field of haute couture and eventually, together with my sister Claire, founded the firm, Fashion Salon the Sisters Oettinger, in Stuttgart.

In 1938, as a result of a warning from a non-Jewish customer who witnessed the infamous Nazi march into Vienna, we dissolved the business and decided to emigrate. My sister, together with my mother, went to the United States, and I went to Palestine in 1938.

After a short period of working in my profession in Jerusalem, I was married to Moshe Rosenbaum, and subsequently we settled in Ramat Gan, where I reside at this time.

CURT ROSENFELD
13 NW 81st Avenue
Tamarak, Fla. 33321

My grandfather, Gabriel Rosenthal, was born in 1834 in Crailsheim and died in 1903 in Stuttgart. My father, Moritz (Morris), was born in 1882 in Stuttgart and died in New York in 1949. My mother, Elenor Rosenthal (née Schneider), was born in 1886 and died in Queens in 1978. I was born in Stuttgart in 1921.

We emigrated in 1940 when the entire family went to the United States. I started to work immediately at the Jewel Lamp Company in East Newark. In 1943 I was drafted and went to England, participating in the Normandy invasion. In 1945 I became a military-government investigator and returned home by the end of that year with a Purple Heart and three Battle Stars. Soon afterwards I started to work for my old company.

I married in 1946 and soon became manager in my father-in-law's leather business. In 1950 I started working for Liebman Breweries, brewers of Rheingold Beer, as a checker in the Brooklyn plant. I was promoted to supervisor and assistant superintendent of the department. In 1979 I moved to Florida for health reasons. I have one son, Martin Jeffrey.

As a military investigator for the military government I went to Stuttgart on several occasions. My main purpose was to look for my uncle and aunt, Mr. and Mrs. Heinrich Schneider, and my cousin, Herbert Schneider. Through a friend of my father who came back from Theresienstadt, I learned that my uncle, aunt, and cousin were living in a small town near Reutlingen. Since my aunt was originally not Jewish and had converted to Judaism, she was able to shield my uncle. My cousin Herbert Schneider was in Theresienstadt but returned safely. My wife and I made it possible for my cousin to come to the United States, and his parents followed. My cousin Herbert Schneider was born in Stuttgart and now lives at 3673 North Pellegrino Drive in Tucson, Arizona 85715.

BRUNO ROSENFELDER
113 East Grant Avenue
Vineland, N.J. 08360

We remember you and your parents very well. Since we left Stuttgart already in 1927, I am not very familiar with the events after 1933. By the way, we took my mother to Switzerland in 1932. My brother Lothar and his wife, Hansi, left for the United States shortly after he came back from concentration camp.

My sister, Claire, was the wife of Dr. Lothar Dessauer in Rapperswil in Switzerland. My youngest brother, Fritz, was born in 1901 and was always very much involved in sports when in 1933 he was thrown out of his *Sportverein* since he was a Jew. He committed suicide because he believed that this would open the eyes of his friends. When that happened, the following headline appeared in the *Stuermer*, the German Nazi newspaper, "Jew Rosenfelder pleases everybody, he shows reason and hangs himself."

Leopold Marx said a few words at his grave from which we will quote literally the following sentences:

> A young man committed suicide because he was thrown out of his Sportverein . . .
> In this coffin does not rest a man as a human being who lived his life and died his death like other people. The body whom we hereby give to the cleansing flame held the life which was thrown away by its owner because he did not think that it was still worthwhile to keep.

267

It was a life of a kind which presently is not estimated very highly any more. It was the life of a Jew.

To experience suddenly as a reality how the bottom of his German sentiments, with which he felt intensely united with all his powers and with his whole soul, was suddenly pulled out from under him, the young man felt that he could neither endure nor survive. And if he, a human being, sacrificed his life, we only hope that his sacrifice was not in vain.

We believe that the true German spirit speaks better through the words of the Jew Marx than through the *Stuermer*.

*LUTZ ROSENGART
250 West 57th Street
New York, N.Y. 10019

Born in Heilbronn in 1904, I graduated from the classical high school, studied law, and started practicing law in my hometown in early 1929 in association with my father, Max Rosengart, who was an attorney there since 1884. He had been a Democratic councilman and was vice-mayor during World War I after obtaining the plurality of votes in the preceding municipal election, and was named in 1930 on the occasion of his seventy-fifth birthday, a citizen of honor of Heilbronn, where also a street bears his name. A lawyer of high reputation, he was a member of the State Board of Attorneys in Stuttgart for twenty-two years (until 1933). In view of his merits and apparently taking into consideration the fact that he had lost in the war his oldest son, a "Referendar," the State Ministry of Justice granted my father's petition not to strike me from the list of attorneys in 1933.

Nevertheless I emigrated to France in February 1934. In Paris I wanted to acquire a bachelor of law degree, but after demonstrations by French students against German refugee-lawyers too successful in their examinations, I went to the old Normandy city of Caen and received, in 1936, a diploma as "Docteur de l'Universite de Caen" *summa cum laude;* my dissertation on a topic of comparative criminal law won a prize from the faculty and was published by the Institute of Criminology of the University of Paris. From 1936 to 1940 I worked in Paris on special assignments for a highly reputed international lawyer, André Prudhomme, who was also an assistant professor in the University of Caen and editor of the renowned *Journal de Droit International,* of which I became a regular contributor. In addition, I wrote articles on topics of criminal law and copyright law.

In 1940 I was interned as enemy alien, sent to a camp near Tours and arrived some weeks later—after a perilous and strenuous march—in Limoges, which belonged to the unoccupied zone of France. Afterwards I was drafted into a labor company stationed in a hamlet near Bellac (Haute-Vienne), from where we were transferred in summer 1941 to another place to work on the construction of a dam; most of my comrades were later deported and perished. Fortunately I had obtained, in 1941, a visa for Cuba after unsuccessful attempts at getting a visa for the United States. I reached Cuba via Spain, stayed two and one-half months in Havana, and finally was granted an American visa. End of 1941 I emigrated to the United States.

For the first two years I lived in Englewood, New Jersey, where my son was born four weeks after our arrival. (He is now an associate professor at New York University and has a two-year-old son.) At the same time I started to work as a clerk in my father-in-law's New Jersey industrial enterprise. Ten months later I took up night studies at New York University School of Law, from which I graduated in 1946. After passing the New York Bar Examination, I kept my meanwhile-improved position in New Jersey until 1949, when I became jobless for more than a year. After six months of work in an export-import business as a clerk, and after many unsuccessful attempts at getting a lawyer's job, I finally opened my own law office in 1952. Since then I have been a single practitioner, specializing in German restitution and decedent estate matters. A member of the editorial board of the *Bulletin of the Copyright Society of the United States,* I published a study of comparative law on co-authorship.

My family was very fortunate in not having lost any of its nearest members during the Nazi persecution. My brother, who had earlier emigrated to Sweden, succeeded in obtaining visas for my parents, who joined him in Stockholm in 1939. My two sisters had left Germany with their families in 1933. But many cousins of mine, alas, have perished.

As to my Jewish background, both my parents were great liberals in religion as well as in politics. In 1920, in line with the revolutionary spirit of the epoch, I founded, with some friends, a modern-styled Jewish youth group, named Juedischer Jugendbund Heilbronn, which I led for several years before and after my university studies. I became later (in 1930) a member of B'nai B'rith, have been a charter member of Leo Baeck Lodge in New York, and belong to Congregation Habonim and various Jewish organizations.

MAX ROSENGART

IN MEMORIAM

Max Rosengart

(Max Rosengart—Bruder meiner Grossmutter väterlicherseits—war
Rechtsanwalt in Heilbronn.)

Max Rosengart,
Deutscher und Jude,
Ihm gelang die Verbindung
Von Religiosität
Mit Klassischem
Bildungsgute
Zu Humanität.

9/25/79

Nicht nur Neffen und Nichten
Gaben acht
Auf seinen Rat,
Auch die Stadt
Hat hochgeacht'
Sein humorvolles Schlichten,
Sein unerschrockenes, gütiges Wesen
Und hat ihn zum Ehrenbürger erlesen.

(Max Rosengart, brother of my paternal grandmother, was a
lawyer in Heilbronn. He succeeded in combining religion with
classical learning. He was highly esteemed by family and
friends for his straightforward counsel, coupled with kindness
and at times with humor. He served for many years on the
town council and was named an "honorary citizen" of
Heilbronn.)

8/1/81

Written by Luise Helen Bronner

*OSKAR ROSENSTEIN

Attorney Dr. Oskar Rosenstein, born in Stuttgart in 1872, was admitted
there at the end of 1903. Late in 1938 his admission was revoked. He was
thrown into prison for several days during the pogrom of November
1938. He emigrated to South America in 1939 and died in Johannesburg
in 1943.

ERWIN I. J. ROSENTHAL
199 Chesterton Road
Cambridge CB4 1 AH
England

Born in 1904, the youngest of six children of Moses and Amalie Rosenthal in Heilbronn, I am the only one alive. Three sisters and my brother emigrated; one sister perished in Theresienstadt.

Without funds during the inflation, I could not go to the university after graduating from high school. I became an apprentice in the Dresdner Bank branch in Heilbronn, but managed a year later to be transferred to Heidelberg, where I began to study Semitic languages and history, besides my apprenticeship, and moved to Munich in 1926, then to Berlin, at the advice of my teacher, Bergstraesser, one of Germany's leading Arabists. Graduating in 1929, and obtaining a grant I worked on my doctors thesis, and for a teachers exam, but the grant ended with Hitler's accession to power, before I reached these goals. However, my dissertation about "Ibn Khaldun's Ideas About the State" was published in *Historische Zeitschrift* in 1932. Later I wrote again and again about his ideas.

Being convinced that Hitler meant what he preached, I was able to emigrate to England, landing in Dover in 1933, at first under a four weeks visitor's visa, receiving great assistance from the Jewish Academic Refugee Committee; a Jewish doctor even took me in his home. Dr. and Mrs. Shepherd became great friends, gave us a luncheon after my wedding to Elisabeth, née Marx, who was my fiancée in Germany and instrumental to convince me to emigrate. Through the help of various people, especially the saintly Mr. Herbert Loewe, I was beginning my academic career by being appointed a part-time lecturer in Hebrew and Semitic epigraphy at University College, London. The meager salary was supplemented by the Academic Committee, and by my reading German to a neighbor in the publishing business.

I called on England's leading Arabist, Professor H. A. R. Gibb, who had reviewed my publication about Ibn Khaldun favorably. A long friendship ensued, but he could not place me. Thus, I mainly taught Biblical Hebrew for thirty-eight years, except for the last few years.

From UCL (University College, London), where there was a very friendly attitude towards refugee scholars, I moved to Manchester in 1936. There a professor came to me and told me that he voted against me, as they did not want any foreigners. But, he continued, since you are now one of us, be assured that we give you all the help and support. I was very short of funds, so when I was invited shortly afterwards to the professorial dinner, I was glad it was at a Friday night, when I could refuse, because I did not travel on the Shabbat, otherwise I would have to tell that I could not afford the five shillings for the dinner! I finally got a full-time lecture-ship in Semitic languages and literature at Manchester University; funds raised by the Jewish community helped.

At the outbreak of war my services were refused by the Home Guard, as an "enemy alien," but I was later declared by an Aliens' Tribunal at Chester as a "refugee from Nazi oppression" and allowed to stay on at Kendall, a prohibited area, but was regularly visited by the local police-men, to the great joy of our firstborn, Thomas Gabriel (1935). To give my lectures I needed every week a new pass, until the vice-chancellor of the university arranged for a pass for the entire term. During the Blitz I led a team of firewatchers in the university and was a firewarden in our street. Again through the vice-chancellor, I had the good fortune to be granted British citizenship early in 1940, and thus saved from internment.

As part of my war work I lectured on international affairs, mainly Anglo-German relations, for various groups, especially discussing Nazism in all its aspects, and of course the "Jewish question." Army groups were included in the lectures. I also was active in Jewish adult education. My reserved occupation as a university teacher ended in 1944, and I then did six months active army service. I was then on loan to the Foreign Office and sent to the Middle East to look after German POW's. I was a civilian, equivalent of a lieutenant colonel. To the disappointment of my children (Miriam joined Thomas in 1938), I was not in uniform. My wife Elizabeth, hard-pressed to make ends meet during my army service, earned extra money doing needlework. I also had the help of an industri-alist, to keep up my superannuation payments going.

The Official Secrets act does not permit to disclose much about my service in Egypt, except that I was editing a weekly paper for the POWs and lectured to them in the desert. Early in 1946 I was repatriated, having contracted infective hepatitis. Recovered, I joined the German Section of the Foreign Office, resigned in 1948. Years later I found my name on the Gestapo list, prepared for the Operation Sea Lion, Hitler's plan to attack Great Britain.

The Society for Jewish Studies, founded by Leo Baeck, gave me a six-month grant to get back into academic work, and I was appointed to a lectureship in Hebrew at Cambridge, leading to readership in Oriental Studies in 1959, after being awarded the Litt. D. degree in 1958 for my published work. I developed a wonderful friendship, 1946–1948, with Leo Baeck, under whom I studied Midrash at the University in Berlin. We lived near each other and had many discussions, and I was drawn into the Society for Jewish Studies, where I often lectured to rabbis. His friendship gave me great strength and enrichment, and we met at the Leo Baeck Institute, founded in 1955. I am still on the board, the second-oldest member! For a few years I was a part-time teacher at the Leo Baeck College for Jewish philosophy. I also contributed articles on Judaism and Islam to the *Synagogue Review.*

In 1957, as the Cambridge delegate to the World Congress of Jewish Studies in Jerusalem, Professor Remgstorf from Muenster, Germany, an active promoter of Jewish-Christian understanding, persuaded me to give lectures in Muenster, during which the Semitist asked my permission, to put my name on top of the list of suitable candidates for the chair of Semitics at Berlin, which I did not give. My four lectures were published in Stuttgart. Later I lectured at Frankfurt University. From that time dates my interest and cooperation in the Christian-Jewish dialogue.

Aside from teaching at Cambridge I was a member of the faculty board of Oriental studies until 1974, a founder member of the Society for Near Eastern Studies, and several times its president. I was faculty chairman and chairman of the Commitee of Management of the Middle East Center, from 1962 to 1977, and in that year I was president of the British Association for Jewish Studies. I received a Rockefeller grant to study constitutional theory and law in modern Islam, traveled widely in Asia, the Middle East, and North Africa. My wife assisted me in finding out about the position of women in modern Islam. A book, *Islam in the Modern National State,* resulted. In 1967 I spent a year as visiting professor for Arabic studies at New York's Columbia University, but had to decline the honor of accepting the professorship of Arabic, free after the untimely death of Professor Schacht. Returning home I was able to teach Arabic texts and lecture on Islamic institutions.

From 1948 on for many years, we had "open house" Shabbat afternoon for Jewish students; many of these young people became good friends, writing to us, or visiting us, when in Cambridge. I also celebrated marriages until a few years ago and buried fellow-Jews; the Cambridge congregation had neither rabbi nor chazan.

Faculty and college honored me with a dinner on my seventieth birthday, and on my seventy-fifth birthday I was presented by colleagues and former students with a jubilee volume, now printing, which will contain a full bibliography of my writings over fifty years. A Japanese (and Spanish) translation of an earlier book, *Political Thought in Medieval Islam,* is a closed book to me!

I wish to conclude with mentioning my visit to Heilbronn last year at the invitation of Herr Pfister, mayor for cultural affairs, to take part in the Martin Buber Exhibition. I also lectured on the *Wissenschaft des Judentums* before an audience of 160 persons, and visited the old Jewish cemetery in Worms.

I was moved when visiting the graves of my parents in the nicely kept

Jewish cemetery and when standing in front of our house in the Caecilien-strasse, both familiar, and strange.

Now, a year later, I can look back with more detachment and feel that we must acknowledge the tremendous effort present-day Germany is making to rehabilitate its former Jews and to recognize what the country has lost by Hitler's *Endloesung!*

HANS AND TOBY ROSENTHAL
4937 West Mercer Lane
Glendale, Ariz. 85304

Father: Leo Rosenthal, born 1885. Was in tobacco wholesale business in Heilbronn until 1938. Died 1976 in Philadelphia.

Mother: Frieda Rosenthal, born 1890. Died 1976 in Philadelphia.

Family emigrated to Italy (Genoa) in July 1938, then to Havana, Cuba, in 1939 and to the United States in 1940. My father mainly worked in the knitting industry until retirement in the early 1970's.

I was born in 1924 in Heilbronn, finished my education in Philadelphia, and have been in the commercial-lighting business since 1952. Founded manufacturer's-rep agency in Philadelphia area (Diversified Lighting Association) in 1955 and moved to Phoenix, Arizona, area in 1974, where I am partner in similar agency. Married Toby in 1951, and we have two daughters, Irene (twenty-six) and Marsha (twenty-three).

I have been a member of B'nai B'rith for many years, various syna-gogues, Kiwanis, was president of Philadelphia section of Illuminating Engineer Society of North America in 1968–69, and am currently presi-dent of that organization's Arizona section.

GUSTAV ROTHSCHILD (by Dr. Werner P. Heyd)

Gustav Rothschild appears in my memory for the first time around 1963, when a school friend, Fidel Bok from Rottweil, brother of the former Staatspräsident of Wuerttemberg and brother of the then mayor of Nordstetten, where Rothschild was born, gave me letters from Israel with the request to answer them. Gustav Rothschild steadily asked questions. They were political questions about the present and its development. Inconvenient questions and uncomfortable questions asking the youth of Germany, about the dead Nazis and the new ones, about the old anti-Sem-ites and the new ones. But especially he wanted to know how the people felt—and not the "public opinion" but the thoughts of individuals—about Israel and the relationship between the Germans and the Jews. Finally he was highly interested in finding old acquaintances and friends from

Nordstetten. It still took a few years until I was able to drive with Shmuel Rodenski through three villages in which up to recently Jews had lived, namely Muehringen, Nordstetten, and Rexingen. Gustav Rothschild's reaction was: "I thank you because now I can talk with our Shmuel Rodenski about my Nordstetten." Here I saw clearly the fate of these people. They had evaded a deadly fate in their homeland but would always bear the mark of the Diaspora. They came to the new country but carried the scars of the old.

His children: His son Gustav became a banker in Halle and came via Stuttgart to Frankfurt, where he was connected with the spiritual German movement of Jews. He was active in the Jewish Bund movement and the Lehrhaus and especially in the sport and business associations.

No miracle, then, that the Nazis went after him very early. Warned just in time by friends, he avoided captivity at the last moment by fleeing to Holland where was able to stay for a time but also with a feeling of uncertainty. For that reason he continued his flight to Prague.

He had given up hope of returning home. Prague became for him a waiting period for Palestine, which of course at that time meant anything but security.

He succeeded in emigrating to Palestine and became the manager of a German department store. In Israel he met his wife, who was one of the last ones to escape from the Warsaw Ghetto. To meet her, to talk to her, was more than a present. Within a few weeks of meeting we were talking together like we had known each other for five years. Since I have met Gustav and Lutka Rothschild several times in Israel in the meantime, my life had become indefinitely richer. After the war the German Jews lost their money in Israel and Rothschild was soon pensioned. He played an important part concerning the economic development of the State of Israel.

When he came to Germany to talk to Weil, Bok, and me, he found that also here my people suffered under Hitler's terror and that really not everyone followed him without thinking.

Actually he never again entered the house of his parents. The Nazis had sold it with all its contents as the house of a fugitive. It was proved to him that the house was sold for DM300 and that the costs of the notary and court had used up the last penny. When shortly before his death he tried once more to find people with photos, books, letters, or even a stamp collection, I could not find anything to give him in the entire village of Berthold Auerbach. Freudenstadt, where he spent his vacation and where he felt quite well, became also the place of his death in summer 1975. His heart failed and he now rests in the country of his fathers.

[*Editor's Note:* Werner P. Heyd wrote a book (Bleicher Verlag) called

275

Schwäbische Köpf in which he writes in much more detail not only about Gustav Rothschild but also about Berthold Auerbach and Leopold Marx. Heyd was born in Stuttgart in 1920, studied theology, German, music and art, wrote various books, and is today the head of the feuilleton department of the *Schwarzwälder Boten*.]

INA ROTHSCHILD
800 Cottman Avenue, # A 324
Philadelphia, Pa. 19111

I was not born in Wuerttemberg, but lived twelve years in Esslingen as wife—and housemother—of the director and housefather of the orphanage Wilhelmspflege, Theodor Rothschild.

When we had to close on the first day of World War II, we went to Stuttgart. My husband then directed and taught in the Stuttgart Jewish School until we left in 1942 with Transport XIII from the Killesberg to Theresienstadt.

There we worked from the first day, my husband taking care of the Wuerttembergers. We began with 1,200 people; after four weeks there were about 400 left. My husband died from malnutrition and pneumonia in 1944. I worked—as in Stuttgart—as nurse together with the Stuttgarter sisters Francisca, Else, Erica, and Ruth Rieser. Ruth and I are the only survivors since the others went East with a transport. Ruth is very sick now at eighty-nine and lives in the old-age home on the Kaulbachstrasse in Munich. Together with Recha Schmal, formerly from Laupheim, and Sister Johanna Gottschalk, formerly from the old-age home Sontheim, we were liberated in 1945 and went to Switzerland, where we again worked with liberated, mostly old and sick people from Bergen-Belsen and Theresienstadt. Then we went together to work in the Jewish hospital in Basel. Recha Schmal and I emigrated to the United States in 1946 with the help of Dr. Schmal from Ithaca and Rabbi Dr. Emil Schorsch, a relative of mine. I started to work in Philadelphia's Mount Sinai Hospital, took my State Board examinations, and worked as private-duty nurse until my retirement some years ago. Recha Schmal died in 1977, as did Sister Gottschalk, in Johannesburg, South Africa.

JULIUS H. ROTHSCHILD
15 Shoshone Avenue
Buffalo, N.Y. 14214

I was born in 1902 in Bad Cannstatt as son of the butcher Lehmann Rothschild. I attended the first school years at the Schillerschule, then two years at the Eitel Gymnasium, and continued at the Realschule until we moved to Stuttgart. In 1912 my father took over my grandfather's share of the Loew's Metzgerei, Nadlerstrasse 17. I finished my Einjaehriges at the Friedrich Eugens Realschule. In 1916 I started as apprentice with the firm Tiefenthal & Halle. Later on, still as part of the company, I finished my education at the Technikum in Reutlingen as textile engineer.

As Tiefenthal & Halle acquired the Mechanische Weberei Krueger & Company in Ulm, I became manager there. I also traveled abroad for the company. Later, as the change in politics created more and more difficulties for Jewish companies, I tried to make a living by selling on the road for the oil company of Leopold Ehrlich. But this became more and more difficult, so I decided to emigrate. In 1938 I left Germany. For the year 1932 until my departure I spent a lot of my time helping the remaining Jewish youth.

Always interested in sports, member of the Stuttgart Kickers, the German-Austrian Mountain Club, I joined the Sportsgruppe Schild der Reichsbundes Juedischer Frontsoldaten. Soon I became leader of the Jugendgruppe and later Vereinsvorsitzender. During my presidency the Sportsgruppe Schild became the most outstanding part of the Reichs-organization. With the help of the members of the Sportsschule, Stuttgart became German master in football, handball, and also outstanding in Leichtathletic. I personally was at that time also a member of the Arbeitsgemeinschaft Juedischer Sportvereine. The achievement I am most proud of was the establishing of friendly relations between the two arch-rivals, Hakoah and Schild. As the Nazis took Hakoah's sport field, I offered them our place for training and we started to play against each other. These friendly relations became an example for the whole of Germany. As I left Germany, I was honored by both organizations and I was, at that time, the only possessor of the golden medal of the Schild and the silver medal of Hakoah.

My father was Lehman Rothschild, born in Bad Cannstatt in 1871 and died in 1955 in New York City. He owned the Metzgerei Loew in Stuttgart, Nadlerstr. 17, and worked last as helper at the Metzgerei of Bloch & Falk in New York.

My mother, Dina Rothschild, née Gailinger, was born in 1879 and died in New York City in 1959.

*MARTIN ROTHSCHILD

Lawyer Martin Rothschild was born 1876 in Cannstatt, where he practiced law from 1912 on. After his admission to the bar was revoked in 1938, he was able to work to a limited extent with his colleague Erich

Dessauer, now degraded to a "consultant," as an "assistant consultant" in Stuttgart.

In 1942, he was deported to Theresienstadt. He died of malnutrition in 1943. Dr. Rothschild shared the fate of most elderly people, whose bodies could not withstand the hunger rations.

RAY ROTHSCHILD (formerly Otto Rothschild)
43 Agate Road
East Brunswick, N.J. 08816

Father: Fred (Friedrich) Rothschild, born 1889 in Nordstetten/Wuerttemberg; died 1946 in Toms River, New Jersey. *Mother:* Mary, née Rosendahl, born 1899; died 1970 in New York City.

My father had a wholesale business in edible oils and soaps in Stuttgart. After immigration into the United States our family settled on a ten-acre chicken farm in Toms River, New Jersey, in 1939. My father had to sell the farm due to health reasons in 1946 and passed away shortly thereafter.

For myself: Born 1923 in Stuttgart—attended grade school, gymnasium, and Handelsschule until emigration to United States in 1938. Lived on chicken farm in Toms River, New Jersey, while attending high school. Started college in 1943 at New York University, entered U.S. Army early 1944, served in Europe, discharged in 1946, resumed education, graduated B.S. degree in 1948, major in accounting. Worked as an accountant, then entered business, first operating coin laundry, then dry-cleaning plant, and in 1955 entered chemical business. Currently president, Perk Chemical Company, Inc., in Elizabeth, New Jersey, also president, Perk Realty Corporation, Rothschild Management Group, Inc. In addition to chemical business have considerable interests in residential apartment buildings totaling about 400 apartments. Licensed pilot, own aircraft.

Married to Erica Rothschild, born 1925. She is mother of our two children, Alan and Susan. Alan is active in my real estate business and partner therein, also graduate of Rutgers University. Susan is graduate of Monmouth College and employed in secretarial work.

278

ARTHUR SAENGER

(Information supplied by son A. Tamir, who lives at Kibbutz Hazore'a, Israel.)

Arthur Saenger was born in Laupheim in 1865 and died in Tel Aviv in 1949. He was associated with Saenger & Harburger, Stuttgart. His wife, Rosa Saenger née Gutmann, was born in 1876 in Heilbronn and died in 1966 in Haifa. Both arrived in Palestine in 1939 and were living with their son, Dr. Siegfried Saenger, in Jerusalem and later in Tel Aviv.

EMMA SAENGER (née Stern)

Emma Saenger (1857–1939) was eighty-one years old when she arrived in New York City. She had been a permanent resident at Wilhelmsruhe, the Jewish Senior Citizen's Home in Sontheim, and saw all her worldly possessions destroyed during the Kristallnacht, including her treasured photographs of her oldest son, Julius, a volunteer in World War I, only a few months out of the university, twenty-one years old, and dead after seven months in the Kaiser's Army. Emma Saenger had to endure son fighting son—having one son, Julius, in the German Army, and another, Herbert, in the American Navy. She also had four daughters and, in happier days, saw them in Schubert's *Dreimaedelhaus* at the Heilbronner Stadtherter.

[For further information about her family, see: daughter THEKLA MAY, son-in-law HENRY MAY, grandson JAMES MAY, and granddaughter ELLEN WEITZEN.]

SIEGFRIED SAENGER
Leanstr. 37
Ramat Gan, Israel

My family was rooted in Wuerttemberg for many generations. My father, Arthur, my grand and great-grandparents, lived in Laupheim (grandfather had a garden business, great-grandfather teacher and religious teacher, and on mother's side a rabbi in Mergentheim). It was a tradition that usually the oldest became a rabbi. My mother came from Heilbronn. I was born in 1899 in Stuttgart, a soldier in 1917, studied medicine, and established myself as a podiatrist in Stuttgart in 1925. Was also very active in the Jewish community and a co-founder of the Jewish school. Married

279

since 1924 to Hilde, née Nuernberg, from Antwerp, a doctor of philosophy specializing in psychology, and later, in Israel, worked as a domestic and then as a French teacher. Her grandparents, Bernhard and Clara Edenfeld, living in Stuttgart, were related to Albert Einstein.

Emigrated in 1935 to Israel. At first a taxi driver in Jerusalem, then in Tel Aviv. Stones were thrown at me often during the riots in Arab territory. A colleague in the taxi before me was killed by terrorists. Since 1940, again podiatrist for the workers' health insurance. At times director of a children's hospital in Affule. Replacing as podiatrist in the whole country from Lebanon to Eilat, I was for twenty years the president of the podiatric organization with seminars for doctors, parents, and nurses, and active in social medicine until retirement in 1967. I had many scientific lectures and publications. Member of the board of an Orthodox religious community, I lived in Tel Aviv until 1967 and then in Ramat Gan, still representing other physicians throughout the country, but now only doing scientific work.

My son, Rolf Raphael, born in 1926, is a teacher of mathematics and physics in religious girls' high school and teacher in a Yeshiva, substituting as director. He was gravely wounded in the War of Liberation. He was strictly Orthodox. Together with his wife, Rachel, from Leningrad, active for the Chabbad Chassidim of the Rabbi of Lubavitch. Daughter, Ruth, born in 1929 and lives in a kibbutz since 1948, now living in the Kibbutz Yassur, three children and two grandchildren.

Brother Erne, born in 1912 in Stuttgart, emigrated to Israel in 1934; co-founder and living in the Kibbutz Hazore'a with family and four grandchildren.

MRS. ALFRED SALFIELD (née Schloss)
6946 Northaven Road
Dallas, Texas 75230

My father was Josef Schloss, born 1888 in Laudenbach near Mergentheim; died 1937 in Stuttgart. My stepmother (mother died in 1929) was Bella Schloss, née Strassburger, born 1896 in Baisingen; killed Riga in 1943. My half-sister, Margrit Schloss, was born 1932 in Stuttgart; also killed in Riga in 1943.

I was born Anneliese Schloss, in Stuttgart in 1922, and lived there until my father's death in 1937. I emigrated to England since my number was too high. I spent most of the war in London and Brighton, partly as maid, partly later doing office work in a war factory. In 1944 I immigrated to the United States, where my fiancé was in the U.S. Army.

In 1944 I married Milton Strauss, born 1907 in Oberdorf near

Bopfingen. I joined him in Texas, where he was stationed as a sergeant with the U.S. Army. After the war we settled in Dallas, Texas, and had two sons. Monty is now a mathematics professor at the Texas Tech. in Lubbock, Texas. Larry passed away two years ago at the age of thirty-one. My husband, Milton, died in 1954.

In 1955 I met and married my present husband, Alfred Salfield. We have a twenty-three-year-old daughter Susie. We live in Dallas, Texas, and are semi-retired. Both my husbands were traveling salesmen; therefore, had little time for community activity. But I took that over instead. I have been very active with Hadassah, had every portfolio imaginable, including that of a president, served on our Reform temple sisterhood board, Council of Jewish Women, B'nai B'rith, PTA, etc.

LISA SAMUEL (née Einstein)
47 Rehov Sokolov
Nahariya, Israel

Father and mother, Otto and Jenny Einstein, were born in Helmingen and Hamburg respectively. They left Stuttgart for Central and North America in 1939. Father died in 1959 and mother in 1963.

I was born in 1911 and was a medical student until leaving Germany in 1933 for England, where I switched to nursing (in preparation for going to Palestine).

I married Dr. Benjamin Samuel in 1940 and spent the war years in Wales, where he practiced. In 1949 we left for the United States to visit our family. We stayed twenty-one years in Los Angeles, both working in our professions and raising three children, Judith, Jonathan, and Jacob. We all were very involved in Jewish activities and never gave up the wish to settle in Israel, which, to our great relief and joy, happened in 1970, where we still don't feel too old to contribute at least some service to our country.

LOTHAR S. SANDER
111 Harris Road
Princeton, N.J. 08540

Born 1922 in Stuttgart
Father: Rudolf Sander, born 1880 in Stuttgart and died 1966 in Brookline, Massachusetts.
Mother: Alice, née Epstein, born 1889 in Stuttgart and died 1978 in Moorestown, New Jersey.
After attending the Schieker Schule and Commercial High School in

Stuttgart, I received an apprenticeship in the printing trade. This training was interrupted by the fact that my father was arrested and interned at Dachau in 1938. Our family emigrated to England in 1939. After working on a farm in England, my father and I were interned in 1940 and sent to the Isle of Man. Subsequently, I was sent by the British government to Canada, where our internment continued for two years until my release in 1942. I was able to arrange to further my studies and entered McGill University to study chemistry, graduating with a B.S. in 1945. I worked in Montreal as chemist and emigrated to the United States in 1947, to join the rest of my family in Brookline, Massachusetts. I held various positions as research chemist in Boston and joined the Research Development Laboratories of National Lead Company in Brooklyn, New York, in February 1952.

In 1952, I married Greta Landwehr, a biochemist from Wiesloch, Germany. We have two children: Steve, age twenty-six, journalist and public relations manager, Denver, Colorado. Miriam, age twenty-four, musician and student living in Chapel Hill, North Carolina.

We are now living in Princeton, New Jersey. I am working as a research and development chemist at Amchem Prod. Inc.–Henkel U.S.A., at Ambler, Pennsylvania. Greta is a research associate in the Department of Biochemistry at Princeton University.

I was elected to president of the Philadelphia Society for Coating Technology for the term 1978–79. I am also active in professional societies, ASTM, SSPC, ACS, and member of the National Research Council. My hobbies are tennis, photography, and chamber music (violin).

SIEGFRIED AND ILSE B. SANDER
713 Westchester Park Road
Springfield, Ohio 45504

Born 1907. I married Ilse B. Frankenstein in 1934 and we lived from 1934 until our emigration to the United States in Stuttgart. Our son. Peter Michael, was born 1936 and Cantor Leo Adler and his wife Lotte were his godparents. The Adlers were very close friends to us, and we are still in contact with Mrs. Adler occasionally.

In 1938 we emigrated to the United States. We did try to leave earlier but found no country to leave for. We tried Liechtenstein and Switzerland (where I had excellent connections), Argentina, Spain, England, and Israel. Finally an affidavit from an aunt of mine made it possible to leave for the United States. We arrived in the United States in 1938.

After working only six weeks in New York we were given the chance to leave for Springfield, Ohio. Life in Springfield was entirely different from

New York, and we appreciated the friendliness of the people from the first day. I worked first for a floor-covering store as trainee, learning how to lay linoleum. The foreman, however, recognized the futility of this plan and I was placed as bookkeeper and officer manager earning $12 per week. From this job I "graduated" in 1939 and "dared" to open my own office in accounting. I worked first from my small residence and later, in 1941, rented a small office in a downtown office building. From there the office developed and grew, so that in 1958 I hired a capable young man who was to become my first partner. Due to his "drive" our practice flourished and grew enormously. In 1968 we built our own building and took in another partner, until we were, in 1977, five partners in total. In 1978 I went on partial retirement and gave up my partnership share in favor of the remaining members. When I am in town I am still partially active but only as consultant and public relations man.

Our life in Springfield has been most enjoyable. We are, I think, fully accepted as full citizens. I served seven years as secretary of B'nai B'rith and one year as president. I headed the Springfield UJA Campaign in 1946, was president of our Reform temple for three terms, and in 1968 I headed the United Way Campaign for Springfield and Clark County. I became member of the board of trustees of our local hospital and served as its president and later chairman for three years. I was appointed to the Blue Cross board of Southwest Ohio and served on it for six years. It would become too lengthy a report if I enumerate all the activities during these years. I would like to mention, however, that in 1944 our daughter, Susan Marion, was born. All this story of "success" would have been impossible without the enormous help of my wife.

Ilse B. Sander, née Frankenstein, born 1909. She went early in life to Nuernberg as an apprentice at an exclusive store for ladies' apparel. Ilse worked there until 1931 and moved from there to Hannover, where she worked until we were married in 1934.

After our arrival in Springfield, my wife was my first assistant in my office and worked as such off and on for many years. In addition she had positions as a saleslady in several stores.

Ilse has been active socially. As a member of the Red Cross she works weekly as volunteer in our local hospital. She was a member of many womens' organizations and served on their boards or as president. For the last ten years she has been a member of the board of Mental Retardation and served as its president for the last seven years. She has served as a member of the board of our temple and as president of its sisterhood and received the "Woman of the Year" award from the Pilot Club International as well as many honors from various other organizations.

To complete this report I feel that our children should be mentioned:

283

Peter M. Sander: Born 1936. Graduated from Brandeis University in 1957. Two years at Bennington College, Bennington, Vermont. Army in Korea until 1959. 1960–61 graduate work at Carnegie Tech in Pittsburgh with master's degree. Assistant professor at Brandeis University in Dramatic Department; 1972 until present, assistant professor in Graduate School of Dramatic Arts at Ohio University, Athens, Ohio. Married and has one son, ten years old.

Susan M. Stone (née Sander): Born 1944. Graduated from Ohio State University with a degree in nursing in 1966. R.N. degree in 1966. Worked as public health nurse in Pueblo, Colorado, and later moved to Orlando, Florida. At present she is engaged in teaching nursing at the Florida Hospital and Vocational School. She is married to Dr. Harry Chase Stone, obstetrician and gynecologist. They have four children.

MARTIN SANGER
2 Hunting Pack Court
York, Pa. 17402

I left Germany in 1934. I attended public school and Realschule. I went to work in the metals industry in 1926 in Ulm, and after serving one and one-half years of apprenticeship was sent to Nuremberg for the same company, where I remained until I left for the United States.

I arrived in the United States and after trying to orient myself for about two weeks, on my third day looking for a job, I found employment as a laborer (metal sorter) with a firm in Jersey City, New Jersey. I remained with the same company until 1946. I advanced in the company through various stages, and the last five years of my employment, I was executive vice-president and general manager.

Then I established in partnership a company in Columbia, Pennsylvania. After my company incorporated, two years after its inception, I became president and remained so until my eventual retirement. In 1979 I turned over my share of the business to my son, who is carrying on a partnership with my former associate's family. I started my company with very limited funds, and when I retired, the company was one of the three largest firms in our industry in the United States. I am now retired and spend about half the year in York at my home and the other half at my home in Florida.

I was married in 1941 to Esther Jackins. We have three children and six grandchildren.

In 1937, I brought my sister and family to this country, and in 1939 my mother came to this country and lived with me until her death in 1954.

META SANGER
8662 Delmar Boulevard
St. Louis, Mo. 63124

Sorry, I did not answer your letter of March 18th. But too much came back to my mind, especially of the last year or months in Ulm, of what I thought the years had closed the memory.

My husband, Julius Sanger, and I, Meta Sanger, née Scheuer, were married in 1929. My husband was a partner with his brother Albert and cousin Sally Leiter in the firm of Glaeser Nachfolger in Ulm-Soeflingen.

In 1939 we left with our three-and-one-half-years-old daughter, Hannelore, for England on a transit visa.

In 1940 we arrived in New York. We then settled in St. Louis, Missouri.

My husband eventually established himself again in business, the same as in Ulm, textile and plastic waste material, together with his brother Max, who already was an American citizen.

My husband died 1977. He was born in 1898 in Oberdorf am Ipf. He was the son of Jakob and Mina Sanger, née Neumetzger.

I was born in 1905.

My parents-in-law also emigrated to St. Louis, Missouri, where they died.

My daughter is married and has three children.

SANFORD H. (SANDY) SANGER
P.O. Box 1406
Mountain View, Calif. 94040

Resident of Mountain View, California, since 1968. Wife, Carol Ann Sanger; daughter, Barbara Ann Sanger, born 1956.

I was born in New London, Connecticut, in 1922. I graduated from Barnard School for Boys, Riverdale, New York, in 1940. A.B. political science, Bucknell University, Lewisburg, Pennsylvania, in 1947. U.S. Air Corps 1942–1946. Licensed pilot, received through the Civilian Pilot Training Program in 1941.

Lebanon-Pacific Lodge #136 F & A.M.—South San Francisco, California. Member—Los Altos Golf & Country Club, Los Altos, California. Member—Lt. Col. John Howard Post #558, American Legion, Los Altos, California. Member—Elks Lodge #1471, Palo Alto, California. Member—Irish-Israel-Italian Society of San Francisco, California. Past president—California Taxicab Owners Association, 1971–1972. Past president—Northern California Alumni Association of Bucknell University, 1958–1971. Director—General Alumni Association, Bucknell University, 1969–1974.

Member—The Horseless Carriage Club, the Reo Club of America, the Auburn-Cord-Duesenberg Club. Past director—Sharon Heights Community Association, 1962–1967, Menlo Park, California. Member—California Trucking Association. Member—Film Air Package Carriers Conference (FAPCC) (APECA) Messenger/Courier. Past member—International Taxicab Association. Past chairman—Diversification Committee (ITA). Founder—1957—and president of Diversified Transportation, Inc., formerly known as Cabs Unlimited, Inc., Mountain View, California. Operator of taxicabs in Mountain View, Palo Alto, Los Altos, and Cupertino from 1957 to present. Also, Falcon Parcel Service and Interstate Motor Carrier, covering thirty counties in Northern California and the State of Nevada. Member—Delta Nu Alpha, National Transportation Fraternity. Bilingual—fluent German.

Consultant—Shulman Transport Enterprises, Cherry Hill, New Jersey, from 1972 to 1977. Assisted in establishing SkyCab Program, including communications, advertising, and formation of a Pick-Up and Delivery Network throughout the United States for Priority Air Freight.

President—1971 thru 1975—Air Surface Associates, Inc., affiliate of Pacific Southwest Airlines (1975–1978, vice-president).

Founder—1978—Sanger Consulting, Inc. Engaged in forming a group of agents (franchises) to service every community in the United States for package express and air freight. This was done for Profit by Air, Inc., an air-freight forwarder (1977–1978). Duties included writing a comprehensive questionnaire to potential agents.

1979—June through August, Sanger Consulting, Inc. Consulted on marketing, sales, and establishment of an airline and package service, including the general interfacing with airborne terminals. Previous contractual arrangements (union) and lack of management time commitments thwarted the program.

Candidate—California Assembly—21st District. Polled 30,000 votes, the second highest of any Republican.

Candidate in Santa Clara County. Lost to an eighteen-year politician by two to one margin. 1976 campaign.

Father: Herbert Hugo Sanger. Born 1890 in Detzbach Wuerttemberg; died in 1967. Advertising specialty business: H. H. Sanger, Inc., 510 Fifth Avenue, New York, N.Y.

WILLIAM SANGER
415 Central Park West
New York, N.Y. 10025

Both paternal and maternal sides of my family originally came from Hechingen. My brothers, Marcel Max and Siegfried Rene (Fred), and I were born in Lyons, France. At the outbreak of World War I my father was in New York, where he had a business. He stayed on and became a citizen.

My mother and we three sons, refugees in a sense, went to Stuttgart, where grandparents and most of the rest of the family lived. There we went to school and stayed till my father came in 1920 and took us to the United States, citizens upon arrival. My brother Max, after a few years, returned to Germany and entered the firm Elias Moos, the "family business" founded by our great grandfather. Max eventually returned here because of the situation in Germany.

Fred died in 1977, leaving his wife, Lucie, and two sons and three grandchildren. Max died in 1979 leaving his wife, Ruth, and one son.

WILL SCHABER
106 Pinehurst Avenue
New York, N.Y.

The irresistible persuasiveness of Walter Strauss convinced me, an "outsider," to add a word or two from my own perspective to these moving accounts of so many fellow Württembergers.

As a Heilbronner, I had many early contacts with members of the Jewish community. From my school years I will always remember the ardent reading of passages from Leonhard Frank's *Der Mensch ist gut* by my classmate Arthur Reis, now in Israel. Later, lectures of the great Rabbi Max Beermann at the Volkshochschule left a deep impression. So did my conversations with the banker Abraham Gumbel, a profoundly knowledgeable student of the origins of World War I; with Alex Amberg, a merchant who had joined the small but stimulating circle of the local Friedensgesellschaft; with Hermann Kern, a wonderfully gifted amateur *Rezitator,* and Isy Krämer, the cantor and music critic.

And like thousands of other Heilbronners, I was under the spell of a chain of Jewish actors and musicians who enriched our Stadttheater, among them the unforgettable Philipp Rypinski, conductor of one of the finest *Carmen* performances I ever heard on either side of the Atlantic. In creative and receptive ways, as performers and donors, Jews signally contributed to the breadth and depth of the city's cultural life.

287

They also contributed to the prevailing spirit of interreligious tolerance. I vividly remember a meeting during the twenties—Nazism had reached its first peak—when representatives of all denominations and political affiliations, from the Communists to the Nationalists, joined in forcefully denouncing all forms of anti-Semitism.

When I first visited Heilbronn after the war and the Holocaust, my old colleague Hans Franke, author of a history of the Heilbronn Jews, remarked sadly: "Our cultural life is in ruins. We painfully miss our Jews!"

It must be said, however, that the city as a whole has not forgotten them. There has been a wealth of exhibitions, lectures, and publications reminding the present generation again and again of the Jewish cultural heritage. For many young people this was, and is, a gripping revelation. And in it lies the hope for the future.

MANFRED SCHEUER
Shave Zion
Israel

I was born in Heilbronn in 1893. I was gravely wounded at Verdun and since then have had to wear a prosthesis on my leg. I was elected to the Assembly of the Wuerttemberger Jews and later to the Executive Council of the Jews from Wuerttemberg.

In 1935 people from Rexingen came to me for talks. I had never before heard of Rexingen. There was Freddi Weill, Victor Neckarsulmer, and Mr. Lemberger. They told me they wanted to emigrate, their permits to sell cattle were taken from them. They wanted to go to Palestine. I remarked they could only go as "capitalists," since they were not Zionists; there were long delays for Zionists from the Hechaluz, so it would take even longer for them. The Rexingers said: "No, capitalists is not possible." They had not enough means.

We then arranged a discussion in Stuttgart in 1935 on a Sunday in connection with a talk by Mr. Vischnitzer in the synagogue. It was filled with young people; many wanted to go to Kenya or Costa Rica.

In an anteroom the problem of the Rexingers was discussed. They knew nothing about Zionism. Why did they want to go to Palestine? A Mr. Pressburger stated that they wanted to go back to the land of their fathers, to return to Jerusalem. This changed my attitude—I wanted to be helpful—and we decided to register the Rexingers and get acquainted with them.

The Palestine Office delegated Franz Mayer, from the National Representation of German Jews. The Rexingers tried to make as strong an impression as possible, and although they really were only cattle dealers, they all showed up in dirty high boots like real farmers. Franz Mayer was so impressed by the appearance of Jewish farmers in Germany that he supported their request for a certificate, which was granted as an exception, for all Rexingers.

Later I visited settlements in Palestine with Pressburger, Weill, and Neckarsulmer. Although the Rexingers were impressed by the big settlements in the south with plenty of cattle, due to the big credits such settlement would have required they finally arranged a settlement through the RASSCO on land belonging to the Keren Kayemet le-Israel, near Nahariya. They received sixteen capitalist certificates; the balance were worker's certificates.

What form should the future collective take? Evidently there were only two choices. Either a kibbutz with no private property and everything administered for the community, or to leave everything in private possession, the economy as well as the family life. However, the Rexingers, despite the resistance of the "experienced" people, desired a new arrangement: land, cattle, vegetables, in short the economy, should be administered as a unit by all, while at the same time each settler should have his own home and property, so that his individual life would be preserved. Practically: the money goes into one pot, but each has his own home. Thus was born the new construction of *moshav shitufi*. Whether Shave Zion— meaning "Returnees to Zion"—really were the first ones to create such a type of settlement is open to debate since the settlement Moledet claims to be the first.

Later new people were accepted, but basically there was not much change in the structure of the village. The "Swabian folk character," as it was later called in many books and magazines, has been preserved.

I myself became the president of the association as well as the president of the Rexinger community before I retired a few years ago.

RUTH HEUMANN SCHIFF
RR 2
48 Street, Box 27
Decatur, Mich. 49045

My parents were Isaac and Blanda Heumann of Braunsbach. They had a retail yard-good business. My father was gone all week and came home on Friday afternoon for Shabbat. Sundays were spent packing the goods my father had sold during the week. My mother came from Buchau, the daughter of Salomon and Cilly Einstein.

I grew up in Braunsbach, went to the regular village school and the local cheder. Our synagogue was in Braunsbach, and the interior was destroyed in the Kristallnacht. Life in Braunsbach had become bitter for the Jews, and every business had a sign, "Juden unerwuenscht" (Jews Not Wanted). In 1941 my parents were deported to Riga and were declared deceased in 1942.

I came to this country in 1939 and lived at first with my sponsors (my father's cousins) in Bristol, Virginia. I went to high school there, and later on took up nursing. In 1943 I got married. By the way, my husband's maternal grandmother had come from Nagelsberg near Kuenzelsau. My husband studied agriculture.

We are farmers and had, until recently, a good herd of Holsteins for which I was the herdsperson. My husband built all the barns and buildings on our farm himself. Now, as it has become too hard for us to continue working with cattle, we have lent our farm to a very nice young dairy couple.

My husband bought several houses, fixed them up, and they are rented. As we have always been very active, it would be difficult to stop working altogether, so I often act as rental agent.

While we did not exactly become millionaires, we have had a good life and are quite satisfied.

HUGO SCHLESSINGER
9400 Olympic Boulevard
Beverly Hills, Calif. 90212

Born in Oehringen in 1891, the former owner of a department store, left Germany after the Nazi takeover, and came to the United States in 1939.

He was active in Los Angeles in many charitable organizations, and including the United Jewish Welfare Fund, Hilda Simons Scholarship Fund, Westside Jewish Community Center, Senior Adult Friendship Club, Center Chorus.

He was honored for his activities by the mayor of Los Angeles with the Mayor's Senior Citizen Award, and by the United Crusade with the "Silver Bowl."

JULIUS SCHLESSINGER

Julius was born in Heilbronn. He moved to Stuttgart as a young man and became a partner in a spirits distillery. He married Martha Flegenheimer in 1913.

They moved to Chicago in 1938, where Julius became a liquor salesman. He died in Chicago in 1952, and Martha moved to New York to live with her daughter and family. Martha died in New York in 1979. They had two children.

Erwin learned the grain business in Stuttgart, then moved to Chicago in 1934 and entered the meat-packing business. After World War II, he started his own company. He was married and had two daughters. He died in Milwaukee in 1973.

Ann married Kurt Wechsler, originally from Berlin, who was a stockbroker. They made their home in New York and had two sons. Both are married. Ann lives in Manhattan.

GEORGE AND KATHERINE SCHLOSS
2220 Avenue of the Stars
Los Angeles, Calif. 90067

I was born in Heilbronn in 1898. After attending Business College I started in the family business of L & I Schloss A.G. in Heilbronn, in 1915, where I remained until I was forced to leave in 1938. I married in 1924 Kaethe Schloss, née Kahn, born in Heilbronn in 1902. Her parents were Sigmund and Anna. We have two sons: Ludwig (Lou), born 1925, and Kurt, born 1929, both in Heilbronn.

Fortunately, after leaving business, house, and all we owned, we could leave Heilbronn together in 1938 and arrived in Los Angeles, California in 1938. We started our business, California Yarn Company, where I am still active today with my son Lou. He married Muriel Levett. They have two children: Peter G. Schloss, born 1951, married, one daughter; and Karen G. Schloss, born 1956, married. Kurt R. Schloss, married Stina Falkborn and have two sons: Mark R. Schloss, born 1965, and Steven G. Schloss, born 1966.

HILDE SCHLOSS
c/o Maja Silberberg
12749 McCormick Street
North Hollywood, Calif. 91607

Dear Walter Strauss:

Do you still remember your father's good old friends, Max and Hilde Schloss? If so, you probably will be surprised to hear from the ninety-six-year-old Hilde Schloss.

I often think of the nice days in Stuttgart, where we played cards with your father and had no inkling that the future had the horrible Hitler time in store for us.

You, as well as we, belong to the lucky people who found a new home and life in America.

Your questionnaire, sent to Maja, brought back many memories. In Maja, I have a loving daughter-in-law, and all week I am looking forward to Sunday, which we always spend together. I am having some difficulties in writing due to very bad eyesight.

So I say goodbye for now, and remembering the good old days of the past, I am sending you my heartfelt greetings.

CHASKEL SCHLUSSELBERG
by his daughter, Eleanor

My father was born in Poland in 1901. In 1919 he went to Stuttgart to work and seek his fortune. He was married in Germany to a woman set up by a matchmaker and had two children: a son, Henrik, and a daughter, Chana. As anti-Semitism grew worse, he had the foresight to send his son to England, to be taken in by a family until Germany was safe again. That was in about 1938. His wife and daughter, who did not go to England, perished in a concentration camp. He himself worked stoking the coal-burning oven in an industrial camp until 1942 or 1943, when he was taken to Auschwitz. There he did whatever jobs were necessary, including being a barber and working in the nearby I. J. Farben factory. In 1945 he was liberated by the Russians and went back to Stuttgart. Besides putting flesh back on his bones, he once again took up selling all kinds of merchandise. I am told he attained an amount of respect and esteem from the community there. He was the honorary religious leader of Israelitishe Kultusve reinigung. While in Germany, he reacquainted himself with a distant cousin, Ruth Hoff, whom he later married in the United States. In 1950 he went to England to take his son to America, where Ruth Hoff was already living. The son, since he had left Germany, had gotten used to life in England and to the family that raised him, so that when my father came to get him, he preferred to remain in England. He thereafter changed his name to Harry Wrightson after the name of the family which cared for him, although he was not officially adopted. He lives in Cambridge to this very day with his wife, Joyce, his son, Julian, and his daughter, Joanna. In the meantime, Chaskel went alone to America, where he married Ruth Hoff and settled in Brooklyn. He immediately got a job dying bristles in a paintbrush factory and worked there until he had a stroke in 1970. In 1953 he had a daughter, Eleanor Schlusselberg (me!), who still lives in New York and is an actress under the name of Eleanor Reissa (after Chaskel's mother). He lived from 1970 to 1976 in a nursing home where he remained the cheerful, strong survivor until his death.

I can be contacted at: Eleanor Reissa Schlusselberg, 457 West 57th Street, New York, N.Y. 10019

Chaskel's son can be reached in England: Harry Wrightson, 14 Almond Grove, Bar Hill, Cambridge, England CB3 8DU.

*JULIUS SCHMAL

Attorney Julius Schmal, born in Nordstetten, District Horb, in 1871. Served as an attorney in Ludwigsburg since 1898. He died in the early days of Nazi persecution in 1935.

His widow, Bella Schmal, was to endure every degree of infamy and persecution. The final indignities she was forced to suffer were her expulsion to Baisingen in 1941 and her deportation to Theresienstadt in 1942 at the age of sixty-five. She was one of the few survivors and, after her liberation, took up residence in Switzerland.

RECHA SCHMAL
See the article on Simon and Grete Schmal.

*ROBERT SCHMAL

Attorney Dr. Robert Schmal, born in Stuttgart in 1886, hailed from a family of jurists. He was admitted in Stuttgart in 1912. Maligned by the Nazi press as early as 1933, he left for Switzerland in 1937 and proceeded to the United States in 1940 or 1941. He died there in 1948.

SIMON AND GRETE SCHMAL
by Stephen M. Schmal
7317 Summit Avenue
Chevy Chase, Md. 20815

My father, Simon Schmal, was born in Laupheim in 1898. He attended the Jüdische Volksschule and the Latein-und Realschule in Laupheim, but attended Gymnasium in Ulm. He studied medicine at Tübingen and Munich, and did his residency in Berlin. After completing his studies and residency, he established a pediatrics practice in Stuttgart–Bad Cannstadt.

My mother, Grete née Schmidt, was born in Stuttgart in 1906. After her high school education, she worked as a doctor's receptionist. She and my father met in 1935, and married in 1936. My father was interned by the Nazis in Dachau in late 1938; he was released because of his father's death, and he and my mother left Germany in the last week of December of that year.

Arriving in the United States, they lived in Kew Gardens while my father studied for the state medical boards. During this period, my mother learned and began practicing electrolysis. After my father passed the state boards and received his license as a general practitioner, he and my mother visited some thirty cities, towns, and villages throughout New York to decide where they wanted to live and work. They selected Ithaca, where they remained until their respective deaths. My mother died in 1975 after a long illness. My father, who practiced medicine until 1978—fifty-one years after he had started in Germany—died in 1979.

My aunt, Recha Schmal, needs to be mentioned in this history, too, because she was an integral part of our family and household for thirty-one years. She was born in Laupheim in 1900. She attended the Jüdische Realschule, the Latein- und Realschule, and the Institut der Englischen Fraülein, all in Laupheim. After spending the six years thereafter attending to the family and household, due to my grandmother's illness, Recha started her professional training in the nursing school in Freiburg. She then worked in Berlin for three years before moving to Stuttgart. In Stuttgart, she worked in the women's clinic and as a private-duty nurse before working as my father's nurse and receptionist for six years. After that, she went to Frankfurt, where she worked first in the hospital of the Jewish community and then as a private-duty nurse. In early 1942, she and my grandmother went to an old-age home in Eschenau, Recha serving as the nurse. Later that year, both were deported to Theresienstadt.

Recha survived—my grandmother died in Theresienstadt—and after spending a year in a relocation center in Switzerland she came to the United States in the summer of 1946, joining us in Ithaca. She attended school to enable her to become licensed, and after receiving her license in 1948, she worked for seventeen years as a registered nurse at Tompkins County Hospital. She retired when my mother, due to her illness, was no longer able to attend to the household. Recha took care of the house but, more important, was a companion to my father and really a surrogate mother to my brother and me until her death. Recha died in 1977.

As for me and my brother, we were both born in Ithaca, I in 1941 and Ron in 1944. We both attended Cornell University after high school, and we both moved to Washington after getting our bachelor's degrees. I received an M.A. in government from American University, Ron an M.A. and Ph.D. in psychology from George Washington University.

I married quite recently, in September of last year, to Debra Villani. Incidentally, we honeymooned in Europe and visited both Laupheim and Stuttgart. I work as a labor relations/employee relations supervisor for the U.S. General Accounting Office after having done the same type of work for the National Labor Relations Board.

Ron, who lives in Fairfax, Virginia, married Marilyn Strauss in 1970. Ron and Lynn have one child, Jesse, who's five and one-half, and they're expecting a second child in July 1982. Ron works as a clinical psychologist in a community clinic in Warrenton, Virginia, and he does some private work also. Lynn works as an art therapist in Arlington.

Debbie, whom I met at GAO when I transferred from the NLRB in 1978, currently works for the National Motor Freight Traffic Association.

I hope that I've provided the information you wanted.

ERICH SCHMIDT
Son: Dr. Thomas S. Smith
51 Old County Road
Bingham, Mass. 02043

The son of Julius Schmidt, textile manufacturer in Stuttgart. Studied chemistry with Professor Willstaedter in Munich, worked one year at the Kaiser Wilhelm Institute in Munich. Afterwards worked in the family factory in Stuttgart. Came to the United States in 1939 as a research chemist until he died in 1965.

He had married Lotte Moos (from Ulm) in 1942. His son, Thomas J. Smith, is on the staff of the Tufts–New England Medical Center as the chief of surgical oncology.

BERTHA SCHNURNBERGER-LOEWENTHAL
18700 Walkers Choice Road
Gaithersburg, Md. 20760

My parents, Salomon and Julie Loewenthal, were born in Buttenhausen, both in 1879. They lived there until deported to Theresienstadt, where they died in 1942.

My father was dealing in horses, together with my uncle Hermann Loewenthal, who was living in New York.

My brothers, Hugo and Karl, also perished. Hugo, born in 1905 was married to Gerda, née Kanter, born in 1909. Their child, Inge, was born in 1935. Karl was born in 1906. Both my brothers were working in my father's business.

My grandmother, Lotte Loewenthal, was also deported, but I do not know any details.

MAX SCHORSCH
47-48 196th Place
Flushing, N.Y. 11358

Parents: Eugen Schorsch, born 1866. Lived in Schwaeb. Hall until 1938. Died in 1944 in Mar del Plata, Argentina, where he lived with my sister

295

Irma, who is still living there. In Schwaeb. Hall, partner in the wholesale business of Flegenheimer & Schorsch. Regina, née Scheuer, born 1876 in Heilbronn/N. Died in 1931 in Schwaeb. Hall.

I was born 1905 in Schwaeb. Hall. I worked in Heilbronn and Frankfurt in banking business. From 1924 until 1938 with Flegenheimer & Schorsch. After Crystal Nacht, Dachau, Switzerland, Cuba, 1942–45 U.S. Army. Worked in chemical business in New York and retired in 1978. Presently living in Flushing.

I am married to Ruth, née Goldschmitt, born in 1920. Children: Madeline, Michael, Deborah, and Ellen, from twenty-two to thirty-one years old. I am a member of Temple Beth Sholom, Flushing.

ILSE SCHOTTLANDER (née Braunschweig)
8038 Zurich
Rainstr. 78
Switzerland

Louis Schottlander from Heilbronn, born 1885, left Germany in 1910. He lived in Zurich, Switzerland, where he married, but went back to Konstanz, Germany, in 1914 to fulfill his duty as a soldier during World War I. He returned to Switzerland in 1918 and since then lived in Kreuzlingen, Switzerland, with his family. He was naturalized in 1933 (when he did not want any more to belong to the Germans).

An interesting detail may be that he made his apprenticeship (about 1901–4) in the house of Julius Sanger, the grandparents of James May.

Wishing you much success.

*WILHELM SCHWABACHER

Dr. Wilhelm Schwabacher, born 1887 in Stuttgart, served the judiciary of Wüerttemberg since 1914, first as district attorney and district court judge. In 1933 he was Landgerichtsrat in Stuttgart. His grandfather, Wolf Schwabacher, was royal court musician in Wuerttemberg; his grandfather on his mother's side, was a superior court advocate. In accordance with the Law for the Preservation of the Civil Service, Dr. Schwabacher was retired in 1933. In the beginning of 1939, deprived of his maintenance payments, he emigrated to Switzerland. From March 1939 on he was able to have a small law practice, and in 1941 he was employed by the Office of the District Attorney of the Canton of Basel. From 1950 on he was acting district attorney.

The very musical Dr. Schwabacher had many friends in Stuttgart, which made it especially difficult for him to leave. After he was dismissed as a judge, he wrote to a colleague: "My local patriotism and love for Stuttgart, which, like so much else is deeply ingrained in me and cannot easily be uprooted, have been severely put to the test!" Dr. Schwabacher, who during the last years of his life was very ill, did live to experience his promotion to Landgerichtsdirektor, in the course of restitution proceedings, in 1950. He died in 1952 in Basel.

CHARLOTTE SCHWABE (née Heilbronner)
as reported by her son, William
3234 Bridlepath Lane
Dresher, Pa. 19025

My mother, Mrs. Charlotte Schwabe, has asked me to respond to your letter of May 1980.

My mother was born in 1899 in Stuttgart. Her maiden name was Heilbronner. She married my father, Karl Schwabe, who owned one of the larger department stores.

My mother had a brother, Dr. Edgar Heilbronner, an orthopedic physician, who emigrated to Israel and founded the Alyn Hospital for Crippled Children in Jerusalem.

My mother's sister, Rosel, married Georg Meyer. She perished in Theresienstadt. Particulars about her may be obtained from Hilde Gutmann, Rua Frad Countinho 554, Apt. 22, Pinheiros, São Paulo, Brazil 05416.

At age eighty-one, my mother is retired. In former times she was active in teaching piano. My father was a piano tuner and repairman, in business for himself and, incidentally, enjoying his independence. He did not at all mind the transformation from a prosperous proprietor of a business to a blue-collar occupation.

My parents had two children, myself and my sister, Eva S. Porreca. I am on the administrative staff of a very large teaching hospital and specialize in human-resource administration. Born in 1923, I am married and we have one child, a boy age seventeen.

My sister, Eva, is widowed and is an art therapist. She was born in 1932 and has two children; a boy, age twelve, and a girl, age fourteen.

FRED AND HILDE SCHWARTZ
4750 NW 22 Court
Vanderhill, Fla. 33313

My name is Hilde Schwartz, née Gideon. I am the daughter of Moritz and Sofie Gideon, née Zuerndorfer. I married Fred Schwartz and we have one son. We retired three years ago. Our son graduated from Harpur College in Binghamton and is now a junior executive for a theatrical literary agency in New York City.

ANNIE SCHWARZ (née Oppenheimer)
140 Ocean Parkway
Brooklyn, N.Y. 11218

My husband's parents: his father was born in Mühringen/Horb, Wuerttemberg, and his mother in Edesheim/Pfalz

Eugene Schwarz was born in 1897 in Mühringen. He attended school there and the Gymnasium in Horb. He had a brother, Leo, who lost his life in World War I.

After his schooling he learned the textile business with Philipp Haas Company, Stuttgart, Alexanderstrasse, bed and table linen and cotton. Later he represented South Germany for the firm S. Fraenkel. In New York he represented several textile houses and did business for them in this city.

I, Annie Schwarz, née Oppenheimer, was born 1906 in Bad Cannstatt. Daughter of Emmy Oppenheimer (née Steiner) and Karl Oppenheimer. They were deported to Theresienstadt. There they lost their lives.

I had one sister, Dr. Alice Oppenheimer, who emigrated to Holland. From there she came to Theresienstadt with her husband and son, and they all lost their lives.

After I finished Ober-Realschool in Cannstatt, I went to the Villa Berg Sanglingsheim/Berg and became a licensed baby nurse.

In 1927 we got married in Stuttgart. We have one son, Edward Werner Schwarz. At the time we left Germany he was nine years old. We went to live at 140 Ocean Parkway, Brooklyn, New York. Our son was drafted and was in the Korean War from 1951 until 1953.

I myself passed an examination to be a masseuse, as I was bound to my home and could work only part-time. My private interests are reading and art. For years I have been a member of United HIAS.

*WILLY SCHWARZ

Attorney Dr. Willy Schwarz, born in Stuttgart in 1898, was admitted there in 1924, and pursued his vocation until 1938. After losing his admission in 1938, he left for Argentina in 1939. Abroad he worked initially in a publishing house and since 1945 as a partner in a commercial enterprise.

298

G. SCHWARZENBERGER
4 Bowers Way
Harpenden, Herts. AL5 4EW
England

Professor Schwarzenberger is director of the London Institute of World Affairs.

Just received your letter of 24 August. I am just leaving on a prolonged international outing. Therefore I suggest that you go ahead with the printing, as after my return I would not have the time to respond to your kind invitation.

All the best.

From the Marx lawyers booklet:

Dr. Georg Schwarzenberger, born in Heilbronn in 1908. In 1930 he passed the first examination *summa cum laude*. In 1933 he was denied the opportunity to take his second examination and was dismissed from his legal internship, although by that time he had already made a name for himself among legal scholars with several publications. As a member of the SPD (Socialist Party of Germany), through his activities in the Socialist Student Union and his appearances in political assemblies he had brought upon himself the hatred of the National Socialists. Consequently he was denounced even by his own colleagues. In 1934 he emigrated to Great Britain with his wife, the legal assistant (Referendar) Dr. Susanna Schwarzenberger. From 1934 to 1940 he served as a secretary at the New Commonwealth Institute in London. Simultaneously in 1938 he launched his academic career, in which he advanced, as early as 1949, to being appointed associate dean of the Law Faculty of the University College in London.

*ALFRED J. SCHWEIZER

Attorney Dr. Alfred J. Schweizer, born in Stuttgart in 1875, was admitted in 1901 and resigned in 1938. During the wave of arrests on November 9 and 10, 1938, he was seized and incarcerated in the police prison of Welzheim. In 1939 he left for England and proceeded to the United States in 1940.

He was married to Elsa, sister of Irma Mayer and Marta Hirsch. He and his wife had no children, but they were assisting war orphans, enabling them to study or to finish their studies. Most of their help was done anonymously.

Only after the war was he able to resume the practice of law to a limited extent by representing clients in matters of restitution. He died in 1955.

WALTER SELZ
Beer Tuviyah
Israel

Our parents, Ferdinand Selz, born 1877, and Mina, née Stein, 1870, started a department store in Weikersheim in 1902, which they had until 1933. After the pogrom in 1933, we were forced to sell the business. My parents emigrated to the United States, where my brother, Arthur, has lived since 1928. Our parents helped relatives and friends to escape from Nazi Germany to build a new life in the United States. They died in 1945 and 1950 respectively.

My sister Meta Mann born in 1903, emigrated to the United States in 1935 with her husband, Carl, and her daughter. They live in Miami Beach. My sister Senta Mayer came to the United States in 1935 and now also lives in Miami Beach.

I, Walter Selz, born in 1907, active in the Zionist Youth Movement JJWB, left Germany in 1934. I married Lotte Wachtel, born in 1905, a physician, and settled in Beer Tuviyah, at that time the southernmost location. We have three married children and seven grandchildren. Our village, Moshav Ovdin, celebrated its fiftieth anniversary.

RENÉ AND HANNE SERKEY (SZOEKE)
118-40 Metropolitan Avenue
Kew Gardens, N.Y. 11415

My family name in Germany was Szoeke. I was born in 1909. I emigrated to the United States in 1937. In Germany I worked in the ladies' apparel industry, and I was employed in the same field in New York until my retirement in 1976.

Hanne's parents were Siegfried and Fanny Mann, née Kohn. Mr. Mann was born in Ulm in 1877 and died in Kew Gardens in 1973. Mrs. Mann was born in Ulm in 1885, and died in Kew Gardens in 1973. Mr. Mann was a lawyer in Ulm. He was a delegate to the Chamber of Attorneys of Wuerttemberg in Stuttgart. He was arrested and mistreated on the night of November 9, 1938. Mr. and Mrs. Mann left Germany in 1939 and after a year's stay in England with their son and daughter-in-law came to the United States in 1940. Mr. Mann was then retired.

Hanne was born in Ulm in 1914. She graduated from the Maedcheno-berrealschule in Ulm and had planned to attend the Hochschule fuer

300

Leibesuebungen in Berlin with the object of becoming a gymnastics teacher. This, however, was no more possible. Hanne arrived in New York from Germany in 1938 and we were married in the same month in New York. Hanne has been working in physical therapy since she came here, and she is also employed as a companion in the Margaret Tietz Center in Queens.

We have two sons, both married. Robert is a mathematics teacher at Richmond Hill High School in Queens, New York; Richard is an attorney in Plymouth, Massachusetts.

We are members of Temple Isaiah in Forest Hills, Queens, New York.

ELSE AND OTTO SEYFERT
Konstanz-Bodensee
Ruppanerstr. 13
Switzerland

We are now already in our fifth year here and feel very happy. We are still busy with our music. My husband plays various concerts with Rothenberger and I am working with quite a few interesting singers, mostly from Switzerland.

With kindest regards.

HARRY SHELTON
668 Riverside Drive
New York, N.Y. 10031

Father: Sally Schleimer. Was owner of a Wohlwert store in Cannstatt. Harry emigrated to the United States in 1939. Parents left in 1940 with brother Alfred to Shanghai. In 1947 went from there to New York. Mother was working as a supervisor for the Westbury Hotel, New York. Brother Alfred went to San Francisco and became a baker. He married and has two children. Harry Shelton is a successful manufacturer of ladies loungewear.

[Given by telephone.]

FELIX SHINNAR (formerly Schneebalg)
I. E. Shinnar
Ramat Gan
Tel Danin
Israel

Educated at the Dillmann-Gymnasium. He was a representative of the Israeli government in connection with the restitution agreements with

Germany. He wrote a book, *Bericht Eines Beauftracten*, about these facts. We wrote him for this study but did not hear from him. Meanwhile, we heard unfortunately that he is very sick.

AENNE SHOMBERG (née Kaufman)
137-47 45th Avenue
Flushing, N.Y. 11355

My husband, Dr. Ernest Shomberg (having changed his name here from Schaumberger), was a dermatologist in Stuttgart from 1920 to 1939. He then left for the United States. After his exam he worked as a general practitioner until he retired in 1970. He was born in 1890 and died in 1972.

I was born in 1891. My maiden name was Aenne Kaufman.

My son, Gert (changed here to Gerald), was born in 1922 in Stuttgart. In January 1939 he went to England with a children's transport and joined us in New York City in November 1939. He served in the U.S. Army during World War II.

My daughter, Liese, was born in 1926, also in Stuttgart. Both children are now married and have their own families.

When we arrived in New York City we rented an apartment and took in roomers and this way earned some money. My husband could study, my children could attend school, and a modest life was possible.

In Germany we belonged to the synagogue in the Hospitalstrasse. We belonged to B'nai B'rith in Germany and also here (Leo Baeck). I also belong to the Thursday Club of Habonim and work as a volunteer in the Margaret Tietz Nursing Home.

MARIANNE SHOTLAND (née Hess Blumenthal)
418 E. Indian Spring Drive
Silver Spring, Md. 20901

I was born in Stuttgart, Germany, as the daughter of Ludwig Hess and Louise, née Levi, in 1920.

My father had become a junior partner of the firm Leopold Levi, Merchanische Kleiderfabrik, shortly before World War I. Returning to civilian life, he married the daughter of his senior partner, my mother. He died one year later, as a consequence of an illness he contracted as a soldier in World War I.

As a young child, I grew up in the house of my beloved grandparents, Leopold and Minna Levi, whose house not only remained a focal point for their immediate family, but for a larger extended family throughout Germany, and many other Stuttgart Jews. My mother remarried in 1923,

302

and my stepfather, Hugo Blumenthal, joined the firm of Leopold Levi, and became a happy adopted Stuttgarter, winning many friends through his amiable nature.

Despite the fact that our family belonged to the Central Verein and the R.J.F., they fortunately never lost the sense of Jewish priority, so that the coming to power of the Nazi regime did not in any way damage our self-image. Due to my father's war record, I was permitted to attend the Maedchen Gymnasium until 1937, from where I transferred to the Israelitische Lehrerbildungsanstalt in Wuerzburg, which I attended almost up to the time when the Nazis closed this institution. It had been attended previously by my maternal great-grandfather, my paternal grandfather, my father's brother, and my, at that time, future father-in-law; among many spiritual leaders of German Judaism.

By the end of 1938, we actively worked on our emigration to America. This preparation was interrupted by the arrest of our Papa Hugo and his incarceration in Dachau, following the Kristallnacht. My brother, Werner, had witnessed the burning of the Stuttgart Synagogue. If nothing else, this brought home to us that civilization had taken a leave of absence and it was time to go. Unfortunately not all the members of our family were able to do so.

Our parents, Werner, and I arrived in New York in 1939, and we all had a very positive approach which helped us to feel at home. We also were happy to be reunited with many relatives and friends who had come before—and some, though not enough, who came afterwards.

We took any available work; my parents worked in a clothing factory, I worked as nursemaid and governess, my brother worked after school and on Saturdays, until we found some kind of foothold. At the same time, we, as well as my aunt, Martha Eppstein, and her husband, did all in our power to get the rest of the family out of Germany.

Our grandparents left literally *mit dem letzten Zug*, and in 1941, started a two-year Odyssey which led to our reunion in 1943. By that time, my brother, Werner, was in the U.S. Army, and I, after attending business college, worked as an export statistician in a large New York office, a job I kept until my marriage in 1946.

My husband, Dr. Edwin Shotland, taught at the Jewish School in Stuttgart. He left for the United States in 1937 and struggled to get back to his own field of mathematics and physics.

After a four-year stint in the United States Army, which he spent in Africa, Sicily, Italy, Greece, Rumania, Bulgaria, and Yugoslavia, he was able to establish himself and can now look back with satisfaction on a career as an applied physicist and on his work in guided missiles, satellites, and the field of communications.

After our marriage, we lived in Bridgeport, Connecticut; Dallas, Texas (where we met up with several other ex-Stuttgarters); and for the past almost thirty years in Silver Spring, Maryland, near Washington, D.C.

We have two sons. Larry lives in Houston, Texas. Mike lives in Colorado, is in the construction business, and has a wife and two young daughters. After our children left home, I began working as a real estate agent.

We have remained in touch with many of our old friends but also have made new ones from different backgrounds. We speak English at home, are involved in U.S. politics, belong to an American conservative congregation and to all kinds of organizations—but we still carry a piece of Wuerttemberg within us. My mother passed away in 1980.

HILDE SIEGEL (formerly Hilde Fleischer Maxwell)
10 Wildwood Drive
Eastchester, N.Y. 10707

My family came from Goeppingen; my grandmother, Mathilde Gutmann, born in 1871, married Max Steiner, died in New York in 1957. Her two children were Clara, born in 1893, and Albert, born in 1896.

Clara married Kuno Fleischer, born in 1880, also in Goeppingen; he was the owner of a paper mill in Eislingen, emigrated to the United States after seven months in England in 1939, worked in paper mills in Orange and Holyoke, retired to New York in 1950, died in 1951. Their two children were Kurt Fleischer Maxwell; born in Stuttgart in 1914, he emigrated to the United States in 1933, worked as an office manager, entered the U.S. Army in World War II, and was killed in action in 1944. I was born in Goeppingen in 1919, emigrated to the United States in 1938, became a registered nurse, worked in the Public Health Nursing Administration. In 1953 I married Hans Oppenheimer, born in 1915 in Stuttgart, and emigrated to the United States via England in 1940; he was a research biochemist with a Ph.D. from the Unviersity of Chicago, and died in New York in 1972. I remarried in 1978 to George Siegel, a lawyer in New York City, born in 1910. I have two children from my first marriage: Joan Oppenheimer, born in 1954, a hydrologist in Tucson, Arizona, married to Horton Newsom, born in 1952. My son is John Oppenheimer, born in 1955 in New York City. My mother, Clara, passed away in 1981.

Her brother, Albert, became a lawyer in Goeppingen, married Martha Eppstein. They were also able to emigrate to the United States, and the family settled in San Francisco, where Albert did office work, died in 1955. They have two sons and three grandchildren.

304

MAJA S. SILBERBERG (née Harburger)
12749 McCormick Street
North Hollywood, Calif. 91607

Thank you for taking the time and interest to record our history, which must never be forgotten. Some of us have undertaken by ourselves to the task to preserve it for family members. Your publication, however, will reach so much further and give a more complete picture of "Our Times."

This is the history of the families Harburger and Schloss. My life is full and busy, since I am still active in my profession.

My father, Rudolf David Harburger, was born in Stuttgart in 1875 and died in Los Angeles, California, in 1954. His business had been Vereinigte Bekleidungswerke Heyman & Schwartz, G.S. Harburger, Adlerstrasse, Stuttgart.

My mother, Leonie Harburger, née Berolzheimer, was born in Stuttgart in 1885 and died in Riga during the 1939 holocaust.

I was born in Stuttgart in 1912. My profession, Heilgymnastin, diploma from Alice Bloch Institute in 1934. At present I am still working as registered physical therapist in Los Angeles. My husband, Kurt S. Schloss (changed his name to Kent S. Sloss in 1943), was born in Stuttgart in 1908 and died in 1956 in Los Angeles. His business in Germany had been import and export of raw materials for the manufacturing of brushes. In the States he was a public accountant.

Our son, Rodney Franklin Sloss, better known as Roddy, was born in Los Angeles in 1943. He is a certified public accountant, a graduate of the University of California, Berkeley, and now director of the controls, evaluation, and audit department of a nationwide firm with the home office in Los Angeles.

In 1962 I married Alfred Silberberg, born in 1909. He died in 1965. He had a daughter, Susan Rose Silberberg Peirce, born 1949.

This is the information about my brothers and sisters:

Elsbeth Harburger: Born in Stuttgart, 1910. Married Manfred Kohl. They are living in Los Angeles and have two daughters and four grandchildren.

Hans (John) Harber (Harburger): Born in Stuttgart in 1911, and died in Los Angeles in 1968. He emigrated in 1935 to Nairobi, East Africa, and fought with the English Army in Africa during World War II.

His Widow, Sara Harber, née Ellenhorn: One son, Kent David Harber, one stepdaughter, Debby.

Margot Harburger: Born in Stuttgart, 1917, and died in Riga (Holocaust), 1941.

Otto (Hottie) Harber; Zelda, née Caplan: Born in Stuttgart, 1919, and his wife is living in Los Angeles. They have three children and one grandchild.

My late husband's parents

Max Schloss: Born in Stuttgart, in 1875, and died 1952 in Los Angeles.

Hilde Schloss, née Kerb: Just celebrated her ninety-sixth birthday in fairly good health amidst family and friends.

My late husband's sister

Else Adler Schloss: Born in Stuttgart, 1904, and died 1968 in Chicago, Illinois.

ELLEN SILK (née Schmidt)
3541 Royal Woods Drive
Sherman Oaks, Calif. 91403

My father, Salamon W. Schmidt, born in Stuttgart in 1891, was a part owner of Julius Schmidt & Company. He died in 1967.

My mother, Dora Babette, née Spiegelthal, was born in Stuttgart in 1902 and now lives in Los Angeles.

I was born in Stuttgart in 1929, the youngest of three sisters. The Jewish school, where I was enrolled, was closed after the Crystal Night, and my parents sent us on a children's transport to England in 1939. We went to a boarding school in Southern England, where we spent the next three years. My parents, leaving most of their possessions behind, were able to come to London, staying in a hostel. We were able to see them occasionally, even spent a summer with them in Wales, when the hostel had been evacuated there.

After the war my parents moved to London again, my father got a job in a shirt-repair factory, my mother worked as a dress finisher. I lived with them, finishing high school in 1948. Later, my father found a position in Luton Bedfordshire, and we eventually bought a house and moved there. I worked for a year in an agricultural research station about 10 miles away, then entered Bedford College, London University, commuting daily. I graduated in 1952 with a B.S. in physiology, then worked two years toward a master's degree at the Post Graduate Medical School in London. When this program was terminated, I decided to emigrate to California in 1954.

I lived with one of my sisters and worked for the next six years as a biochemistry laboratory assistant, later as chief technician at the Children's Hospital of Los Angeles. My parents and my other sister moved to California in 1959, uniting the family again.

In 1958 I married. We have three sons, now nineteen, seventeen, and fifteen. I quit work when my first son was born.

For fourteen years we have been members of Valley Beth Shalom Temple, Encino; I am on the board of the sisterhood. I am active on the board of the Women's conference of the Jewish Federation Council of the San Fernando Valley, a charter member and on the board of the Golda Meir Club of Israel Bonds. I serve on the board of governors of Haifa University. I am also a member of ORT and finance chairperson of the Black-Jewish Youth Experience.

MARIANNE L. SIMMEL
P.O. Box 562
North Eastham, Mass. 02651

The Simmels were not *waschechte Schwaben*, having lived in Stuttgart for only a few years. After my father lost his position in Gera in 1933 (and resided in the local jail in Schutzhaft for a week or so), he was advised that "things were much better" in southern Germany. Other people in similar situations left Germany right then and there. My father even had an offer of a post at the then new medical school at Ankara (there may have been additional offers), but my parents decided, *da kann man doch seine kinder nicht erziehen,* so we emigrated to Stuttgart. Dr. Ludwig Weil was especially helpful to my father when he first began to practice in Stuttgart. Later, when Dr. Weil emigrated to England, my father took over his practice, his car, and even his medical technician and general factotum, Mr. Beuerle. Many other people in Stuttgart showed much kindness to my parents. We children went to school there and came to feel at home in Stuttgart, even if we achieved only limited mastery of Schwäbisch.

Father: Dr. Hans (Eugen) Simmel, born in 1891 in Berlin-Charlottenburg. Physician. Prior to 1933, director and physician-in-chief of the Municipal Hosptial in Gera, Thüringen, and professor at the Medical Faculty of the University of Jena. Moved with family to Stuttgart in 1933, in private practice of internal medicine, some affiliation with Marienhospital. Dachau 1938, very ill upon release, immediately sent to Switzerland, to a sanatorium run by an old friend and colleague. To England in late 1939, and from there, his wife and children to the United States in 1940. Eventually held position as pathologist at a hospital in Warren, Ohio, though only partially recovered from effects of Dachau. Died of these effects in 1943 in Colorado Springs, Colorado.

Mother: Dr. Else (Rose), née Rapp. Born in 1894. Pediatrician. To England in 1939 and to United States in 1940. After my father's death in 1943, prepared for and took New York State Medical Board exams. Held several institutional positions as a physician. Finally was physician for

307

many years at Uncas-on-Thomes Hospital in Norwich, Connecticut, where she died in 1964.

Sister: Eva (Barbara), Mrs. Richard Lehman, 6425 Kenhowe Drive, Bethesda, Maryland 20034. Born in 1925.

Brothers: Arnold (Georg) Simmel, 549 Riverside Drive, New York City. Born in 1926. Gerhard (Friedrich) Simmel, 16-C Venice Court, 41 Conduit Road, Hong Kong. Born in 1930.

Myself: Marianne (Lenore) Simmel, born in 1923 in Jena, Thuringen. Attended Madchengymnasium in Stuttgart. In 1938, Dr. Otto Hirsch arranged for me to go to Stoatley Rough School in Haslemere, Surrey, England. To United States in 1940. Held various unskilled jobs until I entered Smith College in September 1940. Such jobs also part-time while in college, and full-time during vacations. Graduate study in psychology at Harvard University, Ph.D. in 1949. In 1978 resigned as professor of psychology at Brandeis University (though I continue to hold pro-forma title of adjunct professor of psychology). Now working as free-lance designer.

That about does it. I think you will agree, *dass ich die Treppe hinauf gefallen bin.*

I should have mentioned that, as my father's health deteriorated, prior to his death, Dr. Otto Einstein arranged for him to go to a sanatorium in Colorado Springs where Dr. Einstein was on the medical staff.

*ELIZABETH SIMON (née Baruch)

Mrs. Elizabeth Simon, née Baruch, widowed Kiefe, was born in 1908. She passed her first examination in 1930 and in 1933, after having married attorney Dr. Alfred Kiefe in Stuttgart in 1932, she began the preparatory legal service in Wuerttemberg. In the summer of 1933, shortly before her second examination, she had to leave. She and her husband emigrated to Portugal in the fall of 1933. They worked hard to support themselves and their family, and after her husband's death in 1951, she struggled to make a living as a secretary, a language teacher, a masseuse, and finally as a co-owner of a brokerage firm.

*BERTHOLD SINGER

Attorney Berthold Singer, born in Reutlingen in 1866, had been admitted to Amtsgericht Laupheim in 1895, to Landgericht Ulm in 1896, and to Landgericht Rottweil in 1898. He surrendered his admission in 1938 and moved to Stuttgart. In 1939 he left to join his son Arthur in Lisbon and died there in 1942.

RUDOLPH S. SINGER
1 Delcrest Court, Apt. 102
St. Louis, Mo. 62124

I was born in 1899, the son of Berthold Singer, a lawyer in Rottweil. My father was born in 1866 in Reutlingen and died in Lisbon in 1942. My mother, Caroline Gunzenhauser-Singer, was born in 1867 in Bad Mergentheim and died in Lisbon in 1948.

I practiced law in Stuttgart from 1925 until 1934, then was employed at the leather factory Zufferhausen from 1934 until 1938. Mr. Arthur Levi, owner of the firm, was my wife's uncle. My wife was born in 1909, the daughter of Julius Stern and Luise Bernheim-Stern.

I served on the board of the synagogue community in Stuttgart and also on the board of the Volksbuehne.

In 1938 I left Stuttgart with my wife and our two-year-old son, Thomas, for the United States. Our son is also a well-established attorney in St. Louis, which makes it three generations of lawyers.

I have worked here for thirty years as an accountant for a division of Brown Shoe Company.

I have been retired for the last ten years.

MARTIN M. SONDHEIMER
2046 West High Street
Lima, Ohio 45805

Dr. Martin M. Sondheimer was born in 1895 in Oberdorf, attended the Volksschule in Oberdorf, Progymnasium in Nördlingen, graduated from the Ludwigsgymnasium in München in 1914. He attended Medical School at the University of München and Freiburg, and then did postgraduate studies at the Katharinen Hospital in Stuttgart and the Herzklinik in Wien, where he specialized in internal medicine and also studied psychology under Freud and Federn.

Dr. Sondheimer opened his own practice in Stuttgart in 1926 and married Elizabeth Bing, born 1907, in 1928.

He left Germany for the United States in 1938. Here he passed the Medical Boards of the States of New York and Ohio and opened a practice in internal medicine in Lima, Ohio, in 1940. He retired due to blindness in 1979.

Dr. Sondheimer was and still is a member of the United States, Ohio State, Lima, and Allen County Academies of Medicine, the World Medical Association, is a member of the staff of St. Ritas and Memorial Hospitals in Lima and the Fifty-Year Club of American Medicine. He is a member of

Temple Beth Israel-Shaare Zedek and was several times on the board of directors there. Active member of the Temple Brotherhood and B'nai B'rith.

Parents: Father: Julius Sondheimer, born 1862, died 1931 in Stuttgart. Mother: Lina Sondheimer, née Weil, born 1874 in Oberdorf, died 1944 in London, England.

Children: Hannah Sondheimer, born 1929 in Stuttgart. Three children. Daughter Marian, born 1931 in Stuttgart. Married. Two children.

Martin thinks that I should mention his brothers and sisters. Max Sondheimer lives at 83 Greenhill, London N.W. 3, England. Hans Sondheimer died in Florence, Italy. His wife, Grete, lives at 221 Corso Orbassano 10137, Turin, Italy. Hilde Sondheimer committed suicide after being released from Theresienstadt concentration camp in 1945.

HANNA SPEIER (née Lindner)
2236 Crest Road,
Baltimore, Md. 21209

My parents, Adolf and Ida Lindner, née Hirschheimer, had a textile business in Heilbronn. Originally they came from Affaltrach and Lehrensteinsfeld. They were members of the Israelitische Religionsgesellschaft Adass Jeschurun. During the Kristallnacht turmoil my father rescued a Torah from the synagogue. This is now in a Baltimore synagogue. During this time many friends were in hiding in our apartment.

We were four children, two brothers and two sisters, and all grew up in Heilbronn. My brother Max died in 1981. My brother Fred lives at 63 Stadbroke Grove Buckhurst Hill, Essex, England. Max went there in early 1933. Fred was interned there and sent to Australia to work in the British Labor Force. There he married the former Heilbronner, Friedl Schloss. After the war they moved to England. Both brothers were connected with Thomes Plywood, Ltd.

My parents, sister, and I came by way of England to Baltimore, where we arrived in late 1940. They were active with the Chevra Ahavas Chesed, which was founded by immigrants from Germany. My sister Ruth, who lives here with her family, married Jack Barth, formerly of Zurich, Switzerland. Address: 3 Stonehenge Circle, Apt. 2, Baltimore, Md. 21208.

I, Hanna, married Norbert Speier. My husband served in the U.S. Army Medical Department during World War II. We are now retired.

Like many immigrant families we had a hard struggle in the early days here, and with perseverance and hard work we succeeded in building a new life in our new homeland. I sincerely hope that this report will help with your efforts, for which I wish you success.

310

MRS. PAUL STEINBERGER (née Milly Gottlieb)
202 Templey Avenue
Cumberland, Md. 21502

Born in Stuttgart in 1905, I worked as bookkeeper for my father, David Gottlieb, in our business, Nehemias Gottlieb Soehne, lacquer and paints, for fifteen years. The business was established in 1897.

I emigrated to Cumberland in 1937 and started as packer in a knit wholesale place. Later I had two positions as a bookkeeper. In 1965 I got married to Paul Steinberger, formerly Kassel, and retired in 1967. In 1939 I had brought my parents and brother Kurt to Cumberland. My brother served in the American Army during World War II. All three are deceased.

*ALBERT STEINER

Attorney Dr. Albert Steiner, son of an attorney in Goeppingen, was born there in 1896. Since the end of 1923 he was admitted to the Amstsgericht Goeppingen, and since early 1924 to the Landgericht Ulm. The admission was annulled in 1938. In 1938 he emigrated to the United States and could barely exist as a peddler for a brush manufacturer, until he was able to land a job with a merchant of hops. He died after a long illness in 1958.

HELMUT STEINER
Guisan Str. 35
CH-9010 St. Gallen
Switzerland

I was happy to hear that you are well. It is a long time since I saw you in New York. I know how my dear cousin Julius Steiner liked you; therefore, I would like very much to grant your request to write to you.
Personal Data of the Family.
Father: Simon L. Steiner, born in Laupheim in 1864. Owner of a tannery in Laupheim. Very active in the Laupheim Jewish community. He died in 1937, a victim of that time, and is buried in Laupheim.

Mother: Melanie Steiner, née Herz, born in 1872 and died in New York, 1956.

Helmut Steiner, born in Laupheim in 1899. Married 1927 to Edith, née Noerdlinger, from St. Gallen, born 1900, kindergarten teacher.

Son, Heinrich Steiner, born 1931. Doctor of law. Married Marianne, née Wallach, born 1942. Kindergarten teacher. Four children born in Israel, where family lives in Haifa: Daniel, born 1966; Michael, born 1968; Judith, born 1970; Naomi, born 1975.

Daughter, Martha Steiner, born 1935, St. Gallen, kindergarten teacher, married Dr. Vincent C. Frank of Basel, born 1930. One daughter, Simone, was born in Bern in 1968. The family of Frank Steiner lives in Basel.

Re: Helmut Steiner: A tanner by profession, changed in 1926 and entered the firm of Simon H. Steiner, hops, in Laupheim in a leading position. Emigrated to St. Gallen with family in 1936, founding a hops business there in 1937. Firm was closed during the war. From 1946 to 1969 director of the St. Gallen firm, heavy activities on behalf of reconstruction of the firm in Laupheim, and representing interests of the New York hops firm, and especially the European interest of Julius Steiner and Elinor S. Gimbel. From 1946 representing Jewish interests in Laupheim, especially in connection with the old Jewish cemetery, from 1937 widely engaged in Jewish affairs in St. Gallen.

The House of Steiner: There are five generations of the family instrumental in building this firm. Founded in 1845 by Simon Heinrich Steiner, together with his father, Heinrich Steiner, the hops business was located in Laupheim in the midst of a large hops-producing area, and still bears his name. The small business grew in the next generations into a highly respected hops-supplying business which had excellent business relations with breweries in Germany and especially also in nearby Switzerland. The business, however, became worldwide when one son of the founders, Sam S. Steiner, emigrated to the United States and founded there the firm of S. S. Steiner, which soon developed into a leading firm of German hops imports and also created an excellent position in Central and South America. Through the opening of these tremendous areas, the Laupheim original firm developed into one of the leading expert firms.

Another son of the founder, Louis Steiner, directed Laupheim then, but unfortunately died early. His widow, Hedwig Steiner, is well remembered by many older Laupheimers, not only due to her initiative in how she, on her own, with her two children continued the business successfully, but even more for her noble and humane way in which she anonymously helped so many needy people. When her sons were both grown up, they volunteered in World War I. The oldest son, Heinrich, was killed in France. His brother, Julius Steiner, supported his mother after returning from the war, but already in 1923 he went to the United States, where he found his second home-country, and after the retirement of his uncle, succeeded him as president of the New York firm. In Laupheim his cousin Helmut Steiner took his place as director of the firm, which was changed into a corporation in 1930. Following the pressure of the regime he went to St. Gallen, and in 1937 founded the Steiner Hops G.m.b.H.

In the United States, determined Mrs. Elinor Steiner Gimbel, since

312

many years chairman of the board of directors, changed the policies of the firm to a great degree. The daughter of Sam S. Steiner and of his wife, who came from the New York brewing family Liebmann, was at home in the tradition of hops and beer. Her two sons, Louis S. Gimbel III and S. Steiner Gimbel, are now as fifth generation in charge of the business, and this heritage is in good hands.

LOTTE STEINTHAL (née Gunzenhauser)
115-25 Metropolitan Avenue
Richmond Hill, N.Y. 11418

I was born in Stuttgart in 1908 and attended the Roderth School for Girls, from which I was graduated in 1925, and then, after some time in Lausanne, Switzerland, studying French, I attended the Hoehere Handelsschule in Stuttgart to prepare myself for a business career. After graduation I held several positions, mostly part-time, doing office work. After 1931 the office of Brueder Landauer, where I worked until emigrating from Germany in 1936.

I planned to marry my friend of long standing, Werner Steinthal, son of Professor Dr. Steinthal. Since he was only one-quarter non-Aryan, on his father's side, we would have needed the Fuehrer's permission to get married in Germany. Naturally we preferred to leave Stuttgart as soon as possible. We got married in a suburb of London, spending the seventeen days until we could get our marriage license with relatives. Luckily, my father could join us for our wedding but then unfortunately went back to Stuttgart, where he and my mother stayed until 1941.

The day after our wedding we sailed for the United States. Both of us had received affidavits from my mother's cousins, who were quite wealthy and well-known in New York and Cincinnati. They promised to take care of us the first few weeks until we could be settled. To our disappointment, we were presented with a large bill in the small hotel where they had taken a room for us. We then knew that we were strictly on our own. The depression was still on in 1936, and it was quite impossible for my husband to find work in his line as a mechanical engineer. He did some photographic work on his own, making use of a former hobby.

Our son, Rudy Frank, was born only ten months after our arrival in the United States. Happy as we were with our little boy, it did not exactly facilitate our financial situation, but we always got by somehow, my husband doing all sorts of work until he could finally find something in his own line, after the war started in 1941.

In the meantime my parents had arrived and were living with us. For two years we all lived in a small town in Connecticut, where the people did not feel friendly toward us "enemy aliens." After two years we had our fill of the New Englanders and moved back to New York. We have lived here ever since in the same apartment in Kew Gardens. When our son was old enough to take care of himself under my parents' supervision, I started to go back to office work which I continued in different positions off and on until 1978. My husband has now been retired for a number of years. Our son has been with Pan American World Airways for the past twenty-five years and has enabled us to take marvelous trips over most of Western Europe as well as once to the Orient. We have often returned to Stuttgart on brief visits and after all those years have finally been able to more or less forget the bad times we lived through there. We even found some friends who had been loyal and never belonged to the Nazi Party.

Our son married in 1963. They have three girls.

Both my husband and I do not belong to any congregations or organizations, partly due to the fact that we are of different faiths, but not practicing our religion.

RUTH STEPPER
60 Arlosoroff St.
33651 Haifa, Israel

Born in Stuttgart in 1913, I worked in the office of the firm Astroline Company from 1930 until I emigrated in 1936. The boss was Mr. Edgar Baer. The firm was transferred to Christian ownership early 1936, the boss discharged shortly afterwards. I too gave notice then, since I had an opportunity to go to Palestine with my parents and brother Kurt. The new owner wanted to keep me, to train successors, luckily I declined. We were allowed to take 10 marks each with us, and a few cases with dishes and other things were sent later.

There were riots at the same time of our arrival in Haifa, where my mother and I still live. The first years were very hard. There was much unemployment, we did not know the language, there was no call for office workers. I had to work as a domestic at first for various families. Even more difficult was this situation for my parents, handicapped by advanced age; at that time nobody helped the newcomers, not even to get quarters. Everyone was to fight for himself alone. In 1938 I finally succeeded in getting office work with a former German firm, Hausmann Transport, and when they closed in 1956 I began to work as a secretary for United Restitution Organization (URO), Ltd., in Haifa.

My brother, only sixteen when we arrived here, was finally accepted in a woodworking firm; we had no money to let him study, not even for a year. In 1941 he entered a kibbutz, and in fall 1946 he participated in erecting in one night eleven new settlements in the Negev. He still lives with his family in the Kibbutz Mishmar Hanegev. During the war of liberation these settlements were partly isolated and had a difficult existence for many years.

A great many of our relatives, on both father's and mother's side, perished.

BRUNO STERN
2 South Pinehurst Ave.
New York, N.Y. 10033

I was born 1912 in Niederstetten. My father was Max Stern and mother, Rosa, née Landauer, from Michelbach an der Luecke. I was the youngest of three children. My older brothers are Theodore and Justin.

Schooling: Attended first the Jewish Elementary School in Niederstetten and then the Realschule; Abitur in Tauberbischofsheim. Studied dentistry and medicine at the University of Wuerzburg. Completed my dental studies in 1936. I worked at the Juedische Krankenhilfe in Berlin. In the 1930's I joined the Gesellschaft fuer Juedische Familienforschung.

I emigrated to the United States in 1937 and worked first at the Jewish Hospital in Brooklyn, then as an assistant to the urologist, Dr. Abraham Ravich. In 1948 I started in the printing business. I had my own company until 1969, when my firm merged with Wallenberg & Wallenberg, Inc., and later with the St. John Associates, Inc.

In 1948 I married Lisel Wolfsheimer from Weikersheim, Wuerttemberg. We have two children, Carol Linda and Jeffrey Mark.

All my life I was interested in history, especially Jewish history, folklore, and genealogy. I was and am also very much interested in the history of Hohenlohe and the City of New York. Hobbies are photography and tape-recording.

Published: Meine Jugenderinnerungen an eine Wuerttembergische Kleinstadt und ihre Juedische Gemeinde (W. Kohlhammer Stuttgart).

Slide Shows: (1) *My Town, My House, My Family;* (2) *1000 Years of Jewish Life in Southern Germany;* (3) *New York in the 1970's.*

I am now on the board of the Rashi Association, which tries to preserve what is left of the Jewish holy places in Europe.

[We are sorry to say that our good friend Bruno Stern passed away in 1981.]

JUSTIN STERN (brother of Bruno)
21 Bennett Avenue
New York, N.Y. 10033

My parents were Max and Rosie Stern, née Landauer. My father was born 1878 and my mother the same year. Our family lived in Niederstetten for many generations.

My father was a merchant, dealing in hides, leather, and other products.

Both my parents were active in community affairs. My father was a mohel and chasan during the high holidays. He was a member of the board of our congregation and also a member of the Gemeinderat until Hitler came to power.

My mother was the only Jewish member in the Hausfrauenverein of our city. During the time of Hitler, she gave lessons in knitting and crocheting to the Jewish girls of our community.

In 1938 they immigrated to this country and lived in New York until their death.

My father passed away in 1943 and my mother in 1974.

I was born in 1908 in Niederstetten. After finishing high school in Bad Mergentheim, I went to Karlsruhe, where I worked at the old and well-known firm E. Ettlinger and Wormser. Later, I decided to study law and went to the Universities of Munich and Tuebingen.

In 1933 I left Germany. First I went to Paris, where I stayed for three years. Due to the inability to obtain the permit to work I moved again, this time to Argentina. For a few years I lived in the interior of the country and later on in Buenos Aires.

To reunite with the other members of my family, I came to this country in 1945. In 1950 I married Margot Wertheimer. She had been deported from Stuttgart in 1941 to Riga, Latvia, and spent over three years in concentration and labor camps. Her parents, Jakob and Claire Wertheimer, perished in Auschwitz.

We have one son, Martin Larry, born 1953.

Since my arrival here, I am in the import-export business. Years ago I made many sales trips to South America.

My wife and I are active in B'nai B'rith. I am a past president of the Washington Heights Lodge. We belong to the congregations Emes Wozedek, Inc., and Share Hatikvah Ahavath Tora V'Tikvoh Chadoshoh.

316

LISEL STERN (née Wolfsheimer)
2 South Pinehurst Avenue
New York, N.Y. 10033

I was born in 1922 in Weikersheim, Wuerttemberg. My father was Max Wolfsheimer and my mother, Laura Friedsam.

I attended the public school in Weikersheim. In 1933 we emigrated to Kolmar in France and later on moved to Lyons. In 1940 we were detained for a few months in Camp Gurs. We managed to get out and arrived in the United States in 1942. I worked at several jobs until I married Bruno Stern in 1948. We have two children, Carol Linda and Jeffrey Mark.

The Wolfsheimer family was always interested in cooking and I inherited this trait. The specialties from the Old Country are very much looked for now. Some of my recipes were published in Joan Nathan's *The Jewish Holiday Kitchen* (Schocken Books, 1979) and by the same author in the *New York Post*, March 24, 1980.

SALOME STERN (née Plawner)
41 Bennett Avenue
New York, N.Y. 10033

My name is Salome Stern, née Plawner, I was born in 1909 in Stuttgart. My parents names are Salomon and Rose Plawner; they both came to Stuttgart in 1905 and were born in Poland. My parents lived in Cannstatt till 1938; they emigrated to London, England, and then later to New York, where they both died.

I was married to Berthold Stern, son of Berta and Max Stern, also living in Cannstatt. A daughter, Berta, was born to us in 1935 in Stuttgart. My daughter is married, has three children, and lives in New Jersey. We emigrated to Israel 1938 and then joined our families in the United States in 1945. I had one brother, Josef Plawner, born 1907 and passed away at the age of sixty-one years. We lived always in New York since we came here; my husband passed away in 1966.

WALTER STERN
110 Ramile Court
Paramus, N.J. 07652

My parents are Leopold Stern, born 1898, and Henrietta Stern, born 1902. They lived in Oehringen until their emigration in 1939 to the United States.

I was born in 1930, and since 1948 I am affiliated occupationally with

Associated Metal and Mineral Company. My wife's name is Brigitte, and we have two children, ages twenty-three and twenty-one.

HANS STERNHEIM
Somerville, N.J.

After my studies I became co-publisher and editor of a Jewish newspaper in Stuttgart. I married, and a daughter in Israel was given to us. Journalistic enthusiasm filled my soul and mind—a happy man I was! But this all changed overnight when Hitler came to power in 1933. Only a few years later I saw our burning synagogue. The whole Jewish press in Germany was suppressed and the Gestapo-henchmen arrested every Jew they could find.

It was the terrible night of the 8th of November 1938. The next day I was put into the concentration camp of Dachau, together with 10,000 Jewish men of every age group. My old father was carried off to the Buchenwald camp, where, when American armies liberated it, General Eisenhower paled from the horror that he saw. In March 1939 I fled with my wife and daughter over the bridge that spans the Rhine at the city of Kehl. On the other side the French tricolor fluttered in the wind. Shortly before, I saw my parents for the last time—it was a farewell forever.

And now the final tragedy of the condemned began. Soon they were forced to leave their house. My parents were perched in a dilapidated building, together with my mother's widowed sister, Clara, who for a long time was a member of our family. After we had finally arrived in America, in many carefully written letters my parents implored me to save them from the ill-boding dark cloud that hovered over their heads. All these letters had the mark of the censor. My parents I could not save! The newcomer had not a penny of his own, and nobody could be found who would vouch for an old Jewish couple. Still I can feel my soul-rending dilemma of those days.

Despite the fact that my dear ones were living in utter loneliness, they kept their heads high. Never did they lose hope that some day they would be again united with us in foreign lands. They said the daily prayers, and the defaming emblem of the yellow star that they had to wear when they dared to leave the house they carried with dignity. And nearer in this time of waiting for the end, when more and more Jewish men, women, and children were transported in freight cars to the realms of destruction, my parents came to the God of their Biblical ancestors, and like dew flowed courage and resignation in His will on their decaying abode. Thus the ghetto house became a shrine for my father's beloved scroll.

When in these years of suffering our holidays arrived, my parents said the festive prayers. They might have thought with nostalgia of our beautiful synagogue which, when I said farewell to everything that was so dear to me, was a pyramid of debris. But still, a deep tragic tune flows from the letters of my father, and especially from the ones—always written in his calligraphic way—in which he described the celebration of Rosh Hashana and Yom Kippur.

These hours of supplication repeated themselves on the High Holidays in 1941 and 1942, but the latter's Yom Kippur was the last in the life of my parents. Once they were esteemed by the whole population of my native town, but then they became outcasts, that—not without some secret embarrassment here and there—were overlooked. In 1942, four days after their last Yom Kippur, my parents and my aunt Clara were deported to a concentration camp.

NORBERT AND LILLY STIEBEL (née Loewenstein)
150-35 78th Road
Flushing, N.Y. 11367

Norbert: Born 1905. We married in 1934 in Stuttgart and emigrated to New York in 1938. We both worked in Stuttgart in my father's wholesale shoe business, Norman on the road and I in the office. The beginning in New York was hard. Norman worked as a housepainter at first, but after four months he hurt his back in a fall from a ladder and could not work for a year and a half. Then he was in various firms in the shipping department. I could not find office work at first, so for two years I cleaned two apartments every day. This work was very strenuous, and so I became an operator during the war in factories, for six years. After that I succeeded in getting an office job and worked until I retired in 1966. We have no children. We are members of the synagogue Machane Chodosh, Rabbi Manfred Gans, in Forest Hills, New York.

Norbert retired also in 1966 and started to paint pictures and learned ceramics. He is very talented in both fields. We live in our own home.

Facts about my Parents, Simon and Rosa Loewenstein: Father was born 1878 in Rexingen and owned a shoe wholesale business in Stuttgart and Cannstatt. He was in the Welzheim concentration camp together with Rabbi Adler from Cannstatt and Dr. Zuerndorfer from Stuttgart. After he was discharged he could not emigrate quickly to the United States as he had a high waiting number. My brother Sally (now Charles Lowen) tried to get a visa for Rio de Janeiro and succeeded shortly before the war started. My mother died in 1943 in Rio from cancer. After the war ended my father and my brother and his wife and daughter came to New York, where my father died in 1953.

319

D. ELLEN STIMLER (née Sander)
33 West Second Street
Moorestown, N.J. 08057

Concerning my parents: Rudolf Sander, formerly Levi, was born about 1882 in Stuttgart and was the son of Uri and Helene Levi. After the death of Uri, Rudolf took over the management of his father's printing and lithography business in the rear of Gartenstrasse 15 in Stuttgart until he left Germany in the Spring of 1939. Rudolf married Alice Epstein, daughter of Victor and Clara Epstein of Stuttgart in 1918. They had three children: Dora, born in 1919; Lothar, born in 1923; and Frank, born in 1927.

Dora (myself) (who now calls herself Ellen to avoid confusion with her American mother-in-law, Dora Stimler) was the first member of the family to emigrate to the United States in 1939. The rest of the family left Germany about the same time, following Rudolf's two-week incarceration in Dachau in 1938. They marked time in England while waiting for their quota numbers to come through. The escape to England was accomplished through the assistance of Rudolf's brother, Ernest, who was well established in England since 1933.

Following the advice from other young Wuerttembergers who had preceded her to the United States (particularly Trude Hirsch and Walter Hirsch), Dora sought the assistance of the International Student Service and, through their help, landed a scholarship at Radcliffe College. She graduated in 1942 *magna cum laude,* Phi Beta Kappa, with a major in American government. Rudolf, Alice, and Frank arrived in Boston during Dora's junior year, and Dora arranged for Frank to be "adopted" temporarily by the parents of one of her fellow students. Rudolph and Alice were able to stay with a Quaker family until they could get a foothold on their own.

Eventually Rudolf and Alice reestablished a home for their family in Brookline, Massachusetts. Rudolf worked as a sales representative for various printing firms, and Alice found successive jobs as an infant nurse. Frank distinguished himself successively at Boston Latin School, Harvard College, and Harvard Law School, where he was on the *Law Review.* Lothar, who had been interned for a period of time in Canada, eventually rejoined the family and established a career in paint chemistry.

Rudolf died in Brookline in 1966; Alice died in 1978.

At this writing in 1980, Dora lives in Moorestown, New Jersey. She is married to Saul Stimler, a computer consultant, and they have two children: Lynn, unmarried, working and studying in Seattle; and Mark, working toward a mechanical engineering degree. Dora is a New Jersey

320

attorney with a practice in family and school law. For recreation, there is sailing and gardening. Lothar is living in Princeton, New Jersey, working as a paint chemist for a Pennsylvania firm. He is married to Greta, who is a biochemist at Princeton University. They have two children.

Frank has a large home in Cambridge, Massachusetts, where he is professor of law at Harvard Law School. Frank has co-authored a leading textbook on family law, is an arbitrator of labor disputes for the American Arbitration Association, has been a member of many study commissions, and lectures and writes widely in his special areas of family law, welfare law, tax consequences of divorce, and alternate dispute resolution. Frank is married to Emily, who is a psychiatric social worker. They have three children.

Dora particularly regrets the failure to maintain formerly close ties with her contemporaries from Stuttgart and welcomes this opportunity to locate some of the old friends. For contact with any member of the family, please write to her.

*GUSTAV STOSSEL

Gustav Stossel, son of the rabbi of Stuttgart and brother of the lawyer, Dr. Rudolf Stossel, was born in Heilbronn in 1890. Since 1919 he was acting district court judge in Stuttgart; since 1933 regional court justice at the Regional Court Stuttgart. In 1933 he was retired in accordance with the Law for the Preservation of the Civil Service. In 1939 he emigrated to the United States, where for many years he was unable to make more than a minimal living. Only in 1945 did his situation improve, when he was employed by an auto factory. He died in 1952.

*RUDOLF STOSSEL

Attorney Dr. Rudolf Stossel, son of the rabbi and brother of Dr. Gustav Stossel, was born in Stuttgart in 1886. He was admitted in Stuttgart in 1914. For many years he was the legal representative of the tenants' union of greater Stuttgart and environs. His admission was voided in 1938. In 1938 he emigrated to the United States, where, until 1941, he was able to find employment with his brother. The brother had founded a small moving company which folded with his death in 1952.

321

EVA STRAUSS (née Kops)

1 Brentwood Lane
Great Neck, N.Y. 11023

I was born in Stuttgart in 1905, daughter of Adolph and Martha Kops (née Kramer.) My father was born in 1868; my mother in 1878. Father died in 1954 and mother in 1963.

My parents came to this country in 1938 and lived in New York. I have a brother, Walter Kops, born in 1910 in Stuttgart. He now lives in Atlanta, Georgia, and is unmarried. He was with Kops Brothers, New York corset factory, Nemo, which was founded by my father's brothers at the end of the nineteenth century. Later, and until now, he was with the Poirette Company—garments—in the sales division.

My husband, Julius Strauss, was born in Stuttgart/Cannstatt in 1899, son of Solomon (from Geinsbach) and Frieda (from near Heilbronn) Strauss.

My father-in-law and my husband owned a cigar factory in Cannstatt. We were married in 1927 and came to this country in 1935. My husband was first employed by the General Cigar Company in Hartford, Connecticut, where we first lived for one year. Then we moved to Lancaster, Pennsylvania, for thirteen years. Finally my husband became president of the company in 1949 and we moved to Great Neck in 1950. He died in 1979.

My husband and I both belonged to Temple Beth El in Great Neck. I am active in the sisterhood and volunteer in the senior citizen center. My husband was active in the United Jewish Appeal and other organizations.

My brother-in-law, Ludwig Mayer, was in business with my husband and his father and in this country was employed by Kops Brothers until he retired.

I have two children, a daughter and son, both born in Germany. They were seven and four years old when we came to this country. My daughter is single and is now in Boston finishing a course in nursing. She also is an artist—she paints. My son is married to Laura, née Ginsberg. They have two daughters.

KURT STRAUSS

P.O. Box 190
Southfield, Mich. 48037

I was sixteen-and-one-half years old when I left Ulm, Germany (after having graduated from the Realgymnasium there), with my sister Lili and brother-in-law Benno B. Levy and their one-and-one-half-year-old son Werner, when we emigrated to the United States. That was in 1937.

Being unable to take out any money during the Nazi regime, we were able, due to our contacts in Nuernberg, Germany, to take along a quantity of drawing instruments which we could sell in the United States. Of course, every beginning is difficult, and shortly after arrival in New York in 1937, we tried to acquaint ourselves with the outlets where we could dispose of these drawing instruments. After having looked around and contacted as many people as possible, we finally reached the conclusion that our best outlets for these instruments would be pawnshops. Being refugees, these pawnbrokers were the easiest people to approach, and to have received a $25 order was already an achievement in those days of 1937 and 1938. Full-course dinners were available at 50 cents in those days. The sale of our drawing instruments went rather smoothly, although we had a difficult time to dispose of them to stores other than pawnshops. Since those were the days of the depression, we had to struggle for every order. My brother-in-law made the packages, my sister did the books, and I went out selling. Everything was done from our apartment on West 150th Street between Broadway and Riverside Drive.

After having conquered the New York market, I went out of town, first by Greyhound bus and later on in a small car we bought. I was steadily on the road from 1937 through 1943. It was a hard, tough life for me in those days, having covered one half of the United States. In 1943, I decided to get married at the age of twenty-three.

From that time on, we appointed sales representatives in various sections of the country, so I could stay home. We kept on adding other items, especially in the optical field, such as magnifiers, binoculars, etc., which we first imported from Germany and later on from Japan. By 1950 we already had a sales force consisting of six men (mostly refugees) who were selling our goods.

In 1960 my brother-in-law, Benno B. Levy, passed away, having been only sixty years old. At that time I became president of our company, Compass Instrument & Optical Company, Inc. (now changed to Compass Industries, Inc.). In 1957, my sister's son Werner joined our company, and a few years later their other son Frank also joined.

I held this post for almost a decade until 1969, at which time I was divorced after twenty-six years and two sons. Shortly afterward, however, I remarried. This necessitated my leaving New York and moving to Detroit, giving up the presidency and turning over the business to my two nephews, Werner and Frank, while I relocated in Michigan. From there, I conducted our business plus taking care of other states where we did not have coverage.

At first my departure was quite a shock to the entire family, but now

323

everybody is happy with the way things worked out. As far as I am concerned, I made the best move of my life, having found a most compatible wife as a partner. I am earning much less than in New York, but then again, money is not everything—it's happiness that counts.

My father Louis W. was born in Heilbronn 1877 and died in New York in August 1965.

My mother, Frieda, née Einstein, was born in Ulm in 1887, and she died in New York in 1975.

As for myself, I was born in Ulm in 1919. In Germany I attended the Realgymnasium in Ulm and graduated from there after six years. Then, on account of the Nazis, I could not continue my education and emigrated to the United States in 1937. Since making a living was the name of the game, I was forced to go out on the road at age seventeen-and-one-half and sell merchandise. I spent thirty years of my life in New York and the last decade in the Detroit area.

*DR. AND MRS. MAX J. STRAUSS

Max J. Strauss, born in 1894 in Tauberbischofsheim, moved to Stuttgart in 1909. Medal for having been wounded in action. 1919, studies of law at the University Tuebingen. Law degree and doctor of law diploma. Leader of Jewish students against anti-Semitism at the university; 1922 to 1937 practice of law; partner in law offices of Otto Thalmessinger, Dr. Max Strauss, Dr. Kurt Mandry, Thalmessinger II in Stuttgart. 1931–1937, state chairman of the Reichsbund Juedischer Frontsoldaten (Jewish front soldiers); 1937 emigration with wife Gertrud and young daughters, Sibyl and Dorothy. The family settled in Kansas City in Missouri.

Gertrud worked as manufacturer's representative and in other positions until 1949, when the financial position of the family could be considered safer.

Max found, after months of searching, work as a clerk in the claims department of an insurance company and attended night classes at the law school of the Kansas City University. In 1942, Paul Uhlmann, president of the Uhlmann Grain Company in Kansas City, invited him to join his firm and work his way up. 1950, manager of the Country Elevators Department of Uhlmann Elevators Company in Fort Worth, Texas, a branch of the Kansas City, Missouri, firm. In 1952 Paul Uhlmann had acquired the controlling interests of Standing Milling Company in Kansas City and invited Max to join this firm, to take charge of operations of Standard Milling Company's grain elevators in the Middle West. 1964, retirement from Standard Milling Company at the age of seventy. From 1965 to 1971, consultant for international trade in connection with firms in Kansas City and Experience Corporation in Minneapolis, Minnesota. From then on, research studies in the history of the Strauss family, which reaches into the sixteenth century.

Our daughters are married; we have five grandchildren. They live in the states of Kansas, Texas, New Mexico, and California.

Gertrud's parents were Karl Rosenthal and Sophie, née Schloss, in Stuttgart. Karl and his son Erich were partners in the firm M. Rosenthal, Rosenthal, importers and exporters, Stuttgart-Hamburg. Erich was in charge of the firm's Hamburg office and married Maria, née Goldschmidt. They emigrated to Holland in 1937 and settled in Rotterdam. Karl and Sophie Rosenthal settled in Rotterdam late in 1938. With the invasion of Nazi Germany into Holland in 1940, both families had to move first to Doorn and later to Amsterdam. Daughter of Erich and Maria Rosenthal, Elizabeth, was born in 1938 in Rotterdam.

In 1943 both families were deported. The parents and son Erich perished in Nazi camps. Maria and daughter Elizabeth survived and were rescued by British and U.S. combat units. Maria lives in California, retired as secretary from the International Law Department of California University Law School. Daughter Elizabeth is married and lives with husband and four children near San Francisco, California.

The parents of Max Strauss were Nathan Strauss and Johanna, née Saenger. Nathan Jacob Strauss was partner of the firm Gebrueder Strauss, wineries and wine merchants in Tauberbischofsheim. Their second son was Alfred. They moved to Stuttgart in 1909. Nathan Jacob died in 1930. Johanna emigrated with her two sisters, Marie Tannhauser, Stuttgart, and Emilie Erlanger, Stutgart; all three sisters are over seventy years of age—in 1941 via Cuba to the United States. She lived with her son Alfred in Chicago and died there in 1959 at the age of eighty-nine.

RICHARD STRAUSS
Nahariya, POB 5
Israel

Dr. Richard Jakob Strauss was born in Ulm in 1909. His wife Hilde, née Bach, was born in Laupheim in 1911. They married in Ulm in 1933, after he attended business school. Richard was general director of Nahariya Dairy Strauss Ltd.; his wife is now director of the ice factory Glidat Strauss Akko.

A son, Michael, was born in Ulm in 1934. He is now a director of Nahariya Dairy Strauss Ltd.; a daughter, Raya, was born in Haifa in 1940.

Richard's parents were Julius Strauss and Marta Levi. Julius, a metal smelter, was a president of the Jewish community and of the Chevra Kadischa. He died in Ulm in 1937, and Marta died in Israel in 1940.

Richard's sister, Mrs. Alice Haas, was born in Ulm in 1905. His brother, Ruven, was born in 1912, also in Ulm, where he attended high school and took an apprenticeship in a bank. He was later a farmer in Mikveh Israel, Beer-Tuvia, and an employee of the Israeli Health Ministry, now retired.

Richard, after graduating from high school (Real Gymnasium), studied economics in Frankfurt, Berlin, and Tuebingen, obtaining a diploma and the degree of doctor of economics. He traveled to England and France, worked in his father's business. He became a member of the directors of the Nathan Strauss Smelting Works, a consultant to the Ministry of Economics in Stuttgart, was active in the Jewish community and the Zionists with Max Benminger and Herbert Siratach, representing the Zionists in the Ulm Jewish community. He was a co-founder of the Jewish Sport Club in Ulm, director of the Keren Hayesod, also representing the Palestine Office in Ulm. Resigned in the Hitler era from all offices in non-Jewish institutions: Economic Commission, Chamber of Commerce, judge of the Business Bureau, sport and riding clubs, etc.

In Palestine Richard became the founder and owner of Nahariya Dairy Strauss Ltd., Glidat Strauss, and subsidiaries in Tel Aviv, Haifa, Jerusalem, and Beer-Sheva. Arriving with a Capitalist Certificate, he worked on a farm in Beer-Tuvia with his brother Ruven in 1936.

Purchasing nine dunams of land, he was among the first settlers in Nahariya. He built a cow stable, participated in construction in Nahariya, and participated in the Agricultural Cooperative, in part as secretary. He then took over the Education Department. He was also a member of Haganah, training exercises under Chaim Ginzberg, later Dov Levin.

When during the riots no milk transports were possible, we collected the milk and started production in a small barrack, transferred in 1938 to Eyn Sara (Meschek Liebermann). There various types of white cheese, cooking cheese, and cream were made. In 1939 the construction of a small factory in Nahariya was begun, and the cow stable was discontinued because during the Mandate it was not permitted to have cows and work the milk at the same time. So we collected and processed milk from the nearby farms. During that time we worked in cooperation with Thuva, selling their cheese to, among others, hotels and pension houses.

Richard was an auxiliary policeman in Nahariya; later, in 1948, he did military service, receiving Haganah decorations. He was active in placing illegal immigrants and inside activities in restitution matters of both a personal and a general nature after the war. Beginning to give information to in Germany to prepare for possible later relations. He was co-founder of the Organization of Industry in Haifa and of the Rotary Club

326

in Nahariya. After re-entering the German Organization of Economists, he lectured in Germany about Israel in Rotary Clubs and Lodges. During the term of office of the first German ambassador, Payl, he did informative work, including in journals; he was rewarded for this work in 1971 by the BundesVerdienstkreuz First Class (German Medal).

The development of Nahariya Dairy Strauss Ltd. is described in a monograph, from the cow stable to the well-known food concern in Israel, designated as "vital" by the government and military authorities, and as a pioneer of industry in Nahariya.

RUDI (REUVEN) STRAUSS
Nahariya, Israel

My father came as a young boy of five years with his family to Ulm, where he died in the year 1937 at the age of sixty-six. The Strauss family comes from Berlichingen, where they have reportedly been teachers for generations. I believe that somehow all the Strauss's who are related to us have once come from there. Our grandfather's name was Nathan, married to Sophie, née Kutz. My father's name was Julius, and my mother, Martha, née Levi, born in Waiblingen and grew up in Cannstatt.

I was born in 1913 in Ulm, Humanistisches Gymnasium—did not complete studies—then Hoehere Handelsschule der Stadt Ulm, completed at Mittlere Reife. Apprenticeship at the Deutsche Bank, Ulm. After the finished Banklehre, I was sent to France where I studied at the Institute de Vincennes—French and general subjects in French. As I lived with a French family outside, I made good progress and returned to Ulm after about nine months in 1931. Then I started in our father's firm, Nathan Strauss Huettenwerk A. G. Ulm. In 1933 I joined my sister Alice and her first husband, Alfred Hayum, on a trip to Palestine, where I, as a consequence, decided to remain and to immigrate. As I was interested in agriculture, I went to an agricultural moshav settlement and later worked at an agricultural school, Mikveh Israel, near Tel Aviv. During the winter 1935/36 I went to have my own farm at Beer Tuvyiah—south of Tel Aviv and a place quite isolated at that time from other Jewish settlements.

There were several families coming there at the same time. They were all from Germany, and we became acquainted during our stay before. I have to mention one Wuerttemberg family especially, Walter Selz of Weikersheim, whom we knew in Germany from the Juedischer Jugendbund, and who had himself quite a big family in Palestine. In the United States my first wife was Edith, née Guttmann. We had one son but became divorced soon afterwards. My son, Yoek, is today forty-two years old and is a successful businessman. He has three children, two boys and a daughter. After my divorce I lived for some time in Nahariya, where my brother and his family lived, and also our mother, who moved to Palestine in 1938 after the death of our father. I had bought a horse and agricultural appliances and did work as a hired man on the small farm holdings in Nahariya, mainly plowing. In 1941 I joined the British Army in Palestine and was at the Royal Army Service Corps (RASC) first engaged as a driver, later as a clerk, and staying mainly in Egypt.

In Egypt I met Hilde, my present wife. She was a soldier too (ATS) and worked in a hospital laboratory. We met at another old Ulmer acquaintance's house—Otto Levinger—who worked as a textile engineer, installing textile factories in Egypt, where he went as he was not able to get satisfactory employment in Palestine then. Jews in Egypt used to invite the Palestinians (as we were called then) to their houses or make at least one afternoon a week "open house" when we could visit without any special invitation, and even bring friends along. That was in 1942 and in 1945—before demobilization. We married in Egypt. In 1946 we went back to the old "homestadt" in Beer Tuvyiah, where we met with a rather desperate time and situation. The security situation was critical. Economically we stood before ruin. We had our son Nathan in 1947. The harshness of the condition soon got me involved in problems of ailing health, especially during the War of Independence in 1948, and finally we had to leave the farm again and moved to Nahariya. I got employment at the administration of the newly constructed general hospital for the district and worked there until the age of sixty in charge of stores and supplies. Then I worked another six years in a half-time capacity for my older son Yoek, who has a construction business and some smaller industries in the Haifa area. Our son Nathan studied engineering, returned to the army, got married, and has a daughter of eight and a son of four years. His wife, Ruthi, is an architect, and they live in the Tel Aviv area. The army let Nathan finish his studies in the United States, and at Stanford University in California, he received his master's degree in industrial engineering. He regretted not being able to accept a generous offer of his faculty to continue his studies, as his boss had called him back. Well, time has come to pass and I have a grandson in the army now. I am just another old-age pensioner, whose health is often failing, but hoping to be able to stay alive for some more years.

THEODORE STRAUS
5050 S East End Avenue, Apt. 10B
Chicago, Ill. 60615

I was born in 1901 in Crailsheim as the son of Lehrer Straus (Volksschule & Religonsschule). I worked for a while in different cities in Germany and finally made my domicile in Stuttgart, from where I emigrated to America in 1938. My parents had died in 1923, and my family, consisting of ten brothers and sisters all older than I and all married and living in different parts of Germany, tried to escape Hitler's henchmen and only partially succeeded. Four sisters and one sister-in-law vanished with husbands and some children. Some succeeded in escaping to South America; some to Israel, and some to South Africa. I don't want to go too deep into the hardships of us all, so I will go back to my own life—searching for work and finally finding a job paying $12 for forty-eight hours work. For a while I was living together with three other fellows, doing our own cooking and scratching. I changed jobs and worked my way up a little and finally, in 1939, got married. I was happy until fate struck and I lost my wife and child during childbirth in 1943. After struggling for four years I moved to Chicago in 1947, married again, and was fairly successful. I became interested in religious affairs, joined a German-Jewish congregation and the Chevra Kadischa (an organization not connected with any congregation, with about 1,500 family members of German and Austrian background). I became their president for sixteen years and to this date am involved in it.

I now live here in Chicago in an apartment which I own with my wife, Renee. We have no children, but I have close connections with my family. Some I manage to see here in the United States and others I visit repeatedly in Israel and South America. My brothers and sisters are all dead; but my relationship with nieces and nephews is as close as it ever can be.

I am happy and thankful to live in this country enjoying a wonderful life with my wife.

DR. JUR. WALTER STRAUSS

Born in 1889 in Stuttgart and died in 1977 in New York. *Father:* Stephan Strauss (1856–1936). *Mother:* Anna Rosenstein Strauss (1857–1940). *Wife:* Elsbeth Hollander Strauss (1904–1931). *Life in Germany:* active in banking, insurance, sales. Dachau, November 1938—three weeks. Emigrated in March 1939 to New York. Worked as insurance agent; also taught insurance.

Children: Margit (Strauss) Ulrich, born 1928, Stuttgart. Rita (Strauss) Blum, born 1926, in Stuttgart.

Rita S. Blum: Born in 1926 in Stuttgart. Schools—Schieker Schule, Rhodert. Emigrated with father and sister to America in 1939. Lived six months in Illinois with relatives and others until father got established in New York. They lived in New York until 1951. Completed junior high and high school and B.A. from Hunter College. In 1949 married Arnold Blum, also from Stuttgart. Two children: David, a medical doctor, and Ralph, a chef. Lived also in New Jersey for eight years and in Pennsylvania for the last twenty years.

WALTER STRAUSS
19 West 44th Street
New York, N.Y. 10036

My father was born in 1872 in Heilbronn, and my mother was born in Frankfurt in 1882. I was born in Stuttgart in 1905, and since I can remember, my main interest in life was music.

When I entered school at six years of age we all were asked what we were. (I was the only Jewish child in my class.) Some of the other childrens' answers were "Evangelisch" and "Katholisch." All I knew was that I was neither Evangelisch nor Katholisch. Since I had to say something when I was asked, I replied "Musikalisch" and didn't quite understand why the class was laughing. Actually, I wanted to become either a musician or a teacher, but my mother said that I should become either a lawyer or a doctor. Since I could not stand to see the sight of blood, I decided to become a lawyer. However, behind the backs of my parents, I studied philosophy with Jaspers and literature with Gundolf during my first three years. At the age of twenty I received the Ph.D. degree and was told I was the youngest doctor in Heidelberg's history. Afterward I studied law and finished these studies within two years after having written two articles for Professor Ruemelin's *Civil Law* magazine. I then practiced law in Stuttgart until December 1936.

When I left the city of my birth due to the greater and greater Nazi infiltration in December 1936 with my two children, Brigitte (age three) and Frank (age one), I had the intention of becoming a lawyer again. However, to earn some money during my studies I started to sell insurance. Soon I started to enjoy the insurance business and concentrated entirely on it. Against my original intentions, I decided to stay in it and studied at the same time with the American College of Life Underwriters from which I soon received the C.L.U. degree.

In 1939, men like Leo Adler, Rabbi Dr. Auerbach, Theodore Hirsch, Sigmund Kahn, Leopold Levi, and others founded the Organization of the Jews from Wuerttemberg, and I became its chairman. We tried—and sometimes succeeded—to save the lives of many Jews in Wuerttemberg by obtaining the necessary sponsorship documents. In those years we had regular social meetings and concerts. The activities of our organization continued, to a certain degree, all these years, and our present collection of these statements will probably be the highlight of our endeavors.

For the last thirteen years I have been president of the Blue Card (a social mutual-help organization of the Central European Jewish immigration) and have now become its honorary president. Since my Stuttgart days I adored the great conductor Fritz Busch, and we became close friends. After his early death in 1951 I founded the Friends of Fritz Busch Society and arranged many memorial concerts starting in small halls and ending at the Kaufman Auditorium of the Y on Lexington Avenue. In these thirty years, artists such as Judith Blegen, Alexander Kipnis, George London, Sherrill Milnes, Birgit Nilson, Rudolph and Peter Serkin, Martial Singher, Teresa Stratas, and Jon Vickers participated, and they all performed in memory of Fritz Busch without any remuneration.

Fortunately, I was able to bring my father to the United States, where he died in 1944. My mother had died in 1926. My children are Brigitte Saunders, who is a mathematics teacher at Great Neck High School; Frank, who is the public relations director of the Council of Jewish Federations in New York; and Marian, who is a social worker in Boston. I have five grandchildren.

*KURT SUSSKIND

Kurt Susskind was born in Stuttgart in 1906. His first examination was in 1931, dismissed from internship in 1933, left for France in 1934. He returned once again to Germany and worked for an auditor until he left for the United States for good in 1936. He started out as an occasional laborer in restaurants and hotels, worked steadily from 1938 on, and in 1944 succeeded in making a living as an independent account and tax-consultant.

RALPH SUSSMAN (formerly Rolf Sussmann)
110-50 71st Road
Forest Hills, N.Y. 11375

My father, Siegfried Sussmann, was born in 1880, in Stuttgart. He graduated from Gymnasium, spent one year as a volunteer in Paris, and then took over the family business, Gebrueder Sussmann, Schuhgrosshandlung. He came to this country in 1939, where he lived in retirement until his death in 1959.

My mother, Edith Sussmann, née Hecht, was born in 1891, got married, and moved to Stuttgart in 1920. She is now eight-nine years old and is living in a "home" on Long Island.

I was born in Stuttgart in 1921. I attended the Eberhard Ludwig Gymnasium and a private business school. I came to New York in 1938. From 1943 to 1946 I was in the U.S. Army, the last two years overseas. Part of the time I acted as an interpreter and was also back in Stuttgart. I attended City College and received a degree in business administration. Since 1961 I have been with Alfred Mainzer, Inc., publishers and importers of greeting cards, Long Island City, New York, and am now treasurer of this company.

In 1966 I married Gerda Wronker, daughter of Max and Irma Wronker. My father-in-law and his father were the owners of Kaufhaus Wronker, Frankfurt am Main. My mother-in-law is the daughter of Wilhelm and Anna Lichter, Stuttgart. Wilhelm Lichter was partner in the firm Baden-Wuerttembergische Weinbrennerei Hirsch und Lichter, Stuttgart. Wilhelm and Anna Lichter died in Theresienstadt in 1943.

FRED A. SUTTON (formerly Fritz Albert Sontheimer)
7 South 6th Street, Room 218
Terre Haute, Ind. 47807

An old friend of mine, Herbert Lenk of Cincinnati, Ohio, forwarded me a copy of your letter of September 1979 in reference to the Organization of the Jews from Wuerttemberg. I was not aware of the fact that there is such an organization and am very anxious to hear more from you.

I am the son of Bank Director Felix Sontheimer, who died about 1944. I came to the United States in 1939, after spending one year in an internment camp in Holland.

I stayed in New York City until 1940 and moved to Houston, Texas, until I was drafted into the U.S. Army in 1942. I was with the 96th Infantry Division and participated in the invasion of Leyte, Philippine Islands, and Okinawa. I was discharged three years later, after being hospitalized for nearly six months.

After this I returned to New York City in 1946 and worked as an executive trainee for Allied Stores and Peck & Peck until 1947. I then took a position with a department store in Terre Haute.

In 1949 I married a local girl. We have one daughter.

In 1950 I started in business for myself as an independent insurance agent and I am still at it. For several years I have been the secretary-treasurer of the Terre Haute Independent Insurance Agents. In the 1950's I was active with the Junior Chamber of Commerce, had offices local, state, and national as well as international, and I am an honorary life member of JCI, called a senator. For the last six years I have been active in veterans affairs, four years adjutant and two years as commander of the local Disabled American Veterans, Chapter #9. I am active with the American Legion, a member for thirty-two years, presently chaplain, and to be elected as senior vice-commander of the local post 40. Also I am active with the Disabled American Veterans Department of Indiana as district commander and State Color Guard. My wife will take office as state commander for the DAV Auxiliary for the State of Indiana in June, and we will go to the National Convention in Honolulu in July.

My schooling was an apprenticeship with SAPT AG in Stuttgart and Commercial High School in Stuttgart. I took several night classes in New York City and Houston.

I changed my name from Fritz Albert Sontheimer to Frederick A. Sutton in 1940. I remarried in 1968, and I am a member of the St. Stephen's Episcopal Church in Terre Haute since the early fifties.

I have two brothers, Paul F. Sutton at 43 Meadow Way, Willowdale, Ontario, M2H2V2 Canada, and Henry R. Sutton, at 221 Aylstone Road, Wigston-Leicester, England.

RUTH SZILAGYI (formerly Richter) (née Liebmann)
9761 South Ingleside
Chicago, Ill. 60628

I was educated as a gymnastics teacher and also in orthopedic gymnastics and massage (physical therapy). I was for a while self-employed and taught at RJF (Reichsbund Juedischer Frontsoldaten) in Stuttgart and later in Darmstadt. When I worked for an orthopedic surgeon in Frankfurt he was forced to release me in order to keep his Aryan employees. This happened in 1938, before I escaped with my husband, Oscar Richter, on October 6, 1938, the day the Jews were forced to have the word "Jew" (*Jude*) inscribed in their passports. On the train to Aachen most Jewish refugees were taken off the train to be searched. For some reason, my husband and I were spared this procedure. We were on the last boat to leave before the infamous Kristallnacht. The last words I remember a customer uttering at the ticket agent's office were: "Let's get rid of all the Jews."

In this country I acquired supplementary training in both nursing and art. After many different jobs, from chambermaid and waitress on Park Avenue in New York, to hospital employee in Chicago (mainly in the field of psychiatry), I arrived at my present employment as art therapist at the University of Chicago Hospital. I am also a co-op owner of an Art Gallery.

My specialty is batik, and my hsuband's, who is in this venture with me, watercolors.

After Oscar Richter's death, I married Oliver Szilagyi, who practiced law in Hungary and became a librarian in the United States. I became a vegetarian and do considerable work for the Animal Protective League, fighting cruelty, torture, and killing with the organization, as well as with Amnesty International, for all species.

In 1971 I won a Certificate of Merit from the University of Chicago Hospitals as the Outstanding Employee of the Year.

I feel that my roots are planted deeply in the city of Chicago, where I fight for the "underdog," and where my husband and I enjoy cultural events, especially the arts.

ERWIN TAENZER
11 Lantern Lane
Lexington, Mass. 02173

Dear Mr. Strauss:

When I read about your seventy-fifth birthday in the *Aufbau* some time ago, I meant to write to you to offer my congratulations and good wishes. But the articles gave no address. Now that I received the letters from the Organization of the Jews from Wuerttemberg, I make up for that belatedly.

We have been out of touch for well over thirty years. The last time I saw you was, I believe, in 1947, when you invited me to your house for dinner. I still recall your interest in music. You played a record of Mahler's *Kindertotenlieder,* in those days on 78-rpm records. I knew of those *lieder,* but had not actually heard them before. Now we have two different recordings of them ourselves.

If you know of any Wuerttemberger Jews who live in the Boston area, I would appreciate if you let me know their names and addresses.

I was born in 1914 in Stuttgart and grew up in Goeppingen. After completing the Abitur in the Realgymnasium I studied for one year electrical engineering at the Technische Hochschule in Stuttgart. From 1934 to 1937 I was an electrician apprentice in Berlin passed by Gesellenprüfung in 1937.

With the help of my later brother Paul I came to the United States in 1937.

I married Ruth Schiller in 1948 in New York. We have three children: Paul A., born 1950; David H, born 1952; Helen Beth, born 1955.

My wife's father, Joseph Schiller, is from Braunsbach.

From 1943 to 1945 I served in the U.S. Army.

I studied to become an electrical engineer and have been active in this field since the end of the war.

We have been members of Temple Isaiah, Lexington, Massachusetts, since 1963.

My father, Rabbiner Dr. Arnold (Aron) Tanzer, was born in 1871 and died in 1937 in Goeppingen.

My mother, Bertha, née Strauss, was born in 1876 and died in 1943 in Theresienstadt.

335

*PAUL TAENZER

Attorney Dr. Paul Taenzer was born in 1897 as the son of the rabbi and historian Dr. Taenzer. He was admitted in Stuttgart in 1925 and since 1936 served as honorary member in the Oberrat der Israelitischen Religionsgemeinsehaft Wuerttembergs. In 1938 he went on aliyah to Palestine via Switzerland. After acquiring the necessary language facility he once again began to study law in accordance with local rules. After passing his examinations in 1941, he served as an unpaid intern in a law firm for one year and was engaged in a law practice of his own from 1942 on. He died in Tel Aviv in 1945.

ARNON TAMIR (Fischmann)
30060 Hazore'a
Israel

I was born Arnold Fischmann in Stuttgart in 1919, son of Michael and Karoline Fischmann. Attended the Karlsgymnasium. Since 1919 member of the German-Jewish hiking club Kameraden, later Werkleute (working people). In 1933 a few months as apprentice in the Schocken Department Store, then retraining until 1934 volunteer in gardening, then until 1936 in the building trade. Active with the Werkleute and in the community youth group as local group leader. From 1936 to 1938 mainly educational work, with Werkleute, Hechaluz in Berlin and Breslau, and preparing young Jews for emigration to Palestine, in the framework of Youth Aliyah.

I will always remember the work we did on a villa at the Lenzhalde in 1935: for a wealthy Jew from Goeppingen. Also unforgettable is the sympathetic behavior of the German masons and bricklayers who taught me the work in exchange for innumerable bottles of beer. They repeatedly assured me that the anti-Semitic attacks were only directed against the other Jews, not against those like me who worked with their hands. I also remember meeting former classmates, who always said, "Jews do not work," when they saw me in my workclothes.

My parents had been forced to close their factory after the boycott and had a very hard time keeping their heads above water. My sister Lea, who presently is living in Haifa, emigrated to Palestine in 1934, and as I had the same intention, my parents decided to follow us at the first opportunity.

Both my parents were over fifty when they emigrated to Palestine with only small capital and very few possessions. They were able, however, to build up a small dairy business in Hadar Hakarmel in Haifa with many

336

faithful customers who liked to visit the Fischmann's "Salon," which had become a social center in the neighborhood. My father passed away in 1951, and soon after my mother moved into my Kibbutz Hazore'a and died in 1967.

I stayed in Germany without my family. It became clearer and clearer that the dreaded war was unavoidable, and in that case plans had to be made for a help organization underground. It is without doubt that this was of the greatest help to our comrades in Holland, so that when this country was invaded they were able, with the use of false papers, to work amidst regular foreign workers. They also got many of our people out of Holland into Spain, and most of them survived the war. A former schoolfriend of mine, Kurt Reilinger, formerly Militaerstrasse, played a large part in the Resistance movement. After the war he was killed in a car accident.

In 1938, because, through my father I was still a Polish citizen, I was expelled to Poland, staying in a refugee camp in Zbaszyn at the then Polish-German frontier. Organized with young people for self-help action, I emigrated illegally to Palestine in 1939 and entered the Kibbutz Hazore'a shortly afterwards, and am a member until this day.

I married Elisheva Loewenstern; two boys, Haggaj, born 1946, and Shimon, born 1950. For about twenty years I was responsible for planning and building in the kibbutz. At the same time I performed cultural activities, directing musical performances and amateur operas, for which our kibbutz was known in Israel during the fifties. Later active as Regisseur at the theater and radio: Haifa City Theater, directing the Theater of the Kibbutz Movement, etc. On the radio there were performed a few of my own plays, some of which were also performed in Germany, Norway, and Switzerland.

Since 1978 I am the director of the department for Documentation and Information in the kibbutz movement, and active as a freelance contributor to radio and various theater productions.

Radio plays produced abroad: The Lost Stones (autobiographic, about the fate of the Stuttgart Jewish community); *The Station* (contribution of the Israel radio to the Prix Italia 1974); *Kommunikation.*

Attempts in the literary field: Contribution to a memorial book about the Jewish community in Stuttgart, published by the City of Stuttgart; this book reprints parts of an unpublished autobiography. *The first years of Hazore'a* (in preparation).

ERELA TAMRI (née Ries)
Kibbutz Ein Dor 19335
Mobile Post Jezreel
Israel

I was born in Göppingen in 1920; the fourth child of Paula, née Fleischer, and Eugen Ries. My father died in 1924. My two sisters and my brother are now living in England. In 1935 we were driven out of grandmother's house, where we lived, so that the mayor of Göppingen could have a suitable house. We then moved to Stuttgart, together with my grandmother, Emilie Fleischer. She died in 1939. Mother joined her children in 1939 in England, where she lived until 1963, the last two years in the Otto Hirsch House.

As a member of the Werkleute, I went to Mittleren Hachscharah in Sennfeld, near Heilbronn, from 1937 to 1938. On the day of the Anschluss, 1938, I left for Palestine, where I had two years of training in vegetable gardening in an agricultural school for girls in Chederah. Those first years of adjusting to the country, to its climate, to its ways of living, to the language—though I spoke some Hebrew already—were not easy. Besides the personal difficulties here there were constant attacks by Arabs on Jewish settlements, and in Europe, the beginning of World War II (not knowing if mother left for England). Already in Germany I wanted to live in a kibbutz, and so I joined in 1940 Kibbutz Erez Yisraeli Vav of the Hashomer Hazair, whom the Werkleute had joined in the meantime. I entered the kibbutz in its first year of existence, and I am living in it presently, going through all our stages of existence. In the first years, before settling down at Ein Dor near the historic site, in 1948 I worked in vegetable gardens and factories. Here at Ein Dor (we called ourselves after the Bible—historic site), we found barren land, *viel steine gabs*, and now we are a most beautiful and prospering settlement. But back to 1948, the army required eight men, and that was much for a new settlement. We could give five men and three women, and so I volunteered, not being married. In 1949, coming back to Ein Dor, I went on working in the vegetable garden, later in the cow shed. In 1952 I married Reuben Tamri, née Loewenstamm, from Berlin. We have three children, two of them already married. Later I worked as a practical nurse for fifteen years in our kibbutz clinic. Now I have been working for six years in our wire and cable factory, Tel Dor, and am responsible for the braiding section. I hope to be able to be an active member, both at work and in community life, for a good many years to come.

338

GERTRUDE TANK (née Loewenstein)
124 NW 7th Street, Apt. 105
Carvallis, Or. 97330

I was born in Stuttgart in 1892, the oldest daughter of lawyer Dr. Rudolf Loewenstein and Marie, née Lebrecht. Father died in 1922. Mother emigrated to United States in 1939 and died in Newark, New Jersey, in 1958. My sister Hedwig immigrated to United States with her family in 1938 and died in Kew Gardens, New York, in 1980.

After graduating I decided to study dentistry in Philadelphia, because at that time the United States was the world leader in dental education. After graduating from Temple University in 1916, I returned to Germany, practiced dentistry in Stuttgart with Dr. Wilhelm Tank, whom I married in 1920 and divorced in 1928. In 1926, the year of the Hitler Putsch, I immigrated to the United States with my five-year-old daughter, Ursula, and accepted the job as attending dentist at the dental clinic of the Community Health Center of the Federation of Jewish Charities. Two years later, I took charge of the clinic until 1953, when at the age of sixty-one I decided to change jobs and of several offers chose that of associate professor of nutrition research at Oregon State University, changing from practicing dentistry and administration to research on the effect of various trace elements on oral pathology by a series of epidemiological studies, publishing the results in a number of scientific journals. I retired from Oregon State University in 1965, at the age of seventy-three.

My daughter, Ursula, married Dr. William K. Gealey, a geologist and paleontologist in 1941. They live in Mill Valley, California, have two sons and one granddaughter.

Realizing the importance even now, at age eighty-nine, of staying involved and keeping active, besides being a homemaker I have been involved in various volunteer activities, one of them as dental consultant to the Nursing Home Task Force, and among others, reviewing research papers before publication and giving German lessons.

JUSTIN TANNHAUSER
10 Place Jean Jaurès
34500 Béziers
France

Emigration from Germany took place 1933. I was twenty years old and single.

At that time the doors in France were open for political refugees, provided they did not seek employment. This made my existence difficult because I had to earn a living, without the right to. I knew French only somewhat from high school. My new connections to French Jews were very helpful. They supported me much in the beginning, and thank God, they helped me not to be deported. After I got a job for which I was paid secretly, but it became known.

By the end of 1936 I obtained French nationality. Meanwhile, my mother and my two younger brothers were fortunate to emigrate to New York. Three short years, before the outbreak of World War II, my life as a Frenchman was the same as that of the other citizens. After the French lost the war in 1940, I became a refugee again. To escape the occupation by the Germans, I moved to the South of France, which was free. I live there now.

But by the end of 1942, this part of France was occupied too. Everybody knows how the Vichy government worked with the Germans, against the Jews and patriots. I thereafter was deprived of my French citizenship. With the help of faked papers supplied by Christians, I was able to work in the forests but not without daily fears for my survival. I had to give up all connections with my fellow Jews during this time, so as not to be discovered.

In 1944 came the happy liberation here, near the Mediterranean. Shortly afterwards my French citizenship was restored to me. So ended an unforgettable era.

Surviving members of my family meet regularly with the *Buttenhaeusern*, thus to keep up the memory of all our departed friends. Every day given us by God could be an opportunity to remember that, which is most important.

Kindest regards and Shalom!

GRETL TEMES (née Marx)
52 H Jefferson Oval
Yorktown Heights, N.Y. 10598

Thank you for your letter and most of all for all the work you are putting into this most precious project. I am most anxious to give you the details of my family and background. I am looking forward to receiving the publication, as this will become the most treasured heritage to my children and grandchildren.

My name is Gretl Temes. My maiden name was Gretl Marx. I was born in 1920 in Tuebingen. I have an older brother who was born in Buttenhausen in 1913. My parents were Hermann and Hilda Marx-Levy. My father was born in 1883 in Buttenhausen and died in New York City in 1956. My mother was born in 1885 in Muehringen, Schwarzwald, and died in New York in 1962.

I grew up in Buttenhausen, where both my grandmothers also had lived. Both my grandfathers had died before I was born. Buttenhausen was a very small village, beautifully located, where everybody lived in a peaceful, relatively good life until the Nazis took over. I was fourteen years old. All my friends were Gentile and I saw them turned more or less into different people overnight, and that meant completely away from me. I had an uncle in Switzerland (my father's brother), and he invited me to come live with him and his family and finish my schooling there. As I realized at that time that there was no other way to get a higher education, I accepted his invitation. For me it was a big step, from a tiny village with a Jewish school of seven pupils, ranging in age from six to thirteen, taught under one roof by one outstanding teacher—to go alone, leaving my parents behind. As I left, I still remember my father saying, *"Es wird nicht so heiss gegessen, wie es angerichtet wird,"* and so I left, hoping that the whole Nazi system would break down before I would finish my education. We were young. Nevertheless I was fortunate, and my parents were happy to know I was safe.

In 1938 my father was taken to Dachau, and I can say this was the most difficult time for me. I wished I would not have been separated. I was safe but very helpless. After six weeks of being in the concentration camp, my father and several other people were released. I will be forever thankful to the late Professor Karl Adler of Stuttgart, whose heroic work to save Jewish lives paid off. Through his efforts, plus the *eiserne Kreuz I Klasse*, my father was reunited with my mother.

My mother had the foresight to prepare to leave home, but my father wanted to remain in order to liquidate all his assets. He was a horse-dealer and had houses and estates. Only my mother's determination not to stay any longer in Germany saved their lives.

They were in Stuttgart for dental work, and when Friday afternoon came, my father asked my mother, "What train are we taking home?" My mother's answer was, "We are not going home anymore, I have the visa and tickets to go to Switzerland." My mother's mind was made up not to live through another May 1 in Germany.

My parents arrived in 1939 in Basel, and I was more than grateful. My grandmother and aunt (mother and sister from my mother's side) were still in Buttenhausen, and there was no way for us to get them out. Shortly before all the Buttenhauser Jews were deported, my aunt who always was a courageous woman, ended her mother's life and her own with an overdose of sleeping pills. I remember the news as a terrible shock. But when all the other families, old and young, were taken away to concentration camps, we found peace knowing they did not have to suffer.

My parents lived in Basel, Switzerland, for seven years. I had met a man, a refugee from Vienna, fell in love, and got married in 1945. My parents received their American visa in 1946 and left for New York. My husband and I had to wait longer on account of the Austrian quota. Meanwhile, I gave birth to my daughter, Masha, in 1948. When Masha was nine months old we left Switzerland to be reunited with my parents. After three years we became parents of a second child, a boy named Alan.

Masha is married and we gained another son. Our son-in-law is a most beautiful person. They have two children. Robyn is the older one. David is the second one. Alan is single. Masha lives in Putnam Valley, and through visiting her frequently, we came to love that area in upper Westchester, in the midst of beautiful rolling hills. It looked so charming and somewhat reminded me of home. We moved to that area in 1974. We enjoy our retirement, the country setting, and most of all our grandchildren—realizing how fortunate we are.

I would like to express the sincere wish that someone else had gone into a more detailed description of the two most outstanding people and they are: Lehrer und Rabbiner Berlinger of Buttenhausen and Professor Adler, Stuttgart, Buttenhausen.

*FRITZ THALMESSINGER
Last known address:
Pucwar Hiraman POB 117
Kanpur, India

Dr. Fritz Thalmessinger, born in Boeblingen in 1909, passed his first examination in 1932. He had his Referendarship terminated in 1933 but was able to obtain his doctorate in Tuebingen in 1934. That same year he left for India, where he has been engaged in business.

*KURT THALMESSINGER

Attorney Kurt Thalmessinger, born in Stuttgart in 1902 is the son of attorney Otto Thalmessinger, who perished in the Nazi persecution. His admission was canceled in 1933. He left for France immediately. As a German, he was placed in confinement as soon as the war broke out. Later on he served as a soldier in the French Army. After the occupation of France by the Germans, he vanished from sight, and under a false name he worked as a day-laborer in a factory. Since 1956 he has been a legal advisor to URO (United Restitution Organization) in Paris.

*OTTO THALMESSINGER

Lawyer Otto Thalmessinger was born in Ulm in 1872. In 1899 he was admitted to the bar and practiced law in Stuttgart. In 1932 he became a notary public.

In 1933, the notary office was taken away from him. It may be assumed that his admission to the bar was revoked in 1938. At the beginning of 1942, he was forced to give up his residence in Stuttgart and to move to Buchau. There he committed suicide in 1942 to escape certain deportation.

MARGOT TIEFENTHAL (née Bauer)
Dahlheimersgatan 4 a
S-413 20 Goteborg
Sweden

My late husband and I left Stuttgart in 1934, leaving our two small sons behind together with my parents. Our plans then were rather vague, but they included both Israel and the United States. We came to stay in Copenhagen, and afte a while we would send for our sons. My husband then had a good job with a textile firm.

At the very last minute we got my parents to leave Stuttgart and join us in Denmark. My brother, Fritz Bauer, also came to stay with us. This was in 1938. The Tiefenthals had decided to leave for the United States earlier on, so both families were safe.

In 1943, the Germans, who had at that time kept Denmark occupied for three years, decided to start persecution of the Danish Jews. We had friends who helped us hide until we could flee on a fishing boat to Sweden. All of us arrived here safe and sound.

My husband, who was a textile engineer, at first got a job as an ordinary worker in Goteborg but soon advanced to do the work he had studied for. In different ways he worked with textiles until the day he died in 1976.

As for myself, I had a small business making ladies underwear, but as times grew hard here I got myself employed in an office. Now, at the age of seventy-four, I can look back at some years of social work with old and sick in the Jewish Congregation of Gothenburg.

I have two grown sons who are married to Swedish girls. Each of them has three children. Some days ago I became a great-grandmother, and I do not at all dislike this new role.

TRUDY TURKEL (née Kirchhausen)
15 Columbine Court
Baltimore, Md. 21209

My Father and mother both were alive in 1933 and resided in Heilbronn A. N. Rosskampfstrasse 30 at that time.

Father: Julius (genannt Hugo) Kirchhausen; born Heilbronn, 1881; *business,* merchant wholesale (fabrics) 1898–1938, Mittelstelle Arbeit fur Auswanderungen der Juden 1938–41; emigration, June 1941, to United States; residence in Brooklyn, New York, 1941–1959; male orderly at the Hebrew Home for the Aged in Brooklyn; retired to Baltimore, Maryland, 1960; died 1966 in Baltimore.

Mother: Elsa Kirchhausen, née Michel; born, 1894; *business,* housewife 1920 on; emigration to United States to Brooklyn, New York, 1941; worked in New York in a leather goods factory; retired to Baltimore, Maryland, in 1960, where she is still residing.

Irene Kirchhausen Manor—eldest daughter of Hugo and Elsa Kirchhausen. Born Heilbronn, 1921; attended Grundschule und Mädchenrealschule in Heilbronn; participated in the Youth Aliyah Program in 1933 and went on Hachscharah; emigrated to Palestine in 1938, where she became a member of Tel Chai, and Kfar Gileadi, and Yifat. Currently she is director of the Bread Museum at Dagon in Haifa, Israel. She married Dodi Manor and bore three boys. The oldest son, Amos Manor is a resident of Yifat in Israel, is married and the father of two sons. The middle son, Uri Manor, is a retired colonel of the Israeli Air Force currently residing in Tel Aviv, and father of two children, Ranan and Gilat. The third son, Jossy Manor, is currently residing at Nahalal and is married and the father of a son.

Trude Kirchhausen Turkel—middle daughter of Hugo and Elsa Kirchhausen. Born Heilbronn, 1924; attended Grundschule and two grades of the Mädchenrealschule and the Jewish school in Heilbronn; was sent to the United States as one of ten schoolchildren with a children's transport sponsored by the HIAS. The emigration took place in 1938, and the transport arrived on the SS *Hamburg* in New York in 1938. The children were then sent to various cities in the United States, where sponsoring Jewish organizations would take over their welfare. I was sent to St. Louis, Missouri, where I was placed in a foster home. I attended Soldan High school for three years, graduated from there, and was the recipient of a four-year scholarship offered to one girl in the United States by the international sorority Sigma Delta Tau. As the recipient of this complete scholarship I attended the Universities of Oklahoma and Nebraska, living at the Sigma Delta Tau sorority houses and becoming a member of that organization. I met my husband, Harold Turkel, at the University of

344

Nebraska, and we married in 1944 in Chicago, Illinois. My husband, being an attorney for the Social Security Administration, was employed in Chicago. We lived there for four years. We had our first son, Steven Charles Turkel, there and then moved to Independence, Missouri, in 1948. There we had another son, James Stuart Turkel. After four years of residence in Independence, Missouri, we moved to Baltimore, Maryland, where we are still residing. My husband retired from the Social Security Administration after thirty-four years of service. I retired also from the Social Security Administration after twenty years of service. My last position with that agency was disability examiner in the Bureau of Disability Insurance. We have both been active in our temple, Temple Emanuel of Baltimore, of which we are charter members. We both served on the board of trustees many times and for years. I taught in the Sunday School of temple for many years, first as head teacher and then as confirmation class teacher. I have also been active in the Chevra Ahavas Chesed, Inc., of Baltimore. I served on the board of directors of the Women's division for the last eight years and was president of the Women's Division of the last two years. My husband I are both members of the Mountain Club of Maryland. My son Steven Charles Turkel is married to Barbara Holmes Turkel. They live in Mount Airy, Maryland, and have two children, David Andrew Turkel, seven years old, and Amy Renee Turkel, four years old. My son James Stuart Turkel is married to Paulette Micrietti Turkel, and they live in Sykesville, Maryland, and have two daughters, Gina Elizabeth Turkel, four years old, and Jaime Ly Turkel, two years old.

Martin Kirchhausen—youngest child of Hugo and Elsa Kirchhausen. Born Heilbronn, 1932; attended kindergarten in the Jewish School of Heilbronn in 1938 and part of 1939; was sent to England with a children's transport in July of 1939. He lived in England with a non-Jewish family in the country, until later, during the war, when he was sent to a Jewish orphans' home in Oxford. He rejoined my parents in April of 1945 in Brooklyn, New York, where he was sent to school. He later attended high school in Independence, Missouri, where he lived with us. He enlisted in the U.S. Air Force in 1949 and served three years in Korea. After completion of his service, he attended the University of Maryland and in 1964 married Barbara Bradshaw Kirchhausen. They reside in Baltimore, Maryland, where Martin is employed by the Social Security Administration. Barbara is also employed as a preschool teacher. They have four children: Julie Ann, born 1966; Susan Michelle, born 1970; William David, born 1972; Richard Edward, born 1972.

I might add that my grandmother Kirchhausen also lived in Heilbronn in 1933, was sent to Schloss Eschonau bei Afaltrach, where she died in 1943.

*MANFRED (FRED) UHLMAN

Attorney Dr. Manfred (Fred) Uhlman, born in Stuttgart in 1901, was engaged in the practice of law since the spring of 1927. He was politically active in the SPD (Socialist Party of Germany) as a friend of Kurt Schumacher and in the anti-fascist organization Reichsbanner Black-Red-Gold. Tipped off by a sympathetic judge ("In Paris it's very beautiful just now!"), he repaired there as early as 1933 and proceeded to England in 1940.

He was a man of many talents and used them with varying degrees of success. He tried his hand as a writer, as an art dealer, and as a breeder of aquarium fish. Finally he took up painting with much success. His most notable achievement as a writer was his autobiography, *The Making of an Englishman* (London: Victor Gollancz, 1960). While the book is written in fluid style no painful subject is either embellished or glossed over.

Manfred Uhlman lost both his parents in Theresienstadt. His sister, Erna, and her two-month-old daughter, Tana, were to be transported to Auschwitz in 1942. She threw herself and her baby in front of a train.

P.S. When this report was sent to Manfred Uhlman, he answered as follows: Excuse me for not having answered your letter before because I have been seriously ill for nearly three months which is not amazing as I am over eighty years old. I am an English citizen for nearly forty years and don't feel strongly enough about Wuerttemberg which I still love but try to forget.

The article about my career is perfectly correct with one exception. It does not mention my novel *Reunion*, which Koestler called "a masterpiece" and which had a great success in America.

RUDOLPH E. UHLMAN
10 Murchinson Place
White Plains, N.Y.

Born in 1909 in Stuttgart; student at the Eberhard-Ludwig Gymnasium; diploma in 1927; student of law at the Universities of Freiburg, Munich, Berlin, and Tuebingen; Referendar examination in 1931 in Tuebingen. Discharged by the Nazis in 1933.

Emigrated in 1934 to the United States. Studied American law at Cornell University from 1934 to 1936. Research fellow at Harvard Law School from 1936 to 1938.

Since 1940 practicing as attorney-at-law and associated with the law firm of Guggenheimer & Untermyer.

My father was Richard Uhlman (died in 1947 in Chicago). He was a partner of the firm of Gebrueder Uhlman in Stuttgart and member of the Stuttgart Chamber of Commerce. My mother was Alice Uhlman, née Kauffmann (died in 1979 in Princeton). She was the sister of Thekla Kauffmann.

I am married to Hilde Igersheimer, the daughter of the late Professor Dr. Med. Joseph Igersheimer from Goettingen and Frankfurt. We have three children. Our son is professor of political science at the University of Missouri in St. Louis.

My sister Marianne is married to Professor Dr. Klaus E. Knorr in Princeton. My sister Dorothee died a few years ago in Chicago.

I am a member of the Board of Help and Reconstruction and a member of the Leo Baeck Institute.

MARGIT ULRICH (née Strauss)
11 Riverside Drive
New York, N.Y. 10023

I am the daughter of Walter Strauss, formerly of Stuttgart. My father arrived in the United States in 1939 with my sister Rita and myself. We moved to the Bronx. He worked as a special insurance agent for the Royal Globe Liverpool Insurance Group. He also taught several courses in the evenings at the College of Insurance after having obtained a special advanced degree in insurance at that school. He retired from his job around 1955, but still continued to carry on a private insurance business for many years. He died in New York in 1977 at the age of eighty-seven.

I attended Walton High School in the Bronx, received a B.A. from Hunter College, and an M.A. in education from City College. I taught kindergarten, homebound children, as well as reading for many years in both public and private schools. I recently resigned from my teaching job and am currently working for a doctor, as well as doing tutoring on a volunteer basis.

In 1960 I married Ernest Ulrich, son of the late Karl and Grete Ulrich. We have two daughters: Lisa, born in 1962, and Nancy, born in 1964. We live in New York, enjoy the companionship of friends who are both German and American, Jewish and non-Jewish. We spend our vacations in New England and have made several trips to Germany, England, and Norway, both on business and for pleasure.

My sister is Mrs. Rita Blum of 1322 Hillsdale Drive, Monroeville, Pennsylvania 15146. She was born in 1926, graduated from Hunter College in New York, and worked as a French-English secretary. In 1949 she married Arnold Blum, a metallurgical engineer, son of the late

Melanie and David Blum of Stuttgart. They lived in New Jersey until they moved to Pennsylvania in 1959. Mrs. Blum was employed as a tax consultant and is now a secretarial assistant for the Municipality of Monroeville. Mr. Blum is currently a consulting metallurgical engineer. They have been long-standing and active members of Temple David in Monroeville.

Rita and Arnold Blum have two sons. David, born in 1950, is an internist and endocrinologist practicing in New Rochelle, New York. He has two sons—Jason, aged four, and Jonathan, aged two. The younger son, Ralph, born in 1953, is a chef in a large restaurant in Connecticut. He is the father of Jeremy, aged four, and Courtney, aged one and a half.

RENATE VAMBERY (formerly Gerstman, née Liebmann)
7574 Buckingham
St. Louis, Mo. 63105

I left Stuttgart initially in 1934 to study in England and later in Switzerland. I came home for vacations and for the purpose of emigrating to the United States with my parents. I had earned a diploma in kindergarten teaching, which I used working as an attendant with crippled children in St. Louis, until I returned to school, this time to Washington University. There I studied occupational therapy, a profession which I practiced for twenty years in Nebraska and Chicago and, for five years, with the Armed Forces. I directed several occupational therapy departments, mainly psychiatric ones. I also headed a clinic for preschool handicapped children in Gary, Indiana. After my husband's (Howard Gerstman) death, I returned to St. Louis to attend Washington University Graduate School (I had been enrolled in a graduate program at the University of Chicago) and to help my ailing mother and aging father. I used my master's degree in psychology as senior counseling psychologist at Jewish Employment and Vocational Service in St. Louis (where I also worked with handicapped clients). The next ten years were spent at a Community Mental Health Center as a vocational rehabilitation specialist and psychotherapist. At that time I also co-founded a Personal Growth Center. (I attended seminars and workshops on group processes and became involved in group work.)

I was remarried to Miklos Vambery from whom I am divorced. I have served on boards of professional organizations and held offices. I belong to seven professional organizations, nationally and locally. I have been a consultant to the Department of Health, Education and Welfare as "vocational expert" and am listed in *Who's Who of American Women*. I have been active in peace, civil rights, and human rights organizations for many years.

For the past seven years I have been president of the Humanists of St. Louis, an affiliate of the American Humanist Association. I served on the boards of the Ethical Society and the United Nations Association. During the Vietnam War I brought three Vietnamese children to St. Louis for medical treatment, under the auspices of the Committee of Responsibility.

At this time I am deeply involved with Amnesty International and concerned with suffering anywhere and everywhere. After translating

349

my own diaries I now participate in Holocaust Studies and discussions. I am writing and lecturing on holistic health and will have a chapter on the subject published in a *Humanist Counselors' Guidebook.* As a humanist counselor (clergy status) I help people with diverse problems.

Dear Mr. Strauss, I believe you knew my father, Walter Liebmann, who was a colleague of yours, but considerably older. He died more than twelve years ago. My mother preceded him in death by three months. My father, Dr. Walter Liebmann, practiced law in Stuttgart. My mother was Tilly, née Neuburger. Both parents left Stuttgart with me in 1937. My sister was already married and lived in Frankfurt. She and her husband arrived in the United States in 1938. Both parents adjusted well to the new land and the new life. After a few weeks in New York, where my mother's older brother had lived since before the First World War (as editor-in-chief of the German *New Yorker Staatszeitung*), we moved to St. Louis. Relatives on my father's side sponsored us. My father, at fifty-five, and in the depth of the American depression, took a job as bookkeeper. He also obtained a degree in economics from St. Louis University. My mother sold homemade products until she developed severe asthma. This illness can be traced to the day she received the news of the torturous death of her sister Elsa Kauffmann, née Neuberger, in Theresienstadt, whose husband, Dr. Eugen Kauffmann, apparently died of starvation in concentration camp. My mother prepared about thirty newcomers for their final citizenship papers.

Both parents continued to pursue cultural interests, such as music, lectures, and art. My father studied astronomy after his retirement at age seventy-four, following a heart attack. They both became members of the Ethical Society. My father also worked on restitution cases. He was active until the last three months of his life, when at eighty-four, he suffered a series of strokes. My mother had died three months earlier, after many years of suffering.

Other relatives: My uncle, youngest brother of my mother, John (Hans) Neuburger, formerly of Stuttgart (Neuburger Gardinen), almost eighty-six years old, went from concentration camp Welzheim to England, then to the United States. He lived in New York for twenty-seven years, then moved back to Germany in 1967, with his non-Jewish wife. He now lives in a retirement home in Bad Reichenhall. My father's half-brother, Hans Liebmann, formerly of Stuttgart, emigrated first to Israel, then lived in Switzerland until his death in 1974.

LOUISE VICTOR (née Wolf)
Maastorenflat
Schiedamsedijk 177
Rotterdam
Netherlands

My husband, Eugene Victor, passed away in 1980.

My parents, Anna and Herman Wolf, of Heilbronn died in Bergen-Belsen shortly before the end of the war.

My first husband, Otto Victor, and I emigrated to South Africa and worked very hard. Otto joined the Army and fought with the Allies for six years, during the entire war. After his return, he again worked in his original field, hides and skins. He died at age of forty-four.

We have a daughter and grandsons. One grandson is married, and we have a greatgrandson too.

My second husband, Eugen, had one son, George, who died at the age of forty-four. There are a daughter and two sons, grown up and working and unmarried. All of them are doing well.

I live in Rotterdam since 1961 and intend to stay here.

MAX VICTOR
Usonia Road
Pleasantville, N.Y. 10570

Parents: Jacob Victor, born 1870 in Heilbronn/N., and died in 1934 in Heilbronn. Co-founder of Lederfabrik Gebr. Victor. The firm Gebr. Victor was established in Heilbronn in 1867. Mathilde, née Kirchheimer, born in 1875 in Heilbronn and died in 1934 in Heilbronn.

I was born in Heilbronn in 1905. 1928–1932, economic research in Kiel. 1932–1937, Lederfabrik Heilbronn. 1937–1941, in Holland, England, and the Dominican Republic. Since 1941 I have been in the United States; started with brother Victor Brothers, exporters and dealers in hides.

I married Trude Victor, née Strauss, born in 1905 in Frankfurt/M, in 1931.

From 1932–1937 we organized the Juedische Jugendbund in Heilbronn.

LUITPOLD WALLACH
College of Liberal Arts and Sciences
Department of the Classics
4072 Foreign Languages Building
University of Illinois
Urbana, Ill. 61801

Born in Munich, Bavaria, in 1910, as the only son of Karl and Rosa Wallach. I grew up in Laupheim, Wuerttemberg, where my family had settled in 1912. In Laupheim, my three sisters and I attended the one-room Jewish Elementary School and then the Public Grammar School (Latein und Realschule). My father returned to Laupheim in 1919, after World War I, from an Italian prisoner-of-war camp. I concluded in 1929 my formal higher education with the Abitur examination at Ulm on the Danube.

Subsequently, I engaged in the study of two fields: (a) the study of history and philosophy at the Universities of Berlin and Tübingen and (b) simultaneously, in the study of Jewish theology at the Hochschule (Lehranstalt) fur die Wissenschaft des Judentums in Berlin, Artillerie-strasse. I received the degree of doctor of philosophy in history from the University of Tübingen in 1932 and a few years later the rabbinical degree from the named Hochschule. Upon appointment by the Israelitische Oberrat in Stuttgart I was the last Bezirksrabbiner of Göppingen, Wuerttemberg, 1937–1939.

My sister Sally succeeded to emigrate to the United States in 1938, and with her help I was able to follow in 1939, after having spent time with many others in the KZ Dachau. We could not save our parents and sisters. My mother died in 1942 in Laupheim, having been refused medical aid. My father perished in Auschwitz some time between 1942 and 1944, and my youngest sister, Betti, in Stutthoff near Danzig, probably by 1944. My oldest sister, Charlotte, survived in Hungary after intolerable hardships and arrived in 1947 in the United States, but never regained her health. Life was much kinder to me.

I was active as a rabbi in various American communities from 1940–1948, also in 1947 and 1948 as Jewish chaplain at Hendricks Chapel of Syracuse University, New York. I then realized an older intention of mine and started my academic career as a college and university teacher in history and the classics. I had prepared for this from the very begin-

352

ning through my studies and also through the uninterrupted publication of scholarly papers which have appeared since 1933 in German and Belgian professional journals, and since 1941 in American historical and philological and literary journals. After having taught in various American colleges and universities since 1951, I joined the faculty of Marquette University in 1962 as professor of classics. In 1967 I followed an invitation of the University of Illinois at Urbana, Illinois, as professor teaching the classics and mediaeval studies. Of the numerous academic honors and fellowships I received over the years, I am going to mention only a few (*Who's Who in America* and the *Directory of American Scholars,* Volume III, contain a complete enumeration); the election to the honor society of Phi Beta Kappa, Cornell University chapter; publication by the Leo Baeck Institute of my book *Liberty and Letters: The Thought of Leopold Zunz* (London, 1959); a critical account of the beginnings of the Science of Judaism in Germany during the nineteenth century and others. In 1975, colleagues, friends, and former students from Austria, France, Germany, England, Italy, and the United States honored me greatly through the publication of a *Festschrift* with historical, philological, and literary studies written in English, French, German, and Italian, entitled *Gesellschaft, Kultur, Literature: Beitraege Luitpold Wallach Gewidmet,* edited by Professor Karl Bosl, University of Munich and Bavarian Academy of the Sciences (Stuttgart: Anton Hiersemann).

A bibliography of my books, monographs, articles, and reviews, published 1933–1975 in Europe and in the United States, compiled by my wife Barbara, Ph.D. in classical philology, at present visiting professor at the University of Pittsburgh, is published in the above-named *Festschrift,* pages 279–289.

Since 1975, I have published in addition the following volumes: *Diplomatic Studies in Latin and Greek Documents from the Carolingian Age.* (Ithaca and London: Cornell University Press, 1977); *Die Zwiefalter Chroniken Ortliebs und Bertholds,* 2d. ed., (Sigmaringen: Thorbecke Verlag, 1978), (the first edition appeared in 1941 without my name on the title pages for the reasons explained in the two first Prefaces.)

At present I am finishing the printer's manuscript of my large edition with commentary of Charlemagne's *Libri Carolini* written for him by the Anglo-Saxon Alcuin. This work will be followed by a monograph, entitled *Aristoteles Latinus and Alcuin: Newly Discovered Aspects of Syllogistic Mediaeval Logic.* I finally hope to republish a set of Hebrew studies, published in journals between 1938 and 1948, under the title: *Hellenistic Jewish Studies in Hebrew Literature and History.*

Finally, it has been an encouraging experience watching the loyalty shown to me by former Ph.D. students who are now teaching at American colleges and universities. Some of them are planning another *Festschrift, in Status nascendi.* Others are publishing the results of their own studies as books which are undeservedly dedicated to me. Of these I should like to mention for the sake of brevity just two, at the head and at the end of an alphabetical list: Gary B. Blumenshine kindly presented to me his diplomatic edition of Alcuin's *Contra Haeresim Felicis* (Rome: Biblioteca Apostolica Vaticana, 1978). And last, but not least, Barbara Wallach dedicated to me her first book, *Lucretius and the Diatribe Against the Fear of Death* (Mnemosyne, Suppl. 40; Leiden: Brill, 1976). *Vivan sequentes!*

My wife, Dr. Barbara P. Wallach, became, in 1980, a professor of classical studies in the Department of Classical Studies at the University of Missouri at Columbia, Missouri 65201. Our address there is: 1201 Business Highway 63 South, Apt. 201, Lexington Square, Columbia, Mo. 65201.

EMMA WEIL
Heinrich Stahl-House Room 26
Bishops Ave.
London N., England

My father, Sigmund Weil, M.D., was born 1860 in Aufhausen, where our family lived for generations. His father owned an oil mill there. My father was, for many years, the liberal president of the Jewish community in Stuttgart and still active in the community in 1933. He also was on the board of the Jewish Club to assist sick persons, as well as on the board of the Jewish Home for Orphans in Esslingen, where he was honored to show the King and Queen of Wuerttemberg the new buildings and to explain to him the Jewish synagogue service in the orphanage. He was a well-known specialist in stomach disorders, and during World War I he was chief of staff at the Stuttgart Falker Street Hospital, emigrated to England at age eighty in 1939.

His son, Dr. Herman Weil, already in England since 1936 with his family, helped him and also me to come to England by posting a sum of money as a guarantee. My brother was a director of the Salamander Shoe factories in Kornwestheim. He was a lawyer but could not work in England in this profession. My brother died in 1960 during a visit to his married daughters in Johannesburg, South Africa. His wife, Thilde, born Rothschild, died in London in 1978, her mother, née Levy, was a sister of Max Levy, general manager of Salamander. My brother's son, living in London, became a very successful insurance underwriter with Lloyds. His grandchildren graduated in sciences and chemistry from Cambridge and London Imperial College.

I myself was born in Stuttgart in 1892. I had an excellent education, including studies at the Universities of Frankfurt and Munich, where I studied national economy with Professor Franz Oppenheimer and Professor Adolf Weber. I was in New York for nearly two years, 1923–1924. Back in Stuttgart I worked first as a secretary, then I obtained a position as social worker in the Jewish community in Stuttgart, as well as taking care of Jewish welfare problems in Wuerttembrg and Hohenzollern.

In 1939 I went to England, working first as a domestic, and I could not obtain a permit for social work. It was a difficult time, especially during the Blitz. After working in the boarding house Sachs-Pick, I advanced from domestic to telephone operator, and receptionist and information lady.

I celebrated my eightieth birthday in Stuttgart, much honored by the city and also by the new Jewish community. The Stuttgarter newspapers printed articles in my honor, pointing out my former services. Now I am in retirement, but still active in my new circle.

FRITZ WEIL
P.O. Box 236
25.600 Petropolis E DO RIO
Brazil

I was born in Stuttgart in 1910. I went to grammar school, commercial school, and technical college for textile industry in Reutlingen, had several business and technical volunteer positions in Stuttgart, Hamburg, Neuchatel, and the United States. I worked from 1931 in my father's firm knitwear factory, Philip Weil & Company, in Stuttgart. In 1934 I married Elisabeth Charlotte (Liselotte) Emrich, born in 1911 in Stuttgart.

Emigrated in 1936 directly to Brazil and since 1937 am living in Petropolis about 60 miles from Rio. Founder, together with Jacob Adler (formerly lawyer in Stuttgart), of the knitwear firm Malharia Aguia. Partner until 1965. Several months later founded, together with son Roberto, the Malharia Pe-We-Ce Ltd., in which I am still active. Member of the Jewish Community in Petropolis and Rio. President of the WIZO in Petropolis.

My father, Philip Weil, was born in Gailingen in 1876 and died in Petropolis in 1969. He was a partner in the knitwear factory Philip Weil Company. My mother Helene, née Lion, was born in 1889 in Diessenhofen, Switzerland, and lived in Petropolis from 1939 until her death in 1969.

My father-in-law, Adolf Emrich, was born in 1881 in Bruchsal and was a partner in the Wuerttemberg Brandweinbrennerei Hirsch & Lichter of Stuttgart. He was also president of the R.J.F. in Stuttgart and died in 1956 in Petropolis. My mother-in-law, Flora, née Lebrecht, was born in 1888 in Bingen and lived in Petropolis from 1939 until her death in 1970.

My grandparents-in-law were Julius Emrich, born 1856 in Merchingen, who died in 1945, and Lina, née Lichter, born 1859 and died in 1943. Both lived in Bruchsal until 1933, one year in Stuttgart and from 1939 in Petropolis.

My sister, Margarete Weil Reichenheim, was born in 1911 in Stuttgart, married Fritz Bloch in Zurich in 1932, and emigrated to Brazil in 1940. Her second marriage was to Hans Gerhard Reichenheim from Berlin. They are living in Rio de Janeiro. Their son Michael is twenty-six years old and a physician.

I have two children: Roberto, born in Rio in 1937, whose daughter, Silvia, is fifteen, and Mariana Weil Wilberg, born in Petropolis in 1944, whose husband, Alfredo, is Brazilian of German-Spanish origin. Alfredo converted to Judaism. Their three children, Claudio, Felipe, and Patricia, are twelve, eleven, and eleven respectively. They live in Rio.

HERMANN WEIL

Born in 1876. In 1904 he came to the opera house in Stuttgart with tremendous success as a baritone there and all over the world. His most famous role was Hans Sachs. As a Jew he was forced to leave in 1939. He lived as a voice instructor in New York until he died while fishing in Blue Mountain Lake near New York in 1949. He also had great success at the Metropolitan Opera from 1911 to 1917. His first role was Kurwenal in *Tristan*. He was Faninal at the New York premier of *Rosenkavalier*. Since 1911 in Bayreuth his main roles were Amfortas and Hans Sachs. His son changed his last name in the United States to Weir.

*HERMANN WEIL

Attorney Hermann Weil, born in Stuttgart in 1888, was the son of Sanitaetsrat Dr. Sigmund Weil. He was admitted in Stuttgart in 1919. In 1936 he emigrated to England. He died in 1960 at the home of his children in Johannesburg, South Africa.

*RICHARD WEIL

Attorney Dr. Richard Weil, born in Laupheim in 1889, was admitted in Stuttgart in 1919. After losing his admission in 1938 he set out for Australia. He did not reach his destination, as he died on board ship between Indonesia and Australia as a result of a heart attack in 1939.

ROLF A. WEIL
3015 Simpson Street
Evanston, Ill. 60201

Leni Metzger Weil: The Metzgers left Germany in 1939 after Arthur Metzger was incarcerated in Dachau after November 1938. They got a visa to the United States under the French quota because Arthur Metzger was born in Strassburg in 1891. The Metzgers' two younger daughters, Lotte and Ilse, had left with a childrens' transport for England in 1939. Leni emigrated with her father Arthur and Mother Adele, née Gruenwald, to Chicago. Arthur Metzger had been a partner in the Stuttgart shoe-wholesale firm of Neu & Gruenwald. When they arrived penniless in Chicago, they started out doing domestic work on the North Shore. Not much later, however, Arthur joined the Fuller Brush Company like many other refugees. Leni worked in a factory, and Adele kept house in the Hyde Park neighborhood. The two younger girls arrived from England in 1940.

Rolf A. Weil: The Weils left Germany in 1936. Father, Heinrich Weil, had been Geschaeftsfuehrer of Singer Naehmaschinen in Stuttgart. The newspaper *Flammenzeichen* had attacked Singer because they employed a Jew in a leading position. As a result emigration became necessary. After an exploratory trip to Palestine in 1936, during the period of Arab-Jewish unrest, it was decided to emigrate to the United States. My father left in 1936, and my mother, Lina Weil (née Landauer), left with me later that year. Mr. Fuchs, the crooked secretary of the American Consulate, had demanded a gift of a sewing machine to speed up the paper work. In the United States my father worked for Singer and a couple of other companies, then finally started his own small stapler and fastener business. My mother rented a room to help support us. I had been a student in the Eberhard Ludwig Gymnasium in Stuttgart. In Chicago I attended high school and university, where I received B.A., M.A., and Ph.D. degrees in economics in 1942, 1945, and 1950 respectively.

Leni and Rolf Weil: We had known each other as teenagers as members of the BDJJ in Stuttgart and met again quite by accident in Chicago in 1942. After a long period of dating, we were engaged when I got my master's degree in 1945. Later that year we were married. At the time I had a research appointment at the University of Chicago. After some teaching at Indiana University and research for the Illinois Department of Revenue, I joined Roosevelt College in 1946. There I rose through the ranks and eventually became dean of the College of Business Administration and president of the University in 1964.

Leni and I have two children. Susan was born in 1949, and Ronald was born in 1951.

I am serving as president of Self-Help in Chicago, and Leni is treasurer. My biography is listed in *Who's Who in America*. I have received two honorary doctorates, one from the College of Jewish Studies and one from Loyola University. I have published in the fields of finance and higher education, and serve as consultant to business firms. I am on the board of a chemical and publishing company. Leni and I are members of Beth Emet Synagogue in Evanston, and I serve on the temple board. I am also a Rotarian.

Leni and I have been back in Stuttgart as well as in Nuertingen. In fact we enjoyed the hospitality of Leni's gymnasium classmates at their summer home in the Schwarzwald. We also maintain contact with friends of my mother in Nuertingen.

Our parents have all died. Heinrich (Henry) Weil in 1959, the Metzgers in 1969, and Lina Weil in 1977.

We believe in collective responsibility but not in collective guilt as far as the Germans are concerned. This past summer Leni and I were Ehren-gaeste of the mayor of Berlin and found the religious service in the Pestalozzi Synagogue to be a highlight of that trip.

Leni's sisters are: Mrs. Ilse Glaser (high school English teacher), 1511 Dobson Street, Evanston, Ill. 60202; Mrs. Lotte Strupp (married to Professor Hans Strupp, a psychologist at Vanderbilt University), 5058 Villa Crest Drive, Nashville, Tenn. 37220.

JERRY WEISS
Grossinger, N.Y. 12734

My sister, Leni, was married in 1940 to Werner Breit, who came from Beuthen. She was divorced about five years ago. She has one daughter, Doreen Harvey, who is a teacher married to Keith Harvey, also a high school teacher. They have a daughter, Diane, who is five years old. They live in Holly, New York (near Rochester).

My parents were married in 1913. My father, Oscar, ran his textile business, I. Weiss & Company, until he passed away in 1930. My mother did earn her living as a medical masseuse. But that had nothing to do with the New World Club. Her best friend was Joe Adler, who was a director of the club. Joe was the brother of Leo Adler, our cantor. Joe also died some years ago.

I was in the founding class of the well-known Schicker-Schule. Then I attended for six years the Eberhard-Ludwig Gymnasium, then the Staedtische Handels Schule, and then Technikum fuer die Textil Industry.

GRETEL WEISSMANN (née Apt)
210 East 47th Street
New York, N.Y. 10017

Gretel Weissmann was born in 1902. Her father, Hermann Apt, died in New York in 1948. She started as a very hard-working masseuse and now does electrolysis. She has one daughter, Anne Braun, who lives in San Francisco and has three children (ages twenty-two, eighteen, and fourteen). Her sister, Trude Weil, died in Switzerland.

ELLEN WEITZEN (née Beate)
2 Washington Square
New York, N.Y. 10012

Ellen Weitzen (née Beate) was born in 1926. She was a teenager when she arrived on these shores and entered Newtown High School in Queens. After school hours, she was employed in a local bakery and, during summer vacations, as an "upstairs" maid with a wealthy American family. After graduation, she continued her education at the New York Merchandising Institute and two years hence was selected for the executive-training program of Lord & Taylor's department store. Thus her fashion career commenced and continues to this very day on a part-time basis. She is special assistant to the president of Woman's Haberdashers, Inc., a high-fashion organization with three stores on upper Madison Avenue, and an active member of the New York chapter of the Fashion Group. She is married to Frederic Weitzen, chairman of the board of Marboro Books, and has one son, Stephen. He is a sophomore at George Washington University in the District of Columbia.

[For information on the rest of her family see entries for: brother JAMES MAY, father HENRY MAY, mother THEKLA MAY, and grandmother EMMA SAENGER.]

HANSI WELTMAN (formerly Erlanger, née Cahn)
619 Home Savings & Loan Building
Youngstown, Ohio

My maiden name was Hansi Cahn. My husband, Otto M. Erlanger, left Stuttgart in 1937. My daughter, Margot, and I came to the United States in 1938. My husband worked at an uncle's place, earned $15 a week, and had a chance for daily English lessons. I made my first money giving tennis lessons. Later we started our own business of millinery supplies and did very well until the fashion changed—no more hats.

Our brother-in-law, Richard Kahn, and his wife, Friedel, became our partners. We liquidated and went into the spiral business in Sayville, Long Island, which my nephew, Dr. Klaus Feuchtwanger, had. He did fabulously and went to Switzerland. All three studied medicine.

In the meantime our daughter, Margot, married Kurt Wegner from Berlin. She worked and he studied. He earned his doctorate in Buffalo and was also Phi Beta Kappa. He is a pediatrician now doing only consulting work, and teaches at the University in Kent, Ohio. After two years we also went to Youngstown. I worked in a fashionable ladies' apparel store. My husband was a buyer for a furniture store. In 1967 he retired and I worked part-time. In 1969 he died. Soon afterwards I married Dr. Erhard Weltman, who had lost his wife four years before.

Margot became a social worker. She got her master's degree at Columbia University in New York City and worked at different jobs in New York and Youngstown. Four years ago she earned her Ph.D. She is now the director of a big mental health clinic in Canton, Ohio. They have three sons. The oldest graduated from Brandeis University. He is now in law school at Ohio State. The middle one graduated from MIT in Boston, took off for one year, and works for Westinghouse in Pittsburgh. The youngest studies business administration at Georgetown University in Washington, D.C.

My husband has one daughter. She is a singer and teaches voice in Seattle, Washington.

It might interest you to know that my sister, Marie Bruegman, worked for many years for Dr. Tanzer and did a lot for the emigration. She took care of the whole Rexinger emigration. After he left Stuttgart she worked for Dr. Ostertag.

I have three cousins: Dr. Martin Sondheimer of Lima, Ohio; Max Sondheimer of London, England; and Trude Schuelein, who lives with her daughter in Washington, D.C.

My parents were Selma and Emil Cahn. My mother died in Stuttgart and my father in Theresienstadt.

My sisters Stefani Feuchtwanger and Marie Bruegman both passed away, also my brother Martin Cahn.

[Hansi Weltman died in May 1981.]

MRS. PAULA WILSON (née Pressburger)
35-31 85th Street
Jackson Heights, N.Y.

I was born in 1904 in Rexingen. My parents, Sigmund and Blanda Pressburger, died in 1927 and 1930, respectively. I married Paul Herman

Stern in 1933—he died in 1938. I went to England in 1939, where I was married in 1945 for a short time to Arthur Wilson. I came to New York in 1957 to my sister, Ms. Edward Eckstein. I am presently a volunteer at Elmwood Hospital and Self-Help.

JUSTIN WIMPFHEIMER
6 The Glen
Tenafly, N.J. 07670

Father: Leopold, born Ittlingen, 1894; died 1969 in New York City. Business Activity: Self-employed
  Mother: Betty (maiden name, Kohn), born 1901 in Crailsheim, died 1973 in New York City.
  Both parents immigrated to the United States in 1938.
  Justin: Born 1935, Ittlingen. Arrived with parents. Married—wife's name, Rochelle. Two children (twins). Business: real estate. Member Temple Sinai, Tenafly, New Jersey.

JOSEPH A. WINTER
91-41 Lamont Ave.
Elmhurst, N.Y. 11373

I was born in Stuttgart in 1914. My parents were Sali and Max Winter, sister Brunhilde. Died KZ in 1944 unknown. Eggs and butter booth in Staedt. Markthalle, Stuttgart. I left Stuttgart in 1940 after one year of voluntary work at the Mittelstelle/Stuttgart.

In 1941 I was drafted into the U.S. Army. After basic military training with the U.S. Army 4th Motorized Division, graduated Military Intelligence School, Camp Ritchie, Maryland. Took part in Battle of the Bulge (Bastogne encirclement) and Remagen Bridgehead Battle in 1944.

In 1947 married Ursula Hefter, fashion designer. I worked four years in import and export of steel and changed trades under G.I. Bill to go to fashion school. In 1955 I took over the factory of my father-in-law, which made fashion blouses and consisted of four employees. Production increased over the years to thirty-five employees and the manufacturing of better sportswear, dresses, and blouses in Elmhurst, New York.

We have two children. Ruth graduated University of Chicago, Ph.D.— Married to Larry Bloom, lawyer and alderman of 5th Ward, Hyde Park/ Kensington, 1503 East 56th Street, Chicago, Illinois 60637. Two children—Aaron and Gabrielle. Randy—graduate of University of Boulder, Colorado. Master's degree. Teacher in elementary school, Boulder, Colorado.

In touch with a lot of Stuttgarters in the New York area. Love to hear from "out-of-towners."

ALFRED WOLF (died 1981)
VICTORIA ("TRUDL") WOLF
911 Schumacher Drive
Los Angeles, Calif. 90048

[Alfred:] My parents were Cecile and Julius Wolf. My mother died on the Italian steamer *Gerusaleme* in 1937 four hours after she left two of her children in Palestine.

My father died two years later in 1939 after arriving in Brighton, England, to stay with his brother Sidney.

I was born in 1898 in Heilbronn, graduated from the Gymnasium, enlisted in the German Army in World War I. I was twenty years old when I returned to Heilbronn. My first visit was across the street to the Victors. I already then was convinced that I would marry Trudl, then about thirteen, and totally uninterested in men!

My father was very helpful and intelligent in shaping my career. First textile engineering school in Reutlingen, then practical studies in Cologne, Gummersbach, and Forst in factories related to our family business.

After another year at the University in Frankfurt, where I worked for the exam as a diplom-merchant, I was sent to the University of Lausanne, to learn French and prepare toward a doctorate in economics, which I made in 1922.

Only then was I allowed to become a part of the family firm, W. M. Wolf, a textile enterprise of high standing in the field.

In 1924 I married Gertrude Victoria Victor, whom everyone called "Trudl." She had studied chemistry in Heidelberg and Munich, but her mind was always more on German literature and writing. Our daughter, Ursual Julia, was born in 1926; our son, Frank Jacob, in 1928.

When the monster Hitler arrived, we knew that our lifestyle had to change. Trudl, who had published three novels and many short stories, was thrown out of the National Writer's Chamber, unable to work anymore in Germany. Our children should not suffer the indignities of attending an Aryan school. My wife took the two children and went to Ascona, Switzerland, in 1933, two months after Hitler assumed the chancellorship. I stayed at home sadly.

For three and a half years, my connection with my family consisted of a monthly weekend visit. Though they were facilitated through our business connections in Italy, it was a terrible nervous strain for me, because of the German money regulations. In Heilbronn, our company, W. M. Wolf, went through increasing political chicanery and I had no other thought in mind but personal emigration, despite leaving my father behind. In 1936 we found a typical blackmail letter at the staircase and then decided at once. I would leave for my family in Ascona, without a job.

After two months of worrying, I received a letter from a well-known textile firm in Vienna, Bunzl and Biach, with a secure employment offer. I left at once for Vienna.

In Austria the political situation worsened, and in 1938 the little country was occupied by the Nazis. I had to leave and emigrate somewhere else.

I met Trudl Victoria in Zurich (she had just returned from a reconnaissance trip to the United States), and she wanted to convince me to prepare immediately for my immigration visa for the United States. When I demurred, she told me she would do it alone.

Bunzl and Biach sent me to a small place in France, St. Louis, Haut-Rhin, to work for their firm from over there, especially in Belgium, Holland, and Italy. I ran a small assorting plant, a nerve-wracking time with the occupation of Czechoslovakia and the passport problems; I was totally not *en règle*.

Switzerland enacted a new law against too many foreigners, meaning that all non-Swiss citizens had to leave the country before the imminent war. Switzerland had only enough food and room for its own 4 million citizens. Trudl and the children had to leave Ascona and found asylum in Nice in the South of France. A short lived "asylum"! War broke out, the so-called *sitzkrieg* (sitting war). When I visited them in their rented old Château de la Tour, all men of ages suitable for war service had to assemble, regardless whether or not they were Jewish enemy aliens. My first camp was a football field in Cape d'Antibes, then we were transferred to Les Milles, near Marseille, to a deserted brick factory, where the living conditions were scandalous, the sanitary facilities barbaric. I spent the next three months in the windowless, dusty, brick factory, until a few selected people were transferred to a deserted movie theatre where we formed a battalion of French soldiers, with French uniforms, food, and even pay, but without arms. We were building trenches for horses, even though there were no horses! It was a sublimely grotesque decline of the "Grand Nation."

When Italy declared war on France in 1940, Trudl and children had to leave the "Zone de Guerre" and went by car somewhere toward Vichy. On the road at a bridge crossing the Rhône they were captured by a gendarme, who considered them German spies. They were taken prisoner, treated miserably, and threatened with shooting; their documents were taken away, until the so-called Armistice.

Trudl had written about this gruesome episode later under the title "Guilty Without Trial" published in a book *The World's Greatest Spy Stories*. She could make fun of herself as "Mata Hari Wolf."

It took months until we were reunited in the old Château in Nice, but it was a short-lived pleasure. I had to flee again, because of my hasty demobilization and faulty papers, and Trudl, because she got her visa to United States. But the visa was only a nice beginning. She had to obtain all her stolen papers, which had been sent to Algiers, and had to secure exit and transit visas, through Spain and Portugal. When one permit was granted, another one had just expired. It was a devilish game that lasted four exhausting months with bribing and coaxing and not despairing.

For me, who had to leave secretly, it was difficult. I had to spend some weeks in a Spanish prison and give the rest of my valuables to a guard in order to proceed to Portugal. By a stroke of luck we all met at the station in Lisbon!

After a few days in the opulent Portuguese capital, we sailed on different ships to the coveted land of America. I was on the Portuguese ship *Laurence Marquez*, paid for by my former company, Bunzl & Biaca, and Trudl and the children were on the American ship *Exeter*, a present from her American friend Billings.

In New York, we felt like other immigrants, happy and poor! We sent the children to Trudl's sister, Maya Larsen, and husband in Los Angeles. I found a job at the Malden Spinning and Dying Mill in Massachusetts, the first company in the United States I had asked for a job. My first pay was 36 cents an hour. I did the work well due to the practical wisdom of my father twenty years earlier.

Five years later, the Star Woolen Company in Cohoes, New York, heard about me through old business acquaintances in New York, and hired me after an extensive examination for $25 a week. I organized an assorting plant for them, which resulted in various salary raises, especially as I worked voluntarily in the evening in their garnett plant. Garnetts are very high-priced complicated machines to dissolve pieces of fabric into fibers, unknown in Europe.

The boss, Mr. Stein, wanted to keep me and proposed that Trudl and the children should move to Cohoes, but Trudl wanted to go to Hollywood and start her writing career again in a new language. I could not and would not persuade her otherwise. After a tough beginning, she made it in writing scripts, films, and books.

In 1942 I was transferred as plant manager to our subsidiary in South

Pittsburg, Tennessee, a godforsaken little town in the Cumberland Mountains. Not even a Yankee for those inbred Southerners, I was a bloody foreigner, but I was a success as a plant manager. We made pure silk out of discarded silk stockings for the manufacture of powder bags for heavy artillery. I could even prevent a strike at the factory.

My family and I visited each other occasionally, but basically I was alone and missed my children. With the war's end in 1945, I was out of a job again. Nobody seemed to want powder bags for artillery and me!

I went to Los Angeles. Trudl sold books and stories all over the world. But at the end of November a letter arrived from Henry Chanin Company. In 1945 I entered their offices in Atlanta, where I was introduced to the vast enterprise of that man, who was a genius and a drunkard, a life bridge master and the husband of a German refugee, Herma, and the father of two smart sons.

In a three-minute personal interview he said, "I hope we will work together for many years to come," which I did, exactly twenty-three years. I was made a vice-president in 1947 shortly after I became an American citizen.

Trudl and I divorced in perfect harmony and still are best friends. I married an Atlanta lady, Lilian Lazarus, and Victoria married the heart specialist Dr. Erich Wolff. We gave our friends and the entire family an example that one can remain close even after a formal divorce. Lillian died in 1960.

As a sort of therapeutic measure, Victoria advised me to write my life story. I did it. It comprised 1,110 pages.

BERNARD WOLF
Hatters' and Textile Furs
142-01 41st Avenue
Flushing, N.Y. 11355

I arrived in New York City in 1925, as the first Jewish person to emigrate from my hometown of Niederstetten in the early twenties. The decision to leave Germany was a most painful and difficult one. It meant leaving my parents and sister at a time when very few people left Germany for an insecure future in the United States.

After graduating from Realschule in Bad Mergentheim and subsequently from Oberrealschule Schwäbisch Hall (Maturum), I was convinced that, even then, a young Jewish person had very little chance to accomplish anything worthwhile in Germany since anti-Semitism was rampant. I could not follow my father's suggestion to study further in medicine, law, or science. I felt that time was of the essence and the United

States, especially New York City, had appealed to me ever since my childhood.

My immediate financial problems were taken care of by the firm of S. Rosenfelder and Son of New York (a wholesale fur dealer), who employed me in accordance with the wishes of the parent firm in Leipzig, where I had been instructed in the rudiments of the trade. Although I had originally planned to make my way in the world of finance and banking— I was an apprentice for two years in my uncle Stefan Jacobowitz's bank, the Wuerttemberg Vereinsbank, in Stuttgart—I dropped the plan in favor of my firm desire to make a complete and radical change of my future.

From the time I set foot on the soil of my adopted country, I was certain that I had acted wisely. I loved my job, I loved the people I worked with, and I loved the hustle and bustle of this metropolis.

In 1928 I married Emma Nanette Mayer, whom I knew as a young girl of fifteen in Germany, and who came to the United States in 1923 at the age of sixteen. She was the daughter of Alfred and Clementine Mayer of Stuttgart, who were themselves refugees from Alsace-Lorraine as a result of World War I. Our wedding took place in Stuttgart in 1928, to which we returned to be with our parents for the event.

After the Wall Street Crash of 1929 I lost my job, but my wife was always able to find employment in the fashion field. We struggled along until 1936, when I was able to introduce fur fibers into the textile industry. This bit of good fortune enabled us to move to a fashionable midtown neighborhood. I formed the firm of Bernard Wolf, Inc.

In 1939 I was able to sponsor my family, whom I had left behind, to join me here in New York City. I settled my parents and my married sister in Danbury, Connecticut, then the leading city of the felt hat industry in the United States. In the years to follow, I sponsored with my affidavits about twenty persons, mostly Wuerttemberger Jews, and I employed about six or seven old friends and acquaintances in my business. Even those who became soldiers in World War II found a temporary job with me upon their return.

My son, John Clement, was born in 1940, our first and only child. He became editor-in-chief of Amphoto Books and has since formed his own firm of Cook & Wolf, Inc., publishers of photographic books and guides. He married in 1969, and in 1973 our first grandchild, Alexandra, was born, to be followed by Benjamin Wolf in 1976.

In 1978 we celebrated our fiftieth wedding anniversary. Among the guests was Bruno Stern of my hometown; he most likely gave you my name and address, as he always kept in touch with all emigrants of his beloved Niederstetten.

BERT WOLF
29 Lexington Drive
Metuchen, N.J. 08840

My father was Martin Wolf, born in Koenigsbach in 1897, died in 1935. He was a cattle dealer with his father and uncle, Abraham and Isak Wolf in Pforzheim. My mother was Else Loewengart, born in Rexingen in 1909. She married Martin Wolf in 1929 and came to New York with me in 1938. She remarried in 1940 to Ernest Fuerst and moved to Somerville, New Jersey, where she resides now. Mr. Fuerst died in 1970.

I was born in Pforzheim in 1930, graduated from Rutgers University in 1951. I am presently president of Rosenthal Lumber and Supply Company in New Brunswick. My wife, Rita Cominsky, and I were married in 1954, and we have two daughters, Diane Norma, born 1955, and Susan Amy, born 1957.

In 1933 I had three grandparents alive: Helene Gideon Loewengart, who was born in Rexingen in 1881, came to the United States in 1938 and died in Somerville in 1970. Hermine Krieger Wolf, who was born in 1869 in Weingarten, and died in Argentina in 1952. Abraham Wolf, who was born in 1860 in Koenigbach, and died in Argentina in 1948.

I am a member of Congregation Neve Shalom, on the board of directors of the Northern Middlesex County Jewish Federation, B'nai B'rith, and a captain in the United States Air Force.

*EDGAR WOLF
Last known address: Kaiser-Wilhelm-Str. 3
Pension Rossman
7570 Baden-Baden
West Germany

Born in Rottweil in 1903. Passed his examination as a Referendar in 1933, but could no longer serve. He worked for some time in business. He left for Belgium in March 1936 and in September of that year went to Portugal. There he operated a small artisan shop until 1948. Thereafter he worked as a sales representative. He was handicapped by a serious eye ailment. He once again resides in Wuerttemberg.

*FRITZ WOLF
P.O. Box 95
22100 Nahariya
Israel

Just when your letters about your book of the Jews from Wuerttemberg arrived, I also received a letter from Victoria Wolff, my former sister-in-law, from which I quote: "It would be a shame if you would be missing in the book—." You promised to shorten the story of my brother Alfred, and so I hope you have the necessary information to determine all the connections and tie-ins of the family as well as of the Jews from Wuerttemberg in general, a sociological feature which I consider just as important as the individual stories. Assuming this, I restrict myself in this report to my own little "me," to be used as desired or to be ignored.

Born in 1908, I was spoiled, being the youngest, especially as my emotional mother was already thirty-one years old, considered at that time not so young anymore. I was the result of a love-match with a good-looking gentleman and businessman by the name of Julius Wolf, born 1870 and at the time already a partner of the firm later known as W. M. Wolf A. G. (Inc.). My mother, Caecilie Wolf, died melodramatically in 1937, returning by boat from a visit to two of her children in Palestine. The cause of death was angina pectoris, but just as true would be from a broken heart. Due to the strong protest of my father she was not buried at sea, but in Cyprus. All the events, Second World War, German occupation of the island, the destruction of the Jews, and the construction of defense installations have made her grave disappear without a trace. My father died in 1939, having escaped at the last minute before the start of the Second World War to England.

Until 1933 my life followed the course of most well-to-do Jewish boys in Wuerttemberg; three years preschool classes, nine years high school, graduating from the Real Gymnasium in Heilbronn, four years law studies at the Universities of Heidelberg, Munich, Berlin, and Tuebingen, doctor examination and two years practical service in the judiciary. Then, just at the start of the third year, while continuing the training in a lawyer's office came the fall into the reality of the Third Reich. At once, already in 1933 I left Germany. My goal was Italy, where there was Fascism too, but without anti-Semitism. We still had business friends and the country seemed warm to me and not expensive. I wanted to become a hairdresser—today this seems grotesque and even absurd—but at the time it seemed realistic for people whose intellectuality was destroyed by the Huns.

My proud plans, which already included a beauty salon on the Riviera, could not be realized. I tried to make a living representing industrial oil firms, Portuguese cork producers, selling musical instruments (wasn't I musically inclined?), and I even opened an institute for foot supports!

Finally I emigrated to Palestine, thanks to a gift transfer, which at that time was still possible. My brother-in-law, the former lawyer Dr. Oskar Mayer from Heilbronn, who already resided with my sister Gretel in Nahariya, could buy there for me some land—a so-called *Meschek*. I did not know how potatoes, tomatoes, or cabbage grew, and my endeavors to dig a water channel in the wrong direction will be an eternal memory. But I did learn quite fast the job of a gardener and chicken-raiser. Only the prices for the vegetables at that time did not cover the cost; the fruit trees, due to the closeness of the sea, did not bear fruit properly; and the chickens got sick and died.

I got married and we started to eat up our small capital. Hardly two years later my wife, Paula, died and left me with a six-month-old girl, Daniela. Today she is in a high position in the State Health Department, married, and mother of a highly gifted boy, Itai, who is also an international basketball player.

Of course, this was in the future. I was working as a common agricultural laborer, paid by the hour. Then I met Ruth Mamlock, who became my new wife; always in a happy mood, mastering all difficulties with equanimity, realistic, clever, and as clean and shiny as a day in spring. Also extremely good looking at that, she was an ideal life comrade. She gave me a son, Uri, and was a wonderful mother to Daniela, not in name only.

Together we succeeded in building a house, a symbol as well as a refuge. We sustained Arab attacks and hundreds of nights on the alert, English curfews, German air attacks, the fears of the Second World War, and the blockage of the land route to Haifa and the rest of Israel. We saw many people killed and many suffering. We often worked sixteen hours a day, because for many years we had between us four full occupations, or actually five; Ruth was not only mother and housewife, but worked as a saleslady, an employee, a cook, and as a nurse. I myself worked for the post office and gave piano lessons on the side. Ruth and I grew flowers and I sold them, direct to the consumer, so that the entire profit remained in our hands, despite low prices.

During the tremendous changes of the Palestine Mandate into the State of Israel, there was, of course, also tremendous change in our new domicile of Nahariya, situated so beautifully by the sea, 9 kilometers from the border of Lebanon. The small village of mainly German and Eastern European immigrants became a mixture of all different origins, with 30,000 inhabitants, a city with manifold social and political organizations.

All this involved us too. For four years I was president of the Leo Baeck Lodge of B'nai B'rith here, not to mention assorted smaller jobs. I think I contributed my share to the construction of our country, as well as Ruth. I wrote for Nahariya three great evening-filling "musicals"; *The Nahariyade, the Grosse Parnesse,* and *Abrakadabra,* or *The Miracle of the Morgenlands.* The entire text and a good part of the music came from me. I may state they were successful because the times to produce a "musical" in the German language on the stage are long past.

In 1976 Ruth died. I married again; luckily, I may say. My wife's name is Fritzika Horwitz, and so far all has gone well. One should never give up . . . never say die . . .

*HEINRICH WOLF

Lawyer Heinrich Wolf, born 1873 in Schwäbisch Hall, was an attorney in Stuttgart since 1900. Since 1922 he was also a notary public. The notary office was taken away from him in 1935; his admission to the bar, in 1938. He was permitted to continue as a consultant. A former front-line fighter, he could not bring himself to emigrate, for "I cannot live without Germany," as he still put it during the years of persecution. Dr. Wolf was a member, and later president, of the Israelitische Landesversammlung. In 1943, he and his wife, Clementine, née Levi, were deported. It became later known that the transport went to Auschwitz. It is not certain whether the seventy-two-year-old man even reached this inferno alive, for only a few days after the transport left, the few belongings he was allowed to take with him were returned to Stuttgart. They had been found at some railroad station in Saxony.

*HEINRICH WOLF II

Attorney Henrich Wolf II, born in Baisingen in 1902 was admitted in Stuttgart in 1931. He was withdrawn in 1933 and left immediately for Brazil.

WALTER WOLF
3101 N. Sheridan Road
Chicago, Ill. 60657

I am the son of Felix and Anna Wolff, née Moos. My father, who owned the Sueddeutsche Durchschreibbuecherfabrik, died in 1929. My older brother and I kept the business until we emigrated to the United States. Lothar arrived in the United States a few months before my mother and I came to this country in 1936. My father, Felix, was very active in community life in Stuttgart. He was "Kirchenvorsteher" for a number of years.

Mother, Lothar, and I settled in Chicago in 1936. The first few years were hard. Lothar married in 1937 a girl by the name of Hilde Herzberger from Muenchen-Gladbach. They raised a daughter, Doris, and a son, Frank. Lothar stayed in the same line of business as in Stuttgart, working for a company as a salesman. He passed away at the age of sixty-five. He was stricken by cancer and died in 1969. My mother passed away in 1960 at the age of almost eighty. Since 1944 I am a sales representative for a nut, screw, and bolt manufacturer, working in Greater Chicago and 90 percent retired in 1976.

In 1962 I married my childhood sweetheart, Lilo, née Gaertner, who lived in Vineland until that time. She was married to Hans Gutmann until 1962, when she was granted a divorce. Hans Gutmann passed away a few years ago. Lilo's parents, Isidor and Gertrude Gaertner, née Furchheimer, and her grandmother, Mrs. Lina Furchheimer, came to the United States in 1939 and 1940 respectively. Grandfather Furchheimer died in Stuttgart in 1939. He, Max Furchheimer, and Isidor Gaertner owned Lindner & Furchheimer in Stuttgart. Grandmother Furchheimer and the Gaertners lived in New York for a few years and settled with Lilo on a farm in Vineland. Grandmother Furchheimer died in 1958 and is buried in Vineland. The Gaertners came to Chicago with Lilo in 1962. Mother Gaertner passed away at the age of eighty-four in 1976, and father Gaertner celebrated his one hundredth birthday in very good physical and mental condition in August of 1979. He is residing at the Self-Help Home for the Aged in Chicago, Illinois.

My mother, Anna Wolff, née Moos, was born in Hechingen in 1881 and died in Chicago in 1960. My brother Lothar (Leonard) was born in Hechingen in 1904 and died in Chicago in 1969. His widow, Hilde, lives in Northbrook, Illinois, and has two married children and four grandchildren.

I, Walter Wolf, was born in Hechingen in 1905. My father, Felix Wolff, was born in 1868 in Schw. Hall. The entire family moved to Stuttgart in 1906.

Lilo and I are active in Temple Sholom, in Self-Help of Chicago, and in the Chicago Heart Association and other organizations.

AREIH ZAMIR
30060 Kibbutz Hazore'a
Israel

My brother is Dr. Siegfried Saenger, who lives in Ramat Gan, Israel.

My father, Arthur Saenger, was born in Laupheim in 1865 and died in Tel Aviv in 1949. He was associate owner of the firm Saenger & Harburger in Stuttgart.

My mother, Rosa, née Gutmann, was born in Heilbronn in 1876 and died in Haifa in 1966.

My parents arrived in Palestine in 1939 and lived with my brother in Jerusalem and later in Tel Aviv.

I have lived in Kibbutz Hazore'a since 1934.

PAUL ZIPPERT
3008 Offutt Road
Randallstown, Md. 21133

I will be only too glad to add my part to the documentary of Jews from Wuerttemberg and find it a very worthwhile cause. I might remark that in the beginning of your letter, when Dr. Kroner and Dr. Stoessel were mentioned in their nature as rabbis, it would have been appropriate to mention my great-grandfather, Rabbi Dr. Moses von Wassermann, whose contributions to the development of the Stuttgart Jewish community during his office 1872–1893 speak for themselves. [Editor: Of course Paul Zippert is historically absolutely right. We deliberately only mentioned contemporary personalities.] I hope that our efforts to record this documentary will be appreciated by the next generation, and that despite changing modern times, they will be just as sensitive and loyal toward Jewish traditions as we were toward our forefathers.

The roots of our family tree were embedded deep in the Wuerttemberg soil. My great-grandfather, Dr. Moses von Wassermann, studied theology at the University of Tuebingen. He was of the Jewish congregation in Stuttgart 1872–1893. His daughter, Amalie Kaufmann, born in Stuttgart, married Richard Kaufmann, who operated a bookstore specializing in antique books. His daughter (my mother), Helene Kaufmann, and my father, Max Zippert, having returned from World War I, met coincidentally at family Karl Kahn's Seder table, Pesach 1919. They were married and I was born one year later. Together with my younger sister Amely (Adler) we formed a happy family. My parents were very active in the Jewish congregation in Stuttgart. My mother, having graduated from Stuttgart Conservatory of Music, pursued her profession as a pianist and piano teacher for many years. My father was a factory representative, traveling in Wuerttemberg.

I entered my apprenticeship as maintenance mechanic in a machine shop in Cannstatt. After the hardship we Jews had to face under the Nazi regime, I was fortunate to start a new life in the United States with my parents and sister, who had to remain in England during World War II, eventually settling in Baltimore, Maryland. After returning from duty with the U.S. Army Medical Corps in 1946, I entered the field of building orthopedic braces and appliances at a local children's hospital. The same year I met my wife, Bertl Selig, and we were married. We have two sons; Michael, our oldest, is married and is employed in the U.S. Coast Guard, where he rebuilds boats. Our youngest son, Randy, is constructing dental prosthesis at a laboratory. For the last ten yers I worked for Catonsville Community College in maintenance.

Looking back over our lives and existence which had almost been destroyed, my wife and I were able to build a future for ourselves. This should serve as an example to our children and grandchildren, who might be reading these lines, and spur them on to live their life committed to the principles of our ancestors.

Appendices

Dr. Adolf Palm Writes About the Fate of Jewish Students of the Stuttgart Karlsgymnasium on the occasion of the One Hundred-Year Anniversary of the School

The former Jewish students of the Karlsgymnasium are not asking for pity, but they are entitled to demand that what was done to them should never be forgotten. The temptation is growing to erase the memory of these years. Peter Hoffmann, one of the historians of the resistance against Hitler, observed this: "The sufferings and the destructions, which were left by this demon, are nowadays, with the exceptions of the survivors of the death-camps, no longer directly felt." We, responsible for the future, and aware that everywhere people can fall into the abyss of diabolical error and cruelty, will not overlook the fate of our former Jewish students. While many individual cases could not be recorded any more, the few which are known should speak for the unknown.

As a gifted jurist, Dr. Fritz Erlanger (graduated 1922) was at first in Waiblingen, Berlin, and Ulm in government service. His admission as practicing attorney in Stuttgart was revoked by force on May 29, 1933. He emigrated that year to France and reached the academic degree of a *licencié en droits*. At the start of the war he was interned as a German national in the South of France, but was transferred to a hospital in Perpignan with a severe diabetic condition. When the Gestapo extended their influence to the South of France, he was taken in 1943 to the notorious transfer-camp Drancy, a first step for Auschwitz. And in Auschwitz his life ended at an unknown date.

Dr. med. Robert Mathias Gutmann (graduate of 1891) received during his school years ten prize-medals; he was at first only evacuated. However on August 22, 1942, nearly seventy years old and mortally sick with cancer, he was transported to the concentration camp Theresienstadt, in North Bohemia, where he died a miserable death in the first days of September.

Dr. Walter Einstein (Abitur 1920) lives now in Paris. He lost his permit to practice law on May 29, 1933; he was working as a legal adviser to textile firms until 1935, emigrated one year later to France, but was interned in 1940 as a foreigner. When the Germans after the invasion took control of the camp, he was able to escape in 1942, and thereby escape from being sent to an extermination camp. He lived hidden by French peasants until

375

two years later the German occupation troops retreated. Before this happened, his father was shot as a hostage.

Letters from emigrants who left in time reflect their sufferings and humiliations. Dr. med. Fritz Reif (Abitur 1908) wrote in 1968: "The fate of my good old mother—deported and never heard from—was such a painful experience that my relations to Stuttgart were interrupted for years." The final decision to emigrate was made already in 1934, when he heard over the radio about the Laws of Nuernberg. "To remain was incompatible with our self-respect and the future of our children." However, only in 1938 he arrived in New York City. During the First World War he spent over six months of four and one-half years military service in the hospital due to a kidney infection, which he got in the morass of Lithuania as the medical officer of his battalion. The mother of Dr. Max Wolf (Abitur 1908), retired veterinarian-doctor, blind and lamed by two strokes (and her two unmarried sisters) was able to go to Switzerland, because they had naturalized relatives there, but she died six weeks later.

Dr. med. Ludwig Weil (Abitur 1893), until his death in 1960, kept up the connection with his old school. He practiced over thirty years in Stuttgart as an internist. Years after he left one still spoke of the "friendly-earnest" doctor who healed many people not only by his outstanding knowledge and experience, but also through his interest and endeavors for the whole human being. Aside from his warm-hearted humanity, he was the prototype of the stoic sage who tried to lift himself above the earthly endeavors: He said: "The dignity of life and death does not mean too much to a very old man. He relies on love and mercy. And if one reviews one's life, and even if one imagines to have spent it in reasonable decency and fairness, one realizes that without mercy there is no sense in dignity alone."

Of eight members of the family Weil who passed through the Karlsgymnasium, we must mention Professor Dr. Sigmund Weil (Abitur 1899), highly regarded as orthopedist and human being, living in Heidelberg. A few months before he died he thanked his old school: "I always think back in deep gratitude to the beautiful years in the Karlsgymnasium, during which my thinking was decisively influenced. There is nothing better in educational basic principles as the ones taught in a good humanistic institution." Similarly wrote Hermann Jacobi on his eightieth birthday: "During my long life, my humanistic education was of great advantage to me and gave me understanding for all human behavior. I shall maintain in future, too, my closeness and my gratefulness to the Karlsgymnasium."

As the former Royal Wuerttembergian court-sculptor Heinz Fritz created the Bronze Statue of the "Stuttgardia" for the new City Hall in 1905, which also graces the present City Hall. One was looking for a model in schools of Wuerttemberg. It was found in Else Weil, the sister of Dr. Sigmund Weil.

Dr. phil. Walter Strauss left the homeland in 1936. Fortunately a highly regarded lawyer in Stuttgart, he had to work hard to build a new existence in New York, to become later a leading personality in the American insurance profession. Besides this he helped, despite unbelievable difficulties, many Swabian *Landsleute* to emigrate to the United States with the assistance of the Organization of Jews from Wuerttemberg, whose co-founder and president he is. He thereby saved them from such a sure death. He also helped them with advice and suggestions to become familiar in the new surroundings. Together the memory of the old homeland was kept alive.

After the war, he tried to reconnect the German-American relations on a human basis, despite much hostile opposition. To keep awake the German cultural heritage after the death of the great musician Fritz Busch, he founded the Friends of Fritz Busch Society. Besides this, the man, so absorbed in philosophy, literature, and music, never forgot the old school, especially not his old teacher, Professor Dr. Eugen Wolf (Abitur 1905): "I owe him my love for German culture, for German art, and German literature, which nobody could take away from me."

When Walter Strauss undertook in 1965 a trip to the old country and many of his American friends resented this trip, he told them: "We cannot better our world with hatred." Thus he reached truly exemplary humanity, after the insults, dishonors, and being expelled from his homeland.

In the newly developing Israel, where the higher positions were all long occupied, the securing of an existence for new immigrants was difficult. Albert Katz, today still closely connected with the school, and the graduate from 1924, describes humorously how he, coming from a banking position in Germany, courageously entered a hotel in Tel Aviv: With élan, he put a napkin over his arm, imitated like an old-timer the movements of a perfect waiter, and presented himself with success. Later, his pulse was higher when, in the Hilton Hotel in Tel Aviv, guests from Stuttgart arrived, like Chief-Mayor Dr. Klett or when he exchanged school-memories with Carl Schmid: *Carolini fuimus!*

When they had to leave their fatherland, there was everywhere written: The Jews are our misfortune, they are without roots, strangers to our way of life. What occurred at the time in reality was for the first time expressed by the men of the German resistance. In a proclamation to the German people, which General Beck, after the planned overthrow, intended to publish, the "godless race-theories, the miserable crimes, the degradation of the German honor and of the German good name" were exposed. Expiation must be done for the persecution of the Jews "which was done in the most inhuman and pitiless, deeply shameful and never-to-be-made-up-for manner."

Research has proven that more than twenty of the conspirators who were arrested by the Gestapo listed the persecution of the Jews as the prime motive for their action. Especially the murder of the Jews in the occupied territories, in the first place the massacre of Borisov, was one of the most important reasons for the resistance for many of the officers.

In Wuerttemberg, State Bishop D. Theophil Wurm protested repeatedly and sharply to the government and the party against the unlawful actions and the disgusting cruelties. But this is not being mentioned to excuse the others, who did nothing. The guilt remains. Fritz Ernst pointed it out mercilessly without exempting himself: "The first boycott against the Jews on April 1, 1933, was public, and disgusting; not one critical voice was heard, not one protest of the Christian churches." And Hermann Graml said, looking back to the Kristallnacht of November 9, 1938: "The people became gradually insensitive toward the fate of the Jews. The Jews became outlaws."

Karlsgymnasium Stuttgart: Visit from New York
Stuttgarter Zeitung
May 13, 1965

It was two years ago that Ministerpräsident Dr. Kiesinger met in New York with the former student of the Stuttgart Karlsgymnasium Dr. Walter Strauss, who had emigrated in 1936. He was interested in all the aspects of the law and worked himself up after years full of sorrow to a position in the insurance field and tried to help wherever he could. He also worked for the Organization of the Jews from Wuerttemberg, whose chairman he became.

The meeting of our Ministerpräsident with his Schwaebisch compatriot finally led to an invitation to Stuttgart which was realized last spring. A reception was held for the guest on May 11 in the Villa Reitzenstein. The comrades who graduated with Walter Strauss in 1923 were also invited, and with them the two teachers who were still alive, Otto Werner and Eugen Wolf.

Responding to the very hearty welcome speech of the host, Walter Strauss thanked for the trip to Stuttgart, especially his friends who were sitting with him at his table, who stood by him in difficult times, and finally thanked his old school which gave him his love for German culture, which was a passion which nobody could take from him. He confessed that only hesitantly he followed a call to visit his old country. He saw very clearly that he followed a possibly painful course since the revival of so many memories could mean a danger to the peace of his soul, which he finally found after so many years of absence. But in all he said, he found his deepest belief that the world cannot progress by hate. This confession to humanity made a deep impression on the audience. It was an evening to remember. The Karlsgymnasium knows that it is related with a former student who likes to remember his school grateful that its values helped him in the years of his need.

The 1981 yearbook of the Leo Baeck Institute contains a most interesting article: "Persecution and German Popular Opinion" by Ian Kershaw. The article proves by trustworthy reports from Germany from the Hitler years that only a very small part of the German population (about 5 percent) approved of the November 1938 pogrom, whereas 32 percent were reserved or indifferent in their comments and 63 percent displayed disgust or anger. This is a German average. The writer states that in South Germany, especially Wuerttemberg, the percentage opposed was even higher, for religious reasons. One Gestapo office there wrote in 1937 that the Catholic peasantry was more or less "deaf to any discussion of the racial problem," and specifically that in Wuerttemberg the Protestant population showed "human sympathy and religious solidarity" with the Jews and rejected the pogrom on the grounds that "the Jews are human beings too." Among the members of the Confessing Church copies of a text of Karl Barth's "Salvation Comes from the Jews" were distributed. The article says that "the Protestant Church in Wuerttemberg was in an area much affected by liberal values and was very conscious of its own identity—juxtaposed as it was with Catholic areas and having resisted a vigorous Nazi assault on its rights in 1934."

(*Editor's note:* I would like to call attention to the fact that the above percentages refer to the year 1938 and most probably deteriorated during the years that followed, especially after the start of the war.)

Index of Cities, Towns, and Villages

Note: New York and Stuttgart are not indexed because they appear on almost every page.

Aachen, 263, 333
Aalen, 119
Abbazia, 134
Affaltrach, 109, 110, 345
Affule, 280
Aix-les-Pains, 112
Akko, 163
Albany (California), 120
Albany (New York), 69, 70, 226
Alexandria, 79, 97
Algiers, 364
Altoona, 246
Ambler, 282
Amsterdam, 42, 73, 107, 138, 240, 243, 325
Angers, 75
Ankara, 307
Ann Arbor, 69, 261
Antwerp, 30, 179, 228, 280
Archshofen, 101
Argeles-sur-Mer, 24
Arlesheim, 56
Arras, 110
Ascona, 362, 363
Asperg, 9
Astoria, 4
Athens, 284
Atlanta, 193, 194, 259, 322, 365
Atlantic City, 79, 140
Auckland, 15, 16
Aufhausen, 231, 354
Augsburg, 78, 123,266
Auschwitz, 1, 10, 31, 32, 37, 41, 42, 56, 90, 107, 132, 145, 146, 148, 152, 156, 158, 166, 169, 172, 174, 216, 228, 249, 255, 257, 292, 316, 346, 352, 370, 375
Auschwitz-Blechammer, 24

Backnang, 59, 60, 119
Bad. See under remainder of place name
Baden (Germany), 234
Baden (Switzerland), 31, 84
Baden Baden, 14, 80, 367
Baghdad, 237
Baisingen, 20, 21, 22, 57, 68, 116, 135, 147, 148, 153, 199, 280, 293, 370

Baltimore, 3, 54, 110, 111, 148, 149, 155, 169, 172, 173, 241, 245, 310, 344, 345, 373
Bamberg, 42
Barbados, 143
Barcelona, 14, 178
Barmer, 55
Barnet, 220
Basel, 56, 225, 276, 296, 297, 312, 341
Bastogne, 361
Bat Galim, 167
Bayside, 161
Beechhurst, 254
Be'eri, 95
Beersheba, 220, 221, 326
Beer Tuviyah, 254, 300, 326, 327, 328
Bellac, 269
Beloit, 127
Bennington, 284
Bensonhurst, 134, 135
Bentheim, 69
Berg, 29
Bergen-Belsen, 276, 351
Bergenfield, 68
Berkeley, 16, 28, 102, 216, 305
Berlichingen, 243, 262, 263, 327
Berlin, 14, 16, 18, 41, 49, 52, 54, 62, 70, 87, 91, 95, 98, 106, 115, 116, 118, 128, 129, 133, 139, 150, 156, 165, 180, 195, 198, 205, 210, 213, 218, 219, 225, 226, 233, 254, 271, 272, 273, 291, 293, 294, 301, 315, 326, 335, 336, 338, 346, 352, 356, 358, 368, 375
Berlin-Charlottenburg, 226, 307
Bermuda, 195
Bern, 26, 197, 312
Besigheim, 50, 90
Bethel, 91
Bethesda, 101, 115, 129, 308
Berthold Auerbach, 275, 276
Beuel, 263
Beuthen, 358
Beverly Hills, 290
Béziers, 339
Biberach, 255

Bielefeld, 242
Bingen, 356
Bingham, 295
Binghamton, 298
Binswangen, 24
Bloomfield, 104
Blumenau, 159, 160, 165
Bne-Brak, 20, 95
Boeblingen, 342
Bogota, 107, 123
Bonn, 18, 255, 263
Bopfingen, 104, 231, 281
Borisov, 378
Borsigwerk, 24
Boston, 25, 35, 36, 82, 89, 114, 120, 146, 180, 181, 212, 235, 282, 320, 331, 335, 360
Boulder, 151, 361
Boundbrook, 65
Bramhall, 105
Bratislava, 137
Braunsbach, 9, 289, 290, 335
Brecksville, 53
Brentwood, 208
Breslau, 259, 336
Bretten, 43
Briarcliff, 8, 9
Brick-Town, 104
Bridgeport, 303
Bridgewater, 171
Brighton, 280, 362
Bristol, 290
Brno, 156
Brockport, 130
Bronx, 3, 20, 37, 63, 75, 80, 88, 100, 104, 125, 141, 144, 151, 167, 168, 203, 223, 347
Bronxville, 133, 245
Brookings, 260
Brookline, 35, 47, 72, 281, 282, 320
Brooklyn, 10, 15, 41, 43, 58, 60, 61, 68, 73, 108, 112, 134, 170, 244, 267, 282, 292, 298, 312, 344, 345
Bruchsal, 355, 356
Brunswick, 155
Brussels, 1, 24
Bryn Mawr, 138
Bachau, 52, 56, 176, 220, 221, 245, 289, 343
Buchenwald, 24, 63, 200, 318
Buenos Aires, 102, 134, 142, 204, 241, 249, 316
Buffalo, 15, 82, 83, 157, 196, 201, 234, 250, 259, 276, 360
Burgsteinfurt, 12
Burlington, 135

Buttenhausen, 5, 6, 44, 46, 132, 167, 170, 174, 193, 194, 237, 238, 266, 195, 340, 341, 342

Caen, 268
Cali, 231, 242
Calw, 183
Cambridge (England), 271, 272, 273, 292, 354
Cambridge (Massachusetts), 71, 72, 321
Camp. See under remainder of place name
Canandaigua, 25
Cannstatt, 18, 29, 31, 38, 50, 52, 53, 91, 95, 106, 122, 130, 131, 145, 146, 150, 191, 192, 194, 195, 197, 200, 201, 225, 226, 244, 250, 276, 277, 293, 298, 301, 317, 322, 327, 373
Canton, 34, 360
Cape d'Antibes, 363
Cape Town, 213
Carlstadt, 141
Carvallis, 339
Casteljaloux, 24
Catonsville, 373
Centerport, 149
Centralia, 121
Central Valley, 106
Champaign/Urbana, 14
Chapel Hill, 282
Charlotte, 157
Chateau de Tombebouc, 24
Chazerim, 254
Cheltenham, 94
Chemnitz, 204
Cherbourg, 159
Cherry Hill, 246, 286
Chesham, 190
Chester, 272
Chevy Chase, 190, 293
Chicago, 23, 42, 69, 75, 97, 121, 122, 126, 146, 148, 149, 167, 168, 173, 177, 184, 187, 189, 199, 201, 217, 240, 290, 291, 304, 306, 325, 329, 333, 334, 345, 347, 349, 357, 358, 361, 370, 371
Cincinnati, 29, 45, 112, 113, 169, 170, 183, 194, 313, 332
Cleve, 10
Cleveland, 47, 111, 178, 224, 227, 241
Cliffside Park, 110
Clinton, 156
Choes, 364
Cologne, 57, 105, 149, 263, 361
Colorado Springs, 307
Columbia (Missouri), 354
Columbia (Pennsylvania), 284

Columbus, 23, 79, 227
Concord, 157
Constantinople (Istanbul), 149
Contulmo, 165
Copenhagen, 343
Crailsheim, 167, 207, 245, 266, 329, 361
Creglingen, 98, 210, 243, 262
Croydon, 232
Cuernavaca, 231
Cumberland, 311

Dachau, 9, 32, 33, 42, 44, 50, 51, 55, 58, 66, 75, 80, 81, 83, 85, 91, 93, 99, 103, 112, 122, 127, 136, 147, 148, 152, 159, 170, 184, 191, 197, 207, 212, 217, 218, 219, 228, 242, 247, 258, 259, 282, 293, 296, 303, 307, 318, 320, 329, 341, 352, 357
Dagon, 344
Dallas, 154, 178, 280, 281, 303
Danbury, 91, 366
Danville, 111, 112
Danzig (Gdansk), 52, 102, 128, 200, 352
Darmstadt, 35, 333
Dearborn, 105
Decatur, 180, 181, 219
Degerloch, 137, 193
Dellmendingen, 111
Denver, 26, 54, 106, 118, 264, 265, 282
Des Plaines, 237
Detroit, 178, 262, 264, 323, 324
Detzbach, 286
Diessenhofen, 355
Dijon, 98
Dortmund, 71
Dover (England), 271
Dover (New Jersey), 25
Dowagiac, 180
Drancy, 24, 56, 219, 375
Dresden, 189, 215
Dresher, 297
Duenamuende, 200
Duensbach, 10
Dugway, 156
Dunkirk, 223
Durham, 157

East Brunswick, 278
Eastchester, 304
East Elmhurst, 63
East Meadow, 100, 101
East Newark, 266
Edelfingen, 246
Edesheim, 298
Edinburgh, 16
Eilat, 280

Ein Dor, 338
Eislingen, 304
Elizabeth, 246, 247, 278
Elkins Park, 12
Ellwangen, 23, 99, 111
Elmhurst (Illinois), 66
Elmhurst (New York), 25, 73, 123, 133, 202, 361
Elmsford, 52
El Paso, 148
Encino, 307
Enfield, 143
Englewood, 269
Englewood Cliffs, 155
Enschede, 69, 70
Erez Yisraeli Vav, 338
Erie, 86
Ernstbach, 169
Eschenau, 294
Essex, 88, 310
Esslingen, 6, 29, 44, 80, 92, 99, 109, 172, 230, 248, 262, 276, 354
Evanston, 189, 357, 358
Evergreen, 35

Fairfax, 294
Fair Lawn, 34, 68
Farmingdale, 3
Fechenbach, 73
Feuerbach, 18, 90, 176
Fishkill, 68
Florence, 15, 171, 233, 310
Flushing, 41, 71, 86, 101, 103, 121, 199, 295, 296, 302, 319, 365
Folkestone, 218
Forest Hills, 10, 33, 72, 73, 118, 153, 170, 179, 181, 319, 331
Forest Hills West, 174
Forst, 362
Fort Belvoir, 159
Fort Jackson, 141
Fort Lauderdale, 154, 210
Fort Lee, 145, 177
Fort Riley, 208
Fort Smith, 106
Fort Tryon, 67
Fort Worth, 324
Framingham, 207
Frankfurt, 12, 18, 22, 24, 49, 57, 67, 78, 98, 106, 108, 125, 126, 156, 164, 181, 182, 199, 203, 211, 231, 237, 252, 255, 266, 273, 275, 296, 326, 332, 347, 350, 351, 355, 362
Freeport, 228
Freiberg 158

383

Freiburg, 18, 125, 207, 215, 239, 251, 294, 309, 346
Freudenberg, 38
Freudenstadt, 250, 275
Freudenthal, 109, 240
Fuerth, 51, 110, 152

Gablenberg, 176
Gailingen, 152, 168, 221, 355
Gaithersberg, 191, 295
Gan Yavneh, 186
Gary, 349
Gdansk. See Danzig
Geneva, 124, 125, 127
Genoa, 14, 214, 274
Gera, 307
Gerlingen, 198
Givatayim, 12, 13
Glendale, 274
Goeppingen, 43, 62, 89, 94, 172, 174, 175, 216, 219, 243, 245, 252, 253, 256, 304, 311, 335, 336, 338, 352
Goettingen, 150, 347
Goteborg, 22, 343
Gothenburg, 343
Gowanda, 233, 234
Great Neck, 80, 258, 322, 331
Greenvale, 81, 106
Grossinger, 158
Gross-Rosen, 24
Gummersbach, 362
Gundershoffen, 80
Gurs, 142, 219, 317

Hackensack, 252
Hadar Hakarmel, 336
Hadley Wood, 220
Hague, The, 58
Haifa, 28, 30, 40, 91, 96, 167, 202, 217, 254, 279, 307, 311, 314, 325, 326, 328, 336, 337, 344, 369, 372
Haigerloch, 93, 143, 144, 146, 177, 258
Hallandale, 254
Halle, 275
Hamburg, 95, 126, 255, 281, 325, 355
Hammelburg, 129
Hampstead, 241
Hannover, 283
Harpenden, 299
Harrison, 12, 132, 179
Harrowgate, 203
Hartford, 322
Haslemere, 308
Havana, 97, 274
Hazore'a, 202, 210, 243, 255, 279, 280, 336, 337, 372

Hebron, 197
Hechingen, 29, 89, 96, 97, 108, 153, 287, 371
Heidehof, 202
Heidelburg, x, 16, 44, 70, 114, 156, 166, 213, 219, 224, 242, 271, 330, 362, 368, 376
Heilbronn, 12, 13, 22, 35, 36, 37, 38, 71, 84, 85, 87, 107, 108, 110, 127, 128, 134, 136, 138, 139, 140, 142, 147, 148, 166, 172, 180, 202, 204, 208, 209, 211, 248, 253, 255, 268, 269, 270, 271, 273, 279, 287, 288, 290, 291, 296, 299, 310, 321, 322, 324, 330, 338, 344, 345, 351, 362, 363, 368, 369, 372
Helmingen, 281
Hempstead, 226
Herrlingen, 66, 195, 201, 217
Herts, 220
Herxheim, 45
Heslach, 180
Hessen, 104, 209
Heuberg, 58, 162
Highland Park, 122, 173, 184
Hoboken, 42, 159
Hoechberg, 57
Hoechberg-Wuerzberg, 262
Hohenzollern, 355
Holly, 358
Hollywood, 133
Holyoke, 304
Hong Kong, 123, 308
Honolulu, 114, 141, 333
Horb, 32, 68, 69, 107, 135, 152, 172, 183, 298
Horkheim, 209
Houston, 304, 332, 333
Huntington Park, 127
Huntington Woods, 57, 262, 263
Hyde Park, 361

Ichenhausen, 124
Independence (Missouri), 345
Independence (Oregon), 27
Inwood, 137
Irvington, 64, 129
Istanbul. See Constantinople
Ithaca, 294
Ittlingen, 361
Izbica, 154, 179

Jackson Heights, 34, 36, 48, 63, 75, 114, 115, 120, 200, 201, 202, 212, 213, 360
Jaffa, 214
Jamaica, 108, 211, 212
Jamaica Estates, 254

384

Jamestown, 234
Jebenhausen, 93
Jena, 307
Jersey City, 284
Jerusalem, xiii, 1, 13, 96, 142, 143, 148, 149, 156, 157, 198, 215, 221, 232, 262, 266, 273, 279, 280, 288, 297, 326
Johannesburg, 176, 203, 270, 276, 354, 356
Jungfernhof, 169

Kaiserlautern, 137
Kanpur, 342
Kansas City, 72, 324
Karlsbad, 156
Karlsruhe, 95, 105, 130, 183, 216, 247, 316
Kehl, 202, 318
Kendall, 272
Kenilworth, 229
Kensington, 111, 361
Kent, 360
Kenton, 192
Keuka, 229
Kew Gardens, 45, 59, 61, 88, 94, 118, 170, 205, 258, 293, 300, 314, 339
Kfar Hanassi, 232, 233-234
Kibbutz. See under remainder of name
Killesberg, 200, 276
Kirchheim/Teck, 29, 258
Kiryath-Chiam, 29
Kleinerdlingen, 235
Kochanowitz, 24
Kochendorf, 107
Koeln, 25, 107
Koenigsbach, 64, 367
Kolmar, 317
Konstanz, 167, 296, 301
Kornwestheim, 354
Krakow, 70
Kreis Ohringen, 155
Kreuzlingen, 296
Kuenzelsau, 38, 290
Kvutzat Hefzibah, 70
KZ. See names of individual concentration camps

La Jolla, 109, 257
Lake Grove, 97
Lakewood, 100, 102
Lancaster, 322
Landac, 77
Landsberg, 221
Laudenbach, 254, 280
Laupheim, 26, 36, 71, 86, 112, 123, 152, 158, 176, 205, 214, 225, 226, 228, 276, 279, 293, 294, 308, 311, 312, 325, 352, 356, 372

Lausanne, 169, 170, 181, 227, 313, 362
Lawrence, 89
Lebu, 165
Le Havre, 58
Lehren-Steinsfeld, 172
Leiden, 354
Leipzig, 18, 104, 125, 190, 366
Leningrad, 280
Leonia, 4, 5, 9, 152, 168, 176, 195, 196, 201
Les Milles, 363
Levuka, 173
Lewisburg, 285
Lexington, 48, 335
Lima (Ohio), 309, 360
Lima (Peru), 191, 211, 241
Limoges, 268
Lisbon, 10, 11, 44, 151, 195, 308, 309, 364
Little Neck, 236
Little Rock, 193
Liverpool, 105
London, 3, 9, 40, 44, 48, 85, 94, 117, 124, 125, 130, 134, 142, 143, 169, 170, 171, 175, 187, 196, 199, 214, 220, 227, 232, 234, 241, 244, 255, 256, 271, 299, 306, 313, 317, 346, 353, 354, 360
Long Island City, 168, 332
Los Altos, 285, 286
Los Angeles, 127, 128, 150, 151, 157, 208, 211, 238, 281, 290, 291, 305, 306, 362, 364, 365
Louisville, 12, 86
Lubbock, 281
Ludwigsburg, 53, 73, 105, 118, 120, 139, 149, 150, 245, 265, 293
Lugano, 178, 179, 251
Lunéville, 159
Lunéville Baccarat, 64
Lynn, 207
Lyons, 287, 317

Ma'abarot, 186, 187
Madison (Connecticut), 245, 246
Madison (Wisconsin), 15
Madrid, 11, 173, 209
Magdeburg, 104
Mainz, 209
Malines, 24
Mamaroneck, 138
Manchester, 16, 136, 271, 272
Manhattan, 15, 73, 203, 291
Manila, 58
Mannheim, 65, 113, 115, 152, 183, 185, 205, 212, 259, 260
Marbach, 223
Mar del Plata, 295
Markelsheim, 21, 246

Marlboro, 224
Marseilles, 363
Mauthausen, 53, 115, 119
Mazzuvh, 221
Meiningen, 69
Melbourne, 213
Memphis, 129
Menlo Park, 286
Mercersburg, 182
Merchingen, 356
Mergentheim, 3, 6, 21, 63, 78, 87, 98, 140, 153, 246, 247, 254, 279, 280, 309, 365
Merrick, 44, 72
Mesa, 180, 181
Metuchen, 367
Metzingen, 147
Mexico City, 250, 251
Meyerville, 75
Miami, 254
Miami Beach, 29, 74, 77, 212, 230, 245, 254, 300
Michigan City, 260, 261
Middletown, 33, 135
Middle Village, 110, 136, 174
Milan, 184
Miles City, 240
Mill Valley, 339
Milwaukee, 291
Minneapolis, 325
Mishmar Hadarom, 186, 155
Mishmar He'emek, 243
Mishmar Hanegev, 315
Mission Viejo, 150, 151
Moissac, 17
Monmouth, 278
Monroeville, 32, 33, 347
Montevideo, 134
Montreal, 157, 250, 282
Moorestown, 281, 320
Morehead, 23
Morris Plains, 261
Moscow, 203
Mountain View, 285, 286
Mount Airy, 345
Mount Vernon, 138
Muehlen, 107
Muehringen, 123, 167, 177, 230, 275, 298, 340
Muellheim, 226
Muenchen-Gladbach, 57, 371
Muenster, 273
Munich, 48, 58, 66, 67, 70, 91, 121, 125, 127, 156, 159, 161, 163, 171, 174, 184, 214, 217, 218, 219, 248, 255, 271, 276, 293, 295, 309, 316, 346, 352, 353, 355, 362, 368

Münsingen, 119
Murrhardt, 223

Nagelsberg, 290
Nahariya, 32, 70, 71, 91, 148, 166, 182, 208, 281, 289, 325, 326, 327, 328, 368, 369, 370
Nairobi, 305
Nanuet, 168
Nashville, 358
Nauheim, 104, 172, 245
Neckarvaihingen, 150
Neresheim, 235
Nesselhausen, 254
Neuchatel, 355
Neuffen, 146, 194, 195, 196, 200
Neuily-sur-Seine, 239
Neu Isenburg, 124
Neumünster, 1
Neuss, 57
Neustadt, 17, 18
Newark, 339
New Brunswick, 35, 367
Newburgh, 231
New Haven, 53, 246
New Herrlingen, 217, 218
New Hyde Park, 18
New London, 285
New Milford, 167, 168
New Orleans (Kentucky), 79
New Orleans (Louisiana), 116, 118, 264, 265
New Paltz, 97
New Rochelle, 12, 141, 142
Newton, 114
New Ulm, 64
Nice, 363, 364
Niederstetten, 24, 31, 33, 78, 79, 116, 139, 140, 141, 172, 315, 316, 365, 366
Niles, 181
Nochberg, 149
Noerdlingen, 24, 32, 63, 231, 241, 309
Nordstetten, 57, 122, 187, 246, 274, 275, 278, 293
Norfolk, 114, 218, 219
Northbrook, 371
North Eastham, 307
Northfield, 117
North Hampton, 224
North Hollywood, 291, 305
North Miami, 217, 218
North Miami Beach, 217
Northport, 26
North Royalton, 47
Norwich, 308
Nürnberg, 13, 17, 32, 42, 57, 71, 102, 106, 117, 126, 165, 236, 280, 283, 323, 376

Nürtingen, 358
Nutley, 127

Oberdorf, 98, 100, 101, 205, 211, 212, 235, 280, 285, 309, 310
Oberdorf-Bopfingen, 1, 205, 211, 212, 235
Obertuerkheim, 104
Ocala, 25
Odenkirchen, 169
Oehringen, 172, 209, 210, 290, 317
Offenbach, 229
Oklahoma City, 178
Orlando, 284
Oslo, 173
Oswego, 63
Overland Park, 72
Oxford, 44, 345

Palisades, 261
Palisades Park, 127
Palma Nova, 83
Palo Alto, 151, 286
Paramus, 168, 317
Paris, 15, 17, 24, 75, 107, 112, 125, 126, 134, 140, 159, 173, 203, 209, 239, 242, 268, 316, 331, 342, 346, 375
Perma, 47
Patchogue, 164
Peabody, 37
Pearl River, 117
Pernambuco, 230
Perpignan, 56, 179, 375
Perry, 97, 98
Petropolis, 355, 356
Pflaumloch, 235
Pforzheim, 34, 65, 249
Philadelphia, 12, 42, 45, 55, 78, 79, 94, 140, 141, 143, 144, 172, 196, 233, 246, 258, 274, 276, 282, 339
Phoenix, 274
Pirmasens, 140
Pittsburgh, 32, 79, 111, 246, 264, 353, 360
Plaisance-Losse, 24
Plantation, 185
Pleasantville, 351
Plymouth, 301
Point Pleasant Beach, 100, 104
Port Jefferson, 174, 175
Porto, 147
Porto Allegre, 225
Port-of-Spain, 247
Potsdam, 131
Poughkeepsie, 27
Prague, 228, 275
Prechlauermuehle, 124
Princeton, 13, 47, 48, 50, 69, 181, 183, 281, 282, 321, 347

Prittlbach, 58
Providence, 64
Pueblo, 284
Putnam Valley, 342

Queens, 25, 44, 45, 47, 61, 82, 83, 103, 115, 118, 121, 133, 136, 201, 266, 301 359

Ramat Gan, 12, 237, 238, 266, 279, 280, 372
Randalstown, 372
Rapperswil, 267
Rastatt, 148
Ravensbruck, 63
Ravensburg, 213
Reading, 97
Regensburg, 78, 183
Rego Park, 44
Rehovot, 248
Reichenhall, 350
Remagen, 361
Renningen, 72
Reutlingen, 15, 76, 173, 267, 277, 308, 309, 355, 362
Rexingen, 43, 48, 63, 64, 65, 67, 68, 110, 121, 122, 135, 148, 149, 152, 169, 174, 181, 182, 183, 184, 197, 199, 229, 252, 288, 319, 360, 367
Richmond Hill, 21, 301, 313
Riedlingen, 237, 238
Riga, 1, 10, 17, 36, 52, 90, 128, 139, 152, 155, 169, 174, 176, 186, 192, 193, 200, 249, 250, 280, 290, 305
Riga Kaiserwald, 155
Rio de Janiero, 91, 92, 229, 230, 241, 242, 319, 355, 356
Ritchie, 111, 159, 361
Riverdale, 4, 37, 132, 196, 235, 285
Riverside, 185
Rochdale, 1
Rochester, 24, 25, 62, 130, 217, 218, 358
Rockland, 179
Rockville, 55
Rolandia, 123
Rome, 354
Roslyn, 106
Roslyn Harbor, 82-83
Roslyn Heights, 225
Rotterdam, 9, 10, 37, 42, 325, 351
Rottweil, 36, 37, 156, 274, 308, 309, 367
Ruchama, 17

Sachsenhausen, 226
Sacramento, 4
St. Albans, 234
St. Cyprien, 24
St. Gallen, 26, 27, 311, 312

St. Louis, 117, 198, 285, 309, 344, 347, 349, 350
St. Louis, Haut-Rhin, 363
St. Margarethen, 97
St. Michael, 36
St. Petersburg, 80
San Diego, 114, 219
San Francisco, 25, 107, 114, 141, 151, 153, 157, 191, 216, 246, 285, 301, 304, 325, 359
Sanglingsheim, 298
Santiago, 82
São Paulo, 54, 76, 98, 99, 109, 131, 132, 219, 257, 297
Sarasota, 156, 259, 261
Saratoga Springs, 61
Sauveterre-de-Guyenne, 24
Sayville, 360
S.C., 158
Scarsdale, 2, 61, 67, 94, 126, 138
Schaan, 84
Scheveningen, 58
Schloss Eschenau, 345
Schorndorf, 119
Schwaebisch Gmuend, 80, 99, 103, 207
Schwaebisch Hall, 24, 61, 62, 87, 167, 241, 296, 365, 370, 371
Scotch Plains, 32
Seattle, 93, 164, 226, 320, 360
Sennfeld, 338
Seville, 195
Shanghai, 123, 145, 301
Sharon Heights, 286
Shave Zion, 67, 68, 183, 196, 197, 198, 288, 289
Sherman Oaks, 238, 306
Sigmaringen, 353
Silver Spring, 54, 55, 302, 304
Sioux Falls, 259, 260
Söflingen, 33
Sollingen, 250
Somers, 238
Somerville, 64, 65, 318, 367
Sontheim, 138
South Bend, 181
Southbury, 107, 155
South Dayton, 234
South Devon, 142
Southfield, 322
South London, 232
South Pittsburg, 364-365
Springfield (Missouri), 260
Springfield (New Jersey), 10, 45
Springfield (Ohio), 282, 283
State College, 26
Stettin, 259

Stockholm, 84, 269
Stockport, 105
Stony Brook, 83, 175
Strassburg, 38, 129, 137, 159, 239
Stutthof, 128, 193, 200, 250, 352
Suessen, 155, 169, 252
Sulzbach, 241
Surrey, 142
Sydney, 97
Syracuse, 25

Tacoma, 265
Tamarak, 266
Tampa, 259
Tauberbischofscheim, 315, 324, 325
Teaneck, 168, 252
Tel Aviv, 13, 38, 91, 95, 140, 161, 214, 236, 260, 279, 280, 326, 327, 328, 336, 344, 372, 377
Tel Danin, 301
Tel Dor, 338
Tenafly, 210, 361
Terre Haute, 332, 333
Theresienstadt, 8, 10, 29, 41, 46, 58, 80, 90, 92, 93, 94, 111, 122, 124, 131, 132, 144, 145, 146, 147, 148, 149, 152, 156, 174, 183, 188, 190, 191, 194, 197, 200, 208, 214, 216, 225, 228, 231, 248, 252, 255, 256, 257, 267, 271, 276, 278, 293, 294, 295, 298, 310, 332, 335, 346, 350, 360, 375
Thusis, 31
Tierra Verde, 23
Tinton Falls, 261
Toms River, 68, 122, 278
Topeka, 114, 115
Toronto, 25
Tours, 268
Troy, 101
Tucson, 267, 304
Tuebingen, x, 12, 16, 17, 41, 70, 76, 87, 96, 105, 108, 119, 144, 156, 183, 189, 193, 194, 199, 200, 211, 219, 316, 324, 326, 340, 342, 346, 352, 368, 372
Tulsa, 217
Turin, 310

Ulm, xiv, 6, 17, 32, 42, 47, 48, 56, 59, 64, 66, 86, 91, 94, 97, 111, 114, 118, 119, 120, 124, 158, 159, 161, 162, 163, 164, 165, 170, 172, 174, 190, 204, 213, 214, 215, 216, 217, 218, 219, 225, 228, 232, 233, 237, 238, 255, 264, 265, 277, 284, 285, 293, 295, 300, 308, 311, 322, 324, 325, 326, 327, 343, 375
Ulm-Soeflingen, 213, 285

Union, 63, 64
Unterfranken, 73
Untergrombach, 211
Untertürkheim, 74, 104
Upper Montclair, 228
Upton, 175
Urach, 105
Urbana, 352, 353

Vacha, 254
Valencia, 203
Valparaiso, 81, 82, 83
Vancouver, 223
Vanderhill, 297
Van Nuys, 202
Vedback, 49
Verdun, 288
Verona, 238
Vichy, 112, 127, 340, 363
Vienna, 31, 75, 79, 114, 156, 157, 219, 266, 341, 363
Villa Alemana, 81, 82, 83
Vilvorde-Brussels, 24
Vina del Mar, 81, 82
Vincennes, 327
Vineland, 267, 371
Virginia Beach, 114
Visalia, 246

Waiblingen, 191, 327, 375
Walldorf, 44
Waltham, 71
Wantagh, 23, 101, 208
Warren, 295, 307
Washington, D.C., 111, 112, 116, 135, 157, 158, 164, 191, 230, 294, 304, 359, 360
Washington Heights, 34, 63, 89, 93, 137, 177, 247, 316
Weikersheim, 246, 254, 300, 315, 317, 327
Weilburg, 229
Wein, 309
Weingarten, 367
Weissenhof, 200
Wellesley Hills, 146

Welzheim, 3, 85, 228, 231, 299, 319, 350
Wertheim, 38
West Bronx, 168
Westbury, 113
Westerbork, 42, 107, 158, 221
Westerburg, 229
West Lafayette, 115, 120, 121
West Orange, 68, 104, 105, 139
West Palm Beach, 67, 154
Westport, 53
Westville, 260
Wheeling, 78, 79
Whitefield, 1, 16
Whitefield-Bury, 1
White Plains, 117
Whitestone, 99
Wiesbaden, 44
Wigston-Leicester, 333
Willowdale, 333
Wilmington, 47, 144
Wilna, 235
Woking, 142
Wolfsöhne, 33
Womelsdorf, 151
Worcester, 171
Worms, 273
Wuerzburg, 58, 95, 135, 156, 172, 173, 247, 254, 263, 303, 315
Wuppertal, 211

Yad Vashem, xiii, 1, 148
Yaphank, 92
Yonkers, 106, 228
York, 284
Yorktown Heights, 340
Youngstown, 359, 360

Zanesville, 246
Zbaszyn, 337
Zeiss, 200
Zueiz, 109
Zuffenhausen, 24, 208
Zurich, 15, 16, 31, 32, 41, 75, 84, 106, 107, 126, 129, 218, 257, 296, 356, 363